MW01152451

MISSION ACCEPTED
262
WOMEN

Entrepreneurs, Ultrapreneurs, Creatives

& Media

ROCK LEGACY *& Tell All*

THANK YOU

Thank You.
This is a special message to all the contributors and authors.

This book is a beautiful compilation of inspiration and heart centered writings and messages. We know this, but as an author myself I know only too well that it takes dedication, time and for many it takes getting over the fear of putting your words to paper.

To be in a book is a vulnerable thing to do.

That's why most people don't, but you did.

You surpassed your own fears, carved time in your abundant schedule, wrote and probably re-wrote, searched for pictures, and really took to heart the messages you wanted women to hear.

You have all dedicated yourselves. I have seen you help each other in the building of this book. It has truly been a collaborative honour to see the level of care you have for each other, as well your care for the women that will read this book and the respect and patience you have had for each woman's process.

With the publication of this book may you all receive ten-fold the love, and the kindness you have shown.

For all of you that have businesses, projects, and nonprofits, may this book bring an abundance of the right people your way, so your dreams are fulfilled and your success allows you to continue to serve and be served.

Be Well & Stay Groovy
Your Friend in Writing
Deb

ACKNOWLEDGEMENT

There isn't a book I create where I don't acknowledge my two favorite people, and that's my brilliant daughter Chloae, whose love for the written word was from the first time she could get her hands on a book; and my phenomenal son Ocean, who reminds me how much joy comes from being creative. They both inspire me.

A big shout out from YaYa to the always smiling Brynnlee and handsome Kashton.
It's not possible to start, create, build, and sustain a project of this magnitude without a team of global minded people. My gratitude for Dorothea K, Angel T, Emily B and crew, Kris D, Marietjie M, Carmel E, Kathleen C, and all our supporters, collaborators and suppliers is too large to find words for expression. Thank you! Thank you! Thank you! It's too long a list of all the women that have left me in awe of their drive, accomplishments, bravery, boldness, and abilities.

As a little girl, I have always been impressed by those that spoke out of turn but did it in a way that showed grace and understanding. I was moved to my core when I saw sheer, faithful bravery in action of a woman standing up for herself and what she thought was right.
I envied the movement of one and was astonished when I saw one become one plus, plus, plus, and more plus.

It felt right, and I felt right. Watching other women show up, stand up, and speak up made me feel like the drive I had inside me was okay. I felt like I was with my tribe. I didn't feel alone in the quietness of a young teen girl who wanted to make change but didn't know how.

Even though I have been moved by many women, it was two women in particular that caught my attention and moved my soul. They fueled my faith in the power of a woman, they would be Gloria Steinem and Janis Joplin.

I don't remember how I found out about the works of Gloria Steinem, all I know is when I was in my late twenties, I became aware of this incredible movement goddess, and I was in awe. I'm pretty sure it came from reading a womanist magazine.
We all have people that make an impression on us, that make us feel braver just by reading about them or watching them fight the fight. I can't begin to give thanks for all she has done, sacrificed, taught me, taught us, and it was a savoured moment for me to be able to say "thank you" to her personally.

It's so true that we don't always know how we impact others' lives and a split-second meeting with her where I got to say thank you, get a book signed and see her speak live in a small conference hall is something I'll never forget. I am most sure that there are thousands of others that feel the same way.

Janis Joplin, I was lucky enough to grow up in a house with a record player. In my mother's collection was an album called Pearl. I can't tell you how I felt when I first heard that album, I just knew that I was no longer alone. The strength in her voice gave me the strength to get through the many things a lost teenager needs to navigate. She has been a magical inspiration ever since, and to this day there isn't a time when I hear her sing that I don't feel stronger, happier, and more hopeful.

Finally, it wouldn't seem right to not acknowledge where I received the inspiration from to do this book and the summits that went alongside it. It was early in my years of Entrepreneurship, and I was using a wonderful Women's Day Planner. I had used the same planner for years and it was full of beautiful black and white photography, taken by women photographers. Those pictures evoked beautiful feelings when I saw them. One year, as I went with anticipation to purchase my next year's planner, I was told they were out of print. As unusual as it sounds to say that I was semi devastated, it's safe to say I was highly disappointed. I said in my head "I am going to do a book for women one day and I want it to have beautiful black and white pictures just like this one". I was 31 years old. Some ideas need time to brew.

Now, the inspiration for the summits was something very different. I was sitting on my "couch office" late at night working with Netflix on in the background. I looked up at the TV at a time when Netflix was "suggesting" a movie for me to watch. I didn't recognize the movie but had a "feeling" it had something to do with Gloria Steinem. I decided I was too busy and as I put my head back down to work, I intuitively heard "We sent it three times, watch the damn movie". So, I watched the DAMN movie. The movie was called **Seeing Allred,** and I was jaw dropped and inspired in the first 15 minutes. It was the story of Gloria Allred's life and career. All I can say is, after watching the movie the words that came out of my mouth were: "sister if you can do that, I can do more".

That movie was the motivation to create, the very next day, the Show Up, Stand Up and Speak Up Yes You! 22 Summit Series. Thank you, Gloria. I hope to say that to you in person one day, but know this, your movie, your transparency, and your work inspires us all.

This book project is a collection of some of the most gumption-based women I have ever heard about in history. It is a collection of women that are making history as we speak, even if unknown to them, so that gumption, bravery, courage, joy, and peace never go unnoticed, and our sisters that have yet to step into the world of self-funding have an easier path to follow.

Your instruction with this book is this: Keep your phone near by, as surprising as that sounds. All these women are SPECTACULAR, and when you come across a woman that you want to learn more about, then do it! Go to their information and expand your knowledge of them.

We have done something very special. We had added names to this book that will make you feel proud to know of them. You'll want to tell everyone you meet about them and, chances are, you never learned about them or even heard their names before. The INCREDIBLE women in history that you see in this book, we encourage you to Google them, you'll be left speechless, but proud. These women left their mark not just for other women but for all of humanity. I hope this book helps you to become a "gentle to yourself but powerful to the world" kind of person that brings you to a place beyond your wildest dreams.

Your new friend,
Deb Drummond

FOREWORD

CELEBRATING WOMEN

Throughout history, the narrative of leadership has often been dominated by the accounts of men. Hidden, was a parallel story of women standing at the forefront; shaping societies, challenging norms, and driving change with resilience and determination.

Mission Accepted: 262 Women Entrepreneurs, Ultrapreneurs, Creatives & Media, ROCK LEGACY & Tell All emerged from the passion of visionary Deb Drummond, women's advocate, and a pioneer in entrepreneurship. To date, she has built 7 international companies and inspired thousands around the globe. As a speaker, mastermind trainer, and personal coach, she has motivated and educated more than 50,000 people to a higher state of optimal health and wealth.

As an elite International speaker and author promoting women as change agents, I am deeply honored to be part of this project and providing this brief foreword. For more than 30 years I have worked energetically for gender equality and center-staging women in leadership and decision-making roles. I have mentored grassroots and community-based women to discover their leadership superpowers, speak their truths, and transform themselves and their communities. Whether I am speaking at UN meetings, teaching courses on women and gender studies, advocating for women's issues in the political arena, or connecting women, I have had the honor of hearing the stories of women around the world. They are challenging the status quo to accelerate equality in representation, economic opportunities, and attainment of women's rightful places as partners in creating, managing, and caring for the world we live in.

Because of Deb's ability to envision a better tomorrow, she became acutely aware of the need for more platforms for women's voices to be heard. Through this women-focused 262 project,Deb has fostered community and solidarity among women from diverse backgrounds. She has provided opportunities for networking, collaboration and mutual support, and created spaces where women can connect, learn from each other, and amplify each other's voices. In actuality, she has started a movement, a learning community… spaces for women who have the gumption and conviction to move one step forward in abilities, accessibility, freedom, choices, education, respect, fairness, justice, love, peace, honour, and joy.

This table-top book shares the journeys of 262 women who are courageously contributing their energy, knowledge, and skills to positively impact the lives of others and their communities. They passionately share their stories of personal experiences to provide inspiration and information for your well-being and success as you define it.

In conjunction with this book, Deb founded the Show Up Stand Up Speak Up, Yes You! movement. This is a televised, heart-centered project with a reach of over 350 million. This movement is designed to inspire women, and those who support women, and to encourage the solidarity represented by International Women's Day (IWD).

International Women's Day emerged from the intersection of the women's labor and women's rights movements. The day not only honors the achievements and contributions of women, but also reflects on the challenges of women in the past and the struggles they face today. IWD provides a unifying moment for women to raise awareness of the inequalities women still face, rally for change, and celebrate the courage and determination of ordinary women playing extraordinary roles in affecting the history of their countries and communities.

Concurrently, each woman in this anthology is contributing to this movement by sharing their stories to inspire women to see the things they can change and encourage them to action — making what seems impossible, possible.

Through this book, you will embark on a journey of sharing the lives and endeavors of these 262 women who have fearlessly ventured into the arena of change. They share their unique gifts and talents and the wisdom they have gained on their journeys, which often involved breaking barriers and shattering ceilings. These women illustrate the power of perseverance and the potency of passion and purpose.

I believe that every woman has what it takes to be a leader or change agent. I encourage you to read these stories. Let them serve as beacons of inspiration and understanding that true progress arises when diversity flourishes and voices long silenced are finally heard. Find those stories that resonate with your convictions. Find strength in their openness and vulnerability to galvanize your journey in defying conventions and pursuing your dreams. Let us not only celebrate the achievements of these remarkable women, but also heed the lessons they impart. Let us recognize the importance of inclusivity, empathy, and solidarity in our pursuit of a more just and equitable world.

This book serves as a tribute to the countless women who have dedicated their lives to effecting positive change. May it also motivate you to find the courage to express your beliefs, dig deep in understanding your superpowers… your leadership abilities, your value, and unleash your potential for success. Please join this movement and fulfill your passion as we march in solidarity toward a future where every woman, regardless of background or circumstance, has the opportunity to lead, thrive, and create a better world for themselves and their communities.

Cathy Holt
Changemaker Advocate
www.Catherine-Holt.com

BARBARA BROWN

A Mother of 5, a wife, ex-wife, single mom, sister, daughter, friend, hard worker, breadwinner, and industrious thinker. My grandmother was unique, she never took any guff from anyone. She seemed to beat to the drum of her own opinions. She was a tough one, tough for many reasons that she most likely never shared. She never lived in the era of expressing feelings and being vulnerable.
I, we all, called her Grandma Brown.

When I was a child, and in the mood to be stubborn, my mother would say in her tone: "you are being just like your grandmother", and I used to smile on the inside every time she did. This woman that could make the best meatloaf in the city who would make anyone laugh within minutes was definitely my ally. My ally in energy, my ally in gumption, my ally in keeping on, my ally in going all in, my ally in having an open-door policy, my ally in making enough food to feed everyone, my ally in stretching a dollar as far as it needed to be stretched. My ally in all things brave. She was the best crib teacher I ever had.

You had to learn how to count her hand quickly before she famously took a few extra points … lol But the best part about playing crib, was getting to change the records, and making sure the penny didn't fall off the needle. Some people just have a way of making their way into the fiber of how you live your life. She was fabulous, spoke up at a time when women weren't supposed to and made herself known at a time where quiet was expected.

Grandma Brown, we thank you.

Grandma Brown, I thank you.

Stay bold!
Your granddaughter,
Deb Drummond

Show Up Stand Up Speak Up

PLAY CRIB

LUCKY HARRIS

My Message To Women is...

Single or married,
always make sure you know how to take care of yourself financially.

LAUGH OFTEN

DEB DRUMMOND

Motherhood. What a journey! Or some would say what a trip….

I lucked out. I have the pleasure of having 2 of the most incredible humans as my children. Who knew a heart could fill to a capacity that never gets empty? The fun, the lessons, the joy, and the memories just keep going like the never-ending gobstopper in Willy Wonka. Each part of the journey with each of my children is so unique and special in its own way. It was full circle learning for me to see how their own personalities made themselves known right from the start, while at the same time so many things they did were exactly the same.

They both loved to be awake as much as possible & they both had strong creative ways of thinking. Chloae with her love for the written word, art, singing, dancing, and theatre. Ocean with his love for music, art, and fashion. Let's just say it was a household of creative independent thinkers. I want to have my own business! It's one thing when you say that to yourself and another thing when your teenager says that to you. The first time it happened it was from my daughter. As an entrepreneur myself, I was proud of her for wanting independence and happy she loved something enough to want to make a business out of it.

As a mom, I just wanted to make sure it was going to work out. I knew it was going to be an exploratory adventure. It was a big day in the house when her first business cards arrived! Candy Cane Creative cards for old times' sake! Her business adventures went from Art to Children's Clothing to Skincare and we navigated those waters together. When my son told me he wanted his own business it was the same, but also very different. He was more official, he sat me down on the couch and, with a seriousness in his voice that I had not heard before, he made his announcement.

By this time, I had another 15 years of entrepreneurship under my belt, but still the mom in me had all the same thoughts I had with my daughter. There is a new term now to describe what this is: now it's called …

Show Up Stand Up Speak Up

MOMAGER

This is a very real thing that needs to be talked about. What does it take to balance the life of a parent and your child's new business? When do I stop being a mom and be a business advisor and vice versa. It's a dance, for sure, one that makes me forever grateful I coach entrepreneurs for a living. I am happy to say we are enjoying the ride of my son Ocean's success.

We have a rhythm of respect between Mom & Son as well as being business colleagues. My pride is not only in the person he is, but the person he has had to become to handle a thriving operation like Natsukashii Ink at the age of 19. He was willing to work hard behind the scenes, and he did for almost 5 years before he took his company to market. I am here to help any parent that has the same joy of having a young entrepreneur ready to take on the world of business. Ocean and I do a lot of appearances, shows, and events where we share how we have made all this work while creating an international, successful business. Ocean has showings all over the world for his streetwear, fashion, and art and is happy to connect wherever he is, so please feel free to reach out and meet him on the road. You can reach either one of us on the contact page of his site https://natsukashiiink.world/ or at deb@debdrummond.com We wish you incredible success in all that you do and a big shout out to all the Momagers out there!

BE PROUD

CHLOAE DRUMMOND

My Message To Women is...

Don't be afraid of personal growth.
Even if it means you have outgrown your current environment,
you are stepping into the person you are MEANT to be,
and that's everything.

Show Up Stand Up Speak Up

CHOOSE JOY

MICHELE AINSLEY-BAKER

I spent my whole life interested in Art and making life beautiful with Design. Since childhood, I've been captivated by art and dedicated to beautifying life through design. As a youngster, I crafted dollhouses from shoeboxes, fashioning tiny beds and kitchens from whatever materials I could find—often raiding my mother's closet, much to her chagrin. "Michele, where is my dress?" became a familiar refrain in our household. In my teenage years, I resolved to pursue a career in design, inspired by the vibrant fashion and interior design scenes of the swinging sixties, particularly in Europe with icons like Mary Quant and Biba. Despite life's twists, including marriage and motherhood at a young age, I remained steadfast in my determination to pursue design.

Launching a design and sewing company in Britain, I provided uniforms to hotels and employed women with children who could sew from home. A move to Canada with my three children marked a significant shift, prompting me to return to university to chase my dreams. Balancing fashion shows with home and business projects, I found the synergy between fashion and interiors endlessly fascinating, with trends constantly evolving.

My passion project Ruffle's Lingerie, stemmed from a desire to create elegant lingerie for fuller, mature women. With a team of home sewers, I brought my feminine design concepts to life. Concurrently, I ventured into children's fashion with Top Flight Children's Wear, inspired by the last of stylish options for my grandchildren. Hosting whimsical children's fashion shows added joy to the endeavor.

As societal priorities shifted, homes gained newfound importance, prompting me to focus on enhancing both beauty and functionality in people's lives through interior design. Over the years, my commercial design projects have positively impacted businesses and communities alike. My life's journey has been driven by a steadfast refusal to give up and an unwavering belief in myself. To me, belief is synonymous with growth – never ceasing to evolve. Now, I embark on a new chapter as an artist, embracing the endless possibilities that creativity offers. Never finish growing…I am now becoming an Artist.

Show Up Stand Up Speak Up

I have been an Interior Designer and Fashion Designer for over 35 years, specializing in Residential, Commercial and Marine Design. The Marine design is such interesting work with wonderful Clients who are living their passion, the private yachts are so beautiful. Ainsley Interiors & Renovations features Contemporary and Traditional West Coast Architecture. Ainsley interiors is a Family run business including my Husband and two sons as Contractors, this makes for a very smooth working environment and one that we all enjoy. Every Commercial project is carefully reviewed with business personal and building professionals to create an efficient and working business/community environment, also to elevate your financial gain. Services we offer are Colour Consultations Interior & Exterior, Kitchen & Bath consultations, Carpet/flooring supply and installations, Fabrics etc. Healthy Home includes Feng Shui practices and Eco practices. My passion for a Home for Families and generations to come using sustainable materials where possible. Life must be lived in a Healthy Environment for growth, this has an impact on the Mind & Body which is so important in today's world. I taught Interior Design and Architecture for many years, and I learnt that the younger generation craves a well thought out, simple, light, healthy living space, and they tend to follow trends using Natural materials and bringing nature inside which I love to use. After completing four years in Art College in Britain and two years in University in Canada in Fine Arts and Fashion Design I am still learning every day. Honors & Awards I cherish: Governor General Award for Bravery. Canada, Qualification for Acupressure, Black belt in Jin Shin Do, A wonderful Husband and three incredible sons. AINSLEY INTERIORS & RENOVATIONS. ainsleyinteriors@shaw.ca

BELIEVE YOURSELF

KIMBERLY BUTLER

I had just graduated High school by the skin of my teeth. Everyone left the building, and I sat on the Forest Hills High School stairs. This phase was over. I had managed to get through twelve years of hell of learning disabilities of undiagnosed dyslexia. I have been verbally abused by teachers who would call me "stupid." Meanwhile, I was in honors English, Science, and Social Studies. In all my classes, except math, I was an Honor Student. Did it occur to anyone in the educational system?

Maybe the problem was numbers. No. That would happen only 20 years later. Sitting there, I realized I would never fit into a normal working environment. I had plenty of summer jobs where my learning disability reared its ugly head. I had enrolled in the only school that would take me - John Jay College of Criminal Justice thinking of perhaps becoming a lawyer to sue the New York City educational system for abuse. To my wonderful surprise, I came into a City College that taught me how to learn for the first time in my life. They weren't as concerned about numbers and possible careers in accounting as they were in teaching your mind to see things from several directions at once.

I excelled, and my self-esteem rose. At the end of my sophomore year, when it was time to pick a major, I had a very serious conversation with myself while walking down 9th Avenue in NYC. I said to myself I would never go through Law School. And then I remembered something my mother said: "Do what you love." So, I asked myself: "What do I love?" I love movies. Great! Then go to film school. I graduated from the university as an honor scholar at NYU. I started on the path toward discovering that my real love would be photography. Thank you, mommy!

Show Up Stand Up Speak Up

I didn't want to work for anyone. I wanted to be my own boss, sink or swim. The thought of working in an office where most things are based on politics rather than talent caused waves of nausea. It was confirmed the day I went to a job placement office. I walked in, and they immediately asked me to take a typing test. Behind me were two young men my age, dressed in suits and taken in for interviews without typewriters. That was it. That's when I realized that women had absolutely no shot at real success unless they followed their own path, and mine certainly wasn't corporate. And believe me, movie sets are corporate. So, I started my own photo business. I photographed my friends, their families, events, and anything where I would learn and get paid. My three best friends thought I was insane because they had jobs and paychecks on Fridays. What I had was a dragon that lived within me that would not be put into a box and spend my days accomplishing absolutely nothing and being mortally unhappy. Then, the cold calling began. It was hard, but I just forced myself to do it because I knew that the only other option was death by cubicle. The fear of being locked in created energy in me to pick up the phone and call everybody regardless of how big the magazine was and start to break through.

It was possible because while I was in my senior year sitting in the park, Gloria Steinem and other great leaders of the women's movement were marching down 5th Avenue demanding equal rights for women. When I graduated, there was pressure on the male-dominated society to hire women in business. To my great luck and the sacrifices of these pioneering women, I was in the right place at the right time and had the talent. As I am writing this, I want to thank all the people who told me that I was a loser; I was just a girl; I would end up knocked up, and that would be the end of me. Without them stoking the fire in my soul, I would not have had an extraordinary career and become, as Neil Gaiman has said, "one of the most important photographers of my generation." https://www.kimberlybutler.com/

galinovyrva.com

19

BE KIND

JANE ANYANGO ODONGO

I grew up in the rural village called Nyakach along the shores of Lake Victoria in Kenya, Africa. I enjoyed my childhood playing with mud, fetching firewood and water with a bucket on my head. I ended up getting married at the age of 18 and settling in Kibera Slums in Nairobi which made life really tough for me. At 22, I was a mother and a wife, trying to figure out how to organize my life and yes, I did. I stepped out of my miserable life and became a champion in my community and beyond, touching the lives of many.

In the year 2008 during post-election violence in Kenya following disputed presidential elections, my path crossed with the then USA Ambassador to Kenya. The Ambassador recommended me for an opportunity to travel to the USA for an International Visitor Leadership Programme – IVLP 2010 which would later change my thinking. I saw the need to think differently in all I do and to even go into my books and study more.

I have no degree, I still dream of having a degree, not for the world, not for a job hunt, but for my own good and welfare. A lot of research has been carried out in my community – Kibera Slums, some reports connect well with reality on the ground, but others don't. After a lot of work of mobilizing and organizing women and girls in my community and other slum settlements, I decided to start passing the baton, to start telling real stories about my life and my community and start connecting the research to reality.

Anyango Jane
Kibera Slums, Kenya.

Show Up Stand Up Speak Up

"You cannot bring the 'Cs' and the 'Ds' where us 'As' and 'Bs' are sitting!" This is one of the many profiling statements which I have encountered as a slum woman with very little education and, of course, no money. These, instead of demoralizing me, have inspired me to keep going, accessing spaces, and making my presence count. I bring stories of reality to the ears and the world of those who do not understand that, *in life, you give yourself, your best, and that your best may not be the other person's good or even bad.*

Sisterhood is key to me, I have always brought women and girls from diverse backgrounds into my world, I have mentored thousands of girls and women from 5 different slum settlements. I believe in the power of meaningful participation and representation, that is the only way to make the world better for everyone. I have worked in Kibera Slums since 2003, currently I do coordination for various organizations. My life is an inspiration to many, I am an influencer, a storyteller, and an activist, I tell stories that inspire, I share about controversial issues within my community like wife inheritance, polygamy, Female genital mutilation, period poverty and many others.
You want to listen to me? Share your space, I will be available.

Anyango Jane Odongo, https://www.polycomgirls.or.ke/

DANCE ALWAYS

ALEXANDRA DAVID-NEEL
Anarchist

ROSALIE BARROW EDGE
Environmentalist

SISTER ROSETTA THARPE

Guitarist

GERTRUDE BELL

Archaeologist

My Story

BUTTA B-ROCKA

I've been blessed to tour the world, perform on mega stages, work with multiple Grammy winning artists, and be featured in over 800 articles and write-ups. People see the glitz and glam, but my path to success was paved with setbacks. This is just one example.

In late 2018, I suffered a serious injury during a rehearsal. I tore my meniscus and ACL, and dislocated my shoulder. I was devastated, but I was determined not to let my injury stop me from pursuing my dreams. Despite the excruciating pain, I pushed off my surgery date for 4 months so that I could fulfill my prior commitments. I performed in Vegas, LA, Mexico and Chile. During my show in LA, I met Les Brown, a world-renowned motivational speaker, at an event we both performed at. I was immediately drawn to his positive energy and his message of hope, we exchanged information and kept in contact. Upon my return from Chile, my injury worsened, requiring surgery and a full year of recovery. I became unemployed, I underwent physical therapy three times a week, and had to use a walker then cane for months. On the day of my surgery, Les called me and assured me that this setback was a setup for something greater. For eight months, while I recovered, he took me under his wing as his personal assistant. I learned so much from Les, especially how to overcome adversity, believe in myself, and achieve my goals. I am so grateful for his mentorship and support. He has dubbed me his spiritual daughter, endorsed my multiple books, interviewed me on his platform, and supported me at the premiere of my film, "Finding the Perfect Guy."

Though my injury was a major setback, it truly was a setup for something greater. It allowed me to discover and tap into hidden skills and talents, resulting in the birth of my books, my syndicated podcast, my boys magazine, new music, and my film. I'm now back on stage, performing and inspiring audiences around the world. I'm also working on several new creative projects, including a film streaming on platforms worldwide. I'm so grateful for the journey I've been on. I've learned that I am stronger than I thought I was, and that I can overcome anything that life throws my way. I'm also grateful for the people who have supported me along the way, especially Les Brown. My story is a reminder that adversity can be a catalyst for growth. It's a reminder that we are all capable of overcoming challenges and achieving our dreams. If you're facing a challenge in your own life, remember that you are not alone. There are people who care about you and want to help you succeed. Don't give up on yourself. Keep moving forward, and never lose sight of your dreams.

Show Up Stand Up Speak Up

I'm Butta B-Rocka, an executive film producer, director, screenwriter, actress, top-charting international recording artist/songwriter, best-selling author, host of the Transparency Talks podcast, and CEO and founder of Artists Rock the Mic, BBR Media Group, and BBR Indie Films.

I've had the privilege of working with musical titans like Kanye West, Janet Jackson, TLC, Zac Brown, and Collective Soul, and I've toured the globe, serenading presidents and prime ministers alike. My passion for creativity knows no bounds, manifesting in my music, films, plays, and books.

I relish the challenge of generating fresh ideas and bringing them to fruition. I hope my story inspires others to chase their dreams and embrace their creativity. I believe that anyone can achieve anything they set their mind to, regardless of age. People want to do business with me because I'm talented and experienced in a wide range of creative fields, reliable and professional, creative, and innovative, passionate about my work, and dedicated to my clients and collaborators. What makes me special is my unique perspective and my ability to switch lanes and adapt.

I'm always looking for new ways to challenge myself and grow. I can help you with a wide range of creative projects, including writing, directing, producing, and acting in your film, television, scripts, or music project. I am also able to mentor and develop you and help you build your brand and career in the entertainment industry. I am available to perform or speak as a panelist at your private or public event. If you are looking for a talented, experienced, and creative professional to help you with your next project, contact me today to discuss and get started. ButtaBRocka@gmail.com

RISE ABOVE

My Story

DR. MELISSA BALIZAN

As a little girl I remember standing in the hall holding my dad's hand, I was in a peach dress, and we were getting ready to go to church. I had been told that my first word was "pretty". Everything around me was pretty. God made me and everything around me. I learned early on to rely on Him.

I didn't feel like I fit in and struggled with challenges growing up so learned to protect my heart and didn't let too many people close to me. I still am protective of my heart and struggle with letting others see the real me. I looked for ways to help others even as a child. I was involved in Jump Rope for Heart, a program to help young kids stay active and raise funds for heart awareness. Over 60 million women are affected by heart disease, and it is the number one killer of men and women today.

Who knew this young girl who faced many challenges at an early age would become a doctor willing to listen to others. She put forth her best effort to learn and to ask the right questions. Life gives you plenty of 'what if' but if you think you can do something you can. I know I can make a difference in the lives of every individual that I speak with, and I am touched by helping them.

Whether it be helping with a family member or with health issues, I love providing insight and research to help educate my clientele. I remember being in a group called Close Up and going to the capital to learn how the government is run. I was excited to be a part of this and see where all the action takes place. I learned a lot on that trip and made new friends who now stand by me when life gets tough. Sometimes you're given lemons and need to just make lemonade instead of letting things get to you.

You become stronger and more vibrant and can resonate with so many who have been there with the same struggles, challenges, or health issues. I help myself and others by being able to sleep soundly and can jump for joy waking up in the morning, stepping forward using my knowledge, and my degree for the greater good helping to disrupt the system by listening and empathizing with others.

Show Up Stand Up Speak Up

Have you ever felt like no one was listening to you or been told it's all in your head? What if the world of healthcare was health proactive instead of a sick care system? I'm talking about a system where we look at your whole health, physical, mental, spiritual, emotional, financial, and social health. We want you to be happy and have joy in your life. Taking time for self-care and stress management. Let me tell you a story about a young lady who was so busy with her career and taking care of her family that she neglected to take care of herself. One day she was forced to take care of herself and that's when she decided to change the way we look at healthcare.

She decided to disrupt what's going on, no longer allowing insurance companies to dictate what you can and cannot do. It's your choice, your voice, speak up. We can choose who we want to do business with, to be friends with, to laugh with, to love, to cherish. Creating this new health paradigm, we rock the boat, socialize, be well together and help our families be well. We advocate for healthy food choices, movement activities, and activities to keep our brains active to prevent dementia and Alzheimer's. We educate on finance and have ways to learn and grow when we've lost the ability to connect with one another. Dr. Melissa uses her many talents, knowledge, and emotional intelligence to walk alongside you on your life voyage, to guide, to educate and motivate you. Nobody should be told it's all in your head. Dr. Melissa is kind, caring, empathetic, knowledgeable, and wicked smart. It's an honor to serve, love and show up every day.
Learn more https://drmelissabalizan.com/

TAKE ACTION

CORINNE ALLAN

I am many things but the one thing that is the most important is being a mother.
I have always volunteered, I've always given back, I've lived the life of service in my career as a police officer, but my biggest achievement is being a mother.

I chose and was blessed enough to be able to bring another life into this world, my daughter Kevan Bonn.

Watching this little person grow into an AMAZING adult has impacted the way I view humanity. Everyone is someone's child. Everyone is a miracle because being born is a miracle.

This has made me view everyone I meet in a more respectful and humbled way. Because everyone is someone's child, everyone deserves respect.

They say it takes a village to raise a child. My daughter has made me want to be a bigger part of the overall village because being there for another person just feels right.

Show Up Stand Up Speak Up

Emergency Service Personnel—Police, Fire and Ambulance—and Canadian Armed Forces members have careers like no other; we are always on the front line and we are always putting others in front of ourselves.

As a former Vancouver Police Department Officer, I know how hazardous these jobs are. I've watched some of the heroes become the ones who need help.

That's why Honour House and Honour Ranch were created. Honour House is "A Home Away From Home". It provides a free safe place for Canadian Armed Forces, Veterans, Emergency Personnel and their families to stay while receiving medical care and treatment in the metro Vancouver area.

Honour Ranch, near Ashcroft B.C., is a place for self-reflection and growth. Opened in 2019, this retreat helps Canadian Armed Forces, Veterans, Emergency Personnel, and their families deal with operational stress injuries including anxiety, depression, and Post Traumatic Stress Disorder.

Both locations are run by Honour House Society, which is completely reliant on donations, fundraising and volunteers to meet the operating costs and manage each site so they are available when needed. Please take a closer look https://www.honourhouse.ca/ and consider donating.

LOVE LIFE

CARLI WAGER

My Message to Women is...

Live each day with a grateful heart and always put family first.

Show Up Stand Up Speak Up

LOVE PEACE

LIS HOYTE

Having spent 18 years in a coercive controlling relationship, numerous failed attempts to leave, the final straw came when I realised that not even the courts could help me. It was then I decided that no matter how fearful I was, no matter how much my voice shook, and my heart raced when I spoke my truth, I had to leave for the sake of my children, and I did just that. My children deserved better, and I needed to find peace in my heart. Somehow, I believed that was possible, despite the inner battle I faced every day, moment by moment.

It was so important that, as time passed, I banished the blame, not because I believed that the abuse I suffered was deserving or that I wanted to let them get away with anything so to speak, but in fact, the only person that was being affected by this was me. I was hurting myself, and having that burden of hatred in my heart became too much to bear. So, I let go gradually and began to appreciate myself more and more for making the hardest decision I have ever had to make in my life. I had to shift my paradigm, shift my way of thinking which enabled me to find peace in my heart.

I have reframed that whole experience and now have the belief (not just within intimate relationships, but relationships with other human beings) that having the expectation and reliance on someone else to make you feel valued is an unrealistic belief to hold on to. Yet so many of us do it, so many of us place the responsibility in someone else's hands to make us feel good. However, it is a flawed premise to think, that someone has the capabilities to make some else feel happy, when they are unable to do so for themselves.

Once I truly understood this from all angles, my life began to change, all the responsibility and accountability was on ME to make ME happy. What I am grateful for now, is that by reframing this experience, I have allowed myself to move into territory which helps and supports others. I believe that our thoughts create our lived experiences, wanted or not, but knowing this helps us to cultivate a mindset where we must strive to think greater than how we feel, that's where true transformation occurs. My Message is - 'Make choices and decisions that will create peace in your heart.'

Much Love, Lis

Show Up Stand Up Speak Up

The main purpose for starting up my company was to spread awareness of coercive control, support those experiencing this type of abuse, and produce a life coaching programme with the exact blueprint that I used to Break Free from coercive control which spanned for nearly two decades.

My 'Break Free' programme has helped many people to break free from their coercive controlling relationships and find refuge for themselves and their children. My first publication _Break Free (2021)_ accompanies my coaching programme which provides tools and techniques for people to use who are experiencing these types of relationships, furthermore, there is a focus on the importance of the Inner Game for self-healing and empowerment. My Second publication, _Co-Parenting Within Coercive Control (2022)_ is a helpful guide for parents in supporting their children. Spreading awareness of coercive control has been a part of my purpose from the very beginning, which allowed me to become a CPD Accredited Trainer and Expert Speaker within the field of Coercive Control.

Something that has always been close to my heart is how children and young people develop and form relationships, hence the reason why I have now created a Coercive Control Curriculum for Secondary Schools here in the UK to support teachers and the next generation. I believe that awareness is key and having formally been a Steering Committee Member for the International Coercive Control Conference (ICCC) this was a great way to spread awareness of coercive control. I continue to spread awareness on various platforms which include Speaking Events, Podcasts and Zoom sessions sharing my expertise, I am a Facilitator of the VOICE Programme (Victim of Intimate Coercive Experience) which enables me to support different organisations and better serve my clients with a unique understanding not just from a training facility perspective, but from the perspective of someone who has experienced coercive control for nearly two decades. Starting my business transformed by life, while faith showed me my path to peace. lisreallywhat@gmail.com

33

INNER GAME

ELISE SMITH

In the tender moments after our son's birth, as I cradled him in my arms, wrapped in a soft yellow blanket, I was overwhelmed by the miracle before me, his tiny nose, his striking blue eyes. This moment was more than just a dream realized; it was a testament to God's perfect timing. For fourteen years, my husband and I had prayed for this miracle, enduring countless trials and setbacks on our journey to parenthood. The road had been paved with heartache and disappointment. Despite eleven failed fertility treatments, we clung to our faith, finding strength in Philippians 4:13: "I can do all things through Christ who strengthens me."

Through the struggles, I often reflected on the story of Lazarus, waiting in the tomb for three days before Jesus arrived. Just as Jesus delayed his visit to magnify the glory of God, I realized that my own journey, spanning fourteen years, served to magnify the miracle of my son. Each time I share his story, I also share my testimony of God's grace and timing.

Just when we least expected it, on the brink of giving up, God intervened in the most unexpected way. With a single phone call, He turned our sorrow into joy, our despair into hope. "Congratulations, Elise, you're pregnant," the nurse said, her words a balm to our wounded hearts.

As I watch him toddling around my room with a big smile on his face, I am reminded once again of God's perfect timing and His boundless grace. Just as He blessed us with the gift of parenthood, I know He desires to bless you with the desires of your heart, according to His perfect plan. Keep the faith and never give up on your dreams God put them there for a reason.

Show Up Stand Up Speak Up

My journey began with a profound moment of self-discovery. Confronting my Inner Dream Stealer sparked a fire within me to empower others facing similar obstacles. As I pondered this, I realized it wasn't just about my journey; it was about empowering others to overcome their doubts and fears that have kept me and others from achieving the goals that God placed on our hearts.

This realization led to the birth of Divinely Driven Results, my Christian business coaching platform dedicated to helping women entrepreneurs integrate biblical principles into their business strategies. But my journey didn't stop there. I partnered with Millionaire Momentum with a shared vision: to empower one million people to achieve millionaire status while staying grounded in their faith. Now as a co-founder of Millionaire Momentum, we're committed to providing the resources, tools, connections, and opportunities needed to create Millionaire Momentum while keeping God at the center of it all. We do this through our free virtual networking events for men and women, ways to save money and grow yourself and your business, ways to gain on-going exposure for your products and services, and even support in implementing biblical business strategy.

My mission is clear: to empower you to step into your power as a son or daughter of God, fulfill your divine purpose, crush your goals, and overcome your inner dream stealer—all while keeping God as your CEO. Join me on this incredible journey, and let's build a legacy of faith, abundance, and empowerment together. It's time to show up, stand up, and speak up for the goals that God has placed on your heart through the calling He has given you. I would love to hear about the dreams you are feeling called to pursue. Feel free to email me at: Elise@DivinelyDrivenResults.com

KEEP BELIEVING

My Story

ROBERTA SKYE

SURRENDER

In my Free Spirited later 20's I set sail upon the ocean blue, with the intrepid Captain of a 24-foot sailboat, who used only a sextant for navigation. I surrendered to this journey consciously. Standing atop a cliff on Hawaii, overlooking the vast ocean, I said "yes" to whatever was to come.
While I helped record the daily sun sights, I didn't learn to use the sextant. If my Captain fell overboard, I would be adrift on the whims of sea and sail. As our craft was so small, the winds and currents pushed us west of our destination of Tahiti, and we had to beat our way back after a stop at Motu One, a classic coral atoll. Beautiful blue lagoon, pristine beaches, inhabited by a sole couple and their 2 young children.

A total of 6 weeks passed, with no contact from us to our families or anyone else. Imagine that today?!

The voyage was full of exquisite natural phenomena, luminescence turning the sea into a starry aquarium, strange lights, and sky colours, all offering me deep immersion into Nature's magic and mystery.

Show Up Stand Up Speak Up

RECOGNITION

At very distinct times I've been able to sense a disruption in the energy around me. The first was before we could see the coral atoll on the horizon, causing me to pace around the tiny deck. I noticed the horizon had grown a beard, which turned out to be palm trees. Again, when hiking alone in New Zealand, I stopped to set up my tent in the rapidly growing dark, even though I hadn't arrived at the hot spring to which I was headed. An insistent agitation convinced me to pack up and keep going. Within a very short time I came to a clearing by a stream and found the dugout 'sit bath' of the hot spring next to it.

EPIPHANY

Years later, along came a Teacher in a grey and white fur coat - my Beloved Feline, Danny. Seeking any possible help for this small Being who was struggling with many ailments, I attended a pet Expo and saw a sign proclaiming, "you can communicate with your pets". Astonished and curious, I called my first Animal Communicator, and discovered a whole new world of connection and revelation. She was reading his energy even as we spoke the first time over the phone. She never met Danny. I received incredible wise counsel through Danny 's own sentiments.

This was a BIG epiphany that launched me joyfully into a perpetual inquiry into new perspectives on Sentience and Consciousness in our multidimensional life experience. I am now an Advocate for the inclusion of all voices in this co-created experience on Planet Earth, as I fervently believe everything is Conscious and wanting to connect. Bringing recognition and respect to All, with a welcoming heart, is essential to our survival at this juncture in our collective history.

robertaskye@yahoo.ca

RECEIVE GRACIOUSLY

My Story

SUSAN CAMERON

There's nothing like seeing the tangible results of community members coming together to help one another. I've always been a contributor to my local community because it's just always felt like the right thing to do. And perhaps the spark came from watching my father's activity throughout his career. He was part of the Kinsmen, Lions Club, and other non-profits. Whether it's my instincts or my father's modeling, volunteering for and donating to local charities and nonprofits is a big part of my life. It's about giving back.

One that's close to my heart is A Loving Spoonful. I've long donated to this charity, which has provided healthy food to people living with HIV/AIDS since 1989. Shortly after the pandemic hit, I started helping with meal prep one night every week. When I started doing this, I shared what I was doing on social media and other people were inspired to join our meal prep army. It's incredibly gratifying to see the results of our efforts. At the end of a night in their kitchen, stacks of healthy packaged meals are ready to be delivered to people who need them—members of our community who are managing not only HIV/AIDS but also addiction, mental illness, and home insecurity.

My sense of giving is probably also influenced by my time working at the Canadian Broadcast Corporation (CBC) and local radio stations. The nature of those jobs put me at the center of community events, including charitable fundraising efforts. Though I've moved on in my career, the strong sense of community remains. I still donate to a variety of nonprofits and sponsor local events and performances. I often purchase ads in their programs, not necessarily for the business benefit, but because I know my small contribution keeps local non-profit performances going.

In this busy world, it's easy to expect someone else to step up. So many people feel tapped out. Both donations and volunteerism have been on a downward trajectory for the past decade due to several factors. I'm grateful that my career allows me to continue to do both. Over the years, I've been supported by many people in my community. It feels good to pay it forward and give back to the community.

Show Up Stand Up Speak Up

I LOVE being a realtor and not for the reasons you might think.

While, yes, the paycheck is good and it affords me a lifestyle I love, what I find really satisfying are the non-monetary rewards:
Getting to know people and hearing their stories
Supporting my clients as they make one of the biggest financial investments of their lives
Building a large social and business network that I can use to help others
Exercising my problem-solving superpowers
Seeing a wide variety of architecture throughout the city
Learning about my community

The real value I bring to my clients is my passion for what I do. It's so much more than buying and selling houses. It's seeing people through to the next phase of their lives. For most people, a house is a home, an anchor point. It's the place we always come back to. It's where we keep our treasures that remind us of the life we've lived. It gives me great satisfaction to know I make a difference in the life of every client with whom I work. And whether they know it or not, they make a difference in mine.

If you're looking for a realtor who knows the Vancouver market like the back of her hand, email me at susan@susancameronrealtor.com

LOVE YOURSELF

My Story

JULIE JONES

Hey there, I'm Julie Jones, and let me tell you about the incredible adventure of my life! If I had to pick one word to describe me, it's "kind." From the beginning, my heart was about spreading love and joy and having a blast. Growing up as the oldest kid in my family, I learned something super cool: giving back is the best thing ever. I was like a superhero at church events and helping charities. It felt like painting the world with kindness.

School was a bit tough sometimes because of bullies, but guess what? I made friends with the kids who needed a friend the most. Friendship was my superpower – once you were my friend, you were forever a friend. We laughed, talked, and created memories that would last a lifetime.

Then came the best part: my wedding with Mike! We got married on Halloween and used our wedding to help worthwhile causes. Even though we couldn't have our own kids, I made it my mission to help others who needed a helping hand. You know, something happened when my mom passed away. It made me realize that life is precious, and I wanted to spread happiness and be true to who I am. I became a sunshine-spreader, always lighting up the room with my fun glasses and spirit. I truly believed in people. I thought everyone could be unique, and I wanted to help them see it, too. We would do crazy things, wear silly costumes, and have the time of our lives. I always said, "Let's be brave and say yes to life!"

My journey is fabulous about celebrating life, bringing people together, and being kind. And you know what? I want you to remember that you're awesome too. Be yourself, spread kindness, and have a blast. Because just like I do, you can change the world with love, one fun and happy moment at a time!

Show Up Stand Up Speak Up

Stop Waiting Start Living

I am a passionate breakthrough coach and speaker dedicated to helping individuals break free from the cycle of waiting and start living their lives to the fullest. I empower people to overcome their fears, doubts, and limiting beliefs so they can design their life. Through personalized coaching sessions, I work closely with my clients to identify the barriers holding them back and develop strategies to overcome them. By challenging their mindset and encouraging them to act, I help my clients unlock their full potential and achieve their goals. In addition to one-on-one coaching, I offer inspiring speaking engagements and breakthrough sessions designed to motivate and empower audiences. Whether speaking to a small group or addressing a large crowd, I share practical insights, tools, and techniques that inspire people to step out of their comfort zones and embrace change. My dynamic and fun-filled style impacts audiences, sparking a sense of possibility and igniting a desire for positive transformation.

My approach is rooted in the belief that life is too short to spend waiting for the "perfect" moment or circumstances to pursue our passions. I encourage my clients to embrace imperfection, take risks, and embrace the journey of self-discovery. By cultivating courage, resilience, and self-compassion mindset, my clients are empowered to overcome obstacles, seize opportunities, and create meaningful, fulfilling lives. I am honored to play a role in helping people unlock their full potential and create lives filled with joy, fulfillment, and fun! Connect with me at https://www.juliejones.biz/

41

BE BRAVE

My Story

COLLEEN BIGGS

My life was anything but dull. I grew up in a small township in New Jersey and in 1976 my family moved me to bright and sunny Arizona. I remember jumping in the new backyard pool before unpacking even one box that day! I spent my summers in the pool, so much so that my hair turned green one year from the chlorine. I found freedom in swimming. I was happy, weightless, and free. This summer set the tone for what I would be seeking my entire life, freedom.

I spent my years trapped in an abusive family, not being seen or heard and when I was, it usually meant I was in a bit of trouble. I raised myself for many years and finally left the nest at the age of 17 right after I graduated high school. My Mom had a U-Haul packed and ready to vacate the state. Just like that, I had the rest of my adult life ahead of me, alone. The question was, what was I going to do with it? My life took many twists and turns throughout the years, but I distinctly remember reaching my 36th birthday, a single mother of two amazing kids KNOWING that I needed to be the example I so desperately wanted them to follow. To be brave, courageous in my endeavors, a motivator, a person who lives in integrity and blazes trails less traveled. Yes, that is what I needed them to see. From that day forward I had decided I wasn't going to live my life for others, but for ME! And I never looked back.

I climbed the ladder of Corporate America faster, married the man of my dreams that is now my spouse of 15 years, and have become a female that leads others to lean into their fullest purpose to reach their peak performance, inspire change in others, build unlimited success and leave a legacy. It wasn't easy, there were days when I didn't think I had it in me to become the person I knew God intended me to be. The hardest part was letting go to let God lead. I'm not a patient person and success requires patience, trust, faith in you and God, and determination. Do you have the "never quit" in you? I do! It stems from all of those along my path like my Master of Taekwondo that taught me that tomorrow is another day on the journey to my black belt. And my favorite CEO, Ruk Adams, who encouraged me to continue building the leadership skills necessary to become an entrepreneur. They bet on me and showed up for me. We all need a tribe because it's true that your network is your net worth. These valuable lessons that I have learned along the way, good and bad, have molded me into the amazing individual that I am meant to be today. I thank God every day for every experience.

Show Up Stand Up Speak Up

My passion to work with Business owners started back in 2003 at The Little Gym International, Inc.. I spent nearly 20 years at this company learning the way of negotiation, coaching, launching start-up businesses, and many more skills. The greatest lesson I learned was that my individual effort determines my success. Period. This is why I am so passionate about coaching other Women Entrepreneurs to reach their peak performance levels. *It is by making MASSIVE action a discipline, you will break through obscurity, increase your value to the marketplace, and help generate success in any area you select.*

It really is that simple. However, many entrepreneurs believe there is something outside of themselves that they are lacking. The only piece you could possibly be missing is knowledge, and what you do with it, that's it. I'll use food as an example. We all know that eating a Snickers bar is full of sugar and fat and if we eat it, we are adding to our calories and fat count for the day, yet people continue to eat them, even when they are complaining that they need to lose weight. So as entrepreneurs we know our businesses are driven by sales. If you sell more, you make more money, correct? I would say that is black and white, yet the excuses begin when sales are low on why they didn't sell more or drive additional income. I take these fears, and disbeliefs, face them head-on with the entrepreneurs I work with, and mix them with knowledge so they can leverage their strengths, skill sets, knowledge, and experience to drive sales and increase their income. The number one rule in business is to tell everyone about you and your business. I created a community of like-minded, driven female entrepreneurs to come together and network, create partnerships, be seen, be heard, and be visible. https://colleenbiggs.net/

BE YOU

NOOR INAYAT KHAN
Spy

FE del MUNDO
Paediatrician

HILDEGARD von BINGEN

Polymath

LUCY WALKER

Mountaineer

RUTH SMITH

Hi, I am Ruth Smith A true-blue (real) Aussie farmer's daughter.

The ebb and flow of my childhood facilitated the jumping out of Willow tress into creeks, drinking cow's milk direct from the source and roaming productive paddocks with my 3 older siblings. Rural life was simple, lived with integrity and built around community. A handshake was as good as a written contract and if you worked hard physically, the abundance of the land would nurture your imagination, sense of achievement and spirit.

And achieve I did.

I trained hard and competed at state level for swimming, water-polo, synchronized swimming, and lifesaving. I achieved the Australian Royal Lifesaving Society – Distinction Award and went on to become the first professional female Beach Inspector in New South Wales, and perhaps in Australia. I've run my own swim schools, trained countless aquatic professionals and I still can't get enough. Water and I have a divine relationship. Add children and the results are magical until children with challenges enter my zone of influence and the results are spectacular – transformational for individuals, families and communities.

And now? My soul driven passion as a Specialised Aquatic Therapist and Aquatic Mentor is to ensure that my genius of creating and delivering learning methodologies that tap into the power of water and the spirit that resides in challenged bodies and minds becomes a university degree. Aquatic Therapy is quite remarkable and has astonishing results for the students I am honoured to work with. Aquatic therapy uses the properties of water to transform the lives of children with additional needs and/or challenging behaviours. This cutting-edge modality improves self-regulation, motor planning, fine and gross motor skills, co-ordination, confidence and proprioception development. Their impulsivity reduces as does their anxiety and sensory sensitivities. Research confirms that children with challenges and their families are more likely to socialise with friends when they feel more confident in their child's water safety ability and awareness. I am changing lives.

"Life is Simple … Just add Water."

Show Up Stand Up Speak Up

It seems I was born with water in my veins. As a child I often wished that gills were standard issue for humans. Water and I have always had an inseparable connection. For forty-two years, teaching and coaching swimming in pools in Australia and overseas has been my genius. My early career in the disability-care field introduced me to hydrotherapy, The Halliwick Method and influential mentors. Water is my 'impact vehicle', the medium through which I facilitate the transformation of lives, especially when children with intellectual or physical challenges are added to the mix. As National winner of the 2022 Australian 'Teacher of Aquatics - Access & Inclusion' award, my work leading the Aquatic Therapy industry in Australia has been recognised by our national peak body. What is Aquatic Therapy? Put simply it's the leading edge, water-based healing modality that utilises specialised equipment and techniques to enhance students' proprioception, motor planning, self-regulation, fine and gross motor skills, cognitive focus, muscle tone, communication and co-ordination. Water safety and propulsion are also common therapeutic goals. Working with 'neuro-diverse' and physically challenged youngsters is a soul-driven, heart led mission that inspires me. Simply, it's a privilege from which I derive inexplicable and immeasurable satisfaction and sense of self-worth while changing lives.

Working with this challenged cohort is often like looking into another's soul. At other times it's as if they have allowed me to cross over their threshold and I am invited into their world. Maybe only fleeting at times, but it is there I have my greatest impact. My intended legacy is to develop both research and university-level post graduate courses and continue the development of the next generation of specialised aquatic professionals. My dream is to have a Centre of Excellence for Aquatic Therapy, a purpose-built pool in Australia where the allied health professionals have a multidisciplinary approach for clients from around the world all under the one roof. It would also be a place of education for specialised aquatic professionals from all around the world. I am looking to create a strategic alliance with an allied health professional, company, entity, or peak body to grow the impact I have in this space. So, now you know a little about me. If you are open to a conversation, I can be reached at rsmithuki1@gmail.com

DIVE DEEP

SHARON MEFFORD

My wanderlust was sparked at an early age.

As the daughter of a military officer, I had lived in 9 different states by the time I was 18. Every two or three years, my parents, 4 brothers, 3 sisters and I would all pack up our lives, say good-bye to our friends and head for the next posting.
I used to jokingly tell people that we moved often to stay ahead of the cops…until my dad found out. He did NOT think it was funny.

In some ways, this was challenging. I had no say over when or where we would live next. So, I tried to find some sense of control in other ways, such as what I ate. I sometimes insisted on eating breakfast food for every meal. And though I would have loved a dog, the suggestion of pets received a firm no from my parents. Moving that many kids was hard enough without furry creatures running around.

But it was also interesting to explore new places. How many people can say they've truly experienced that many different parts of their country? To visit a place is one thing, but to live there gives you a real sense of what life is like.

Then I met my husband, and we bought a house together. Suddenly I was anchored to a single location. It felt foreign and kind of uncomfortable. Boring even.

And that's when the travel started: Norway, Cancun, Australia, New Zealand, France, Italy. We spent several weeks touring Western Canada by motorcycle. On every trip, I've met new people and experienced new things.

Some people who grew up moving around a lot have found comfort in staying put as adults. Now that I get to control where I'm going and when, I think I'll always be drawn to the variety of new places, people, and experiences.

Show Up Stand Up Speak Up

"What is your Why?" or "What is your Purpose?" is a question asked entrepreneurs frequently. Looking back as a recovering "people pleaser," I realized I was trying to make the person asking the question to feel good. It led to many starts and stops for 20+ years and much frustration for me.

My mentor introduced me to many ideas through Bob Proctor and his Thinking Into Results program. The first step was a big goal, and I thought, "Here I go again." My mentor discussed what I wrote and asked me a question, "Sharon, are you Intellectually Enamored, or Emotionally Excited with your goal?" It took for her to say to me many times, "It does not matter to me what your goal is, I just want you to feel the excitement of your goal every time you say it." Her repeating that opened a floodgate of ideas that really meant something to me, and I now have an amazing goal that scares and excites me. I went from burnout while working long hours with students, advocating for them in school and on the job, and not knowing what to do when I retired from that job to my current state of focus. This due in large part to nourishing my Mind, my Body, and my Spirit in my daily work on self-image and setting boundaries.

This is motivating me to get up early in the morning and work on me. I now know that, to help others, I need to take care of myself so I can give to others what I have received from my mentor; a powerful feeling of excitement to start the day, clarity of goal, all-in commitment, and improving self-image daily. Best of all, I love myself and my goal! You can reach me at: sharonmeffordent@gmail.com

BE YOURSELF

MARCY SCHACTER

My Message to Women is...

Fearlessness is a learned habit that gets easier over time.

Show Up Stand Up Speak Up

LIVE LARGE

EMILY BASSETT

In the face of challenges, I've always lived by the mantra, "If there's a will, there's a way," a guiding principle that has shaped my journey and continues to do so.

Life's journey, peppered with its share of highs and lows, took an unexpected turn at the young age of 13 when I lost my father. The sudden shift from carefree adventures to grappling with resilience and independence was a stark reality. Life doesn't come with a manual, and this truth hit me hard. Yet, amidst poorly articulated condolences, family disputes, and internal frustrations, I sought solace in the understanding that we're all crafting our stories, navigating uncharted territories, and learning along the way.

So here I am, contributing a chapter to a book that celebrates the incredible paths women have forged, hoping that my story resonates with you. I encourage you to keep writing your own handbook, discovering silver linings, and staying focused on your success, for it's closer than you might imagine.

On the next page, you'll dive into the story of my company, a testament to paving your own way and determination. Startemup emerged in a humble Pickering, Ontario grocery store break room, a random shot in the dark to begin freelancing after losing my job as the CMO of a travel company and the end of all my relationships in Copenhagen, Denmark, during the height of the pandemic. Building a network in North America from my marketing development in Denmark seemed like a distant dream, but as clients flowed in and positive feedback echoed, it became a tangible reality.

The official birth of Startemup took shape when I joined forces with my co-founder, Connor Rutledge, transforming it into a full-service corporate Digital Marketing Agency. The initial year brought financial, familial, and friendship challenges, testing our persistence and patience. However, each setback became a lesson, guiding us to the remarkable present.

While you read this whole book, I hope you can curl the corners of your mouth, find yourself a smile and take that with you always.

Show Up Stand Up Speak Up

START. Seriously, whatever it is, the hardest part is just to start. I take immense pride in being the founder of Startemup Marketing Solutions, offering digital marketing services globally. If you're reading this book, I can be certain you've seen some of our marketing as we are so proud to be the marketing team behind this project! We pride ourselves on joining YOUR TEAM in the capacity you need it. With our structure and organization, my co-founder and our team offer account managers as 'your personal CMOs.' Not only that, but your 'CMO' has a team underneath them that genuinely CARES. Startemup was born from the need to have an agency that understands every business needs marketing in a different capacity at a different time, and offering one service and pushing it onto clients may not truly be what's best for everyone. Not every industry thrives with ads, a fancy website, or even social media. We focus on what's going to be the highest converting for you - so when you win, we win.

Just like this incredible network of women who have come together to create this book, you can also get noticed for your achievements - and we would love to help get you there! Discover some of our work and book a coffee chat to explore how we might just be everything your business needs. www.startemup.ca Explore our social media management, ads management, SEO strategy, website design, development and management as well as full marketing strategy packages on our site.

STAY WILD

My Story

SUSAN ISAAC

We almost lost her the first night! We got a call asking if we would rehabilitate an orphaned fawn; could we pick her up immediately. She was no bigger than one of our cats. She wouldn't lift her head and refused to eat. Her condition meant we were running out of time to save her. She needed goats' milk every hour. We were force-feeding all afternoon, but she was too traumatized to move. She would only survive if she took a bottle instead of force feeding. She survived the first night thanks to my animal whisperer husband's idea to sleep in a small room and take one of our cats with him. With air mattress in hand, fawn, husband, and cat went to bed. After forced feedings every hour the fawn became curious about the cat. By late evening the fawn stood and voluntarily took her first bottle of milk, sharing with sister cat. We adopted a rhythm of daily care and named her after the surrounding fast blooming buttercup flowers. We discovered the joy of making Buttercup's welfare top priority and became completely smitten. I learned new skills like napping in tall grass, lying quietly for hours, one hand resting reassuringly on her back.

Buttercup was growing up, healing from losing her mom as we were healing from a head-on vehicle collision that happened 3 months before Buttercup's arrival. Our focus on Buttercup helped lift our spirits and strengthened our immune systems. I had daily therapies for numerous injuries. I was shocked to learn that my well-worn warrior approach wasn't the key element in healing. My hard-driving style of exercising often reversed my progress. A new approach of rest, surrender and patience was proving to be more effective. When I resisted this tactic, the universe provided the prod I needed to return to my daily naps with Buttercup. As my pace slowed down, I started to long for my 10-year-old self who painted, drew, laughed, and sat for hours watching a spider crawl up a tree. I was starting to listen to my heart's desire.

Buttercup and I healed together during that warm summer, both longing to experience the world well-loved and whole. Weeks later Buttercup's release occurred, and she began to explore forest life as a wild deer. As for me, my big release and exploration of the creative world as a whole-hearted wild woman, had just begun.

Show Up Stand Up Speak Up

After age 10, I abandoned the subdued whispers in my soul asserting my artistry. My fearful heart didn't know the way. At age 47, I stepped out of the familiar professional world, and the universe strode in. I was mentored and loved every step pf the way. My soul often felt raw and exposed, but I continued to show up. Eventually, listening to my artistic passion became more natural until one day, I quietly owned that I was an artist and had a unique style! There is inherent risk creating glass art with fire. High temperatures can alter an original vision in unpredictable ways. Certainly, it's a daily reminder about the crucible of human life, but the gift of emergence as someone new and whole has been invaluable. I am now proudly unpredictable, wild, and a little dangerous. My first glass pendant design was the butterfly, symbol of transformation, a talisman to help me find my true voice. My one-of-a-kind adornments resonated with others who sought to express themselves and I realized that I was uplifting others through my art. Once, touching her talisman, one woman exclaimed, "I feel powerful when I wear my pendant!" The glass designs for pendants have evolved into the foundation of my digitally designed wearable art and home décor. Imagine, images of glass on fabrics. My vision continues to unfold. It all started through napping in the tall grass with Buttercup so many years ago. That 10-day old fawn taught me to start with silence, presence, listening to my desires and make my warrior spirit second. What are my next steps as I explore new horizons creating, teaching, storytelling, collaborating? I will let you know after I metaphorically take a few naps in the tall grass with my beloved Buttercup. www.susanisaacdesign.com

FLY HIGH

NERYL THOMPSON

My Message to Women is ...

Be a disruptor, change the pattern, shift the energy,
be unexpected.

Show Up Stand Up Speak Up

BE UNEXPECTED

My Story

LINDA L. NARDELLI

A Woman's Way

I am fascinated by how we can bring our vulnerability to the presence of women and be heard—not only by the mind but also by the heart and belly. When a woman listens with empathic awareness, she lets her body feel the words being spoken; she moves close to the other's feelings, which is freeing. Unfettered, a woman's walls fall away, and she blossoms like the lotus flower rising from the mud into a magnificent expression of her glory.

How can we stay true to who we are as women and revel in the abundance of such captivating sensitivity? How do we hold a pristine vision of who we are when we live in a world based on a hierarchy where feminine power is not revered? We must come together and set aside the three lies we inherited. The first lie is that we are lesser, the second is that we are better, and the third is that we are equal. We're not lesser, nor better and certainly not equal. We don't all have the same opportunities in life. We're given alternate circumstances and experiences. We're different, each on a distinctive path expressing our unique design. Yet, as a world society, we are ruled by these three untruths that define our self-worth and the value of others. When we are seen as lesser than others, we struggle against injustice, work hard to measure up and compete for power. When perceived as better than others, we gain a false sense of security and control that we go to great lengths to maintain. To level the imbalance, we believe that we are the same, which fools us into projecting our perception of reality onto others, demanding that they be like us.

How do we embrace authenticity and inner truth when this hierarchal power defines us? That question has led me to the heart of being a woman, disentangling myself from the overarching pecking order of patriarchy and opening myself to the way of the feminine. The more I embody my feminine wisdom without self-doubt or apology, the more I cease overextending and exhausting myself. I become adept at receiving what I need to sustain my endeavours. A woman's way isn't about struggling to meet her needs or gaining a higher rank in society; it's about being present, available, receptive to what emerges in every moment, and ecstatically alive.

Show Up Stand Up Speak Up

Spiritual Mentor & Counsellor, Author & Artist

As a healer, for many years, I naively assumed that to heal meant to fix and make everything better. In time, I realized that healing is a spiritual practice that is not about changing who we are but instead falling in love with life as it is. After all, change is inevitable, but not by chance nor by projecting our will onto reality. Transformation occurs when we develop an intimate connection with our wants and needs and, ultimately, our self-value.

In my spiritual counselling practice, I help people connect with their desires and surrender the pressure to actualize them. We get so caught up in the *how to* that we lose sight of our *why*. Furthermore, we tend to believe that we must explain and justify our *why* to the extent that we disconnect from our feelings and intuitions. My healing work is about developing an intimate relationship with all aspects of the self, body, mind and soul to propel our choices and actions from the whole self. Healing is not about eradicating the parts of the self we dislike. It's about welcoming all aspects and being curious about the guidance they hold. In this way, we cease evaluating ourselves and others through the lens of right and wrong.

In my work, whether in healing sessions, mentorship circles, writing, or creating art, I look for a way back to the center and harmony. In my book, *Mystical Intimacy*, I explore the fulcrum point between our spiritual integrity and human experience, fostering an intimate relationship with our longing. As we move closer to the core of the longing, to its purpose and essence, we cross a threshold from the mundane into the mystery, freeing our creative potential and, as women – our right to be who we are. Visit www.lindanardelli.com to nurture your soul and uncover the wisdom of your human nature.

YOU'RE WHOLE

CHRISTINE BLANCHETTE

Poetry in the classroom

I always loved going to school. Not sure exactly why, but I believe it was my love of learning. Each morning, I would be already dressed and my school bag ready at the door. I would also look for the bus making its way down the rural road to pick up me and my two brothers. When the bus got close enough, we would run down the hill from our house. Despite the short distance from the Hobby Farm in the Eastern Townships in Quebec, I would often be early waiting at the stop to make sure I wouldn't miss it. When the bus didn't show up for some reason, I was sad.

Despite my shyness, I enjoyed being at school. It was also a chance for me to have my own independence. My passion for writing started in elementary school where I wrote my first poem. I will recite some of it here:

"I am all by myself, there is nothing to add, but sweet music burning on a stand. I am all by myself with love and grace" Little did I know later some of my poetry would be published. I caught the writing bug from my mother who would often read and write.

When the moment came to spread my wings, it was while sitting at the kitchen table and filling out my college application. I was nervous while filling it out because I knew this would be a big transition for me to be away from the farm. I remembered telling my dad I want to go to school, and he responded, "you do, Chris". The very words were exciting but scary, but, with the nod of approval from him, I knew there was no looking back.

My zest for life began at an early age. I did enjoy growing up on the hobby farm. In fact, we had a pony, pet pig and we could stretch our eyes as far as we could. It is known as the land of rolling hills and wide-open spaces. While in my teens, I was fearless taking the train and bus to Montreal, and cross Canada on my own. I would journal often while on these solo trips and thought it was an adventure. Later, I discovered my mom had kept all my cards from my travels, from Banff, Alberta, to South Korea.

My love of writing led me to become a successful, nationally published writer for various publications covering health, nutrition, sports medicine, and fitness pieces. I also created my own column. Looking back on my youth, it all started putting my thoughts on paper and turning it into a poem such as "The Cake Scheme". Writing is therapeutic and, if it wasn't for my love of going to school and discovering writing, I wouldn't be sharing my story here. It has opened doors in many areas, and I am still honing my craft. Maybe a whole book one day. Stay tuned!

Show Up Stand Up Speak Up

Little did I know my passion for running would lead to creating my own TV show. I am a living testimonial to...**FOLLOW YOUR PASSION, LIVE YOUR DREAM**....because that's what I did. I can't remember not having an interest in media, though it became magnified after working at Rogers Television and seeing firsthand how the stories were created.

I believe everything happens for a reason, though I wasn't so sure on one spring day back in 2008. That's when I got laid off from my Postmedia advertising job during tumultuous economic times; and I wasn't sure what was next for me. As a natural extension of writing, my attention circled back to broadcast media. Considering my TV interviewing experience, I thought the timing was never going to be better to create my own TV show. I had an epiphany while working on my laptop. First thing I did was send off my proposal, which took a long time, about two years, to get accepted by Shaw TV in 2013. This led to creating my first TV show, "Run With It", which is Canada's only running, fitness and health show, airing currently on TELUS Optik TV, as well as Video on Demand, The Healthy Living Network and now, Live Streaming. On Run With It, I interview fitness-conscious people, from Olympians, physicians, wellness professionals, and celebrities who follow a healthy lifestyle, to people of all walks of life with an inspirational tale to tell.

A couple years later I created another show, called "The Closing Act", which is a music and entertainment show. The Closing Act profiles movers and shakers in the entertainment industry. I can't even imagine not doing what I do today. My platforms are vehicles in which to promote fitness, healthy living, events, and interesting people that tell fascinating stories to inspire others. Recently, I began to teach Freelance Producing at the College Level, to help those who are interested in launching their own program. My advice: Finding a mentor/support is vital. Contact me at www.runwithit.ca to learn more.

PASSION DRIVEN

SARA TROY

Wisdom is often spoken of as if it were a commodity, easily acquired or traded. However, my life's journey has taught me that true wisdom is far more profound. It is not something that can be handed over; it is a treasure earned through the intricate odyssey of life. Wisdom, to me, is that pivotal moment when universal truths permeate my being, resonating deeply with my heart and propelling my spirit into meaningful action. It is the innate ability to discern precisely what I need to know at exactly the right time.

My path to this understanding has been one of rigorous introspection and self-discovery. It certainly hasn't been easy. I've experienced periods of profound disconnection from my soul's messages, and my heart has been broken more times than I can count. Yet, with each fall, I made the conscious decision to rise, emerging stronger and more resilient each time.

This journey has fundamentally been about reconciling my heart with my soul, allowing them to function in harmony. This reconciliation set me free, fully embracing and expressing my true self. Now, I stand unapologetically as myself, wholeheartedly embracing every aspect of my being. In my eyes, this is the essence of wisdom – a delicate dance with life's complex melodies, a process of continuous learning, growth, and resurgence.

For too long, I denied my true essence, cowed by fears of ridicule and judgment. Deep within me was a profound knowingness, an understanding of truths I couldn't articulate. I could see the potential in others and help them recognize it, but I remained alienated from my own humanity, feeling like an outsider.

In my efforts to please others, I lost myself, conforming to expectations that never truly suited me. However, a profound realization struck me – no matter what I did, it would never suffice. It was clear that I couldn't become the person I was destined to be without embracing my soul and allowing my human self to merge with my spiritual essence.

This realization marked a turning point. I stopped trying to fit into roles that were not meant for me. I began to understand that external validation or standards did not dictate my values and journey. By aligning my human self with my soul, I discovered a state of divine wholeness. This unification allowed me to be authentically me, balancing my earthly existence with my spiritual depth. In this equilibrium, I found my true self, liberated from the fears of judgment and free to be who I was always meant to be.

Show Up Stand Up Speak Up

Self Discovery Wisdom is ready for the clicking. Twelve years ago, when I was first invited to join a podcast network, I remember asking, "What's a podcast?" It seems almost amusing now, considering how integral podcasts have become in my life. Fast forward twelve illuminating years, with eleven of those spent on my own network, and the journey has been nothing short of extraordinary. Having my own podcast network has afforded me the honor of interviewing countless remarkable individuals. Each conversation and each story shared has been a treasure trove of inspiration and insight. From each guest, I've learned something new, something profound that has contributed to my own understanding of the world and the diverse tapestry of human experience. Their stories of resilience, innovation, compassion, and determination have not only enriched the lives of our listeners but have deeply impacted me personally. Reflecting on these past twelve years, I am filled with gratitude for this journey. From not knowing what a podcast was to leading a network and engaging with such extraordinary souls, it's been a path of continuous growth and inspiration.

Hearing so many incredible stories through my podcasts, I felt a compelling need to expand their reach. This led to the birth of Orchard of Wisdom.org. It's a platform where we showcase the wisdom and skills of the amazing individuals I interview. Our latest project, "Our Forgotten Children," features fifteen authors who share vital perspectives on what needs to change for the welfare of our children. And there's more on the horizon - we're launching the Self Discovery Coaches anthology this autumn. So, while my journey began with podcasting, and it will always be my first love, I'm proud to say we've grown into something much more. We're not just about podcasts anymore; we're about spreading knowledge, inspiring change, and empowering voices. www.selfdiscoverywisdom.com

DISCOVERING ILLUMINATIONS

TERESA COLLINS

I see you! You are my sister of Light. How many times have you dimmed yourself? The time is now, Light Sister, to become Fearless. It is in the becoming that you will learn to Shine brighter than you ever thought possible. If You Can't Beat Fear, Just Do it Scared. There isn't a single formula for coming into our light. The truth is, it's scary.

The judgment that you fear may actually come; the friends that you fear you will lose may really leave; the life that you fear will change will indeed change in more ways than you can imagine. So, the question that naturally comes to mind is, why open up in the first place? Your Soul knows. She has been whispering to you for a long time.

As a lightworker, coming out of your spiritual cocoon has less to do with your comfort zone and more to do with the people you're here to serve, the message you're here to teach, and the change you're here to create. In other words, your life purpose has more to do with the collective whole rather than just the fear. From this perspective, are you willing to withhold your wisdom, guidance and light from the people you're here to serve?

Are you really prepared to slow down the ascension of the planet because you're scared of your life changing? Do you really want to play it safe and stay in your comfort zone when you know that your purpose could help create real, powerful changes in the world?

It's time for you to truly rise up, little butterfly of the light. Unwrap your wings. It's time to rise up to who you are and to what living your purpose means. Doing so involves coming out of your spiritual cocoon unapologetically, even if that will bring about messy life changes and uncomfortable emotions. You owe it to the people you're here to serve, to yourself, to all of us, and to the world.

Staying in your spiritual cocoon puts a cap on the amount of light you can nurture and express in the world. In other words, how can you truly work your light when you're not letting it shine fully?

If you have found this chapter, it is not by coincidence. Source is speaking directly to you. Reaching you wherever you are and igniting the flame of your soul.

Close your eyes and feel into these pages. You have been Activated. Time to Shine Butterfly. Unwrap your wings and show the world your true colors.

Show Up Stand Up Speak Up

For over a decade I have been igniting and activating thousands of women all around the world. It's your turn. I am the owner of Blended Spirit Wellness & Academy.
I am a Mama of 2 kids with challenges. In fact my kids were the whole reason I activated my healing to begin with. My oldest got really sick and modern medicine wasn't working, so Spirit led me down an incredible and profound journey to become the healer my family needed.

I was born Psychic and have added a huge amount of skills to my toolbox including Reiki, Counselling, Life Coaching, Hypnotherapist and so much more.

My clients are often those who have experienced a large amount of trauma in this and past lives and my Specialty is being an Alchemist. Shifting the Trauma to Wisdom effectively and thoroughly. Often unlocking and activating their natural healing gifts.

Ways to work with me include One on One sessions available both online and in person at my Surrey Studio. Take one of my many Reiki and Spiritual Development classes on my online academy. Join one of my many in-person classes or community events. Book a free 15-minute chat to see how we can connect. www.blended-spirit.com

BE FEARLESS

SONYA VAN STEE

Life is too short to live on other people's terms.

As I write this, it's only been a week and a half since we buried my Dad. Despite my grief, I am feeling so grateful and blessed to have had forty-six years with him. As we prepared for his funeral and people began sending messages and condolences, it really struck me what an impact Dad had on everyone around him, from someone in the next bed in the hospital to people that knew him for many decades. He had a way of making people feel comfortable around him as well as inspire people to become more than they already were, and yet he never once apologized for being authentically himself.

And then I realized – I actually *have* apologized for being myself at times! I have spent so much time worrying about what others think and what they want me to be or how they want me to behave that I lost part of who I am. Don't get me wrong – I have done a *lot* of work on myself over the past few years and I'm not ashamed of who I am. That being said, I recognize that I still have some work to do.

I am one of seven siblings, and each of us is somehow simultaneously the same as the rest and completely different! One of them said to me last week, "Sonya, thank you for being you." What a wonderful compliment! It made me tear up because it showed me how much I've grown and allowed the true me to show up more than my carefully manicured version of how I thought others wanted me to show up. His comment showed me that I am indeed on the right path!

Armed with Dad's memory to inspire me and urge me on, I will continue to work on myself and on becoming the best version of myself. I will take all the things I've learned over the last years and step up my own game as well as mentor those who have come to see me as their leader. Like Dad, I want to impact each person I come into contact with and inspire them to be the most amazing version of themselves! I know Dad would be proud.

Show Up Stand Up Speak Up

It's not as important what we do as what we leave behind.

As a kid, it was never my dream to become an entrepreneur. I wanted to become a nurse or perhaps a teacher: I never dreamed of working for myself or being my own boss. But when, as a teenager, I was introduced to the concept of Direct Marketing, I was sold. I fell in love with the dream. This was going to be amazing, and I was going to rise to the top of my company!

Unfortunately, I didn't really understand the "how" part of the concept and failed miserably, but I held onto the dream all through college and beyond. I tried a few other companies and still never really got anywhere, but then it all changed! I took an online marketing course that taught me how to connect with people on social media and brand myself in a way that people actually want to follow me and do business with me!

It was crazy! I went from never having more than a handful of people join my team to signing up more than fifteen people in my first few weeks of joining a new company! Since then, I've moved once more after discovering I was allergic to the products I was promoting, and my team has tripled what I had in my last company, which was over triple what I had done previously.

But the best part is hands down the impact that I am privileged to have in the lives of my team and their families. They are getting for free what it took me years of failure and tens of thousands of dollars in training to learn, and I am both thrilled and honoured to give it to them. cheeryperson@hotmail.com

YOU'RE POWERFUL

MICHELLE NEDELEC

When I'm happy, you can hear it. I tend to hum, talk, or even sing when I'm happy. I don't think someone needs to be happy all the time and God knows, my family appreciates the silence when I'm concentrating or getting other things done, like sleep. I'm like the happy 5-year-old who's super cute when she's sleeping and quiet. That makes me laugh.

Apparently, even when I was 2 years old, in the dead of winter, I would put on my snow suit and boots and hike over hills and under barbed wire fences to go and visit my neighbour, Maria Markovich. She had the best stories! We'd talk for hours about her husband and her boys, escaping Czechoslovakia and anything else that came up.

When I was 5 years old, I noticed that the neighbour's house down the road was on fire. I ran back to my house and told my mom and dad. I asked them what they needed and they said, "Shovels, buckets and people!" As they left to go help, I got on the phone and called all the rest of the neighbours requesting, you guessed it, shovels, buckets, and people. By the time the fire department got there everyone had helped to almost put out the fire and we saved most of Jackson's house.

I think it's important that kids are encouraged to voice themselves, their happiness, their curiosity, and their input. You never know what they're going to create with it, who they're going to become, and how they're going to improve the lives of others.

Yes, I use my voice in all I do today.
Sometimes, it's just because I'm happy.

Show Up Stand Up Speak Up

Rock the World,
Shake the Foundation
of Dependence, and
Move People to
Stand on Their Own.

My mission statement has served me and all of my businesses.

It's not meant to fiercely create independence; it's meant to foster epic self-empowerment. It applies to me, my business partners, my teams, our clients, and their clients! It's too easy to claim victimhood to the market, the government, and the 'powers that be'. But… once you see that you are capable of so much more; going after your dreams, overcoming the past, even figuring out technology, or building a legacy that carries on beyond your time here on Earth, then you step beyond simply running a business and you set out on a journey of self-discovery and self-actualization. One thing I currently do is run 5 podcasts. Yes, 5. I am a special kind of crazy. The kind of crazy that embraces my kind of sassy. I run The Business Ownership Podcast, currently top 1.5% overall and in business. I also run The Little Blue Pill For Business. It's all about getting it up and keeping it up, and of course, we're talking about revenue and profit.

I understand that it's all about the 6 inches between your ears, so I interview some of the hottest people in the industry who are blowin' and goin' so that we can help you get in on some action. So, if you like a little tongue-in-cheek and not just physically, this podcast is for you.. Life is too short to take it all so seriously, and besides, you'll never know where self-actualization may take you unless you're willing to have a little fun with it! I'm Michelle@AwarenessStrategies.com and I'd love to help you spark the fire that makes you, you!

BE SASSY

CAROLYN MCOUATT

My life's exploration has been to embrace "Freedom" as my guiding force which empowers me to "Soar" and succeed with heart and mind in harmony.

Energy fuels my purpose-driven life. It's my lifelong quest to align with my purpose and make a big positive difference in the world, empowering others to do the same. I'm driven by the profound connection between truth, self-awareness and manifestation. Taking full responsibility for my thoughts, feelings, and actions is paramount – it's Living and Leading above the Line.

My mission? To infuse the world with love, vitality, enthusiasm with an appreciation for what is, all while serving from my highest self. I find strength and wisdom in community, where healing and liberation thrive. Nature's embrace nourishes my soul, grounding me in the present moment, and guiding me with inner wisdom.I approach life as a humble student, always eager to learn and grow. What inspires me? Being present, grateful, and embracing simplicity. Letting go to lead, making space for grace, and delving within to win for true victory. In our collective journey, let's embrace the power of the heart-mind connection, empowering each other to shine and soar in 2024 and beyond.

SUSAN JAREMA

In the tapestry of my life, I've been a lifelong entrepreneur, wanna-be artist, mother, and an explorer of yoga philosophy. From my first entrepreneurial ventures at the age of four, to my extensive 25+-year journey in marketing, I've embraced the ever-changing landscape with curiosity. My online journey began in 1995, navigating the emerging digital space to harmonize technology with authentic expression. A near-death experience in 2010 transformed my life. Beyond the hustle of entrepreneurship, I now wear the hat of a yoga teacher, a student of Buddhist self-mastery, and a champion of sustainability.

In a delicate dance of yin and yang, I strive to navigate the dynamic interplay of business strategy, technology, and inner exploration. Passionately blending marketing with collaboration, I help others to stand out and create an impact in the world. Community is the conduit for collaboration where collectively we can magnify success, share experiences and support each other.

You can find me on the mat, beach, mountains, or Zoom, embracing entrepreneurship and Zen, forever learning. Balance is a lifelong journey of the intricate dance of yin and yang. Embrace the journey, for in it we discover the essence of life itself.

Show up Stand Up Speak Up

Susan and Carolyn, friends for over 20 years, initially crossed paths teaching business classes. Their connection was reignited in March 2020 during a Grand Canyon hike, just days before the world was thrust into a global shutdown. Gazing at the vast canyon, they sensed a global shift and the fear that would be present for businesses recognizing a need for a new form of connection. The Grand Connection was born from the inspiration derived from the expansive wonder of the Grand Canyon and the need to serve the suffering businesses around the globe. Grounded in collaboration, the Grand Connection holds three core values: connect, create, and collaborate. This ethos fosters a win-win-win relationship where businesses share resources, skills, connections, and opportunities to collectively thrive, and their clients receive more value. The Grand Canyon serves as a symbol of their connection and inspiration, representing the infinite potential of a new way of connecting with an open mind and heart amidst the challenges of life and business. At the heart of their philosophy is the principle of Grand Giving.

The Grand Connection recognizes that success is amplified through meaningful connections, serving first and mutual support. Their journey through life's challenges has reinforced the significance of not navigating those struggles alone and resourcing the community to find answers and solutions. "Alone we can do so little; together we can do so much." - Helen Keller. The Grand Connection invites entrepreneurs to be part of a thriving caring community that values collaboration and meaningful connections. In the spirit of "together is better," the community strives to uplift each other and leverage collective expertise for mutual growth. Members actively contribute to a broader purpose, emphasizing the transformative power of connection, creating opportunities together through collaboration and celebrating shared. success.hello@grandconnection.ca

EMPOWERING
COLLABORATION

My Story

MARY LUMMERDING

Have you seen parents in the store who cannot control their child? I had one of those kids. Taking my son Marc grocery shopping was so traumatic that I would cry when I got home. The beginning of my true growth began with raising my son. At age 5 Marc was diagnosed with ADHD (Attention Deficit and Hyperactivity Disorder), thanks to trained day care workers who recognized the signs. Shortly after, his dad was diagnosed … ADHD is hereditary. I read books about parenting and ADHD. A support group called the Learning Disability Association was helpful. I had a cause and I started to grow out of my shell.

Cooking was an activity that my son and I could enjoy together. Marc liked chopping vegetables and he enjoyed being helpful. I appreciated sharing my love of cooking with my son. Another helpful avenue was growing and selling vegetables at farm markets. We grew many different varieties. I enjoyed convincing people to try an apple cucumber and multi coloured carrots. I created radish bouquets with 7 varieties. One day, my husband said we had too many peppers. I wrote a sign that said: 'Today we picked a peck of peppers' which attracted attention. One more story: we had misshapen carrots. The sign said: 'Wonky carrots for kids-young and old'. Yes, growing and selling is an interesting challenge. It helps to be creative and have fun with your work!

When Marc graduated from school I had 3 binders of reports. I went to school meetings and if the school representatives didn't have a report, I pulled it from my binder. One day I met with a group of strangers about my son. I put an 8x10 picture on the table. I could see the faces around the table pause and realise that we were dealing with a person. Advocating for my son helped him, and it helped me too. When Marc became more independent, I joined Toastmasters to continue to build my confidence. The members spent 3 years getting me to speak up. Eventually a member realised that my voice was stronger whenever I talked about vegetables. That was my passion!

My mission today is to help everyone in the world be able to cook for themselves and enjoy their time in the kitchen. All the bits of my life are coming together to create my current endeavour as a Cooking Coach.

Show Up Stand Up Speak Up

If you'd met me fresh out of high school, you wouldn't have imagined I'd become a chef. I was a nervous, shy introvert. I cooked at home because my mom didn't like the daily chore of cooking for 5 kids.

I decided to try cooking for a living. I chose a 2-year Culinary Management program in Toronto. It was a magical time that offered unique opportunities. One special event was held at a castle called Casa Loma. I still recall seeing one of the chef instructors with a student in the ballroom, just the 2 of them swinging around the massive space in their chef uniforms.

I also had work opportunities at the Banff Springs Hotel and the Sheraton in Toronto. I was the buffet queen at Banff Springs. After college I moved to Victoria BC to live with my sister – still struggling to figure things out! Eventually I worked at the award-winning Herald Street Caffe. We made and served fresh pasta. The chef used fresh food from local producers. The Herb Guy would come into the restaurant each week with bags of luscious basil for pesto, rosemary, and other herbs plus edible flowers. I stopped working as a professional cook when I had my son. Cooking at home was easy but sometimes it was boring. I developed ways to make it fun, easy, and interesting.

Fast forward to today. As a personal Chef and Cooking Coach, I help my clients to discover the true value of cooking in 3 ways: social with family or friends, health and financially. Turn on the music – it is time to dance and cook! From my client, Michelle: "It was a treat to have a Chef in the kitchen to answer all my questions". Contact me at ChefMary@kitchentimes.org to explore your cooking journey-online or in-person.

ENJOY COOKING

VALLI MANICKAM

My Message to Women is...

Celebrate and love yourself daily for the powerful woman you are.

Show Up Stand Up Speak Up

YOU'RE FABULOUS

My Story

AMANDA MAY

I have intentionally crafted my life to be a continuous adventure. This involves exploring the deepest levels of my consciousness to understand the beliefs underlying my worldview and the lens through which I experience it. It also consists of seeking out the beauty of the world around me, from hiking the majestic Machu Picchu to finding stillness on the yoga mat. Another aspect of this adventure is experiencing authentic connections with others, where I can appreciate and learn from their spiritual path. However, my wildest adventure has been becoming a mother to two children born 20 years apart. My son showed me responsibility, playfulness, and unconditional love. My daughter has taught me to connect with my heart and let go of areas where my masculine energy no longer serves me. They are the most fulfilling thrill of my life.

Living deliberately means taking actions that support my goals and align with my core values. I set a theme each year, such as "love without limits" or "simplify and scale," and evaluate my actions based on that theme and my core values. I believe in cultivating gratitude, integrity, growth, reverence, and creativity. These values help me to see the gift in all experiences, to be honest and free of manipulation, always to strive to be the best version of myself, to respect and honor others, and to have the passion and courage to create something out of nothing.

Beyond the fancy dresses, designer purses, and elegant events, I truly value my love for adventure. I also appreciate the small things in life, like fresh, warm gourmet donuts, standing at the shore with the smell of the water in the air while fishing, and the awkward yet enjoyable sensation of getting the hiccups. Although I am a strong and resilient person, I lead a simple yet fulfilling life. I have found a perfect balance between being productive and enjoying the present moment. In the past, I used to be constantly busy, but now I have learned to appreciate the beauty of just being myself and enjoying the present moment. I take time to invest in myself and my well-being. I prioritize activities that nourish my mind, body, and soul. These include quality time learning about my life and spiritual partner, working out to challenge my physical limits, reading books to expand my knowledge, journaling to gain wisdom, decorating to express myself, and spending time with my dogs to feel their unconditional love. May you be happy and well as you find your sweet spot in life.

Show Up Stand Up Speak Up

My mission is to empower women to embrace and celebrate their femininity, both inside and out, through beauty. I have created various avenues to achieve this goal, such as serving as a salon manager at Caesar's Palace in Las Vegas, being an on-air guest with Home Shopping Network, and working as a C-suite executive for multi-million-dollar brands. My love for beauty started during my teenage years when my grandmother taught me how to blend eyeshadow colors properly. Although I wasn't allowed to, I would sneak into my sister's makeup and often get in trouble for trying to put glitter on my cheeks for Sunday school. I graduated from high school with my beauty license and followed my intuition to move from a small town in Ohio to Las Vegas, a city that felt grand, luxurious, and limitless. I knew that there was something special for me there. By having a clear vision and taking action towards it, I manifested a beauty career I am passionate about. Over twenty years, I worked with the women's director of the United Nations to build a self-sustaining women's project in the province of Venda, South Africa. I have also developed an Award-winning all-in-one makeup wheel, ran makeup teams for Miami Swim Week and New York Fashion Week, was a national trainer for America's Top beauty brands, and owned a top permanent makeup and advanced skincare academy.

Additionally, I am an author and beauty editor for an international luxury lifestyle magazine. The first two decades prepared me for the next two: Beauty Boss turned CEO. I am now in a position to lead teams in multi-million-dollar companies and work alongside brilliant minds in beauty and business. My vision for the future is clear: step back into international speaking and philanthropy initiatives, become a best-selling author, sit on advisory boards, scale and sell companies to reach my ultimate goals. I want women to feel confident in living bold lives in their divine feminine space, believing they are worthy of everything they desire. www.AmandaMayBeauty.com

LIVE DELIBERATELY

NATALIE CURTIS
Ethnomusicologist

KATHARINE McCORMICK
Philanthropist

CARRIE MATILDA DERICK

Geneticist

AVIS & EFFIE HOTCHKISS

Motorcyclists

My Story

DONNA VACHON

"Trust the journey, you've got this!"
Easier said than done, trust me I know.

This small mantra is the one that helped me through the hardships of my life. At the time I may not have known why something was happening, but I had to trust the journey and not fight the unknown outcome. We all try and fight what is happening vs, what is supposed to happen. Giving up control is the hardest thing to do in your <u>own life</u> after all. I work in the construction safety industry and love my job 100%. I had money in the bank, I was driving a car I loved and was proud of, also had so many truly amazing friends and family. I was living the dream as they say.

In the Summer of 2018, my best friend and I walked into an appointment for me to be tested for breast cancer. We knew this appointment wasn't going to go well. Funny how your instincts just know what you are about to walk into. As we suspected it was indeed Stage 3 Ductal Carcinoma and it had spread to my lymphatic system. This was the day I lost control of my wonderful life. Now, I must listen to the doctors, and do the treatment that frightens me and would hopefully kill the cancer faster than the two of them were killing me combined. To add to this news, I had to accept losing my long, beautiful thick hair due to chemotherapy, losing both of my breasts, and having a full hysterectomy… effectively removing everything we use to identify as women. Unbeknownst to me at the time I would also endure 20 surgeries over the last five years, just to reconstruct myself to feel like a normal woman again.

Trusting the journey was the hardest thing out of all that mentioned above. To some of you, that might sound strange, but having faith is a struggle when you are dying from treatment with no promise of survival through the seeming abyss of poison and pain.

Show Up Stand Up Speak Up

Today, I am still here to write this book entry, I am back to work full time, and I have a beautiful relationship including an amazing Bonus Son.

The message here is that trusting the journey is what brought me to this beautiful day.

I am grateful to be alive and share my life with all my supporters and feel the love I suspected I may not ever again.

vachon2010@gmail.com

BE FIERCE

My Story

TABYTHA TOWE

Born to Smile

I was born in Canada to immigrant parents with two younger siblings. We all have different personalities but love each other, so we grew up with fond memories and yet some difficult times, as anyone does. I left for a while, but now we are reunited and strong and keep expanding.

My parents ran restaurants for a few years, and we children would either "help" with entertainment (we sang karaoke) or try and set the tables properly. I suppose, in a way, I was conditioned to be in the service industry one day. My family has dined on exotic meals our entire lives and has had open appetites. I have a taste for adventure!

I've always loved taking care of others; maybe that's elder sister syndrome. But I love animals and am back in touch with nature again. I've worked with rhinos, turtles, and elephants. I've been blessed. Music fills me; though I cannot play an instrument nor hold a tune, I still sing anyway. I go to many concerts. My whole life, I've been fond of arts and culture - movies, food, language through books, or exploring foreign words and worlds; I'm a bit of a writer at heart. I love the ocean, though I have an inner ear imbalance, so being in or on the ocean is both the best and worst. I tell cringy dad jokes. I wear mostly thrift clothes. I have fun tattoos. Like to volunteer or help others. I'm a big lover with a tough exterior until you get to know me. I have a wild laugh. I'm very stubborn yet loyal; it must be a dog sign zodiac characteristic. I'm not good at sports, but I am competitive anyway. I don't think I'll ever marry. Definitely a sun chaser. I want to protect sharks, get my motorcycle license, and be a great person. I'm thankful I'm free, embrace how I feel, and sometimes get to dance!

Fare well!

Show Up Stand Up Speak Up

'As every one of us has a story, so does every cocktail' Me

Leaving home to travel abroad, I embarked on a journey filled with beauty and challenges. My career began at the bottom, navigating through various roles in diverse establishments, facing the stereotype that women couldn't excel in bartending. Twenty years ago, I had to prove my skills by asking patrons about their cocktail preferences to demonstrate my expertise. My experience taught me that success in this industry isn't just about skill but also attitude. It's demanding yet rewarding when customers leave satisfied and safe.

As I've grown, my role evolved from a bartender to a mentor, emphasizing organization and training. However, the physical toll of late-night shifts prompted me to innovate. I'm now transitioning into a cocktail consultant and designer, utilizing my creativity to host events and create menus. With over 150 original cocktails to my name, I cater to unique tastes, recently designing a Spanish-themed menu in Mexico.

Looking forward, I aspire to be my own boss, allowing more time for travel and loved ones. My goal is to provide unforgettable experiences, hoping to one day plan your event. Cheers to future adventures in hospitality! Spiritedevents@yahoo.ca

FREE SPIRITED

JOHANN CALLAGHAN

The best days of my life were the summer months when my mam took us on mystery day trips. We'd pack our bags with drinks and snacks, and off we went—to Foto Wildlife Park in Cork, Butlins Mosney Center in County Meath, or sometimes even a day trip on a boat to England. Ah they were the good ole days. But life wasn't all sunshine. It threw some serious challenges which turned out to be a blessing in disguise. Having an alcoholic dad, dealing with multiple cases of abuse, becoming a teen mam, losing my daughter Megan, and going through a difficult marriage—all were challenging. However, years later, I realised something significant. My whole life experience has been a project about getting over a core wound of feeling insignificant. Losing Megan in 2007 pushed me to a breaking point, questioning why life was so hard and was it worth it.

Then came a game-changer. A lady named Vanessa invited me to an inner circle session. Weirdly, no one else showed up for six weeks. It was just me and Vanessa doing deep, intensive work. It opened my eyes. When I slowed down and asked my subconscious mind powerful questions, I discovered stuff about myself I never knew. "OMG, I'm so powerful! I create my own reality!" Forgiving myself for years of blaming and shaming myself, transformed my life. Being kind to myself and giving myself permission to have fun gave me so much freedom. None of it was my fault, and it's not yours either.

In fact, seeing what I didn't see before, opened up a whole new world of possibilities. Today I want to share that with the world so that you can find freedom, peace of mind and sleep with ease at night. So, here I am today—with my beautiful daughter Leah and my wonderful husband and a whole new view of life. If you're not growing, you're dying. Albert Einstein said it best. "The most important decision we make is whether we believe we live in a friendly or hostile universe." So, do you want to learn and grow from your adversities? You were born to do just that.

Now, I want to share this with the world. Do yourself a favour and think about what's not working in your life and ask why. Be kind to yourself and forgive yourself. Sleep on it and see what unfolds.

The journey to empowerment begins with a good night's sleep.

Show Up Stand Up Speak Up

As a Certified Sleep Science and Health Coach at Therapeutic Healing, my mission is rooted in the belief that true well-being begins with therapeutic healing. I guide professional women and entrepreneurs on a transformative journey, emphasizing the crucial role of self-care and the cornerstone of a good night's sleep. So many people are working too hard, grinding and hustling, and have experienced burnout, as I did, or are very close to it. Most people don't value sleep and don't know how to rest; physically or mentally and it's a big problem in our world today!

With a deep understanding of one's relationship with sleep and rest, I empower clients to take back control of their lives, ensuring they awaken each day rejuvenated, restored, and ready to embrace life to the fullest. International speaker and featured in media worldwide, I am the creator of the S.L.E.E.P. Success Method, a transformational framework for sleep success. With a combined 10+ years of study, teaching and coaching, I teach and transform through my online courses, programs, workshops and summits. I also host The Empowering Family Health Podcast.

Nothing gives me more pleasure than seeing my clients achieve more and be more in their life for themselves and their families as a result of sleeping better and changing their lifestyle to support that. So, if you want more energy, better performance and less stress with better sleep, then let's get on a complementary 15-minute call and see how I can help. I believe EVERYTHING is better with better sleep!
https://linktr.ee/johanncallaghan_sleepcoach

SLEEP WELL

My Story

BRENDA FOLLERT

I've had a love for music and big dreams since I was a little girl, singing in front of my teddy bears. I wrote a poem in fourth grade that I remember made it into the public library, after winning a poetry contest. The songs my mom and dad sang and played on their guitars, quieted the animosity in my home, and brought the greatest sense of love, warmth, and connection in my family. A place I felt most validated and affirmed with one of my love languages, words of affirmation, as I was always encouraged as a young girl of a gift that I carried.

I always felt I would do something great, but life, as per usual, didn't turn out the way I envisioned. It slowly crushed those dreams, and little by little, replaced my confidence with insecurity, my belief with doubt, and my heart with fear, anxiety, depression, and hopelessness. My life became about surviving, not thriving. My dreams felt far away, like they were impossible. I was left with the impact of trauma from abuse that I would need to deal with face to face.

Layer by layer, I slowly began to put myself back together, gaining clarity and healing through the only source I know, my Heavenly Father. I often think, if I could change it, would I? The answer is always the same: no, because I know these things, as hard as they were, having endured them, made me who I am. I am stronger than ever because of them. My pain has become my superpower! Eventually, my faith led me to programs and people that brought healing and purpose back into my life. God began to place me in positions where I was using my gifts that I continued to pursue. A spark came back into my life, I have hope again, I feel alive again. I am on a path to purpose, and those dreams that I felt as a little girl no longer feel out of reach.

Show Up Stand Up Speak Up

All my memories are intertwined around music.

The nostalgic songs that tug on my heart strings, resonate deeply and remind me of moments that are dear to my heart. Songs enhance moments, building memories with friends and loved ones. They bring tears to my eyes when I feel like nobody understands me and speak directly to my heart as if to say everything will be ok.

All the different roads that I have taken have led me back to my passion, like metal to a magnet you will always be drawn back to your deepest heart's desires. After years of going in the wrong direction, it was my faith that led me back to my heart and passion. I am finally following those desires, and doing what I believe I was created to do. I'm writing and producing music, and I am also impacting and inspiring the lives of others as a transformation coach. Stepping into the pursuit of my dreams, I have helped others break limitations and unproductive patterns/mindset to rise to new levels, become persistent, and consistent, in committing to every goal they have in place to reach their best self.

Whether you need direction or help to believe in yourself or someone to believe in you until you can learn to believe in yourself, let's live on purpose together! It is my hope that through my music you will find hope healing and encounter the love of our Heavenly Father as I have. I hope to connect with you whether through my music or through one-on-one coaching. If you want to be inspired and encouraged, please connect with me. I'd love to chat more. Bwurtzfollert@gmail.com

LIVE PURPOSELY

NICOLE GRIBSTAD

God has walked with me for as long as I can remember. I feel overwhelmingly special to have had Him speak to me audibly about His identity at the young age of five. Although I've gone through numerous ups and downs filled with joys and sorrows, peaks and valleys, and wins and losses, the presence of the Lord has never left me.

I've finally found this beautiful inner peace and joy and knowledge! It fills my heart and moves me into song and dancing in my spirit that I just can't keep to myself! This excitement of hope and bliss is my personal life force that pulls me forward extraordinarily no matter what. With new biblical insights every day, I wake up and show up more confident unlike those days of my younger self.

Growing up with a weak immune system, year-round allergies, and a humble home life as an immigrant, I used to wake up stressed and overwhelmed with mere desires to just survive not knowing if I actually would. Low energy and cloudy thoughts were my constant companions. Even though I still get exhausted frequently, tired or not, my Holy Spirit energy propels me unstoppably forward despite the storms that come. I can't think of one single thing that my God hasn't brought me through in the ebbs and flows of life. Time doesn't stand still for anyone, have you noticed?
Ready or not, life goes on and on. While every wave and every ripple effect made me feel powerless and defeated before, I now feel Godfidently powerful.

Now I have such certainty of who I am and whose I am, and my identity is found in God rather than
what my circumstances, experiences, and status in the world tell me. I now know my worth is purely found in my identity in Christ, my Lord and Savior, as His adopted child. In Him I am wholly accepted, washed clean white as snow and a Daughter of the King. I invite you to this everlasting joy and relationship with the Father of all Creation, all existence in the universe.

Every good and perfect gift comes from the Father of Lights who gives all hope, all joy, all promise and abounding riches in Christ.

Show Up Stand Up Speak Up

God Sized Dreams

Immigrating from Canton to California at 7 and growing up with the culmination of my family, church, and school made up my world. However, local news of threatening gangs, violence, broken homes, and minority low-income circumstances weighed on me. Through it all, our limitations stirred me with determination, especially with our cramped two-bedroom apartment.

This drove me with visions for a more comfortable lifestyle focused on meaningful work. My insatiable dream of making a difference to better the world consumed me. I've always known that the Lord was calling me to something bigger than myself.

As the Lord pursued me, I'm thrilled and glad to say that I am the founder of The Godfident Life Masterclass, an acclaimed Best-Selling Author and dynamic Motivational Speaker, who embodies the essence of transformative empowerment. As a seasoned Deliverance Mindset Minister and an insightful Practical Bible Application guide, I am a beacon of wisdom for those navigating their faith journey. With my unique role as a Homeschool Parent Wellness Advisor, I expertly tailor my guidance to uplift and enrich the family unit. I specialize in equipping Christian professionals, who are driven yet caught in the throes of overwhelm, confusion, and anxiety. My approach is not just about finding solutions; it's about embarking on a journey towards purpose and clarity. My strategies pave the way for a harmonious blend of fun, fitness, freedom, and fulfillment, transforming both personal lives and professional endeavors into realms of boundless possibility. Join me and discover how to turn your aspirations into tangible, exhilarating realities in both life and business. "In him was life, and that life was the light of all mankind." John 1:4 NIV nicole@godfident.life

BELIEVE

My Story

KERRI KAUFMANN

My mother has been battling epilepsy for as long as I can remember. As a child, I witnessed her daily struggle firsthand. I didn't fully understand the complexities of her condition, so I became the person who constantly tried to make her happy and uplift her spirit in any way I could. Even at a young age, I showed her love and offered any advice I could come up with. I wanted to be her best friend and without hesitation, I always gave her my love and support. Our bond was unbreakable. I devoted my time to finding solutions like surprising her, by cleaning the house before she woke up, making breakfast, and even doing her hair and makeup. Although I may not have possessed great skills back then, I tried my best to make my mother happy. She always put her children first, so I wanted to give back in any way I knew how. My mother would confide in me about her problems, and I became her listening ear. I was always searching for ways to bring her joy.

Although epilepsy was not well understood at the time and is more so now, I would still describe the current attitude towards it as; blind arrogance. The procedure was meant to prevent her from harming herself or others, but it only added to her shame and low self-esteem. These experiences further impacted her perception of the world and exacerbated her struggles with epilepsy. Witnessing my mother endure these battles inspired me to explore holistic approaches. She became my inspiration to delve into the mind, body, and soul connection. I developed a keen interest in finding a better way. I became curious about understanding why people get stuck and unknowingly began helping myself in the process. This led me on a soul search and travelling was one of the key elements in my journey. Unaware I had accumulated a pile of conditioning, it was as if I were a wandering soul, unable to ride the waves of life. Whenever life threw me a curveball, whether it was in personal relationships or just everyday life, I found myself unable to manage it at times. I was keen to align to my higher self and finding the best me within me, became my mission.

A friend reached out to me and asked if I wanted to take a Reiki class with her. That was a turning point for me. Reiki connected me to a level of existence that embraced the present moment and allowed me to delve deep into the underlying emotions that needed to be resolved. Reiki allowed me to cut through the noise and distractions of everyday life and helped create a space of deep presence and inner connection. In the midst of the chaotic rat race that defines our world, Reiki has provided me with a profound sense of deep connection and calm.

Show Up Stand Up Speak Up

Reiki is not only a practice for inner work but also a means to connect with others on a level that I believe everyone can benefit from. In a world that often feels disconnected and fast-paced at times, it is crucial for us to stay grounded and continue genuine connections with ourselves and others, however that may look for you. We must remember the importance of nourishing these connections to stay elevated amidst the craziness of our lives. Taking a moment to find peace within ourselves and to connect with others is essential to me. Incorporating tools like Reiki, meditation, and a safe space to connect etc., can offer a profound amount of support. It allows us to tap into a source of inner peace and healing, and enables us to navigate, the fast-paced world with a sense of calm, and clarity. Reiki serves as a reminder that amidst the chaos, we can find moments of tranquility and connection, both within ourselves and with those around us. When we approach others with mindfulness and a sense of understanding, we create a deep level of connection that grounds us to our environment.

By acknowledging and embracing the diversity of experiences and struggles that exist, we develop a sense of empathy and compassion. This allows us to connect with others on a profound level, transcending superficial differences and finding common ground in our shared humanity. When we can truly listen and understand one another, we create a space where healing and growth can occur, and why not together? In this way, for me, Reiki became a powerful tool, not only for personal calm, but also for building bridges of connection with others. It reminds me that we are all connected, and by nurturing these connections, we can become more rooted in our environment. Through the practice of self-care, we can cultivate a deep sense of empathy, understanding, and unity, creating a more harmonious and compassionate world. Together as one consciousness. kerrikaufmann007@gmail.com

CONNECTION MATTERS

JANICE PORTER

Being a grandma to a toddler has brought more joy and surprise into my life than I could have imagined. While her bright eyes are watching the world with wonder and excitement as she sees so many things for the first time, I am watching her with wonder, seeing many things anew.

Last summer, I took her to the playground, and instead of engaging with the brightly coloured slides, monkey bars and climbing walls, she beelined it to the pile of sand in a neighbouring parking lot. Who knew a giant pile of sand could be so much fun?! The joy in her face as she climbed up, jumped on and rolled in this mound of sand was priceless. It definitely made me rethink my perspective on such things—dirt is so not my thing—to going with the flow, enjoying watching her have fun even though her choice certainly wasn't one I would have made when I was a kid. She's so different from who I was as a child. I don't think I was ever as energetic and free-spirited as she is. I was quite fearful and she seems to have no fear. Though only four years old, she learns so fast! She has already developed strategies for playing games like UNO and Snakes and Ladders. She loves to win and yet accepts defeat graciously.

I have a lot to teach her, and I have a lot to learn from her, which means we are never bored. She is extremely active, innately curious and fiercely independent. It's no surprise that being a grandma to this firecracker is the biggest joy of my life. Spending time with her is all-consuming and each stage of her short life has brought different phases of joy and pride. When I was impatiently waiting to become a grandma, I couldn't know the depth of how it would feel. Now that I am, I know why my heart yearned for this so much.

Show Up Stand Up Speak Up

Sending out kindness is so needed in today's world and I'm on a mission to spread that message. The good news is that spreading kindness is as simple as sending a card. I can't tell you how many times I have received a call or note saying "you have no idea how much your card meant when it arrived". Why cards? They are a symbol of human connection that has, unfortunately, largely gone to the wayside. And this connection is important in both personal and business life. After all, businesses are run by humans for the benefit of other humans.

I have worked hard over the years to build business relationships and teach others how to do the same, using online and offline strategies. Online, I focus on using LinkedIn and show my clients how to attract the people they can help—clients, referral partners and strategic partners. Staying connected and nurturing those new relationships comes next and I am passionate about this part. I use a "tangible touch" follow up system—physical cards—with clients, prospects, associates, and friends, to stay connected. I celebrate and appreciate them on a consistent basis. When you send out a REAL card to someone "just because" with no agenda behind it, not only do you brighten their day, but you brighten yours too. I challenge you to experience the joy of sending out kindness and joy in the form of a card in the mail. Email me at janice@janiceporter.com and you can send one anywhere in the world for free as my gift to you.

Let's spread kindness, one card at a time!

STAY CONNECTED

My Story

DR. PAULA GORDON

In my 4ᵗʰ year of medical school, I witnessed the important role radiology plays in diagnosis, and decided that I would specialize. I had the good fortune to be accepted into the residency program in Vancouver, where Dr. Peter Cooperberg, one of the original gurus of ultrasound, who had introduced this relatively new test, worked. After completing my training as a radiologist, I did an additional "fellowship" year training with him, qualifying me to become the head of an ultrasound department. But there were no jobs in ultrasound, so I started my career working with Dr. Linda Warren, one of the pioneers of mammography in Canada, in her practice that did a high volume of mammography. I learned that specialty on-the-job.

In 1985, we acquired a new ultrasound machine with a high-frequency probe that allowed study of organs close to the surface, including breast. I just happened to have these 2 unrelated skill sets, and started doing ultrasound on women with breast lumps: either lumps that were feelable, or masses seen on mammograms. It worked. I quickly found that ultrasound could find feelable cancers that were missed on mammograms, largely because of dense breast tissue. I started doing needle aspiration of cysts, and needle biopsies of masses, using the ultrasound to allow me to see the needle going where it needed to go. Those needle biopsies proved to be highly accurate, and enabled women to avoid unnecessary surgeries. In the process of doing those exams, I encountered other masses that turned out to be cancers. They were not feelable or seen on the mammograms. That wasn't supposed to happen, based on all the research done to that point. I published my research in a major medical journal in 1995, and I suggested that ultrasound could be used as a supplemental screening tool for women with dense breasts. That didn't go anywhere.

In 2004, a woman in Connecticut named Nancy Capello was diagnosed with stage 3C breast cancer, only weeks after she'd had a negative mammogram. She was incensed that her cancer had hidden in her dense breast tissue, but although all the doctors knew about her breast density, none had told her. Her single-handed advocacy led to legislation that all women in Connecticut be told their breast density, which is now finally catching on in Canada. Thanks to patient advocates, 6 Canadian provinces tell all women their density, and some provinces cover screening breast ultrasound with public health insurance. Stay tuned for continued progress!

Show Up Stand Up Speak Up

My most important message is that women should get screening for breast cancer starting at age 40. Mammography is the gold standard and can reduce deaths from breast cancer by 40%. When cancer is found early, women can be treated successfully with less aggressive therapy: less surgery, and some can avoid chemotherapy. The ideal would be for all women to have a mammogram annually. If left untreated, cancers grow and spread, and this happens faster in younger women who haven't gone through menopause. So, if we want to find them as early as possible, we should screen annually, not every-other-year. Women need to know that there are false alarms: sometimes something shows up that needs another look but turns out to not be cancer. Like cysts or non-cancerous tumours. Once a woman has a mammogram, she should be told her breast density. Density refers to the proportion of normal breast tissue and fat, and it varies from woman-to-woman. Forty-three percent of women over age 40 have dense breasts, so it's normal and common. The only way to find out if you're dense, is on a mammogram. You can't tell by size or feel. There are 2 consequences of dense tissue: cancers can hide in dense tissue, so can be "missed" on mammograms. And women with dense tissue are at a higher risk of getting breast cancer than women with non-dense breasts. They should do breast self-exams (all women should!).

Go to www.knowyourlemons.org and learn what else to look for. Try to have supplemental screening. Importantly: advocate! All the progress made in the past has been thanks to patients: women who've had cancer who want other women to have an easier time than they did. We need more women who haven't had cancer to help. If you're in Canada, contact info@densebreastscana.ca. In the USA, contact contact@dense-info.org. In the UK, contact breastdensitymatters.uk@gmail.com The best way to ask a general question is to forward your question to info@densebreastscanada.ca, or "tweet at me." @DrPaulaGordon

GET SCREENED

ERIN BIRCH

I woke up on my 44th birthday and did the math! Yup, my life was half lived! I laid in bed absolutely SHOCKED! Where had the time gone? I was only a few years out of high school, wasn't I?

I asked myself a series of questions: Am I happy? Am I fulfilled? Is there enough fun and adventure in my life? What about passion? Who the hell am I, anyway? Am I where I thought I would be at this age? Am I going to have to work until the day I die? I sure as heck won't be able to retire at 55 and travel the world like I dreamed of when I was 20! Did I want the second half of my life to carry on like it was, or, did I want to make some changes?

This midlife realization was a blessing! It led to an awakening and a personal transformation. It led me to decide to do what I needed to do to be happier. I understood that my happiness was up to ME and no one else!

I became single. That was a big decision and the hardest thing I have ever done.

I started on a personal journey of rediscovering and reinventing myself! I closed my business as an artisan jeweler and started a business in marketing, a business I could do from anywhere in the world, the beach or the bistro! I fell in love with building my business and I became successful quite quickly. A very big part of my success was that I also realized I needed to BECOME the person who COULD be successful. I became aware that the limiting beliefs, the beliefs I had about myself, would hold me back … not just from success, but from the joy and happiness that I desired. I completely rewired my mind and upgraded my self-concept and identity! I got rid of the belief, the BS story that I had believed to be true about myself since I was a kid, that I was stupid and would never amount to much. I stopped playing small and started to play big! I went after what I wanted! I began to truly understand that I was a CREATOR!

And now it's my passion and purpose to help others understand they TOO are creators, have worth, and are worthy of all they desire. YOU are worthy of all that you desire!

Show Up Stand Up Speak Up

My purpose and passion is to help beautiful souls like you become the best version of themself! To create all the prosperity and abundance you desire! To BECOME the person who is able to attract into and create the life that sets your soul on fire! To create an extraordinary life! A life of no regrets!

One of my biggest inspirations came from reading Regrets of the Dying by Bronnie Ware, a palliative care nurse who was at the bedside of thousands of people when they died. She saw a pattern with her patients! The same regrets repeated: I wish I had laughed more, had more fun, traveled more, taken more chances, said how I really felt, stayed in touch with loved ones, etc. No one said they wished they had made more money and kept a cleaner house! They were all regrets about not living MORE! Not longer, but more! That hit me like a ton of bricks!

For me, it's not about making a ton of money but being able to have freedom, flexibility and be able to do what I want, when I want! It's when I impacted MYSELF that I realized I could help others with how I had been helped! I am a business and personal transformation coach. I help people get rid of the ROOT CAUSE of many issues like: limiting beliefs, trauma, anxiety, depression, allergies, phobias, negative behaviors and more. I use several different integrative techniques and strategies to help people create lasting change. I help people become LIMITLESS so that they can live their best life! No regrets. Hey, I've spilled some beans about me now let's hear yours! If you would like to connect, I would LOVE that! You can find me on Facebook or at www.erinbirchcoaching.com

CREATE JOY

STANICE MARKHAM

The best is yet to come!

Growing older may be inevitable, but *feeling* older, *living* older, now that is up to you. That is your choice.

So much has shifted for me recently, opening me up to more. I know this is truly my time to shine, and I can proudly say I'm up for the challenge. But it wasn't always this way. Growing up, a lot of us were taught that women should just be lovely, well-behaved people-pleasers, sacrificing their own wants and needs for those of the greater good.

The good news is, once again, you have a choice. The beauty of attaining that certain age as a woman is the much deeper understanding of yourself that accompanies spiritual maturity. When you get out of your own way, you realize you've gained enough life experience to recognize your strength and endurance, to appreciate your long-term perseverance and hard-won wisdom. I would say learning to love yourself isone of the most challenging yet most rewarding accomplishments in life. You can't fully achieve your goals unless you build them on a foundation of self-love.

After fifty, I think women are far more accepting of themselves as amazing multi-faceted beings, flaws and all. They're more comfortable in their own skin. It's a time of really coming into your own power, connecting with your inner "opulence", as I call it, that richness of being, that personal greatness that sets you apart from the rest.

As a stylist and fashion designer, the pieces I showcase through my business Kimono Envy are designed to remind women that they are exceptional, each in their own way. Once you reach your prime years, you begin to glory in your uniqueness, and take pride in how far you've come. There's just not the same angst over attaining everyone's approval. You simply do what you want, what's best for you and your loved ones, without running it by every girlfriend you've ever had to get their opinion. What other people think of you is none of your business. I am the managing director of a province-wide women's networking group in my area. One of my featured speakers describes it this way. In your twenties, when you walk into a social situation knowing no one, you're secretly fretting, "Gee, I hope these people will like me."

When you're in your fifties, you sweep confidently into the same situation, thinking, "I wonder if there's anyone interesting here I might like." Once again, the choice is always yours.

Show Up Stand Up Speak Up

I am an avid philanthropist, chairing community organizations, and a leader in the entrepreneurial community, living my dream of working as a fashion stylist with my signature line of gorgeous kimonos. And I love it! The positive interaction with my customers as they choose their favourite pieces, ensuring they walk away with the perfect kimonos complementing their tastes and lifestyle, brings me so much joy.

All this is in stark contrast to my challenging upbringing, which led me to leave an abusive home life at age thirteen. Truthfully, I didn't have any foundation of self-love at an early age. Because of my childhood, though, I was always the caregiver, eager to save others, and dedicated to working with organizations designed to aid women in crisis. Giving love, help, and support: that's where I excelled. At my first "real" business conference, I watched a woman on stage speaking about success. I remember thinking, "I could NEVER do anything like that!" Shortly after, I put up a photo of myself at the microphone on my vision board, and, sure enough, in time, the Universe did its Law-of-Attraction thing. When I became the founder of the Edmonton chapter of 100 Women Who Care, there I was, up there successfully speaking on stage, and educating the crowd. Eventually, managing a popular business networking group gave me the confidence to realize my dream of starting my current fashion business, Kimono Envy. On the December eve of the last full moon in 2019, I went to bed asking for some new and exciting changes in my life. Upon awakening, never mind sugar plums, I had visions of kimonos dancing in my head. They were all I could think about! I'd never done anything remotely similar before. I didn't even know how to sew! Forget going unnoticed. These stylish kimonos are fashion-forward cloaks of *visibility* that put you in the spotlight!

Whether it be helping the community as a whole, through my philanthropic efforts or working individually with my Kimono Envy fans and followers and the numerous clients I support through my unique nutritional business, empowering women to look and feel their best is my passion and my legacy. Changing people's perspectives, opening their minds to endless possibilities: my life's goal is to continue making that positive difference. diamondstanice@gmail.com

BE BRAVE

KAREN HALL

I've spent exactly half my life in New Zealand and half in Australia, but I'm a Kiwi at heart and always will be. I grew up on a farm enveloped by fresh air, open space, green grass and animals - life was quintessentially rural, down-to-earth and uncomplicated.

It's no surprise that animals and the outdoors have continued to be a big part of my life, even when I traded Auckland for Sydney's suburban sprawl. My travels have taken me to a multitude of countries: hiking, biking, white water rafting, kayaking, canyoning, scuba diving, skydiving and tourist-ing. I love exploring new places and can't sit still long enough to read a book - active holidays are definitely my jam.

My parents instilled in me a love of service, so volunteering has always been a passion, with Special Olympics kids, the local Soup Kitchen and at charity events. Through this I've learned that life isn't just about ticking off a bucket-list; it's about the people you meet along the way, the hands you hold, and the hearts you touch.

I describe myself as an introverted extrovert, balancing my energy between being with people and less 'peoply' activities, including snuggling with my doggies and gardening. And weirdly, organising and decluttering my home. There's something oddly satisfying about decluttering the physical to declutter the mental. Do you agree?

So, that's me - a Kiwi by heart, a wanderer by soul, an introverted extrovert with a passion for adventure, a soft spot for service, and a (not-so) secret love affair with storage.

Show Up Stand Up Speak Up

When I plucked up the courage to start my own business in 2015, having done the Corporate grind for 20 years, I was blown away by the support and belief others had in my success that I very much lacked in myself.

This insight led me to create a Marketing agency, Reputation by Design, that specialises in proactively amplifying the reputation of businesses and their owners. While the main benefit of our services is increased trust, credibility and ultimately revenue, it's an added bonus that is even more meaningful to my 'why' - igniting confidence in business owners.

There's nothing like winning awards and accolades and getting positive online feedback to ignite your self-belief and quiet the negative self-talk. And this is backed up by research: women run almost 40% of small businesses but only win 13% of awards internationally - a significant driver behind this imbalance is the hesitancy to nominate ourselves for recognition.

Through our strategic support, we've empowered countless women to step out of the shadows of "I'm not good enough" or "Next year my business will be ready" and into the spotlight of multi-award-winning success within months. The transformative power of such journeys remains a constant source of inspiration.

I'd love to hear your 'why' and how worthy you know you are! Let's chat at:
karen@reputationbydesign.com

NO REGRETS

My Story

NATALIE LAVELOCK

'Leave it'. He said.

"What?" I replied

"Leave it all and follow me - You can trust me"

"But…but I worked so hard for this. And, my family, they're depending on me. We have bills to pay. What if someone gets sick - I won't have insurance. We'll lose our home; we'll lose the farm. I don't know if our marriage can handle this. No one will understand"

"I know. It feels scary. You don't HAVE to do this. It's your choice. I heard your cry for help. I heard you ask for a change; something new. This is it - the answer to your prayer. You don't have to do this. And if you do…I've got you baby girl. You can trust me. Don't be afraid."

Don't be afraid. 365 times that phrase is used in the Bible. 365 times - one for every day of the year. Coincidence? I think not!

Fear is the one thing that we are equipped with to help keep us safe. To help keep us alive. And yet so much of the time, fear keeps us from realizing our full potential. And so, I started to contemplate, what would it mean to live fearlessly? I'm not talking about going out and doing stupid stuff fearless. I'm talking about fully going for it in life. I'm talking about not letting temporal things rob me of the fullness and fulfillment of my God-given destiny. Somehow, I mustered the courage to take a Leap of Faith and say 'No' to the overwhelming fear and insecurity that threatened to mute the message I was called to deliver, and 'Yes' to the gift I was created to share. In the years that have passed since that day, I've come to discover that, if God's called me to it, he's going to be right there with me through it and the safest place I can ever leap is into His arms! And I'm so grateful that, not only did the worst NOT happen, but I now have a successful coaching & consulting business that has given me a life I love, sharing my gifts and shining an even brighter light than I could have imagined.

Would I say that now I'm immune to fear? NO.

Fear is a part of life. I experience new things to be fearful of every day. It's the awareness of that fear that gives me the power to choose the direction I want to go in and it's my faith in God that gives me the courage to take the first step.

Faith is the antidote to fear. When Faith is present, there is no room for fear.

So what'll it be sister - fear or faith?

Show Up Stand Up Speak Up

It's Time to Find Your Fearless!

Do you want to help more people?
Do you want to make more money?
Do you want to create a business that allows you to make a bigger impact while living a life you love?

Natalie Lavelock believes God has given you a unique mission to fulfill on this Earth and that your business is an extension of that mission. Her mission is to encourage and equip faith-based business owners, like you, to fulfill their God-given mission while creating a life they love in the process. There's no doubt you're being called to step up in this season, the only question is, "Are you willing to face your fear and answer the call?"

Natalie is a faith-based speaker, best-selling author, trainer and program development specialist who works with successful coaches and speakers who want to create greater significance by developing their Signature group programs, advanced training and certification programs.

If you're ready to move from success into significance, creating your legacy, and equipping the next generation of leaders, and you want to do it in a way that is aligned with your faith, then now is your time!

www.NatalieLavelock.com

FIND FEARLESS

My Story

NATASHA SAMSON

My business IS a big part of my spiritual path. It continually reflects areas for personal growth and self-acceptance, pushes me out of my comfort zone, and requires me to take action while also surrendering to DIVINE timing, not MY timing. I have realized that in business, my outer attainment is a reflection of my inner attainment. I have been a seeker for as long as I can remember.

As a little girl, my birthday wish every year was to become a happy person, a mystery that was anchored within me to solve. Through my 20's, I followed the prescribed path through university and landed the exact engineering job I wanted. But I found myself further from my birthday wish. I engaged in a relationship, being unconsciously controlled, and bullied by my partner, not having the skills yet to defend myself or even communicate. Whittled down to an almost ghost-like version of myself. I was in my early 30's and everything in my life was wrong.

Growth begins here. When you step off the prescribed path and accept the hero's journey, you are presented with obstacles and triggers, divinely assigned to you, that turn you into the hero destined to help others. Mustering the courage to leave that relationship when my core wound was not wanting to "end up" alone, was the first of several relational tribulations. I left my corporate job and started my business. This afforded me the freedom to work part time while I dove into the science of Ayurveda and Yoga. Over the next 10 years, I grew in my spiritual path, improved my mental and physical health, all while offering my knowledge to help others along the way.

Growth is always ongoing. I was ghosted by a romantic partner, tearing my world apart and further revealing unhealed abandonment triggers. I lost touch with my intuition and became distracted by the outside noise. I was divinely guided to explore energy work, where I found the power of healing myself on an energetic level and connecting to my soul's highest vibration. This has made a profound change in my business and my life. I understand now that this time of "aloneness", once a core fear, was a gift that afforded me space to do the deep work, dive into psychology, develop my intuitive nature, be fully present, and learn through the people who seek the guidance I can offer. I do not know where my journey will take me. I am ok with that. I have faith my gifts will help people in a profound way to find *their* "happy", and I surrender to the divine timing of it all.

Show Up Stand Up Speak Up

Natasha is an intuitive healer with an engineer's mind who has been studying, teaching and counselling for more than 15 years. Her love and passion are palpable to everyone who works with her or attends one of her events. She offers her gifts and skills with a servant's heart and is a medium for divinely inspired healing. She is dedicated to sharing her deep understanding of healing the mind, the root cause of suffering, through engineering, ancient science, and intuitive knowledge. She draws from both the physical and philosophical wisdom of Ayurveda and Yoga and her own intuitive knowledge to connect with the root cause. As someone who is solution-oriented, she uses her natural problem-solving skills to find patterns in all aspects of your life and offers accessible tools, specific to you, to unblock your path. "I Want More from Life!" Is the theme of her offerings, incorporating physical practices to shift the energy of the mind, food choices that will enhance your well-being, daily rhythms to help the body run efficiently, psychology to overcome limiting beliefs and internal blocks, as well as yoga, strategic movement, breathing and meditation.

She integrates these applied sciences to engineer the human psyche towards greater happiness and contentment, all with the spiritual undertone of Mind, Body & Soul healing. Natasha hosts retreats, offers courses, workshops, and keynote speaking engagements. I have chosen this path because I am always trying to grow. I believe in the value of revealing the root cause of our physical and psychological issues so to remove the obstacles that are holding us back on our path. Ram Dass once said, "We are all just walking each other home," "home" being our true Self, the Divine or pure love. I am here to help walk you home. https://nourishyoufirst.ca/

NOURISH YOU

HAZEL YING LEE
Pilot

NAN ASPINWALL
Sharpshooter

MARY S. PEAKE

Educator

ANNIE LONDONDERRY

Bicyclist

SHELBY AVANN

"Fall in love with as many things as you can. Love is the only thing in life that matters."

I grew up as a girl with a major love for horses, and who ironically was also allergic to them. I spent my weekdays riding, and weekends showing. From the time I rolled down my pony's neck in a show because she HAD to eat grass, to the times later in life when I was speeding around a jumping course, cutting corners and trying to beat the fastest times of the day.

My second love was learning about equine reproduction and bringing life into the world. I travelled to Kentucky and Australia to do internships and jobs where I gained experience seeing the full circle of life while also meeting great people and seeing beautiful places with varying cultures.

My third love is traveling. I have grown to enjoy longer periods of travel time away. I started with a university exchange in Finland for 4 months, an internship in Kentucky for 6 and then a year in Australia. I had shorter trips to many other countries in between, but I always loved getting to live and experience the culture of a place and of the people where I spent an extended period of time.

Love number 4 is pole dancing. Pole became my way to express my emotions, my creativity and my sexuality. It became a huge outlet for me when tough times with my family happened. The studio holds my community of wonderful women, who get to witness one another grow in their confidence, their grace and sometimes some newly found wild and sexy personas.

Love number 5 is that for reiki and the gift it gave me to connect to the universe in a way I had never experienced before. When I learned how to do energy healing, I not only learned how to connect to the universe and its beautiful gifts, I also learned how to connect to mine. My gifts of healing people with my hands, and not just during reiki, but in everyday touch. I learned how to get in touch with my intuition, to discern it from my ego and stories. I connected with a spirituality that never fit with religion or the name God.

It connected me, to a very true version of myself.

Show Up Stand Up Speak Up

I chose to be an intimacy coach and healer because it allowed me to blend all my interests and healing into a powerful service for other humans that I knew needed the same thing. I wasn't getting the connection, intimacy or honestly the sex I needed and felt unsatisfied, unseen, hurt and lonely. Looking back now, I realize I didn't have the best relationship with myself. I was codependent with a lot of people and wasn't giving myself what I needed. I wasn't setting boundaries, I would let people be mean to me and still keep them around because I didn't want to be alone. Basically, I was lacking a lot of intimacy with self.

'Reiki gave me the lesson of spiritual intimacy. Learning about attachment styles, the worlds of tantra, kink and all other sexuality really gave me this empowered way of learning how to communicate and understand my emotional and physical needs. I needed to learn how to communicate with myself on so many different levels. What I found the most interesting was the level of shadow work and communication the world of kink offered. The people I have met in this realm are the most amazing, secure, healthy, well-spoken humans with pretty great relationships where everyone involved seems to feel seen and accepted. Who doesn't want that?

I would love to help you create that intimacy you desire! Consensual conversation is always a must, so know that coming into a conversation or a session with me, you always have a choice. Reach out to me at www.shelbyavann.ca. You can also search my name on your favorite podcast platform to hear me as a guest on many podcasts!

TRUST LOVE

My Story

MONYA STEENBERG

It is the final practice before the next qualifying day to enter nationals. By 5:30 pm that day all other athletes had left. It was only my coach and me at the long jump pit. I had to jump a 5m land before I could go home. Those days no cell phones existed, and for me it was a walk home. In the last attempt to help me gain height, my coach brought a running hurdle and put it between the jump step board and the long jump pit, to see if I could land it. I walked back to my jumping sprint, dropped my head down, prayed, and whispered to myself "You can do it". I was exhausted but I knew giving up was not an option. Afterward, I walked home in the dark, barefoot, tired, and covered in sand. After 4 hours jumping non-stop, it was now 9 pm. When I arrived home my parents were furious and couldn't believe I had been there the entire time, jumping. I went to have a bath and afterward realized, I did it! I had one vision and goal that was embedded in my mind. Giving up just because I was so tired of jumping, was not the answer. Landing my 5m mark was.

For my final racetrack sprint qualification in Cape Town, I flew down with my coach. Behind their fancy take-off blocks, I stood there proudly with my wrapped-up feet and looked up at massive stands to run the race my soul yearned for. Without Spikes for the tartan track, 10 min before my 100M, I ran down to the First Aid to wrap my feet in sticky plaster, to avoid running my skin literally off my feet. The sprint of a lifetime, and I ran it full-heartedly.

Lacking financial means to go to university I completed a diploma that usually takes 4-5 years in 2 while working full time. I slept maybe 1-2 hours at night while my flat had books all over my floor, then went back to work at 6 am. I took myself 1 year earlier out of high school, put myself through my last year to start my working career immediately. Not a single person understood why. However, by age 26 I was Purchasing Manager for 25 Ships, self-unloading carriers & bulkers utilizing a $15 Mil budget.

Show Up Stand Up Speak Up

I came home with a new baby, just us two walked into the house and then it hit me. She became the WHY behind my endless drive to build something bigger. I will build and my daughter will learn, lead, and help the world. In 2020 I started online businesses: Nutrition & Weight Management Coach and digital products marketing. I had one goal, to build a legacy for my child and family. To break the cycle and create generational wealth. I wrote one post, not realizing that I inspired others, and it opened doors.

They can learn and build digital products others can download online instantly and sell themselves! At the same time make 100% profits. Helping others become healthier & build income utilizing social media and Digital product building is my passion.

You might not understand in the moment why you are going through what might seem like the hardest thing on this earth; thinking you are failing but know that you are Limitless in the spirit. The moment you understand the separated functionality: Brain VS Spirit, then a new world opens. Other people's thoughts/opinions/ Mind – are not to concern you. THEY OWN IT, NOT YOU.

I am a mom with a passion for helping elevate others! I am on a journey to build a future that will be LIMITLESS. Greatness lies within, follow her voice....

TikTok: monyathesteen

EMBRACE RESILIENCE

My Story

DR. L. IMANI PRICE

"I always knew I was a leader and would have an impact on the lives of others." My leadership journey began early in life. In elementary and junior high I was reprimanded by school authorities for what they perceived as leading student protests against unjust policies and biased treatment. I may have but reprimands didn't deter me; they only strengthened my resolve. I stand up for what I deem right, regardless of the consequences.

I attribute much of my development as a leader to my parents' unwavering support and guidance. They recognized and nurtured my innate leadership qualities, instilling the values of independence and critical thinking from a young age. Being the eldest daughter of a Mensa father and a brilliant mother meant we talked about everything in our household, and our thoughts were valued. It was an environment that fostered a sense of empowerment and confidence. As I progressed to high school, my leadership style evolved, manifesting in my attire. Instead of embracing the casual looks, I wore classic blazers, pearls, and a briefcase. I never felt like my peer group and spent much time alone imagining a life I had never seen. Don't get me wrong, I was a popular student. Though I was involved in various activities and held prominent positions, I knew greater was coming.

Throughout adulthood, I've held numerous leadership roles, but titles alone don't' excite me. Instead, the process of envisioning possibilities and working toward their realization inspires me. As the Managing Director of the eWomen Network DMV Chapter and the Founder/Owner of Women's InnerFitness & Wellness Center, a Counseling Center, I recognize that being a strong leader involves vision and fostering relationships. It is through collaboration and mutual support that we can achieve our greatest successes. I am grateful for the opportunity to surround myself with dedicated individuals who share my vision and passion for making a difference in the lives of others. Leadership, I have come to realize, is not a solitary journey but rather a collective effort, fueled by the strength and unity of like-minded individuals. For anyone feeling isolated or misunderstood, I offer words of encouragement. You are not alone in your journey; your uniqueness is a testament to your potential for greatness. Embrace what sets you apart, believe in your voice, and passionately pursue your passions. Remember, true fulfillment lies in connecting with like-minded individuals who share your vision and values.

Show Up Stand Up Speak Up

My service to others is a calling that started with my decision to become a psychologist. I am a Licensed Psychologist, U.S. Army Veteran Psychologist, and CEO of Women's InnerFitness & Wellness Center, a telehealth group practice serving Maryland, DC, Virginia, Florida, and Colorado. But it all began in high school when friends were drawn to me for help with their problems. My gift did not go unnoticed; as a matter of fact, my 11th-grade psychology teacher told my parents that I had a future as a psychologist. That observation became a prophecy. My psychological priority is helping empower, inspire, and motivate women to ask for what they need and to know that seeking counseling is OK. My holistic approach focuses on the mind, body, and spirit to provide support and guidance on how to cope with life's challenges. By addressing mental, physical, and spiritual health comprehensively, women are encouraged to actively participate in their well-being to create a more balanced and peaceful lifestyle. Why focus on women? Women have been conditioned to believe that we can and should do it all: perfect mothers, wives, caregivers, friends, church members, and career women. We often put everyone else above our own needs. Putting pressure on ourselves to be "superwomen" and juggling an endless to-do list, we end up overworked, overstressed, and running ragged with no time for personal happiness. We become burnt out, which wreaks havoc on our health. But it's high time that women declare we need "Me time."

Our needs are essential, and it's time to prioritize self-love to stay healthy in mind, body, and spirit. It's an act of courage and self-love to ask for what you need. I encourage clients to shift their perspective to what is good about their lives and serving others, which fosters hope throughout our communities and can create a global ripple effect.
drprice@wifwc.com

LIVE WELL

SANDY RUTHERFORD

We each have SO MUCH to celebrate about our lives. Seeking out the lessons learned and celebrating them raises your vibration and serves as a powerful foundation for taking center stage into your inspired destinies! I'd like to share a little of my life story because like yours, mine is rich in learnings. The fun is figuring out how to apply these learnings along the way in preparation for grander roles in this lifelong journey. Here are 2 short stories of my life journey that have brought me to where I am today.

There's no business, like show business I have a show business background. My mom was the first female conductor of the Royal Alexandra Theatre in Toronto, and she had her own TV series on CBC for years. She was also a director and producer of many shows and was very proud of her show business journey and legacy. I am an amateur singer with a Judy Garland type voice and have performed many times including with my mom (most fun experiences ever!), and I started and directed musicals at my high school.

Learning "the show must go on" (I always push forward and guide my clients to do the same) and on time -no excuses, no procrastinating! The time is NOW – when opportunities show up, you jump on them, and YOU show up fully participating every day. I had not directed shows before jumping in to start them at my school, but I was passionate about them and trusted that I was capable and had it within me to make it happen. And I did. For 21 years I was a part of the volunteer Committee that ran the Horse Show at the Royal Agricultural Winter Fair in Toronto and directed the Horse Show for 11 years. We dressed in long gowns every night for 9 days, the men were in black tie and tails or "hunting pinks". I would cue each event in the shows, making on the spot decisions when things didn't flow as expected (which happened often as you were dealing with the unpredictability of animals). My decisions affected a team of over 30 helping to run the shows, as well as the event participants and audience.

I rose to committee leadership at a young age and in a "man's world". Almost all on our committee were successful male business owners and corporate executives. The vast majority gave me their full respect and admiration, supported me and allowed me room to grow and evolve. I learned to trust my gut/instinct and make on the spot decisions. It worked out well each time.

Show Up Stand Up Speak Up

You have a very powerful life story to tell – past, present and future, and of which you can be proud! You have everything within you now to take center stage and step into your inspired destiny! My passion is showing people how much is possible for them and getting them to push for the heights of dream goal successes that are within their reach. Success is a process, an exact science, but we're not taught it. I teach it with passion and inspiration, with guts and glory! I mean Come On! The success that lies within your reach is staggering! People hungry for wonderful new destinies partner with me to help them cut the C.R.A.P. (Counterproductive Really Asinine Programming) and accelerate their success because most people. Know they are capable of much more. Don't know how success works so they underachieve. Don't know how to get past what stops them.

Trained and mentored by and having worked with Bob Proctor, I help people accelerate success by opening up and embracing their gifts (and you have SO MANY you have not yet opened!), immersing them in a guided proven success system with the support, guidance and accountability that is second to none, and upping their commitment to quantum leap their results. How? Our Unstoppable Success System, Self-Image of Your Dreams, and FASTPATH to Success are just 3 of the incredible programs that will change your world because they get at the issues stopping most people from breakthrough success: lack of clarity of desire, an unsupportive self-image, and inability to internalize these powerful teachings. To cut to the chase, when you cut the C.R.A.P. to do the right things, with the right mindset and in the right environment, success is made easy! Check us out at www.inspireddestinies.com

115

PLAY ON

My Story

CATHERINE CURRY-WILLIAMS

I grew up in Bensonhurst, Brooklyn, the youngest of four sisters, my dreams seemed distant. A latchkey kid by age 14 and at 18, I ventured from Brooklyn to Hollywood without a clear plan. I did what any young girl without a plan would do, a waitress by day and acting classes at night; with some success in television commercials rather than the envisioned acting career. Life took unexpected turns and had other plans for me. In 1997, married for just a year, I eagerly awaited the arrival of my first child, a boy—Shane, a name carrying both Irish and Hebrew meanings of divine grace and a gift from God. Our home was adorned with his tiny clothes, a carriage, a crib, and a cozy bedroom, waiting for his arrival. Shane was born as a beautiful, perfect baby, but joy turned to confusion as he struggled to take his first breath. Rapidly, a team of nurses whisked him away, leaving us in shock and disbelief. Nine days in the NICU filled with uncertainty, we didn't know what was wrong with our precious 6Ib 7oz baby boy. On the tenth day, the devastating news came:

Shane was diagnosed with spinal muscular atrophy, a rare genetic disorder. The best-case scenario was a life confined to a wheelchair, but the worst-case scenario unfolded as Shane only lived for two weeks. The pain and devastation were incomprehensible. In the aftermath, grief engulfed me. The best of times had turned into the absolute worst. Nine months later, still grappling with darkness, my sister-in-law shared an article about another mother who had lost her son to the same genetic disorder. I sought her out, and our conversation brought comfort to us both. She told me that doing something good in her son's memory had brought her a sense of peace. From that moment forward, a spark of hope ignited within me. I would seek to create the first Universally Accessible Playground in the western United States in memory of Shane. This inclusive space would bring children with disabilities and their able-bodied peers together, a place where, if Shane had lived, he would have been able to play from his wheelchair, fostering both physical and social development.

With the support of a village, Shane's Inspiration was born. What started as a local initiative blossomed into a Worldwide Inclusion Movement, with 80 playgrounds on five continents and an education program touching lives in 3o countries and five languages. Shane's Inspiration exceeded my wildest dreams. Currently, I enjoy each day inspired and grateful to have my daughter Grace and a village of friends that I call family. I am the co-founder and president of She Angels Foundations. We are a movement that empowers young women and girls to help solve critical unmet needs. I discovered that pain doesn't have to define you—it can be your inspiration. Through unity and collaboration, we can create a ripple effect, leaving a lasting impact.

Show Up Stand Up Speak Up

Catherine is a dedicated advocate and co-founder of Shane's Inspiration, a renowned non-profit established in 1997 in memory of her son Shane. Passionate about inclusivity, she has led initiatives to create inclusive playgrounds and developed educational programs for children with disabilities.

In 2020, Catherine expanded her impact by co-founding the She Angels Foundation. This foundation awards grants every month to grassroots organizations that are female-founded and operated that provide mentorship and resources to young women and girls. Her commitment to empowering women is evident in her advocacy and speaking engagements. With a wealth of experience, Catherine strives to make a meaningful impact globally. She shares her passion for philanthropy through teaching and speaking on its profound potential. Catherine's contributions have earned her numerous awards, including being recognized as one of L'Oreal Paris' "Women of Worth." In 2018, she was honored as one of the "Women of the Year" for the State of California. In 2022, Catherine received the Women's Empowerment Network Award. Additionally, she was named the BRA Networks Visionary Woman of the Year award. She has had written articles in the Huffington Post, Canvas Rebel, and Bold Journey magazines. She has been interviewed in People Magazine, USA Today, Good Housekeeping, Sunset Magazine, Exceptional Parent Magazine, Westways Magazine, Los Angeles Times, Los Angeles Magazine, L.A. Parent Magazine, Los Angeles Family Magazine, Daily News, and Westside Weekly. TV appearances on the Today Show and KTLA. Excitingly, Catherine is scheduled to deliver a Ted Talk in Fargo, North Dakota, further showcasing her dedication to effecting positive change in communities worldwide. ccurrywilliams@sheangelsfoundation.org

EAT CAKE

My Story

DR. ROBIN RISE

My "5-foot minus 1inch", plump, ample-bosomed Polish grandmother took me into her lavender room where she has her Mother Mary shrine, candles, and rosary. It's the private place we go to REALLY talk. I'm the 5'11" granddaughter who inherited her bosom who asks her the deeper questions, the questions about HER, her feelings, her life. She tells me her pain and bliss, her traumas and triumphs. Stories of Poland, escaping to America. Losing her first husband, burying her first son. I know her unfulfilled dreams, her talent for prose and music, unknown except within her lavender room. This day, she grabs my hands and unobtrusively slips a very tightly folded $100 bill. I joke "Grandma, are we doing a drug deal?" She snickers, then says "I want you to have this, from warm hands." My throat still gets a lump as I remember those words. Not an inheritance from cold hands after she leaves this world. Instead, I knew this was a sacrifice, a sacred gesture saying, "for your life to be easier". This is the baton pass. In her lifetime, women couldn't vote or even dream of college. She couldn't have a bank account. She had tucked away a $100 bill-a fortune for her, kept hidden from grandpa in an old cigarette case from WWI.

I felt her baton pass her warm hand to mine. It's my call to action. The women of my family worked, struggled, and fought for everything they had. My grandmother lost her fingertips, crushed under a stamping press in the factory where she worked. Her schooling ended at fourth grade so that she could help support the family—so her brothers could go to school. I still see her waving her handkerchief in that warm hand as I walked across the stage to get my diploma. I'm standing on her shoulders, feeling the support of the women who came before to allow me to have the opportunity that they did not. Our global village can only thrive when women plant trees in whose shade they know they shall never sit. It's what women do.

We nurture the future. We sacrifice from our lives so that our children can have better lives. We don't harm our home, our earth, our kids. The mother energy that knows it takes a village, that we are each other's keeper, that we are here for love and peace for all. I am propelled to action by the women who did what they had to do to better the future. These women did not have the freedoms to do as they pleased, simply because they were women. Thanks to them, I can vote, drive, and have a bank account, but there remains work to be done before our daughters have the opportunities, respect, and equality they deserve. May we make our matriarchal lineage proud—past and future—by what we do today, right now, with warm hands. Roll up your sleeves. There's plenty of work to do.

Show Up Stand Up Speak Up

My prayers to be petite didn't work. Since the 5th grade, I've been 5' 11" with these too-large boobs that I didn't want. I stand out, even when I don't want to. There's never been anything about me that says I'm supposed to blend in, be quiet, or play nice. I'm a change agent. A visionary. A disrupter. When the emperor has no clothes, I say so. An optimist, minus rose-colored glasses. There are big problems to solve and I'm ready. Now it's time to amplify my "bigness". I became a Psychologist because it allowed me to study healing, change, and transformation. Always learning and up-leveling has lead me to study with amazing people across multiple disciplines. Obsessed with finding each person's ideal tools and path to guide them to live the life they were born to live.

Now the mission is bigger. I have daughters, and the situation for women across the world is only minimally better. Not good enough. We can tend to our children and future generations better. It's what women do. In these past 35 years, I've architected my legacy organization, Woman Optimized. Using emerging technology with a new, feminine approach to business and life as we know it, we can heal what's broken. It's not just WHAT we do, it's HOW and WHY we are doing it that matters. We're creating a world where women are empowered to lead, innovate, and transform all industries AND their lives. Together we're building something that has never existed before. Confronting these systems that have limited women's power, WE are collectively unstoppable. Uniting and collaborating, creating a circle for all women to sit in, is more powerful than this existing hierarchy. This is more than a business model; it's a movement. As mothers, caretakers of all the world's children and creation, we profoundly 'innerstand'—know—that a healthy interdependent community and individual success are inextricably linked. Together, we are healing our global village, one woman at a time. When women have all we need, we build a longer table, not a higher fence. Want to talk women's issues? Equality? Leadership? Future of technology? Psychology? Neuroscience? Ethics? How to change the world? Let's talk. Feel the same BIG mission? I'd love to know about you. Connect with me here: robin.r@womanoptimized.com

STAY SURPRISED

My Story

SUSAN FLERCHINGER

In life, unexpected events can shape our path and ignite a fire within us. For me, it was the sudden passing of my father—an event that shattered my world and sparked a deep contemplation of the impact I wanted to have in this lifetime. Thankfully, I sought solace in the divine, reaching out for guidance and clarity to navigate the seas of loss. The first whispered prayer— "Dear God, What legacy do you want me to leave?"— gave me pause and provided an opportunity to uncover the greater purpose that I was uniquely and magnificently designed for. Through prayer, meditation, and soulful introspection, I began to discern the subtle messages and signs that the universe gently placed in my way. Trusting in the wisdom of God, a new path was revealing itself. On a soul-stirring hike through the captivating landscapes of Italy, a profound connection enveloped me. It was as though I became one with the breathtaking beauty of God's creation, transcending the boundaries between heaven and earth. In that moment, clarity unveiled a life-changing purpose: to foster a world where individuals embrace their inherent worth, experience boundless love, and feel genuinely valued.

This revelation led me to explore energy healing modalities, prompting a courageous departure from my two-decade long career in software engineering. Embracing the unknown, I discovered untapped potential and spiritual gifts within myself, bringing great joy in helping others in their physical, emotional, and spiritual well-being. I happily reclaimed my natural positivity and joy-filled heart and smile. As my husband and children wonderfully supported my new path, we consciously deepened our bonds through love and celebrating each one's value. Life-affirming relationships have proven to be essential to living a purposeful life that aligns with our true selves. Amidst all the changes, I also discovered that being intentional enriched our experiences of travel, play, school, and work. In this journey of growth and change, I nurtured an intimate connection with the divine. I realized that one can move forward with unwavering faith in God's magnificent plan by surrendering, embracing blessings, seeking clarity, and taking inspired action. I gratefully discovered that the unparalleled support from angels' manifests miracles beyond measure. I encourage you to tune in to the whispers of your soul, heed the divine guidance that gently nudges you, and, with a resounding 'YES,' embrace the extraordinary life awaiting you. Let your journey be a living testament to the boundless potential that resides within you. What courage can you muster to heed God's call? What awaits when you embrace divine guidance? Imagine the incredible possibilities that unfold when you say 'Yes,' and allow this to resonate and inspire others to shine brightly alongside you.

Show Up Stand Up Speak Up

Deep down, you know that you are destined for something greater! You are not alone! You are made to soar! Every woman has a unique divine call, leading to a life of purpose, fulfillment, joy, and positive impact. Embracing it allows you to take charge of your life, grow, thrive, inspire, and become your best self. In community, we elevate each other, amplifying our impact and potential. You can unlock your extraordinary life by tapping into the divine within yourself. Imagine navigating challenges with unwavering support, clarity, and insight, while making decisions aligned with your authentic self. My journey took a dramatic shift when I experienced a deep personal connection to the divine on that hilltop in Italy, sparking a mission to bring healing to the earth and humanity. As an intuitive healer and celebrated author, my purpose is to empower you to reclaim your vitality and align with your divine calling. With my intuitive abilities and profound connection to angels, I empower ambitious professionals like you to revitalize your physical, emotional, and spiritual energy. Utilizing energy medicine, angel therapy, intuitive healing, and engineered methodologies, we heal chronic pain, release limiting beliefs, revitalize relationships, resolve past traumas, and countless others. These processes unlock your true potential for transformative growth, allowing you to be fully present and better equipped to build a future aligned with your purpose and core values. My heart overflows with thankfulness that I can be an integral part of unfolding miracles: neck pain vanished, social anxiety conquered, cysts disappeared, and so much more. Are you ready to tap into your greatest resource? If you're feeling discontent and unfulfilled, let's rejuvenate your spiritual energy, renew your mind, and embark on a path aligned with your divine calling at our spiritual spa retreat. I want to learn about you and support your journey. Connect with me, Susan, at FormedToSoar.com. You have the power to create a life that surpasses your wildest dreams.

Just one decision can make all the pieces fall into place. Embrace it. Own it. Shine Your Light. The time for transformation is now. susansenergy@gmail.com

SHINE BRIGHTLY

My Story

LESLIE CAPPS

I am a storyteller at heart, captivated by the spirit of humanity. My life has been a mosaic of experiences: dancing in a Caribbean parade, applying dung to a Tanzanian hut, rafting in Costa Rica, climbing the Grand Teton, owning vast lands, real estate ventures, and exploits like off-piste skiing and kayaking on the Yukon River. These aren't hobbies; they're chapters embracing the beauty and complexity of the world and nature.

My journey of unconventional storytelling began in 8th grade, when I tried out for the boys' basketball team. Influenced by Gloria Steinem and Title IX, my goal wasn't about personal achievement. It was about setting a precedent, challenging norms, and empowering others. The experience was rough and the lack of support from women in my conservative community was disheartening. Yet, it underscored the transformative power of stories in shaping our identities and societal roles. Years later, an encounter with a pitbull named Wadi on the side of a Wyoming interstate taught me about the unspoken connections that stories forge. Managing an apartment complex hours from home, I came across Wadi stranded by the roadside. My initial reluctance gave way to compassion, and I couldn't leave him there alone. Winning his trust with Mexican food and patience, I realized that sometimes, stories are not just told; they are felt. Wadi's howls were more eloquent than any words, speaking volumes about empathy, loss and unexpected friendship.

Stories are more than a timeline of events. They mirror our journeys, our struggles, and celebrate our triumphs. They weave a tapestry of human experience, as rich and diverse as a buffet at an international food festival. Through these stories, we find common ground, shared laughter, and the occasional tear, making the world feel like a cozy neighborhood. And in this tapestry, there's a special need for heroines – for bold and unapologetic voices that dare to write new chapters and conquer new mountains. By choosing our own paths and endings, we not only empower ourselves but also light the way for other women to embrace their beauty, strength, and boldness.

In the end, our stories are more than personal histories; they're bridges to understanding, sources of joy and sorrow, and beacons of hope and resilience. By embracing and sharing our narratives, we create a world where every voice is heard, every experience is valued, and every individual is seen for their true authentic quirky self.

Show Up Stand Up Speak Up

Think of me as a bit of a marketing MacGyver meets Bear Grylls, minus the wild animal encounters (usually). This is the place where creativity and strategy collide in the most adventurous ways. My journey's been as varied as a Netflix series – from intense boardrooms, where opinions are as strong as the coffee, to hands-on DIY projects, discovering the joy in creative problem-solving. Here, we blend these experiences into unique marketing and sales strategies. Think of me as a chef, but instead of whipping up pastries, I'm crafting campaigns that resonate with people's hearts and minds. We operate on the belief that it takes a village to build a business. In our village, women are the ones who hold up the sky – with one hand – while expertly juggling a million things with the other. We create marketing campaigns based on a tapestry of stories, each as unique as those funky socks you secretly love. Our approach is as customized as your morning latte. We mix strategic planning with a dash of psychology and a sprinkle of quirks – because that's where the real magic happens. We specialize in out of the box thinking to showcase what makes you fabulous. Why do I do this? I thrive on the thrill of seeing a strategy resonate, lighting up faces with recognition and joy. It's about making business fun – the kind of fun that sparks creativity and genuine connections. In essence, leading Wild Woman Marketing is being the conductor of an orchestra where every instrument is a story waiting to be heard, every melody a strategy waiting to be played. And every woman has a song waiting to burst forth. It's some beautiful music! I'd love to hear your stories and the music you've created. Connect with me: Leslie@wildwomanmarketing.com

BE BOLD

KRIS CAMILLE DE JESUS

Born under the energetic and passionate sign of Aries, my life has been a vibrant journey fueled by a love for music, a thirst for travel, and a genuine joy in connecting with new people.

Music, like a constant companion, has been the soundtrack to my life. Whether it's the invigorating beats of rock or the soulful notes of jazz, I find solace and excitement in the diverse rhythms that life offers. Concerts and music festivals are my temples, where I lose myself in the euphoria of live performances, surrounded by like-minded souls sharing the same passion.

My insatiable wanderlust propels me to explore new horizons. Traveling is not just a hobby; it's a soul-nourishing pursuit. From bustling cities to remote corners of the world, I thrive on the excitement of discovering diverse cultures and landscapes. Every journey is a chapter in my ongoing story, filled with the thrill of the unknown and the joy of expanding my worldview.

In the digital realm, I've found a unique way to channel my energy and skills – as a virtual assistant. Working in this dynamic field allows me to blend my technological acumen with my innate desire to assist and connect with others. Through the screen, I become a bridge, helping individuals navigate their tasks and challenges seamlessly. The virtual world is an extension of my Aries energy, where adaptability and quick thinking are key.

Meeting new people is not just a hobby; it's an essential part of my life's narrative. In the virtual landscape, I forge connections with individuals from diverse backgrounds and cultures. Each interaction is an opportunity to learn, grow, and contribute positively to someone's day. Whether troubleshooting technical issues or offering guidance, the virtual assistant role allows me to bring my Aries warmth and charm to the digital space.

In the tapestry of my life, music, travel, and virtual assistance are the vibrant threads that weave together a story of joy and fulfillment. As an Aries girl navigating this dynamic existence, I find purpose in the harmonies of life, the exploration of new landscapes, and the connections formed with people around the globe. With every click of the keyboard and every new destination explored, my journey as a happy Aries girl unfolds with a spirit that's as boundless as the universe itself.

Show Up Stand Up Speak Up

The inspiration to be a virtual assistant stems from the unique intersection of my skills, passions, and a profound desire to make a meaningful impact. As a tech-savvy individual with a driven spirit, the dynamic nature of the virtual assistant role aligns seamlessly with my personality.

Moreover, the flexibility of working as a virtual assistant empowers me to create a work-life balance that suits my adventurous spirit. It allows me the freedom to pursue my love for travel and music, enriching my life with experiences that, in turn, enhance my ability to relate and connect with those I assist.

In essence, being a virtual assistant is not just a job for me; it's a manifestation of my passion for technology, my desire to assist and connect with others, and a vehicle for personal and professional growth. It fuels me with a sense of purpose as I navigate the virtual landscape, contributing positively to others' lives and embracing the ever-evolving challenges and opportunities that come my way.
dejesuskheizy@gmail.com

CHOOSE KINDNESS

My Story

ANNIE GIBBINS

My Beloved Grandmothers, Irena Volkova and Mary Montgomery,

As I sit down to pen these words, I feel the weight of gratitude and love that has been nurtured by your active presence in my life. Your wisdom, love, and spirit shaped me into the woman I am today, and I am forever grateful for the life lessons you taught me. When faced with challenges, I draw strength from the memory of your love and support, symbolised by the ring I wear in your honour and twirl when stressed. At 56, I find myself surrounded by the warmth of a love story that has spanned 36 years with my husband, James. I still enjoy Thai dinner on Friday nights, kayaking on the weekends and am addicted to adventure shows Survivor and Ninja Warrior. Inspired by your captivating tales, I have embarked on bold adventures to Everest Base Camp in Nepal, Mt Kinabalu in Borneo, The Overland Track in Australia, and many more. Nature has become my canvas for creating cherished memories, a refuge from the stresses of everyday life.

My journey has been one of leadership and accomplishment, balancing the demands of a CEO with the responsibilities of raising five children, including two sets of twins. My impulsive nature has become a tool for innovation and lateral thinking, turning perceived impossibilities into achievable goals.

Your influence, dear grandmothers, has instilled in me a rebel spirit that refuses to conform to the mundane. I am driven by the belief that change, when embraced, leads to newfound energy, success, and joy. Being grandmother of two beautiful girls brings me immeasurable joy and my heart sings every time we spend precious time together. The simple pleasures of walking and talking with my hiking friends makes me feel happy, healthy and connected. And the exhilaration of skiing down snow-covered slopes in winter is a feeling I treasure dearly, even if it means planning holidays around ski resorts! I have learnt to embrace my quirks and find joy in the little moments of laughter, just as we did when I was a child. Though you have both passed on, your legacy lives on in me. Your wisdom, love, and unwavering support continue to guide me on my journey. Thank you for investing in me, for loving me for who I am, and for celebrating the woman I have become.

With boundless love and everlasting gratitude, Annie xo

Show Up Stand Up Speak Up

As a Grand Stevie Award-winning Women's Success Coach, my vision is rooted in a world where women possess the agency and means to achieve financial independence. This belief is not merely a professional stance; it's a personal commitment derived from a profound understanding of the transformative power that economic empowerment holds. In my perspective, economic empowerment grants women the freedom to make informed choices, contribute meaningfully to their communities, and lead lives that are both sustainable and fulfilling. This philosophy is not confined to rhetoric; it guides my every action and fuels a personal goal – to empower one million women globally to achieve financial independence. Why is this goal pivotal to me? I firmly believe that financial independence is the key to unapologetically living a life you love. Witnessing women soar to heights of success and self-discovery brings me immense satisfaction and purpose. This drive is rooted in the stories of my two grandmothers, remarkable women who served as inspirational role models in their time. Their potential was constrained by a lack of financial independence, limited by societal expectations and gender-based dependency. So, in 2015 when I founded Women's Biz Global, my mission was clear: to empower women globally and guide them on the transformative journey to financial independence. It's a commitment that transcends professional success; it aims to break down barriers, dismantle stereotypes, and create a world where every woman has the tools to shape her destiny. The journey to financial independence is not just a goal; it's a catalyst for societal change, propelling women toward self-discovery and empowerment. I am dedicated to leading this charge, inspired by the resilience and untapped potential of women worldwide. Together, we are shaping a future where financial independence is not just a dream but a reality for every woman. annie@anniegibbins.com

POWER UP

AGNES MacPHAIL

Politician

MARY EDWARDS WALKER

Doctor

CHARLOTTE COOPER STERRY

Olympian

DICKEY CHAPELLE

Photojournalist

My Story

TRISH SPRINGSTEEN

Way back in the "Jurassic Period" a long time ago, a young girl left high school and took her first steps into the big world. She was an introvert and very shy. Her passion was reading and being with a small group of friends. She didn't stand out and wasn't very good at meeting people. The thought of speaking or owning a business was not on her radar. In fact, if you mentioned anything like that to her friends and people who knew her, they would have laughed. So how did that shy introvert end up owning a business, being the author of 19 books, speaking on national and international stages, doing videos, appearing on podcasts, national TV, radio, emceeing events and teaching others to speak and stand out. My journey is one of self-discovery, belief, making mistakes, learning, realising I had a story and resilience. Yes, that young girl is me and yes, I am still an introvert but not quite so shy. The first milestone on that journey was learning to believe in myself. It took me a long time to realise I had a message, had stories. It took a long while for me to own my uniqueness, to say I am awesome and BELIEVE it. When you believe in yourself it is a solid foundation to be who you are and own it. You can build on that to explore the world. To get there took mentoring, being part of a group of likeminded people who believed in me, who supported me and pushed me.

The second milestone was the day we lost our son Craig to suicide 3 October 2007. We woke up that morning with a family intact, a 23-year-old son with the world at his feet and a daughter married and living in America. We went to bed that night shattered, lost and broken. Our 23-year-old son chose to leave us. We did not know why and to this day we still do not know why, only that something powerful must have driven him to make that choice. There was and still is so much love in our family. Each day I get up in joy and live to the full because I know that you never know what the next day will be bring. My husband and I chose to live and remember our son – there are so many good memories. Resilience, love and being you was the lesson learned. Today, I am unequivocally me – I celebrate my uniqueness. Everyone is unique. I speak and share my stories; I help others to speak and share their stories. I reach out and grab opportunities and live because you don't know what the next day brings. So many milestones and only space to share two. I love purple, even though I am subtle about this love many people are perceptive and notice. I am often asked about my love of Purple … it's me being unique, being authentic, being genuine, believing, living.

Show Up Stand Up Speak Up

Three phrases that speak to my heart: Show Up Stand Up Speak Up = Owning Your Uniqueness.

My clients work with me because they know I can help them be the Unicorn in their business. I help them have the confidence and self-belief to own their uniqueness, step up, speak, and share that uniqueness. I know from personal experience how empowering it is when you believe in yourself. My passion is giving you that foundation to build on. When you believe in yourself, you find the confidence to grab the opportunities that come, the confidence and courage to step outside that comfort zone and grow. Together we delve deep into your business to find the gold nuggets to repurpose and leverage, avoiding content overload and allowing you to make it easy for your clients to reach you. These lessons I learnt from my journey as an Introvert Speaker: Resilience, courage, listening to feedback, understanding your potential, embracing change, learning from mistakes, knowing your strengths, being aware of opportunities and connecting with others; will allow you to grow in your business and your personal growth.

One of my mantras is I Believe in You Until YOU Believe in Yourself.

My other mantra is 60 Seconds of Insane Courage: take 20 seconds to acknowledge the negative thoughts, 20 seconds to replace them with the positive and 20 seconds to say yes, step up and grab opportunities. For every one business there are several others doing exactly what you do. Don't be selfish – your clients need you. My passion and mission is to help you own your Uniqueness and Show Up Stand Up Speak Up. I am awesome, I am unique. So are you. Take a deep breath - have the courage to be the Unicorn. trish@trishspringsteen.com

BE UNIQUE

My Story

DEE LIPPINGWELL

Just like my mother told me, you can do anything you want.

If you have a dream, don't let anyone stop you from becoming the person you want to be or doing the career you want to do.

Don't let anything stop you. If you want it, then just do it.

Show Up Stand Up Speak Up

Vancouver born and award-winning photographer DEE LIPPINGWELL began her self-taught professional photography career over 45 years ago. Her love of music propelled her into shooting local musicians and her success on that level led her into shooting world-famous performers that we are so familiar with today. Through her hard-edged determination and a commitment to her craft, Dee has had her candidly striking photographs published world-wide. She has received many honours, including being inducted into the BC Country Music Hall of Fame and the recipient of Canada's Famous Women Award, earning this distinction by being published in every major newspaper in Canada. Most recently her whole collection of work, including negatives and digital images, has been accepted into the National Music Centre - Studio Bell in Calgary, Alberta - the greatest honour to date in her career.

Dee has produced 3 photographic Art Books showcasing legendary artists such as Bruce Springsteen, Bob Dylan, Johnny Cash, Jerry Lee Lewis, The Judds, Brooks & Dunn, Loretta Lynn, Vince Gill, Alan Jackson, Martina McBride, Reba McEntire, Dwight Yoakam, Tim McGraw, Randy Travis, Kenny Chesney, Keith Urban, Sugarland, Carrie Underwood, Dr Hook, Fleetwood Mac, Tom Petty, U2, Jeff Beck, Kiss, Rolling Stones, Eric Clapton, Queen, Who, Police, and many more!
Connect with Dee at https://deelippingwell.ca/

BE YOURSELF

My Story

DIANNE JAMIESON

Have you ever felt the weight of being labeled "Too Much" or felt the need to alter your true self to avoid pain? I've been there too—tired of shrinking myself to fit into others' expectations, tired of the internal "shoulds," and tired of fearing the potential hurt that comes with being real. This is not about lacking self-worth, self-esteem or people pleasing; it's about self-preservation, about safeguarding our hearts from the sting of rejection. My defining moment took place when I was just five years old. The sunlit sky above me, I danced with abandon on the front lawn, reveling in the pure joy of the moment—before "living in the moment" became a buzzword. But then, those around me ridiculed my bliss, calling it "silly" and "pointless." The pain of their words cut deep, etching into my very soul. In that instance, I internalized the belief that being my true self equated to pain and wrongness. This belief laid the foundation for decades of living under the scrutiny of my inner critic, constantly modifying myself to avoid being hurt. Can you relate? Perhaps your story is one of being too smart, too quiet, too energetic, too blunt, too____? Always feeling like you don't quite fit the mold. My journey spans across continents-exploring varied careers, pursuing degrees and competing athletically---looking for a place where being myself was not only acceptable but celebrated. Therapies, coaching, mindfulness practices—I've explored them all, seeking to rewrite my subconscious scripts and narrative. It led me to penning my thoughts in this book, finally just putting myself "out there". I've realized that society rewards conformity, praises overachievers and often misunderstands those who don't fit neatly into predefined boxes. What if we're not the ones who fit? What if we possess boundless energy or a spirit that compels us to stand up against injustice? Such authenticity often comes with backlash, causing us to retreat into our shells to "fit in."

Three Practical Tips: Spend time with those who understand you, providing an outlet for your true self. Cultivate self-awareness, self-care, and invest in your personal growth. Seek opportunities that align with your natural strengths in both personal and professional realms. Being part of this book became a challenge of its own. With a barrage of stories in my head, where should I begin? Perfectionism added procrastination to the mix. Comparing myself to other women's clear messages, I found myself drowning in self-doubt. Can you relate? So, if any of this resonates, let's take a step forward together. Let's stand up, show up, and speak up as our true selves. What if we embrace authenticity and encourage others to do the same? The possibilities are endless, the liberation immeasurable. Let's unapologetically embrace the power of being ourselves.

Show Up Stand Up Speak Up

Step onto a path of self-discovery and empowerment, where we'll chart a course toward embracing your authentic self and thriving in its brilliance. For over three decades, I've committed myself to guiding individuals, teams, leaders, and organizations through transformative journeys. Be it overcoming challenges, conquering obstacles, managing stress, or enhancing business, my purpose is to lead you to a more fulfilling and effective life. My expertise spans diverse domains—from outdoor experiential learning to corporate programs, individual coaching, counseling, and consulting. With a wealth of proficiencies across profit, non-profit, government, and private sectors, backed by a repertoire of over 20 subjects, I specialize in aiding leaders in tackling mental health challenges within the workplace. Picture us creating a roadmap from your current vantage to your desired destination. Our collaboration will tap into my toolkit, selecting strategies that resonate deeply with you. My passion exceeds mere knowledge—it emanates from genuine compassion for those facing difficulties. Having witnessed the toll of judgment and lack of empathy, I am resolute in creating a secure space where you feel understood, valued, and empowered. I believe in cultivating self-awareness and equipping ourselves with skills to choose our responses and positively impact those around us. I am devoted and relatable, embracing fun, diversity, and adaptability. Be it structured settings or a more organic approach, I'll meet you where you stand. Your journey is unparalleled, and I am here to guide each stride. Remember, this is your life—a canvas for complete experiences. Let's shed self-imposed confines, judgments, and uncertainties. Together, we will unveil the extraordinary individual you've always been, steering you toward the life you envision. No longer restrain yourself. The time has come to Show Up, Stand Up, and Speak Up for the remarkable individual you are. I am here to support every stride you take.

Feel free to connect at: dianne@diannejamieson.com

PLAY EVERYDAY

NADA LYON

My story starts in Dubai, where I was born into a conservative family. My family was very diverse, and at a young age, I was exposed to a variety of religions, cultures, and customs of the twelve nationalities that my family was part of. Despite my versatile upbringing, I never identified with any religion. Little did I know that experiences from my childhood would lead me to find a deep spirituality that would define my life and my future.

When I was fourteen years old, I was in a car accident that would change my life forever. In that accident, I was declared dead for several minutes, and I vividly recall my soul leaving my body. Instead of finding fear in those moments, I experienced deep clarity, a clarity that I hadn't found in the rules and regulations of religion. Instead, this clarity allowed me to begin my enlightened journey.

It was at fourteen that I became aware of the power of spirituality, but it wasn't until much later in life that I understood how to use my experience to speak on the spiritual realms of human experience. Like so many of us, I struggled in ways that left deep scars. I participated in toxic relationships that encouraged me to bury my light and hide my true self. I experienced financial struggles that forced me to live in my car while I tried to make ends meet. And then, I found inspiration to change.

The reason I was determined to take control of my life arrived sixteen years ago in the form of my son. To this day, he is my inspiration to be a better person, and ultimately, my inspiration to create change. When this newfound light arrived in my life, I was suddenly transported back to that time at fourteen years old, when my soul left my body for a few brief moments and the enlightenment that ensued. I was reminded of a great healing power, and I realized I was finally ready to embrace my spiritual gifts.

I began to study metaphysics and became obsessed with self-development, healing, and biohacking. I discovered the invisible threads in this world that keep us stuck and unmoving and learned how to release these threads, and in turn, the toxic relationships, past traumas, poverty, and mindset that we don't have enough to fully thrive. Then, I began to share these discoveries with others and show them how to take hold of the spiritual powers in their lives and use them to heal, not only themselves but others. Sometimes, I picture that scared young woman living in her car, or the fourteen-year-old after the accident, and I imagine telling her about the woman she has become. "She is a published author, a mother, a wife, and a business owner," I would say. "She helps women all over the world find the power in their own spiritual gifts. And she is only getting started."

Show Up Stand Up Speak Up

I am a firm believer that everyone has been given spiritual gifts to share with this world! For some, it may be the divine gift of healing the body through movement or the sacred gift of ushering new souls into this world. My divine gift was clear at a young age: I was placed on this earth to teach others how to access the spiritual realm and harness the powers of divine relationships and spiritual self-mastery. This mindset was the center of my entrepreneurial journey and continues to inform my business decisions today!

I am the founder of New Earth Masters and the co-founder of the Divine Union Academy. Both organizations were created to help people from all walks of life understand how to access their spiritual gifts and use them for healing and enlightenment. I run these companies with my husband who is also my business partner, which is a beautiful representation of the power that divine intimacy holds! Together, we have supported thousands in their mastery and dream love lives.

New Earth Masters guides people on the path of divine mastery through online courses. These courses show participants how to further connect with their innate spirituality and use it to heal, create, and transform lives. In addition to taking people on a spiritual journey from an online platform, New Earth Masters also hosts spiritual retreats all over the world to help individuals connect with their higher self and create community through elevated living.

Divine Union Academy is for those looking to redefine and magnify their love story. This program guides people into sacred intimacy through understanding the dance of Masculine and Feminine Energies for Lasting Love. By diving deeper into the masculine and feminine realms, this academy allows couples to create a foundation of respect, friendship, commitment, and trust so they can step fully into Sacred Intimacy and Soulful Sexuality. I look forward to guiding you on the spiritual journey that lies ahead! https://www.newearthmasters.com/

137

BE DIVINE

LISA KARASEK

I lived through what experts call a tragic life experience.

My next 48 hours were spent walking the city in utter shock, and then I went to sleep for two years.

My body totally shut down.

The heaviness and the depth of what happened woke me up from that long, deep, and surreal sleep. Realizing I was in my 40's and not yet dead, I had to get out of that bed and get back to my life.

Now in my 50's I focus on maintaining clarity for myself, and my peace. I practice being in flow.

Show Up Stand Up Speak Up

I am a writer and a poet.

I am a naturally gifted healer in the quantum time/space continuum - I work across all timelines, lifetimes, and dimensions. I am an educator, and I am a conscious development practitioner. I facilitate teaching your body how to release trauma and tension, and regulate your nervous system.

I'm dedicated and passionate about helping you work with the dynamics of your self-relationship and update your states of being by powerfully guiding you to a healthier, happier, and more purposeful life. I believe this is the key to most Mind Body Spirit disease and illness.

www.LisaKarasek.com

ALWAYS AUTHENTIC

LAINIE STROUSE

You've probably heard the saying, "Life is a journey". Well, mine has definitely been one so far. Often, we don't take a minute to acknowledge how far we have come or what we have accomplished, we just think about the next thing to do. I have been guilty of that. As we learn about ourselves and the world, it is valuable to acknowledge losses, mistakes, successes, and lessons.

One mantra that gets me through a lot is "I can only do what I can do." It may seem basic, but if you really understand it, it is life changing. We don't have control of others' behaviors, pandemics, weather or a million other things. The more we let go of unrealistic expectations and society's ideas of what a woman or a man is supposed to be, think, feel, and do, we can just be authentic. Once I let go of all the fears and anxiety associated with trying to make sure everything is perfect, I became happier and more effective. I love reading biographies of interesting people throughout history to better understand who they were and how they became legendary.

One thing stood out to me. No one who has achieved anything great did it by being perfect. Read any biography and it is filled with a curvy path of failures, challenges, and messy personal lives amongst the successes. We can strive for unattainable perfection or greatness. I want to give and receive joy, laugh, and make memories. I want to travel, enjoy amazing experiences, and make friends with people around the world.

I honestly believe that if you manage to avoid any mistakes you haven't tried to achieve much. I don't judge anyone for living their way, but some of us want a big life and have big dreams. I hope I leave the world better than when I came into it, even if no one knows that it was me.

Show Up Stand Up Speak Up

What makes someone successful in business? Effective leadership is essential. As a leader it is important to understand the difference between fault and responsibility. If you hire someone and they make a mistake it may be their fault, but it is still your responsibility. Leadership is not about pointing the finger. We need to look at the root of problems to find actionable solutions. We need our employees, colleagues, and investors to believe in us so we must believe in ourselves.

Many women believe the rules are different for them, but I believe that if we don't buy into that, we can rise above the cliches by being undeniable. Funders want to feel that a great idea will be executed with excellence. They must believe that you are the right person to lead the team. How do you get them to believe that? It's not by you flaunting or apologizing for being a woman, a minority, or any other group. Be your best self, wow them with your expertise, and make sure you are great to work with. Investors want to make money. They need to believe in you. Some may want to support diversity, but there are many of every race or gender vying for the few opportunities available. How do you stand out? You must be undeniable. You must be so good that there is no doubt. Find what you are excellent at, love and how you can bring value to the world.
lainie.strouse@gmail.com

BE UNDENIABLE

KELLI KEY

The year was probably sometime in the late sixties and I and my cousin Melanie could be found stretched out in her bedroom with a huge make-believe town made from things located around the house. Who was this town made for you ask? Barbie and all her fabulous friends. You see in this town, in the late sixties, Barbie gave us the ability to dream of what we wanted our lives to look like when we "grew up." With our beds made of shoe boxes, and bed linens made of a hand towel, pillows made from fluffy cotton balls, our world could be anything we could imagine. This was before the now infamous "dream house" or corvettes or even extra clothes for our Barbies. Everything that happened in that bedroom in a small west Texas town, came from our imagination. And Oh Boy, did we dream big! Our Barbies could be a schoolteacher one day and whisk away on an "airplane" made of a handheld broom duster as a Pan Am flight attendant the next.

We dreamed of traveling the world to Italy, France, and England. My aunt Earlyne could sew up a storm and would make us Barbie clothes and she could create anything we dreamed up. I even believe she made our Barbies Pan Am flight attendant clothes if memory serves me correctly. My favorites were when we "styled" our Barbies with fabulous evening clothes and used pliers to cut off the ends of my aunt's sewing pins so we could make "earrings" for our Barbies. A Barbie's outfit is never complete without her accessories!

These little girl dreams served us well! Melanie became a schoolteacher helping to shape generations and to plant those dreams inside the hearts of our youth and I grew up to help women understand their value and help them identify and unlock their little girl Barbie dreams. We have both have traveled the world too, but not on Pan Am of course!

Show Up Stand Up Speak Up

"It is literally impossible to be a woman," according to America Ferrera in the Barbie movie. I think we can all agree she is right. In this world where everything shows up on social media, the magnifying glass seems even larger and the weight of it hard to carry.

Even in writing this, I almost felt as though I wasn't enough or what I had to say wouldn't have an impact … and wouldn't be perfect. Life is messy! WE are messy! It doesn't have to be perfect; it just needs to be real.

I remember working my first corporate job in the early 80's. I had my briefcase, power suit, pumps, and pantyhose (gag) and I was all set to conquer a man's world. I knew that if I just worked harder than the men, came in earlier and stayed later, I could be seen, recognized, promoted. All along, the men literally had it right. They worked hard, showed up to the meetings, but had mastered the art of compartmentalizing things and knew how to flip the switch and end up on the golf course. Meanwhile, you guessed it, I was at the office "working HARDER."

So, here I am 40 years later, and just now learning how to flip the switch and to play like the men. This can be especially challenging these days when work fits right into the palm of our hand. As a woman who had a "near miss" cardiac event, I am here to say Don't Wait. Get yourself and your happiness in order. It gives you a crystal-clear view of what is important.

I am empowering women across the country helping them regain confidence, stand out, and create their dream lifestyle. I LOVE helping women discover what truly brings them joy, because it doesn't have to be impossible to be a woman!

Let's connect. Kelli Key keybeelievers@yahoo.com

DON'T WAIT

My Story

DR. SOPHIA YEN

At 15 years old, I was sexually active, wanted to be a doctor someday, and could not afford to be pregnant. It would derail my future if that were to happen. As a Planned Parenthood volunteer, I ran a pregnancy test, but it was not for me, it was for a 13-year-old girl. It came back positive. I would give her all her options: keep the pregnancy, give the baby up for adoption, terminate the pregnancy. She chose to keep the pregnancy. I realized that her life was going to become very difficult from here. Teen pregnancy, would she graduate high school? College? Would the father stay? Help? I would go on to college, medical school, startup and more.

This loss of future potential could have been prevented if we had provided her: comprehensive sexuality education, confidential reproductive healthcare, a goal to strive for and confidence that she could achieve that.

This is my motivation for what I do: to make women's lives better, to help women advance and achieve equality, and we will all benefit.

Show Up Stand Up Speak Up

I am an Adolescent Medicine specialist, which is a subspecialty of pediatrics. "Sex, drugs, rock 'n roll, some acne, and some sports medicine." My focus is on birth control, menstruation, preventing sexually transmitted infections. I also earned a Master's in Public Health in Maternal Child Health, focusing on obesity.

I am a Thought Leader: Anyone with a uterus and anyone who cares about those with uteri should know about #PeriodsOptional. You don't have to bleed every month (menstruation) and life is better without random blood every ~28-35 days for ~38 years of our lives (12 years old to 50 years old). See my TEDx talk. I love to talk about birth control and menopause and the theme: #StopSuckingItUp. Did you know the #1 cause of missed school/work in a person with a uterus under the age of 25 is painful, heavy periods? If you have bad periods, please see a doctor. No need to suffer. Same for menopause i.e. if you are suffering from menopause symptoms, no need. See a doctor; we have medicines for that!

I am an Advocate: I pray for the day that we no longer have to fight for: women's equality in the workplace, in academia, in caregiving for young and old (where we do more than our share); bodily autonomy; or religious freedom. If you're inspired, contact me and let's do good in the world together https://www.linkedin.com/in/sophiayenmd

DO GOOD

My Story

DIANE BRANDON

We truly never know where we're ultimately headed in life. This is something we've all heard before and it's quite true for me. From my earliest memory at birth (yes, I've always remembered what I thought when I was born), I thought I was here to perform – acting and singing. In school, I had an avid interest in it, singing in the choir, performing in talent shows, attending a local summer workshop on acting, etc.

In college, I majored in French, but also sang in the glee club and chapel choir, in addition to getting up my courage to be in a play. The floodgates opened and I continued to perform on stage for many, many years. I was the stereotypical actor having day jobs (from being a manager in the corporate world to owning my own store to teaching voice privately, etc., etc.) while pursuing my passion at night. Oh, how I loved to act and perform on stage! Then came two separate triggers for a shift on my path: attending metaphysical classes (metaphysics had always been an interest of mine) and my "epiphany of self-esteem." Suddenly my desire to act and my passion for it had disappeared, evaporating like smoke in a breeze, which really took me aback. I needed extra income and suddenly found myself doing "readings" for others. Talk about something coming out of left field! I hadn't even known I was intuitive. Sure, in grad school I had acquired tarot cards and the *I Ching* – but doesn't everyone? I struggled for the first few years working with my intuition, not knowing what I was doing or how I was doing it.

This, despite my getting positive feedback from clients repeatedly. I started to research what intuition was, trying to get a grasp of this "thing" I was working with, apparently fairly well, according to clients. I found others with similar interests in metaphysics and attended lectures and conferences, while also devouring books on the topic. New research was being done in this area and I availed myself of as much as I could find. I started writing articles for metaphysical publications and began speaking, teaching, and presenting (much to my surprise). I've always been driven to understand concepts and found myself formulating my own theories and ideas. This then led to writing, again to my surprise as I hated writing papers in high school, college, and grad school – four books and counting at this point. I found that I love working with others, whether in private sessions or teaching and speaking to groups.

I love seeing the light bulb go off as students discover their own abilities and I love seeing clients make progress in their private lives, finding more fulfillment and self-understanding and acceptance. The path has not been direct, but I know that I'm doing the work I should be doing. Funny how we can find ourselves doing something we love, even if we didn't set out to do it!

Show Up Stand Up Speak Up

"You've helped me transform my life." Imagine my delight reading this in a note that a client sent me! Then imagine my surprise reading the same feedback verbatim from other clients. Talk about a positive feeling! This is one aspect of my work with others. However, it's not the only one. I love helping others to overcome their self-doubts. I love helping others to heal past hurts. I also love assisting others in discovering their previously unknown and hidden talents, especially intuition. I love facilitating others to uncover the meanings of their nighttime dreams and learn how to use their rich messages as a tool in their lives.

It's very gratifying when I lead someone who's never meditated before on a personalized guided meditation and who looks calm, centered, and at peace when they come out of it. The same is true when I do regressions for others or use healing techniques. I love seeing clients unfolding and developing like a flower unfurling its petals, becoming richer and fuller in themselves. Stimulating others to learn, open up to new spiritual realms, and realize some of the vastness of this cosmos lights me up. Likewise, I love reading that one or more of my books or articles spoke to a reader and made a difference in their lives. To me, it's all about reaching and facilitating others on their paths in life – no matter where they are on that path. There's always more to learn and experience that can add positive benefits to us as we move on our paths through life. It's a blessing to me and oh so gratifying to be able to make a difference in others' lives! I'm richer for my interactions with the delightful clients I've worked with. dianebrandonauthor@gmail.com

EMBRACE YOURSELF

My Story

BARBARA FRANKSON

There are 3 seasons in my life. The season of survival started with my conception with my father that I never knew, my innocence being taken without my consent at the age of 7 or younger (I can't recall the exact age it started), and my mom leaving me at the age of 3 in Jamaica to go to the U.S.A to establish a better life for her family. Arriving in U.S.A at the age of 9 into a world that tried to strip me of my ethnicity, showing me where I was separate and not equal, being bullied by my peers from the age 9-17 when I decided to take my voice and power back. Losing my mom at the age of 19 only to find myself homeless and living in my Volkswagen Rabbit in the garage of the from which I would later graduate.

A stranger found me and gave me shelter with no strings attached; at a time in my life that I was so angry with God for taking my mom; because, although I was 19, I only had her in my life for nine years. I encountered my father twice, and both times I ran because my only conversation with my mother regarding my father was where she showed me him from afar and instructed me to run if he approached me. I saw my father twice in my life, and both times I ran. The absence of the first man that was to emulate love and set the bar high on how I was to be treated by men left me spiraling and looking for love in all the wrong places. I married the first man that asked me and believed this to be love only to be abandoned by him in the sixth month of my pregnancy. I was still in search of love and got married to the second man who asked me after our second date only to start divorce proceedings 3 months later. This brought me to my seasons of both success and significance.

It was in this place that I searched for a different kind of love. A love that was there all the time, but I was walking in so many layers of pain that I could not find it. God's love. I had a father that loved me that I spent time getting to know, and I intentionally stopped dating for 3 years. During this time, I found myself and my purpose, my reason for living. My pain prepared me for the passion for my purpose. John Maxwell says, "once you taste significance, success just won't do". I found significance when I was speaking internationally, and God worked through me to speak life into the broken hearted with my stories of pain. There are women all over the world that God will use me to set them free and lead them into being transformed into the full manifestation of their being.

Show Up Stand Up Speak Up

In my seasons of survival and even success, I felt pain that at times left me with a feeling of being paralyzed; but God picked me up and carried me until I could learn to crawl, walk, and run. I am at a place in life where I now realize that my pain prepared me for the passion for my purpose. I am using my voice; the gift God has blessed me with to lead people (especially women) out of being paralyzed with pain, and fear into a life of purpose and hope. I created coaching programs that teach women to use the very thing that has been paralyzing them to propel them into a life of purpose, significance, and fulfillment. These programs help them to remove the mask of expectations, pain, hopelessness, and unfulfillment. They inspire and motivate and transform them from the inside to step into the best version of themselves, and to walk in their God given purpose. I also use my voice as an Inspirational International Speaker to ignite a person's spirit by using the very pain that tried to kill me; however, God used it to transform me so that I can transform others with my stories. What makes me different than other coaches, and speakers is my journey, and my ability to speak to the spirit of the man/woman instead of their flesh (aka egos). My purpose in life is to walk into every door God opens and create a transformational movement that changes individuals, one life at a time. When people change it creates a domino effect. Each morning I wake up having peace and fulfillment, where chaos and emptiness once lived. Walking in my God given purpose allows me to use it to transform lives. I am God's vessel of change. secondchances@bfrankspeaks.com

BE PURPOSEFUL

ELENORE PAN

In the eloquent words of my cherished yoga instructor, we are truly blessed to have discovered yoga in this lifetime. For me, yoga stands as my sanctuary, shelter, and anchor — I now can't imagine a life without my practice.

I was first introduced to the world of yoga at 16. A rebellious yet intellectually curious teenager, it was suggested that I try out yoga and meditation by my mentor at the time, who is very spiritual. Initially approaching yoga as a physical exercise, I quickly excelled. Yet with meditation, I didn't gain immediate insights. In hindsight, introducing these practices to myself early proved to be one of the wisest decisions I have ever made.

A pivotal moment in my yoga journey unfolded during college. I was overwhelmed by the pressure of a highly pre-professional environment, where every smart kid had a speech about their consulting, banking, or software engineering career plans. Needing a reset, I spent a summer in India pursing my 200-hour yoga teaching certificate. There, my Indian yoga teacher taught us the 8 limbs of yoga. For the first time, I realized that the physical practice of yoga, or ASANA, is merely the third step in the philosophy. My teacher emphasized, "We practice asana to make our physical body strong and flexible, so that we can sit in meditation longer without pain." This insight completely reshaped my practice— confronting physical challenges is to fortify the mind, and I need to move past anxiety to discover clarity and peace.

Post-graduation, the demands of a bustling Hollywood career led me to neglect my practice. Engulfed in the chaos, I procrastinated on my practice frequently. Time elapsed swiftly, and it wasn't until the onset of the COVID pandemic that I re-committed to a regular, strong practice. Confronting anxiety and uncertainty on a whole new level was rather humbling, and yoga and meditation became my guiding pillars through the tumult. The challenges helped me realize, I possess the tools for creating abundance and finding spaciousness within myself, not externally. Through meditation, I found a higher frequency.

Despite the return to normalcy, I maintain my practice routine. As I stand on the other side of adversity, I am now more grateful than ever for my yoga mat that serves as a life raft. In so many ways, yoga and meditation molded me into a more empathetic and centered film producer.

Show Up Stand Up Speak Up

I've always known that a career in filmmaking is not all sunshine and rainbows, but the realization hit hard when I transitioned from school to the professional world. I still vividly recall the challenges of seeking my first job in Hollywood post-graduation without existing industry connections. After many hurdles, I was excited to land an interview at a top talent agency, even though it was just a trainee position with minimum wage.

In the waiting room, I sat alongside a tall, blonde Caucasian man in a sharp suit. Our brief and friendly exchange revealed both of our nervousness. Glancing at his resume, I noticed that he graduated from UPenn. Our conversation took an unexpected turn when he shared that the person before us, a Harvard graduate with a producer father, had just interviewed for the same position. It struck me then how stiff the competition really is in this industry, and success requires more than just hard work. Over the years, I have heard more No than Yes, and developed a thicker skin. Despite numerous moments of self-doubt and encounters with seemingly insurmountable challenges, I didn't give up. My journey is shaped equally by betrayals from people I trusted and unexpected kindness from people who didn't owe me anything. In Hollywood, you experience the full spectrum of humanity.

Reflecting on my path as an Asian female producer, I take pride in maintaining my passion for storytelling and team building despite the ups and downs. The experiences, both positive and negative, have deepened my respect and understanding of the weight of our work as content creators. I am now more mindful of the person I am becoming and the impact of my choices. I am committed to navigating obstacles and exploring uncharted territories in the industry. elenorepan530@gmail.com

STAY FEARLESS

OLYA ZHILINSKAYA

My life is an exciting adventure, and the sky is just the beginning for me! Since I was little, I yearned to make a difference in the world, to leave a lasting impact, and to create a life that was extraordinary.

When I was 20, I made a bold decision to leave my sweet home in Crimea and move to Vancouver, Canada, on my own, with $300 in my pocket and my heart brimming with excitement. As an immigrant I've encountered many challenges and hardships along the way, and I always viewed them as opportunities for growth and self-discovery. I took risks, stepping outside of my comfort zone and pushed myself to the limits. I knew that, to live a big life, I had to be willing to take big risks.

I learned from my failures, using them as steppingstones towards success. I believed that failure was not the end, but a necessary part of the journey towards greatness.

Big life was not just about my personal success. It was also about making a positive impact on the world around me. I was always determined to make a difference and leave a legacy of compassion and kindness. It was about finding joy in the little things, embracing the present moment, and cherishing the relationships I formed along the way. I surrounded myself with positive and like-minded individuals who supported my dreams and inspired me to be the best version of myself.

Yes, I achieved great success in my career, traveled the world, and made a tangible impact on the lives of others. But what truly made my life big was the love, laughter, and happiness I shared with my loved ones.

I want my story to serve as a reminder to all of us that living a big life is not just about external accomplishments or material possessions. It is about finding your passion, pursuing your dreams, making a difference, and cherishing the moments that truly matter. It is about embracing the challenges, learning from the failures, and never giving up.

So, dear reader, what does a big life mean to you? Are you ready to embark on your own journey and create a life that is truly extraordinary? Remember, it is never too late to start. The world is waiting for you to shine your light and live your big life.

Show Up Stand Up Speak Up

I am Olya Zhilinskaya.

I am merging the science of your body with the power of your soul to heal and create a life of unlimited abundance.

I self-healed my physical body via lymphatic system and osteopathy. I connected my body and mind via Face Yoga. I self-healed my emotional body via NLP, Time Line Therapy and Hypnotherapy. I found my Higher Self via my unconscious mind.

Now I am Whole and Magnificent! And I am here to guide you towards your own source of light and greatness!

You are Magnificent and I know you are ready to spread your wings and shine bright!

I always meet people for a reason, so let's continue our conversation:
faceyogaqueen@gmail.com

DREAM BIG

My Story

GRACE CW LIU

My life has been focused on "communication". But not just speaking and the notion of putting words together to relay a thought. From an early age, I realized that there are complexities of true communication that can pave the path for efficacy or breakdown. I learned the hard way. I was raised in both Eastern and Western cultures. My parents are Chinese, but we lived in Canada and the US. Out of necessity I learned the communication "rules" for both cultures. For instance, it was okay to be assertive in the classrooms, however, that was not the case at home with my parents. Little did I know that the pressures of these unspoken rules and learning to weave language to cope was activating my purpose and molding me into a Speech-Language Pathologist I was to become. I recall early on explaining to my parents that idioms such as "I'm cool" meant I was doing well and had nothing to do with temperature as well as helping them to pronounce vocabulary words. Looking back now, it was the start of my journey in learning how to bridge and build relationships through communication. I went to the university with a plan to major in Pharmacy. Things didn't go according to my plan…they went perfectly instead.

Failing physics lead me to feeling lost and unclear about the direction of my future. I went to the career services department, wrote down all the majors, put it on the board, grabbed three darts and resolved to let chance choose my future path. My trusted friend and 'sidekick', determined to exaggerate this "monumental moment", blind-folded me. The verdict of my dart-throwing-fate: marine biology, psychology, and speech-language pathology. At this moment, my choice was clear. Marine biology and psychology were not desirable, so Speech-language pathology it was! I soon discovered my passion and love for a career path entrenching in helping people with stroke, traumatic brain injury, and other disorders with their communication problems. Fate? Coincidence? Or just an example of how life guides us to align with our ideal path and purpose? I will leave you to decide.

After graduating I landed a job as a speech-language pathologist in Scotland where I learned to incorporate humor and fun while bridging culture and communication. With the heavy Scottish accents, I found my students playing with the sound of my last name: Liu which is pronounced "Loo" and phonetically is the Scottish word for "toilet". Everyone giggled each time they would address me as Ms. Liu. And from this humorous revelation and examination I began to carefully cultivate my "communication types" that later would become the cornerstone in my career of identifying the unique difference of all people and how they are designed to communicate efficiently. Through my challenging upbringing I have become an expert at resolving communication breakdowns and I now work with patients and private clients teaching them how to transform their own lives through the power of correct communication.

Show Up Stand Up Speak Up

GraceSOULutions was born with the belief that there is a solution to every problem, including communication and conversation problems. Everyone can find the solution they seek by using the guidance of grace that is in you, with the grace of spiritual support, and me, Grace, Communication coach and navigator. Healthy communication, the cornerstone of any successful relationship, extends beyond mere words. Grace's unique strategies empower conflict-phobic and introverted women to openly communicate their thoughts, feelings, and desires, fostering a deeper connection with their partners. Grace aims to transform the way individuals perceive and engage in communication. Grace is passionate about helping her clients shift communication in all areas of life, so they experience more harmony, are understood, more impactful, find resolution quickly and effectively and are supported by their partners, peers, work associates, and families. Embracing an analogy between communication and art, Grace emphasizes the various communication tools akin to an artist's palette. Words, tone of voice, and body language are the brushes and colors that shape the canvas of conversation. Just as there are different forms and styles of art, communication comes in various types, including written, verbal, and non-verbal. Identifying your Human Design along with your four primary communication styles—nurturer communicator, fireball communicator, diplomatic communicator, and humorous communicator—Grace highlights the importance of understanding one's Human Design and style for effective communication. Drawing a parallel to a garden, she encourages individuals to cultivate their communication, weeding out destructive patterns and setting healthy boundaries. Grace's dedication to her philosophy stems from her belief that communication is the key to building and sustaining relationships. She urges everyone to treat communication as a game rather than a daunting daily task, fostering a sense of ease and fun in expressing thoughts and feelings. Now that you know more about my passion for communication I would love to know more about your personal journey with your communication in your relationships. Contact to schedule a complimentary session at www.GraceSOULutions.com

155

BE AMAZING

SUZANNE GRINBERG

Lawyer

G̲A'A̲XSTAL'AS

Negotiator

FANNY ROSENFELD

Athlete

AMELIA JENKS BLOOMER

Editor

ROWENA LIST

It saddens me that 50% of the world 's population lives on less than a dollar a day. A lot of those people don't even have one pair of shoes, let alone a whole closet full that they don't wear. I believe we can make the playing field more even by consciously consuming rather than being consumed. We can make our own lives more fulfilling by thinking long and hard about how we would like our legacy to live on and how we can help to enrich the lives of others.

Reflect upon the times when the smile on your face matches with how you truly feel inside. Show up for yourself – and others, and stand up and speak up to share your values, and watch the magic that unfolds.

Show Up Stand Up Speak Up

Getting It Together empowers people to live their best lives. I educate people to embrace minimalism, reduce consumerism, and illuminate what holds them back in letting go.

At the heart of Getting It Together is encouragement for my clients to create new habits. Healthy habits. And to also understand the cost of clutter in their lives. Material possessions add to the mental and emotional weight that drags most people down. My passion lies in helping and supporting people to understand what comes from clearing their spaces and simplifying their lives.

I feel most of service when speaking to a large group of individuals who are eager to learn the keys to a successful organized lifestyle. My goal is to leave audiences with a fresh perspective on their lives and possessions, urging them to re-evaluate their priorities.

My passion for this work stems from a deep desire to make the world think differently about stuff and how "things" don't make us happy -- living a fulfilling life does. Helping others does.

Rowena@gettingittogether.ca

REFLECT UPON

My Story

MELISSA MCCLELLAND

I felt like I'd lived a thousand lives before I'd turned thirty. The chapters of my life, out of context, would appear disjointed; like a vast anthology of stories (much like this one), each authored by a different individual. And in a way, they were. Every unforeseen plot twist birthed a new incarnation of my being, each one more determined than the last to write a better, or at least less painful, chapter.

But as fragmented as these chapters may seem, an underlying theme threads them together: absolute, intrinsic confidence. This confidence wasn't born out of clarity, positivity, or strong self-esteem. It was borne out of unshakeable self-trust, even when there were a million reasons to believe I would fail. And sometimes that's all you have. You will never truly know what you're capable of until your back's against the wall; when there is no safety net. That's when your true potential is realized. You'll know beyond a doubt how badly you want it by how fiercely you're willing to pursue it. In your darkest moments, self-trust becomes your lifeline. Self-trust grows stronger with each use, like a muscle. Whether by choice or by force, you will have many opportunities to flex this muscle. And when choice is taken away from you and you're forced to bet on yourself, know this: These events are often the greatest catalysts for transformation, helping you evolve into a better version of yourself.

At 16, I chose to fight for a better life. I had no safety net, and yet, I had to make a move. I took radical responsibility for my future at an age when my peers were giggling about their latest crush with their friends at the mall. I left home with no belongings, no money, and no reason to believe I'd survive. But I had absolute confidence that the path ahead would lead me to a better place than where I started. And that energy - that absolute, intrinsic confidence - is what I've relied on to fuel my success since.

Never underestimate your power. Bet on yourself, even when life gives you a million reasons not to. Self-trust will carry you further in life than you can possibly imagine.

Show Up Stand Up Speak Up

I spent many years hiding who I was and censoring my voice. When people I looked up to told me I was "too much" or discouraged me from speaking up because "the powers that be" wouldn't take kindly to my innovative perspectives, I listened. As a child in school, I got the reputation of being somewhat of an instigator - although not in the confrontational sense - I just wanted to know WHY. I was curious! Why do people do things this way? I was unwilling to accept information at face value without justification just because someone told me that was the way it "should" be. I was especially perplexed by why people continued to do things that they disliked simply because that's how someone else told them to do it.

As I entered the world of entrepreneurship with my first business, a marketing agency offering done-for-you campaigns for coaches, consultants, and personality-based businesses, I found myself at a crossroads: being well-versed in marketing best practices, but overwhelmed by the amount of sleazy hard-selling behind most strategies in the online advertising space, popularized by "gurus" that said it worked. But it felt so disingenuous to me. So, I refused to incorporate these tactics into my own company's methods, and instead committed to mastering marketing strategies that prioritize authenticity and genuine connection so you can grow a successful business without compromising your values.

I believe the best way to show your dream clients that you're the perfect match for them is by infusing more of YOU and your voice into your marketing. If you're a passionate mission-driven entrepreneur who's got a message to share, refuses to have your voice silenced, and wants to grow your business's bottom line in a way that feels good to you – I'd love to connect with you. melissa@medior.net

161

TRUST YOURSELF

KATELYN SILVA

I arrived after work to pick my babies up from school. Just a normal day. When I got to my oldest, he looked up at me with tears in his eyes and asked me, "Mama, where were you?" See, he had one of those performances where the class has practiced, and they sing and dance for the parents. But I had missed it…

He said, "I looked around and all the other kids' parents were here, but I couldn't find you."My heart was shattered.

'What am I doing? If something happened to me… would my kids just remember me working? Am I always going to miss out on those precious once-in-a-lifetime moments as their mom?' Something had to change.

As a child, I had always known two things: when I grew up, I was going to be a mom and an author. I was a mom. But I was stuck in restaurant management just doing what I thought would pay the bills and feed my family. I felt stuck, drained, and longing for that purpose from my Heavenly Father – what I knew I was supposed to be doing. I didn't want to look back with regret, wishing I had taken a leap of faith and stepped into the gifts I had been given! God had given me a vision… and I decided to pursue it.

That was when I picked up the manuscript I had put on the back burner and dusted it off. For years I had tried to finish it, but I kept getting stuck, moving things around, just feeling overwhelmed and not sure how to bring it all together. With a sudden influx of clarity and focus on what really mattered, I started making real progress. In just six months, the first draft was completed, and I started pursuing the publishing journey.

That book was traditionally published with a small publisher… and it didn't quite turn out how I'd hoped. But you know what? It opened the door for me. I started to hone my process, pursue other book ideas, and invest in what it would take to really become an author. That led to the day my prayers were answered and things started to shift. My husband and I agreed I could quit my job and focus on being a mom full-time – and of course the book world! It's not perfect, but I get to share those once-in-a-lifetime moments with my children every day! I'm still learning, there have been a ton of mistakes along the way. There was a beautiful breaking of surrender and a radical encounter with my Creator that transformed me from the inside out and healed my soul and my body. And my kids have gotten to grow right alongside me.

But beyond all that… what's that moment for you? Have you looked around and thought, *This isn't what I'm meant for?* It's time to step into your purpose, say, "Yes," and do what you've been called to do.

Show Up Stand Up Speak Up

When I was little, my mom always inspired and encouraged me to write. I remember creating stories or getting lost in adventures all throughout my childhood. And I had a knack for teaching my peers too. I lost her when I was only eight, but to be honest, all my pursuits are to honor her and remember her. My first book was kind of a disappointing flop. But instead of giving up, I went all in. It took a few books and a ton of investment and learning, but finally, I published my first bestseller. Others started asking me… "Wait, you're a mom, you're working… and you're publishing multiple books? How?!" It became one of those things where the daily, regular life is entangled with what you do. At work, at church, on coffee dates… I started helping friends, co-workers, and loved ones pursue their books and dreams. I released my next bestsellers, all the while letting others learn through my process. And I was learning more deeply what they needed too. The blocks and hurdles and challenges and how to help them not just publish, but use their book as a launchpad for opportunities, growing their audiences, and starting to create legacies. I launched We Write Books out of a passion to guide faith-filled women to boldly share their story and use it as a catalyst for growth, impact, and legacy, because no one else has your unique voice and perspectives. I really believe that! I also host the 1 Minute Writing Tip podcast to feature fellow authors, and Coffee Date with Jesus to share hope. The world is waiting for your story, and I would love to hear it and help you craft the roadmap to achieve it. Connect with me at: katelyn@wewritebooks.com

SEEK FIRST

RUBY CAREY

My Message To Women is...

Be fierce, pushy, opinionated, and do it with love for them
but mostly for yourself.
Stand with your sisters and teach.

Show Up Stand Up Speak Up

One of my first memories was bouncing on my mother's couch singing "California here I come", I knew then I was destined to leave my small town and see more of the world. I come from a broken home and money was scarce, so work was the way out and through this method I hoped to oversee my own future. I was the kid that tried her best to find jobs to save money for my adventures to be. I collected bottles, babysat, and did chores for neighbours. I quit school in grade 11 to leave my little town to visit my father in Boston. I eventually found myself in Vancouver meeting new friends and one day I agreed to accompany a friend to a job interview for summer employment with the Canadian Military Summer Youth Employment program. As it turned out he didn't join but I did, hey it sounded like an adventure and it was only for two months, I was looking forward to serving and being a part of the team. I worked my way up the ranks from Private to Warrant Officer while completing my bachelor's degree. After releasing from the military, I moved back to the Lower Mainland, and I took a position with the Public Service working with the RCMP in Human Resources. After a couple of years, I transferred to the Okanagan and took a part-time for Veterans Affairs. I love doing home renovating, studying about wine, volunteering, travel and cooking. I can usually be found outdoors with my Blue Heeler named Lester B. Pearson.
ruby.carey@shaw.ca

GIRLS RULE

My Story

LIZ SVATEK

I've had many careers over the years, but the one that always amazes people is that I am a recovering standup comedian. I say recovering because occasionally, whether in my parenting, my coaching business, or just at a dinner with friends, the standup comedian comes back for a brief but meaningful performance. People roar with laughter and tell me how funny I am. And I love to make people laugh. Laughter is a gift. A connector. Humor is a healer. Healing us and connecting us even in our darkest times. I believe comedians aren't born; they're made. Funny people often become funny because of tough situations. Robin Williams was left alone a lot as a child, a poor little rich kid raised by nannies. Kevin Hart's dad was a drug addict who was in and out of jail. Many times his father would rob and steal from his own family. Jim Carrey was very poor, and his family was homeless. Jim dropped out of school to support them.

It's true that comedy often comes from tragedy. It's a relief to laugh. I have always been funny, but I became a comedian when I realized that being funny could lighten the mood around my house. My father was full of rage and my mother and I easy targets, but humor brought us all together. My father was a great storyteller and I learned how to set up his stories and punchlines for greater effect. Comedy requires skill, intelligence, and a unique perspective on life.

I use comedy in my parenting when I am unable to reach my teenagers. I use comedy in my coaching when my clients are feeling swallowed up by their problems. I use comedy in my 20-year marriage to keep the magic going. Whenever someone learns I was a standup comedian they always ask how I was able to do it. How was I able to get on stage and perform. They say it sounds scary. Here's the truth about being a comedian. Comedians will risk failure, getting no laughs, making a fool out of themselves all to connect. To have the feeling of deep connection, to be seen and heard and understood. When I meet someone and we share a laugh, I know we share so much more. We share the value of the power of connection.

Show Up Stand Up Speak Up

I'm a midlife, mindset, and empowerment coach but my business really started when I bottomed out at 49. I was just one year away from turning 50 and I was unhappy in almost every area of my life. I remember thinking, "Is this all there is?" And then I kept drinking wine, saying I was fine, and refusing to ANSWER THE CALL. The call to freedom. The call to meaning. The call to change.

I decided to RECLAIM myself physically, mentally, emotionally and UNLEASH MY INNER WARRIOR. I drew hard boundaries with family. I took radical personal responsibility for my health and fitness. I left a well-paying job that I hated (golden handcuffs) and embarked on an entrepreneurial adventure. Turning 49 was the catalyst for change in my life. I turned pain into purpose to start living the life I knew I truly yearned for. Now I lead other women to do the same.

Many of us refuse the call of the Sheroes Journey. Hang up on it. Put it on hold… but the call will only get louder, stronger, and more painful. Beginning the work of evolving, changing, and becoming different is terrifying… AND it's the most satisfying, beautiful, spiritual, meaningful journey of our lives.

Women aren't born Warriors, we become them. I have embraced the little girl inside of me that I had forgotten. I had suppressed her to protect her. Now I know that when you heal the girl, the Warrior will appear. Women always say to me: "Where do I start? I don't know if I'm ready." And I say: "You don't have to be ready… you just have to be willing." That is the Sheroes journey and how you become a Warrior Woman. liz@lizsvatek.com

IGNITE YOURSELF

My Story

IRIS DUPLANTIER RIDEAU

Rising above circumstances

I was born in the sultry embrace of the Crescent City, New Orleans, back in '36. Even as a child, I learned the art of survival, the delicate dance of passing for white, taught to me by my grandmother's gentle hand. But the shadows of racism cast long over the South, and at twelve, I pleaded with my mother to seek refuge in the sun-drenched promise of Los Angeles.

Life in California wasn't without its trials. At fifteen, the weight of responsibility bore down upon me as I found myself with child, forced to bid farewell to the classroom and embrace the solitude of night classes. Determination coursed through my veins like a wildfire, refusing to settle for the mundane existence laid out for women of color.

With grit and resilience as my only companions, I carved a path of my own, securing a front-office position at an insurance agency, where my skills spoke louder than the hue of my skin. And in '67, I took a leap of faith, founding my own insurance empire, a beacon of hope for minorities and women alike.

Collaborating with Mayor Tom Bradley, I spearheaded L.A.'s first Affirmative Action Program, a testament to the power of unity in the face of adversity. Rideau Securities and Investment Firm emerged from the ashes of doubt, paving the way for a career marked by milestones and accolades.

But it was in the serene embrace of the Santa Ynez Valley that my true calling awaited. Amidst the whispers of history, I stumbled upon an abandoned adobe house, a relic of times gone by. With a boldness born of necessity, I breathed new life into those weathered walls, birthing Rideau Winery from the ashes of neglect.

As the tendrils of success wrapped around me, I never forgot my roots, my duty to uplift those around me. In a world where glass ceilings loomed like storm clouds, I shattered them one by one, guided by faith and unwavering self-belief.

Today, as the sun sets over the vineyards of Rideau Winery, I stand as a testament to the resilience of the human spirit, a beacon of hope for generations yet to come. For in every trial, every triumph, I found the strength to persevere, to rise above the confines of circumstance and chart my own course through the winds of fate.

Iris Rideau

Show Up Stand Up Speak Up

My journey from the streets of New Orleans to the heights of entrepreneurial success is a testament to resilience and determination. Born into a poor Creole family before World War II, the specter of racism loomed large in my life. Despite the obstacles, I refused to be defined by society's limitations. Starting with a job in a sweatshop, I recognized the value of education and pursued it relentlessly, despite facing discrimination from school counselors who refused to assist a black student.

But where others saw roadblocks, I saw steppingstones. Landing a front office job at a small insurance agency, I seized every opportunity for advancement, balancing work and motherhood while continuing my education. In 1967, fueled by a desire to break barriers, I founded my own insurance company, specializing in serving marginalized communities. My success caught the attention of Los Angeles Mayor Tom Bradley, who entrusted me with overseeing federal programs and managing the city's pension fund—a groundbreaking achievement for a woman of any color. Even in retirement, I couldn't stay idle. Channeling my passion into winemaking, I founded Rideau Winery in the Santa Ynez Valley, driven by a determination to create the best. Through hard work and dedication, Rideau Winery flourished, uniting people from all walks of life with its Creole heritage and renowned cuisine.

In 2016, I sold the winery, but my journey was far from over. Inspired to share my story, I embarked on writing my memoir, chronicling my remarkable life between two worlds. From humble beginnings to entrepreneurial success, my story is a testament to the power of perseverance and the pursuit of dreams. FROM WHITE TO BLACK: One Life Between Two Worlds Iris_rideau@comcast.net

BE RESILIENT

CHLOE MORGAN

When I look back and see how far I've come, it almost seems like another life. The woman I see looking back in the mirror is far beyond recognition of the woman I used to be, as I reflect on the struggles I've endured.

I've battled and overcome many addictions but one that has been my greatest battle and now greatest victory, I thought I'd live with for the rest of my life was an eating disorder. I realize I'm one of the few to survive something so destructive and detrimental, when there are many that do not, as its nature seeks to destroy.

When I accepted I couldn't solve this issue by myself and began working with an amazing prayer counsellor, I remember feeling like God had opened the door of the dungeon cell I was in and calling me out into freedom, but I was still bound as my identity was deeply rooted in the illness.

About 15 years ago when my adoptive father was dying of cancer, seeing him in this position shook me to the core and I remember thinking, "He can't help what's happening to him, but I can help what's happening to me". After his passing I came to the place where I couldn't live one more day with this in my life and I went up for prayer in a church, as I usually did out of desperation, as I lost my voice again to bulimia. The pastor prayed for me, and it was like a miraculous healing took place. I didn't get my voice back right away, but God healed me from the eating disorder instead! It was literally night and day and as time went by, I experienced a freedom I had never experienced before. It's been a journey and process for my mind to heal, but today, I can stand firm saying that I'm totally set free and now a witness to anyone struggling. if I can make it, so can you.

With God all things are possible. I thank the broken girl I once was and chose to love her because she got me where I am today. I understand I needed to go through that struggle for years as it taught me to never give up and that if I could overcome that, then I can overcome anything... and I continue to.

Show Up Stand Up Speak Up

I'm Chloé Morgan, an International Recording Artist and DJ. From a very young age I've always known what I was born to do. I began singing, acting, dancing and playing musical instruments from 4 years old and always felt like the stage was my home. In 2014 I hit a rock bottom lowest point of my life, after a broken heart and seeing all my world around me shatter into pieces. I'd become a fragment of who I was. I lost everything and went back home to the UK with just a suitcase of clothes to my name. January 1st, 2015, I was prayed for by a group of friends, which was so powerful and transformative. I began the healing process by going to counseling, healing ministries, bible studies etc., I was at it all!

As the reality of my life set in and how my poor choices had led me to this place, I struggled with the thoughts of not wanting to live anymore. However, God kept showing me my dream that He gave me as a child, that vision was the only thing I could see. I thought "I can see it, then it can come to pass". My mother bought me a DJ controller at the start of that year, and within a couple of months, practicing day and night, I got my first opportunity in a nightclub in Essex, UK. I committed to my healing that year and exactly one year after I was prayed for, I went back to Canada and my career took off as a DJ and led me to releasing my own music with many incredible opportunities I have been blessed to be living ever since! If my story inspires you, I would love to hear from you. info@chloemorganmusic.com

KNOW THYSELF

My Story

TAYLOR ULLOM

Giving up? Before you do, hear me out. I've been there too. 2015-2021 I felt like I lost everything in my world all at once. People died, I lost my 26-year marriage, children left home, and suddenly I lost myself. Funny how seven years of devastation ends up as a one liner in the middle of a best-selling book. It only adds to my point. When you find *your why*, you find *your purpose*, and in your purpose, you find the most authentic version of *yourself*. That version of you is meant to exist, and life will find a way to bring it out of you. You are meant to change the world, just by healing and loving yourself. Do you want to know how it ends?

You will create the life you can thrive in. In that place, every dream you've ever had for your life, exists. But it takes letting go of everything you thought you were supposed to do according to societal and family norms and expectations. Here's what I learned. I had to break to become bold, becoming bold I became beautiful and happier than I've ever been. So BE BOLD! Unapologetically become the most authentic version of yourself! You can't fail. Let it break, let them leave, and lose the person you thought you were.

This is your life to live now…don't be the person that holds you back. Do it scared if you must. You might be thinking to yourself, "What if I fail?". Let me challenge you with this little mind twist, "What if you succeed"! There is only one way to find out!

Show Up Stand Up Speak Up

Air Force Veteran, National Development Director at Guitars For Vets, and developing podcaster for "What is Your Why?". What is Your Why? Where I introduce you to people who inspire me! We will learn what drives their passion, purpose, and impact in the world, in hopes that inspiration is contagious, and we all catch some!

I started this podcast to highlight individuals and stories that celebrate setbacks turning into success, grit and resilience, passion and purpose! These are the things that inspire me! The reminder that just because it's hard doesn't mean it's impossible! People and places that make me want to dream bigger. I know inspiration is contagious and I am going to sprinkle that magic everywhere! I would love to hear your story! Guitars for Vets (G4V)- The purpose is to help veterans discover the healing power of music through guitar playing and community. I did not start this nonprofit. It began in 2007 in Milwaukee, WI. I joined in 2015, starting the first chapter in Nebraska. In 2020 I was hired to help develop our program from chapter growth to national fundraising. I'm invested until this nonprofit becomes a global name; this program saved my life.

Since joining the leadership team, we have partnered with nonprofits with aligning purpose and values, graduated thousands of veterans, increased volunteerism, and built longstanding community and corporate support. However, every day I meet people that haven't heard of G4V. We can't help veterans if they don't know we exist. My mission is to make G4V a household name around the globe. My goal is to raise millions of dollars, build long standing partnerships, and grow a program that can expand beyond veterans. whatisyourwhy72@gmail.com

BE BOLD

FORBES RILEY

As someone who grew up disillusioned by Disney fairy tales that the princess was always saved by a "man", turns out finding my Prince Charming DID change my life. It elevated every aspect of my and has not only enriched my own existence but has also upleveled my capacity to make a positive impact on the lives of others.

Our love story began with a serendipitous encounter with my fitness product SpinGym, in a Las Vegas hotel room. What began as a simple exercise workout video became THE moment when our paths converged, and two hearts connected. As our relationship blossomed, so did my sense of purpose and the desire to share the love and happiness we found with the world.

Thank you Mr. Joshua Self. The last 7 years have shown me the TRUE meaning of love, caring and like your last name, being SELF(less). Maybe its okay if we live Happily Ever After.

Show Up Stand Up Speak Up

Giving Women the Permission to be Successful!

From my beginnings as a film/TV actress to celebrity host of more than 197 infomercials and live home shopping (QVC), I've generated more than $2.5 Billion and learned plenty of lessons along the way. Today I'm proud to have 28K students enrolled in business coaching and productivity skills teaching the art of the perfect pitch and the true secrets to influence people in all aspects of life.

At the heart of my coaching philosophy lies the belief that effective communication is not just about sales and persuasion; it's about connecting with people on a profound level.

Perhaps I will see you in a future training or when I speak on stages around the globe - it will be my honor to give that empowering hug in person.

Please enjoy my free gift www.FreeGiftfromForbes.com to learn to quickly maximize your networking impact.

DANCE OFTEN

My Story

TONI CARUSO

Two weeks before my 16th birthday, my world shattered, I lost my father. Guilt consumed me as I believed I played a role in his death. Dad, a tireless worker juggling roles as a drive-in theater projectionist and doing his two-week tour of duty as an Air Force Reservist. This July day, he was exhausted when he came home between jobs. I dismissed him when he sought respite on our couch. Little did I know that this seemingly trivial act would alter the course of our lives. My father left for work that evening, and he never returned.
That night driving home, he fell asleep at the wheel, colliding with a tree. Miraculously reaching a nearby home, an ambulance transported him to the hospital with assurances of recovery. Yet, fate had other plans – his chest crushed; his heart stopped.

I took the blame. It was because I didn't let him sleep on the couch that he didn't make it the last two miles of his drive home. I sat with this for days. My birthday came and went, it wasn't much of a celebration. My sister noticed I wasn't myself and point blank asked what was going on. I told her. I killed dad. She then revealed to me that it wasn't my fault, he would fall asleep at the wheel occasionally no matter when and where he slept. It was his fault and his alone.
In the aftermath, I witnessed my mother's devastation, unprepared for what lay ahead. The responsibility fell on my shoulders to navigate finances, fend off deceitful contractors preying on her vulnerability, and keep things together. Independence became my armor, no one was going to take advantage of me. I had an amazing journey, incredible occupations, my life was my own and I was in control.

I was that single boss-lady not needing anyone. However, life took an unexpected turn in my 39th year. A remarkable man entered my life, captivated by the independent spirit I had honed over the years. Patiently, he dismantled the walls surrounding my heart, emerging as my partner.

Through his support, I discovered that life unfolds in mysterious ways, with events beyond our control. The lessons learned were etched into my soul: resilience in the face of adversity, the importance of self-reliance, and the value of allowing someone to stand beside, behind, and in front of me. Though good and bad things happen there is a plan – we need to keep moving forward.

Show Up Stand Up Speak Up

My name is Toni, and I'm an Eventaholic. I'm a July baby, stuck in the middle of summer. My birthdays were the same six neighborhood kids, coming over to swim in our above-ground pool, like we did daily, this day we added ice cream and cake. My sister Melodie, on her April birthday, she scored cupcakes at school and a massive, themed party with numerous presents. Little sister envy took hold. Fast forward to middle school, and I'm done with the pool parties. I decided I had to take charge of my celebrations, so I started promoting them before school even let out. That's where the addiction started. I went from orchestrating school dances to corporate events. even getting certified in event management. If I wasn't organizing someone's events, I would have my own. There is no 12-Step program for Event Addicts. I was riding that event-planning high. This went on for years and grew into my own successful event business! Then March 2020 hit. Total withdrawal. No more parties, no more purpose. I was stuck on the couch feeling sorry for myself and thinking: What's next?

Enter Sandra Yancey from eWomenNetwork – a 45-minute Zoom call, and suddenly, she pulls me out of my depression and gets me back on track. My mission now is all about coaching and training speakers. I've been that silent observer at the back of countless events, watching speakers, some good, some bad. I determined they didn't know what they didn't know. So, I help them share their authentic message and clue them in on the whole business side of speaking. Who knew being a summer baby would lead to speaking on the stage and loving every minute of it? Life's funny that way. Embrace your circumstances, you might just become who you're meant to be. Toni@ToniCaruso.com

STEP ONSTAGE

SHEILA JACKSON

My wings brush the sun,
My dance echoes the ocean,
Me, in love with flight.

NATASHA MCCREA

I crack the whip and spread the love while being uptown and downtown all at once. I believe the richest palace in the world is in the heart of the women sitting right next to me, on any given day.

I am your silver linings cheerleader. And when my ship sails, I will have truly "lived the dash" while encouraging those who have had any level of connection with me to do the same.

Being a perpetual risk-taker has led me to this beautiful life. Love is my mantra and I truly believe the world would be a better place if we all reactivated the love intelligence we were born with. Cheers to failing forward, to loving ourselves and others a little more each day and designing the lives we truly want.

Show Up Stand Up Speak Up

They say to pick one thing and do it well. But we've never been good at bending to the status quo. We'd rather explore our passions and give the world something great to experience. Whiskey rested in French oak and syrah barrels - with notes of caramel, spice, smoke, and California sunsets. Yes!

And we're so much more than what's in the glass. Jackson McCrea is a revolution. We're bringing women into the conversation on whiskey. Seeing and being seen is our greatest currency. So, let's start spending it - freely and unapologetically.
https://www.jacksonmccreawhiskey.com/

BREAK RULES

My Story

ELISA CHOY

Economist and Seer of the Future. Why? My favourite question as a child was Why?... followed by... But Why? Why do people say mean things? Why do people fight in wars? Why am I here? I was plagued with a fireworks brain, popping Why questions nonstop. This insatiable curiosity wrapped in a tenacious analytical mind was annoying for some, like my mother. But I've since carved out a career and reputation for answering these questions, using data.

I am in my happy place when I'm analysing data to understand people and how I fit into the world. In the early 80's, my family migrated from big city Hong Kong to small town Adelaide, South Australia. My brother and I were the only Asian kids in the whole school. Being racially different didn't bother me at all. It must have been my thick (but softly smooth) Oriental skin. What *did* bother me however, was that I couldn't understand why I was different in other ways and *why* I didn't fit in. I didn't even *want* to 'fit in'. Fitting in meant following rules. To me, some rules were just plain stupid. Remember COVID? Not knowing why, I was different continued to afflict me into adulthood and it was deeply frustrating - like being a loaded gun with nowhere to shoot. I was highly talented, overachieving, and ambitious - none of which could help me in answering a lot of my 'why' questions. I didn't feel that I entirely 'fit in' to the corporate world and spent most of my 20's and 30's trying out different versions of me - I was a rebel without a cause, a smart ass with a smart tongue, a good girl yet a clown, a smiling assassin, and an arrogant high achieving b*tch (who proudly labelled herself an 'Intellectual Snob'). I bounced around like popcorn between jobs and careers. I had lived many different lives in search to find myself and yet always ended up being suspended in the middle, landing on nothing.

Or so it seemed for so long. Apparently Saturn was in permanent residence on my astrological chart. Who would have known that I was meant to be swimming upstream to learn a few lessons. So, when I hit 38, a series of life changing events miraculously exploded in my face, turning my world upside down and decimating everything I knew. I have since affectionately called this time, "Hiroshima". Those 'why' questions were burning more than ever, and I was forced onto an inner quest of discovery for the truth amongst the sludge of noise called ego. It took many years and wasn't easy. Now in my 40s, I am relieved to say that some of those questions have finally been answered. I know who I am and how I 'fit in' to the world. I know 'why' I exist. I am a warrior for the truth.

I use my deep analytical mind to piece together the mosaic of data to form a picture of the world. I can explain why people behave the way they do through data. I share my insights with the world through speaking, writing and research. I happily accept that *this* is my role, and how I fit. Best of all, it's on my terms. The Why questions don't stop and have taken me to many places, and now I know why.

Show Up Stand Up Speak Up

Wrapped in feathers, leather, and bright pink lipstick. I fight for a better world for all. I don't use weapons: I use words, backed by data and the gift of insight. As an economist and data strategist, I turn maths into English to turn data into decisions. I analyse people, culture, and society to predict how people will behave in the future — and I'm unabashedly accurate.

I have predicted industry trends, social movements, reality TV winners, and major elections in the US and Australia. But I can't predict horse races, the Super Bowl or the price of oil – these don't rely on market sentiment. But anything that requires understanding the behaviour of people, is fair game. And I love it when I get the game right. I founded Australia's first AI-powered strategic market research company – Maven Data – to harness the power of big data and technology to provide predictive insights for leaders across industry, government, and academia. We use the largest dataset on earth (the open internet) and artificial intelligence to analyse petabytes of data in minutes. Our insights are uncannily accurate because we measure emotions in the content that people engage with online, in the privacy of their digital devices (but not in a creepy way, I promise). Why is Maven Data better than legacy market research methods like surveys, polls and focus groups? Because people don't always speak the truth and are biased.

We're all human after all, and that's okay. But decision making for strategy, marketing and policy cannot rely on the opinions from a mere handful of survey participants. This will not reveal the whole picture. Without a macro view, you run into blind spots. Take election polling…not accurate. We now have the power of abundant data and state-of-the-art technology. Why measure the sky with a ruler? Maven Data is taking market research into the 21st Century with gusto – it's exciting times! We share what we see with full transparency. Sometimes these insights (truths) are hard to hear, but data doesn't lie. The world is complex, and change is changing. Maven Data helps people understand their world to make better decisions. And with better decisions comes a better world for everyone. For more information: www.elisachoy.com

STAY CURIOUS

BLAIR KAPLAN VENABLES

As a child, I was happiest amongst the trees and surrounded by water. Little did I know that the Ontario-based summer camp that I would spend time with as a child would set me up for a life full of outdoor adventures and exploring. Every summer, from ages eight to 17, I would escape to a magical island where I got to leave all of my family drama and trauma behind. I was always my best self at summer camp. Little did I know that when I became a full-blown grown-up, I would reignite this feeling living in the mountains of British Columbia.

I go into the forest to quiet my mind and find myself. I get lost in the bark patterns and the leaves movement. My ideas dance with the wind as it brushes against my skin. My imagination is set on fire while inhaling and exhaling with the nature surrounding me.

Hiking, camping, canoeing, paddleboarding or sitting on the beach is when the fully authentic me shows up in this world. Here is where I am at peace. In nature, I'm inspired. In stillness, I create. Here is where I strengthen my resilience muscle.

Who would have thought that I would be a sober, 38-year-old, childless, parentless birdwatcher? This was not on my vision board, but I'm rolling with the punches from life.

I am resilient (especially when frolicking in nature).

Show Up Stand Up Speak Up

I'm a grief and resilience expert. I was born in the mid-1980s in Winnipeg, Manitoba, Canada, into a family marked by my father's addiction and the eventual dissolution of my parents' marriage. Despite these challenges, I harboured a deep connection with my father, though his addiction led to his absence from our family when I was just seven, leaving me feeling abandoned and unloved.

My entrepreneurial spirit was ignited early, inspired by a family legacy of entrepreneurship. At 12, I became an Avon lady, selling makeup door-to-door to afford my own. While attending a professional development weekend in my early 20s, a moment happened that profoundly changed my life by enabling me to forgive my father and accept him, flaws and all. This reconciliation allowed us to rebuild our relationship. At the end of 2018, we learned that my father was terminally ill. I began to share our story of his addiction, my forgiveness, and our resilience. Our story was inspiring people to make positive changes in their lives. We decided to honour my dad's legacy and to keep inspiring people when he was no longer on this planet, that we would write a book. We would gather stories of resilience from around the world and start the book with his story and end it with min.

In March 2019, our social enterprise, The Global Resilience Project, was born. This initiative became a platform for sharing stories of resilience through our published books, the Radical Resilience podcast, our merchandise line, events we host or attend and strategic partnerships. By sharing these narratives, I've aimed to inspire others to find their own paths through hardship, emphasizing the importance of resilience and strengthening your resilience muscle. The Global Resilience Project plans to empower over 88 million people to strengthen their resilience muscles by August 2025 (when I turn 40 years old).

My goal is to turn my pain into purpose, help the world cultivate resilience, and find gratitude in every moment. The stories we share through The Global Resilience Project are testaments to the strength found in vulnerability and the unyielding power of the human spirit to overcome. Connect with me blair@blairkaplan.ca

YOU'RE RESILIENT

FANNY MENDELSSOHN

Pianist

HILDA OAKELEY

Philosopher

EMILY WARREN ROEBLING

Engineer

MARY WHITON CALKINS

Psychologist

My Story

TAMMY REA

A little background....my parents were kids when they started having them. They had little education, life skills, parental skills or means to provide for their family. We were poor, dirt poor, I was their third child arriving the summer of '69. We lived in a broken-down school bus! Yes, humble beginnings and my starting point in life. I have lived a very interesting, un-common life, one that taught me the value of people, that my worth had little to do with things, titles, or fancy shoes. I am very proud of my humble beginnings and the experience of poverty and how society implies your expected outcome. NOT SO! I measure my success by the distance I have travelled from the circumstances into which I was born. I am proud to say I have delivered the life I promised myself when I was five years old.

Riding a motorcycle is one of my favorite pastimes, it's when I feel most ALIVE, and it nurtures my soul. I love my life and never pass up an opportunity to indulge in whatever blows my hair back. The open road, the freedom...it simply captures my essence!
I love having fun, seeking adventure, walking the line, being spontaneous, saying yes to the absurd, indulging, facing fear, dancing whenever ... where-ever, chasing the unknown, stretching myself, experiencing hair-raising exhilaration moments, finding mischief, laughing until it hurts and sharing these experiences with whomever cares to join me. I love deep meaningful conversation with total strangers, who doesn't?! I can also spend days in my PJ's, drinking coffee and reading. I love to learn. My life philosophy is "ongoing incremental improvement" constant evolution! I don't have a big life agenda, I'm here to help others, to share lived experiences and to be the good I desire in this world.

I love being a woman, I know my power, it's up to me to unleash it and I do so often. I have an incredible eco-system of amazing woman who bring so much meaning to my life, I'm forever grateful! I am a champion for all, leave no woman behind!

Show Up Stand Up Speak Up

My first experience with money, or the lack of, was in kindergarten. I wasn't a huge fan of school, too many rules and the kids were not very nice to me. I don't blame them, I was considered a select mute, refused to speak, frequently wet my pants, had rotten teeth, and would only use a purple crayon to color my artwork ... allegedly a big deal to everyone but me! Different doesn't make friends easily.

This day was different, they were serving hotdogs for lunch, and I was excited! All the kids lined up with their little white envelope in hand patiently waiting their turn to collect a delicious HOTDOG! I wasn't sure what the envelopes had to do with lunch, but in line with the other kids, I started to rehearse those words everyone reminded me to say, "THANK YOU"! Speaking was torture for me, but I could do it for a hotdog. Finally, I was at the front of the line. The teacher smiled and asked me if I had my envelope, I shook my head no. She then asked if my mom had sent MONEY with me to buy a hotdog. I was ready to cry, and I shook my head again, no. That's when the teacher used her manners and said, "I'm sorry Tammy, you won't be able to participate today" and ushered me out of the line. What ignited my ambition that day was a determination to figure out this money business so that I never missed out on a hotdog day again! I learned not to ask my parents for money, it made my mom cry when she didn't have it to give. I was determined to take care of my own needs and I have!

I recently celebrated my 34th year in banking, I have dedicated my life to helping others understand money and create financial plans that offer hope. Small incremental improvements can have generational impact. Each barrier removed sheds light on a path forward and everyone deserves the opportunity to leave their current circumstance in pursuit of their dreams. I'm living proof! tammy.rea@td.com

ACT NOW

My Story

KATHLEEN CARLSON

Be The Village

After chatting with a good friend about life, kids, and the whole "it takes a village" theory. I got to thinking – how many of us actually have a village these days? You know, that tight-knit community where everyone's got your back? It whisked me back to Eft's Lane, the one-mile country road where I grew up. That trip down memory lane was so much fun. Things came to mind that I had long forgotten and my appreciation for those experiences swelled. As a kid I had little idea how good I had it and just how generous our neighbors were. It was more than a street; it was my extended family. With six kids and hardworking parents, we were on our own a lot. Looking back, we were never really alone. It seems the neighbors had an unspoken agreement to watch out for us.

We didn't have much, but I felt like the luckiest kid. My biggest dream was to have a pony, and guess what? Max had Buttercup, a pony I could ride anytime if I brushed him. So, I kinda had my pony. No pool at our place, the Mackey's and Granetier's had one. Countless times, we'd ring their doorbell in swimsuits, and they'd say yes. Swimming pool? Check! Summer meant hours at the apple orchard and apples for horses on a nearby farm. Those trees were my buddies. The memories kept coming! The Curd family's Honda '78 – a community treasure we all shared. Sandy, next door, had the coolest Barbie dolls. I practically lived there, playing like they were mine.

Oh, and I laughed out loud when I remembered the Halloween Mrs. Valero caught us soaping her windows. She made us clean them up and then took us inside to get a special treat. Most weekends, you could always find an extra kid or three at our house. My mom was their favorite and the fridge was always fair game.

Today, my husband Jack and I have the party house. The house where everyone is welcome to come, play, stay, and be loved. Nothing makes me happier than when our house is full of family, friends, and laughter. So, my friends, let's keep that village spirit alive. Open homes, warm hearts, creating our villages wherever life plants us. Because with love and laughter, we're living our best lives.
Kathleen Carlson

Show Up Stand Up Speak Up

Growing up in an industrial town dominated by imposing steel mills, women's career options were limited to mall jobs and food service. I chose a clothing store to start my journey. On the day I began college for computer programming, I was offered an Assistant Manager position and later promoted to Store Manager. They expected me to quit college; I didn't. As fun as it was to work with clothes, I knew I deserved more than slightly above minimum wage. My dad's advice was to find a good company, work hard, and they'd take care of you for life. At 21, armed with $800 and my faithful dog Maggie May, I traveled 2200 miles to find that "good company."

Not long after landing a job, I entered their management program. It was a Fortune 50 giant where I spent 33 years, climbing ranks, managing millions in sales, and navigating complex issues. My sweet spot became mentoring and developing my teams. The corporate culture was tough, marked by hard work, long hours, and intimidation. Over time, I learned the vast difference between managing and leading. Changes came, but none as dramatic as the company's shift towards prioritizing shareholder value. People took a backseat to profits, bringing increasing pressure and struggles for me and my colleagues.I knew I had to change. Leaving behind my position, salary, and everything it entailed, Straight Up Executive Consulting was born.

Today, I guide female leaders facing similar challenges, helping them thrive both personally and professionally. Whether building their own companies or working for others, I intuitively guide them to live by their values, guilt-free as they empower others to do the same! Let's chat—you deserve to live Your Vision, Your Life, Your Way. https://www.straightupsuccess.com/

189

EMULATE PEACE

My Story

BETH ELSFELDER

What do you do when the greatest desire of your heart isn't possible?

The desire to be a mom was ignited in my heart when I was just 10 years old. My parents brought my baby sister home from the hospital and I remember being in awe of this tiny human. I instantly felt a bond with her unlike anything I had experienced before.

When I got married, I felt such excitement at the possibility of having a family of my own. Unfortunately, after months of trying, tests, and infertility treatment, a diagnosis of "unexplained infertility" was given to us. In the meantime, many family members and friends began having children of their own and although I was thrilled for them, the pain inside of me continued to grow. When my 9-year marriage ended, my thoughts and emotions took me into a dark night of the soul that I thought would never end as I explored all the reasons why motherhood escaped me. What was wrong with me? What finally lifted me out of the darkness was the daily unconditional love of my two dogs.

A spark of hope was reignited when I married for the second time, but was snuffed out when, after a year of trying to get pregnant with holistic and medical support, I again heard the words "unexplained infertility." I tried for two agonizing years to convince my husband to bring a child into our lives by adopting or fostering one in need, to no avail. I was back in the pit of despair, questioning everything about my life and why I was here on Earth. Around this time, I attended a spiritual retreat and was amazed at the unconditional love and support of the team, the speakers, and the community who beautifully shared their love and wisdom with all the participants. The tidal wave of affirmation that washed over me was life-changing, and I knew I would find a way to move forward in my life to freely give the same unconditional love to others that I had just received.

Eventually, I was invited to speak about "changing the world" and was divinely guided to share my infertility journey even though the wound was still fresh. When I finished my presentation, I was given a Dr. Suess t-shirt with the words "Mother of All Things" printed on it. This gesture touched me deeply, immediately followed by an "aha" moment: my yearning to love, nurture, and care for my own child could be transformed and expanded to include ALL living things… humans of all ages, animals, nature, and Mother Earth herself. I had been doing this all along! The clarity of vision I received in that moment opened my heart more fully and gave me a true purpose I could fully embrace. No matter what challenges I face, my life will be incredibly beautiful as long as I continue to live and serve from a place of love, forgiveness, and understanding.

Show Up Stand Up Speak Up

Have you ever been kissed by a wolf?

From an early age, I felt a special connection with animals. In my late twenties, I became interested in holistic health for myself; as I welcomed animals into my home, I wanted to make their lives as natural and healthy as possible, too. My research led me to an incredible Holistic Veterinarian and my animals thrived under her care. I was so excited when the Vet asked me to work with her that I blurted out "Yes!" without even knowing any details. The years I worked with her were priceless as I regularly witnessed incredible health transformations of the animals and I was thrilled when she encouraged me to provide healing sessions for the animals as well. I found my calling! In 2013, I moved to Colorado and began volunteering at The Colorado Wolf and Wildlife Center while I considered how to share the gift of energy healing in my new community. The center was a magical place for me to share my love of wolves and my favorite daily chore was pen cleaning because I could interact with the animals while I worked.

On one such occasion, I was approached by a beautiful female wolf and as I was scratching her neck, she looked directly into my eyes and shifted her body so that my hand was on her heart chakra. The energy started to flow, and she visibly relaxed for a few minutes, gave me a kiss, and walked away. It was a beautiful moment of heart-to-heart connection that changed my life and shortly thereafter, Spirit Wolf Energetics, LLC was born.

Through my use of Reiki and Healing Touch, the healthful vitality of pets and the people who love them grows. It fills my spirit to witness positive shifts in the physical, mental, emotional, and spiritual health of the person or animal I'm working with – this includes different species of animals, including the wild ones. I offer both in-person and distance sessions and would be happy to talk with you about how I can assist you and your pets in reducing stress and achieving optimal health with energy healing. You can connect with me at spiritwolfenergetics@gmail.com to learn more.

191

HONOR YOURSELF

IRENE STRONCZAK-HOGAN

My Message To Women is...

Embrace your journey.
Lead with resilience and thrive at every age.

Show Up Stand Up Speak Up

EMBRACE CHANGE

My Story

NANCY BOYD

Life gave me edges to sharpen myself against, but it never dulled the sweetness of the beauty I see. Being super smart cost me, especially when I was a child; I was often either punished or shunned because of it.

My earliest memories weren't happy ones; they were filled with poverty, abuse, and struggle. Our family moved 27 times before I was 11 years old; in my 8th year I was pronounced dead three times; later I battled addiction to alcohol and by Divine grace was granted sobriety – which is precious to me. I work hard, one day at a time, to give something back to the world. I've had to face chronic illness, betrayals by business partners and lovers, and being falsely accused of things I did not do. Healing took time and skilled helpers, each of whom lifted me and gave me strength and dignity. I released shame and found self-respect.

When I was grown, an astrologer told me that I came encoded with a message: Evolve Or Die. People sense that – and get scared. It took me a long while to understand that making people comfortable around me isn't my job; it's theirs. I now deliver that message with compassion and clarity; it's part of my purpose for being here.
I'm still full of questions but my answer always comes back to love. Maybe that's because I know what it is to be hated and feared for who I am, for what I believe, and for who I love.

I'm a private person, and because there are still places in the world where people like me have to stay in a narrow closet, I don't talk much about my personal life. But I know it's important for people to understand that who you love is only a piece of your life; it's not the whole picture. And I'm very much a whole-picture kind of gal.

My wisdom came at great cost – and with many blessings. Today I know that while I was once victimized by people I should have been able to trust, I am now a healed survivor/thriver. I walk in dignity, live in presence, and love with joy and amazement. I see beauty everywhere, celebrate it with wild abandon, and dedicate my life to creating the kind of world from which no one needs to recover.

Show Up Stand Up Speak Up

Change Makers are very special people. Many of them bear the scars of abuse, poverty, trauma, illness, PTSD, or some combination of all of those. What makes them so special is not the story of their past but the story of the future they are helping to shape – one where everyone is seen, safe, and valued for who they are.

These are the people I serve through my company Bright Wings, Inc. and the programs we develop through The Soul Path Academy. I'm a Healer, Coach, and award-winning writer. In 2009 I was honored to be named International Coach of the Year. I've been featured in O Magazine and appear selectively at intentional living summits and events.

From working with hundreds of change-makers and survivors, I have come to understand these things:

– People are tired of living at a shallow/shadow level; they are ready to go deeper, and dare the inner journey it takes to get real.

– The world is going through upheavals of transformation the likes of which we have never seen before.

– Ethical leadership is in high demand.

– Healed and healing survivors/thrivers are the emerging leaders our chaotic world needs right now, to carry us through the turmoil of transformation that we expect to see for the next few decades and beyond.

Consciousness workers, change-makers, and healed and survived thrivers of all kinds are my tribe. I'm always thinking of ways to build community and share tools that lead us to better places. That's what I'm up to. How about you? I'd love to hear your story too! If there's a way I can be of service to you on YOUR journey, count me in. You can reach me (and snag one of my books for free here: https://brightwings.com/about

GIVE LOVE

My Story

MICHELLE RIKER

I discovered my destiny when I picked up a paint brush for the first time. I found meditation, a desire like no other. I found my destiny.

My grandfather was a talented artist, my mother and father could both draw. I designed my first clothes and shoes at age 12, trying to keep up with trends we could not afford. But it never dawned on me that I was a true artist. Funny how, looking back, the signs were always there.

It's what money can't buy that's more important to me and that's called integrity. To be authentic, to be real, to be free and of course to have the love of my small family.

Yoga, sound baths, other spiritual practices, music, and time on the beach help me to breathe freely.

I am a survivor, a warrior, and a believer.

I believe there are no mistakes. The universe will conspire where energy flows and where it flows it grows.

Show Up Stand Up Speak Up

In pursuit of the American Dream, I started my first company while I was pregnant with my son at age 22. The company was called Chrome Angels, making candles with cast iron icons such as skulls, hearts, crosses, and stars. They were covered in Swarovski crystal, placed onto leather straps, and wrapped around fragrant candles. I would drive with my son in our '67 Buick GS400 to boutiques across California. After our first Las Vegas magic show project, my candles caught the attention of celebrities and trendy boutiques around the country. Business took off! And, for a while, we were flying high.

With the 2005 economic crisis, high-end candles became nearly extinct. That, coupled with a split in my marriage, was a huge challenge. But with another God-inspired idea I started making hats and boots in what had been my candle factory and my garage. I created WBFV, "Walk By Faith Vintage". The boots were made at a factory in Los Angeles, while I did all the unique and distressed finishes, which gave the brand its DNA. Though the challenges were strenuous, my hard work paid off. Free People and other brands picked up the line at a show in New York City. But again, the magic happened in Vegas at the very first FM Platform Shoe Show. That is where I met shoe guru Steve Madden.

He flew out to meet me in LA and I was soon off to Mexico to create and develop what would become the Freebird shoe brand with the most ambitious, determined, and creative family-owned factory in Mexico. Traveling back and forth between LA and Guanajuato, Mexico, almost every other week for the past 15 years has not been easy. It was hard taking that time away from my son, even though he reminds me that I inspired and encouraged him to be an entrepreneur. Sketching, correcting, and finishing thousands of samples has taken a toll on me physically. I have realized that I am just getting started. 50 is the new 30. michelleriker@freebirdstores.com

BE FREE

My Story

ANDI SWEENEY BLANCO

I find a quickening in my pulse whenever a pattern is broken in any day's routine. It can be in the environment, such as a thunderstorm rolling in and promising a more adventurous day than expected, or in the form of a person coming into my path for a brief or long moment of connection.

A pursuit for constant spontaneity has followed me in my everyday life and work. Rather than finding comfort in routine, I find it more comfortable to flow with what every shifting moment may bring, as I learn and trust in my own capacity to figure out how to make a trajectory out of what comes next. Stories are born from the unexpected, and so the chase for the unknown persists. This comfort may have stemmed from a theatre background, where improvisation brought unexpected moments of laughter and connection for audience and performers alike.

There's a glimmer that catches the eye when someone is fully here, now, present in space and in themselves. I call it "close to the surface," because it is as if their essence is living on the surface of their skin, and their eyes shine with a light that is overflowing from within but also welcoming in what is all around. That freedom to "be" is the greatest kind of power, in my view, and I've hungered for it since I was young. I would observe cliques at school and group dynamics, where certain energies affected the whole flow and thinking of a whole group of people. I preferred one on one connection, because I found real moments there where I got to see into another person and get to meaningfully take part in their story.

I believe we are here for connection, and thus service is at the center of everything. If we can truly see another and have them feel loved and seen, from us existing, we have accomplished a mini miracle in the story of creation and carried it forward to unfold into more profound moments.

Show Up Stand Up Speak Up

I'm an actress, documentarian, producer, and theatre director based in Los Angeles, CA. I currently host a documentary series called "The Fixers" which does build projects for communities around the world. I am a builder and do some carpentry on the show, but mainly I connect with the community of each country we visit to help tell their stories and champion their dreams. I exist to empower and equip people to achieve the freedom to be fully themselves and create systems of thought and habits in their lives that help their gifts come alive. I have always loved people. I find the deepest moments of growth when I am connecting with another person and getting to the root of what is important to them in their journey.

This started for me as I fell in love with theatre at a young age and began developing characters and stories in collaboration with other artists. I worked professionally as a stage, film, and TV actress from the age of 6 until now, loving how imaginary worlds merged regularly with the themes in my every-day reality. Born and raised in Monterrey Nuevo Leon Mexico, I've had the privilege of exposure to different cultures and languages as I moved around a lot, which set a passion for travel and creating bridges of understanding between cultures and ways of living. I continue to produce and develop stories in hopes that people will feel improved and inspired to live their life with more intentionality, awareness of others, and child-like wonderment.
Instagram: @Andi.global

EMBODY HOPE

LINDA FISK

Looking back now, I can see that the challenges I have faced throughout my career have been the launchpad for my biggest successes, teaching me the power of perseverance, tenacity, and steadfastness, combined with forgiveness, kindness, and grace. Grit was evident in my resolve and my stamina to reach seemingly impossible goals, based on achieving the life I envisioned for myself. And, grace was needed along the journey to accept my limitations, my slow progress, and my setbacks.

Grit determines that life challenges will neither define nor defeat us. It is the toughness, courage, bravery, resiliency, and the spirit that drives us forward. It is the backbone, inspiration, steel nerve, and the vision that you cling to. Your grit is where your perseverance meets your passion. They collide to create your purpose, your mission, and your meaning.

Because of my passion to achieve a long-term objective, to create a life that I envisioned for myself, I was absolute in my perseverance of effort - even when that effort led to painful, embarrassing, or humbling experiences. I had the kind of mental toughness that is often described as "grit." One of my first lessons in grit was in grade school. I was considered to be clinically shy, unable to hold eye contact with any strangers, or utter a word. Over time, I developed a penchant for repeating my words with a pronounced stutter. Social settings and high-stress environments made it nearly impossible to speak, as I became more and more self-conscious of my pronounced stutter. Stuttering became a lifelong struggle that required a lot of grit. But, it also required grace.

True grace recognizes that lessons are often learned through experiencing the result of a failure, a bad decision or a mistake - and learning from it. Grace does not remove consequences or attempt to protect you from your bad decisions, but rather allows for the recognition of the mistake, the forgiveness of the failure and the resilience to incorporate the learning into our forward progress. Grace is embodied; it is an attitude, a characteristic and a belief - and as such, it has a contagious effect on others, including your team and your company.

Grace is freely given favor and mercy, a sense of generosity and kindness, moral strength, a favor even when it is not deserved. It is understanding and forgiveness borne out of self-discovery and self-acceptance. It is an undeserved, unmerited, unearned embrace of acceptance. It always turns heads, opens minds, softens hearts, and leaves people in awe.

Show Up Stand Up Speak Up

In my career, I have learned that true success is consistently doing the work that ignites your soul. Finding your purpose by positively impacting others. For me, I realized that creating and supporting personal and professional breakthroughs for women in leadership was my definition of success. I believe my purpose is to accelerate the success of women in leadership around the world, by connecting them to the resources, networks, tools, experiences, diagnostics, and relationships that advance their unique purpose. In fact, creating a confidential and supportive community designed to accelerate success of each member is the highest value I can offer. I believe it is more important than ever to be intentional about seeking out, investing in and forming the kind of genuine and strategic relationships we need, as women in leadership, to thrive both personally and professionally. No one grows as a leader without support from others.

High performing executives tend to value the perspectives of other leaders, as well as the wisdom that comes from lived experiences. But, most leaders don't have a "safe" environment where they can share openly. All women deserve to have a safe leadership community where they can meet inspirational leaders, create lifelong friendships, and be surrounded by people that are invested in their success. Because executive women often face cultural and political hurdles that men typically do not, they benefit from an inner circle that can share private, confidential information to land the best position and secure the most advantageous opportunities. They need a safe space to be able to be open, transparent, and vulnerable – and receive the kind of support, encouragement, and unbiased advice that they need to grow.

Being in a community of other leaders allows you to have an outlet to continuously learn and improve in a confidential setting. The best advice I can give? Build a large network, but have a close inner circle of women that support, champion, advise, and encourage you. Contact Linda Fisk linda@leadhershipglobal.com

201

PRAY OFTEN

My Story

MELANIE MCSALLY

Personal Journey to Freedom

In the tapestry of life, each thread represents a choice, a moment, a leap. For me, the quest for freedom was a calling that whispered to me over the years. It all began with imagination at age 4. Imagination allowed me to be anyone and do anything—a spark that unknowingly ignited a lifelong quest for freedom.

My path to entrepreneurship began much later at 43, but the seeds were planted in those childhood days of exploration. Adventures on construction sites and the worlds I created in my mind to escape bullying were not mere escapades; they were the foundation of a deep-seated desire to live a life unbounded by limitation. The question was never about starting a business but about living unshackled.

For over a decade, I pondered what drives me, letting the question simmer like a stew, enriching it with experiences, stirring it with connections, and seasoning it with lessons. This contemplation led me on a journey of incredible twists and turns. I traveled the globe as a student of life. I built businesses that thrived on the principles of passion. I met people who reflected back to me the possibilities of life.

Writing a book on freedom was a reflection of my journey thus far, yet it was merely a chapter in an ongoing saga. My understanding of freedom has since evolved into encompassing every facet of existence. True liberation came when I understood that freedom was a state of being that I could choose in each moment. The question of suffering or liberation became a guiding light. In every relationship, challenge, and seemingly mundane decision, I found the opportunity to choose freedom. I transformed the way I viewed success as a measurement of joy. I was only bound by the limits I placed upon myself.

As I share my story, I do so not as one who has reached the pinnacle of understanding but as a fellow traveler on the journey of life. To those who feel trapped, whether by circumstance, fear, or self-doubt, I offer this simple yet transformative truth: freedom is not a destination but a way of being. It's found in the realization that every moment presents an opportunity to choose differently. And so, the only question that remains is not how we find freedom but how we embrace it. In this moment, in this conversation, in this very breath, liberation awaits. Will you choose it?

Show Up Stand Up Speak Up

From a young age, I had a knack for solving puzzles, a trait that hinted at my future. I assembled a wheelbarrow before I could even read, leaving my parents in awe. As life's complexities mounted, my imagination became my sanctuary, a place where I could bend reality. This urge to create and explore steered me away from traditional paths and towards a future free from conventional constraints. Faced with limiting choices, I consistently sought new avenues, crafting an unconventional journey that eventually led me to entrepreneurship. This transition was more than a career shift; it was a leap toward freedom, affirming the power of forging my own path.

Embracing this journey was fraught with challenges and moments of self-doubt, yet it was also immensely rewarding. Encountering skepticism from others became routine, but a fellow entrepreneur's words, "Melanie, you're the exception to every rule," became my mantra. This affirmation fueled my resolve and reminded me that the norms need not apply to me. "Do I really have to?" became a question I'd ask whenever confronted with supposed absolutes. I earned the nickname "the fixer," not just for streamlining tasks but for guiding others to strategies that resonate with their core essence and authentic selves. My business evolution became about embodying a beacon of possibility, demonstrating that success is attainable on your terms. This realization freed my business to adapt and thrive, allowing me to leverage my full range of talents. Using intuition, innovation, and technical prowess, I illuminate the path to freedom, liberating clients from constraints and proving that freedom in business is not just a dream but a tangible reality. I'm Melanie McSally, and this has been a little bit of how I found liberation in business. What's your "Be Liberated" journey? I'd love to read about it: mmcsally@wyzetribe.com.

BE LIBERATED

RANDI JO PIEPER

In the tranquil embrace of dawn, as I sit here with my trusty pen in hand, pondering the simple joys that make life a whimsical journey, I find myself drawn to the front window and the canvas of the morning sky. A symphony of colors unfolds before my eyes, as if nature decided to play with a palette of reddish oranges and baby blues, creating a masterpiece to start the day.

Meanwhile, in the background, the coffee maker hums its morning melody, promising a brew that could rival the elixir of life itself. Ah, the simple pleasure of sharing a cup with my husband or any unsuspecting houseguest who may grace our doorstep.

As I scribble away in my journal, mapping out the adventures that we have had or lie ahead, my mind wanders to the mountains, where cascading waterfalls and snow-capped peaks await. Oh, the allure of nature's symphony, where the melody of chirping birds and rustling leaves serenades the soul.

But why stop there? The countryside attracts with its own blend of sights and sounds, promising a sensory feast that tantalizes the senses. And who can resist the call of the ocean, where the salty breeze caresses the skin, and the lullaby of waves brings solace to the weary heart?

These moments are the treasures I hold near, the gifts that make life worth living. For amidst the chaos of everyday existence, it is these fleeting moments of serenity and joy that remind us of life's true purpose.

So, I urge you, to seize the day with gusto, to savor the simple pleasures that surround you, whether it be a backyard barbecue with neighbors or a spontaneous adventure into the great unknown. For life is too short to be lived in the confines of routine and monotony. And as I put pen to paper, weaving the tapestry of my dreams, I am reminded of the magic that lies within each of us. For it is through the simple act of writing, of capturing our thoughts and desires on paper, that we breathe life into our dreams and set them free and soar into being.

May your days be filled with laughter and love, with adventure and serenity, and may you always find joy in the simple pleasures that make life truly magical.

Show Up Stand Up Speak Up

Nine years ago, I experienced a loss that shook the very foundation of my being – I lost my mother. She was my confidante, my mentor, and my coach. Her understanding of the stress I faced as a probation officer, witnessing firsthand the relentless cycle of trauma and poor choices, was unparalleled. With over 40 years of experience as a nurse, she had seen it all and understood the complexities of human behavior.

After her passing, I found myself struggling with grief and searching for a way to navigate these emotions that engulfed me. It was during this period of darkness that I made a pivotal decision – I hired a life coach, someone who not only helped me process my mother's death but also guided me towards a path of self-discovery and empowerment.
Through probing questions and unwavering support, my coach encouraged me to tap into the wisdom and strength that my mother had instilled in me. I realized that I possessed the capacity to be a source of guidance and inspiration for others, just as my mother had been for me. Embracing this newfound calling, I embarked on a journey of transformation, transitioning from a state of burnout to a beacon of hope and resilience. Drawing from my own experiences of loss and trauma, coupled with my background in the criminal justice field, I began coaching others who were navigating similar challenges.

My approach to coaching is rooted in empathy, understanding, and a deep appreciation for the complexities of the human experience. I recognize that behind every individual lies a unique story, often shaped by hidden struggles and unspoken pain.
If you find yourself yearning to reignite joy and passion amidst life's trials, I invite you to connect with me. https://sociatap.com/randijo/

IGNITE WITHIN

My Story

DR. JAISRI M. LAMBERT

Ancient Ayurveda, the world's oldest holistic medical science, has advocated self-care for millennia, as part of a complete system of natural living from birth onward. It's not new to consider that the first hours of the day belong to spiritual practices, preparing the body and mind for each diurnal cycle, and that the evening hours are for winding down in preparation for sound, dreamless sleep, to rejuvenate cells, tissues, and functions, such as endocrine (hormonal) health.

Ayurveda has discussed extensively about right use of time, called 'DinaCharya' or the importance of being fully in the present moment, whether in service of family or others, or in responsibility for our own physical and psycho-emotional well-being.

Of course, food choices play a great role in giving emphasis to freshly prepared, local, whole, natural, seasonal, simple foods, not only for the immediate energy needed for daily activities, but also for the post-digestive effects of assimilation, elimination, and influence on the mind, moods, and inner space.

Women are the real heads of household and are therefore the keepers of healthy habits and routines influencing the family and the generations. Knowledge of Ayurveda is more sought out by women, perhaps because of our natural inclination to the need (not desire) for harmonious living. As Ayurveda has not appeared in our western cultural backdrop, we are learning as adults, mostly in response to unresolved stresses and symptoms.
Women are the ones suffering from modern pressures to be and do everything perfectly and are so relieved to find Ayurveda support for restoring the needed values of simplicity and contentment, to live a happy life and experience a peaceful passing in due course. The end of life is meant to come by itself when the breaths are complete, and not from disease.

Imagine yourself feeling empowered to opt away from chemical birth control, constricting your breasts into a bra or corset, and working when you're so tired, for example on the first flow days. Imagine you live in a natural support system of healthy solutions to the inevitable down cycles of life, with true support for your needs, without suppression. Imagine a world where you put your well-being first, especially in the critical arenas of digestion, rest, and elimination. All creativity and goodness can flow from there.

Show Up Stand Up Speak Up

Jaisri was born in Scotland in 1947, became an immigrant child at age 3, coming to Vancouver, Canada with her parents and 3 sisters. Her thirst for understanding life and its mysteries began early, and slowly led to discoveries including the French language and the transformational potential of meditation. Migraine headaches began at age 17 and continued to her mid-thirties when Ayurveda came to bless her life with knowledge of the laws of healing. Meanwhile, investigations into naturopathy, all available forms of bodywork healing, and vegetarianism unfolded.

A great turning point came in 1986, when Dr. Robert Svoboda appeared in her life and said, "I think you should meet my teacher, Dr. Lad". The name resonated like a soft gong, reverberating something compelling and deeply true. From 1988 until the present, Dr. Vasant Lad became Jaisri's primary mentor and slowly influenced all major life decisions towards service. Jaisri felt she could not get enough exposure to learning Ayurveda in depth and took every opportunity to study and share its wisdom and goodness.

In 2017, she was awarded the Ayurveda Doctor designation from the US-based National Ayurveda Medical Association, which she had helped found many years prior. Nowadays, she is semi-retired in Surrey, BC, and enjoys gardening, traveling, teaching, friendships, mentoring and writing. The Canada Ayurveda Research & Education Foundation became a federally registered non-profit organization in 2017, to help champion integration of holistic care into the Canadian public health care system.
Connect with Jaisri: www.ayurveda-seminars.com.

TRY AYURVEDA

ZITKALA-SA
Activist

ROSIKA SCHWIMMER
World Federalist

MARIETTA BLAU
Physicist

KATE WARNE
Detective

My Story

DANIELLE LORASO

In my 37 years of life I've held many titles. My most prized title is that of Mama to my bright light 6-year-old daughter, Grace.

Grace came into this world as a major extravert. As soon as she learned to blow kisses, anyone that even came close to looking her way while we were out in public received one or as many as it took for the person to return the gesture. She learned to speak early and would mimic the conversations she heard on our weekly trip to Dutch Brothers. She would ask anyone near-by, in her sweet two-year-old voice "hey! What do you have going on later?". One day, as we were checking out from Target, the cashier handed me a pile of change, explaining that it was for the piggy bank sweet little girl that was brightening days around the store. Following a visit from her "kindness elves" we developed a night-time journaling session in which we shared what we were grateful for throughout the day.

I was blessed to have a support system that allowed Grace to stay home while I worked. Grace was a professional at interacting with adults. Grace entered kindergarten the day after her 5th birthday delighted for the new adventure ahead. She learned a lot that year and as expected she made a ton of friends. Her teachers would provide feedback that she was the friend that would always be there if someone got hurt or was just feeling sad. Kindergarten graduation came and it was time for the yearly awards. A long list of certificates were given from "future lawyer" to "best artist" "future musician" and "biggest helper", although I knew that any of those could have been given to my Grace, none of them were the perfect fit. Finally, the teacher got to "kindest heart", from the moment she said it, I knew. Many of her friends knew it too, they clapped and squealed "that's Grace!"

After the ceremony, Grace skipped over beaming with glee. I was beaming too. I am so lucky to be the mama of the girl with the kindest heart. My Grace.

Show Up Stand Up Speak Up

My seventh-grade dream to make a difference in the world has evolved into a global mission of generosity. The spark for this initiative ignited in August 2018 when I encountered the concept of "glad giving" and observed the rising trend of paying for the person's order behind you in the drive-thru. Inspired by these acts, I conceived a unique idea – loading a digital gift card, sharing it on Facebook, and allowing anyone who came across it to use it. The message was straightforward: "I'd like to treat you today; if you see this and want it, it's meant for you." My intention was to do something simple and fun that could help brighten the day of those around me. The initial response to my first share was diverse; some were hesitant, doubting it was meant for them, while others questioned why I chose this form of generosity over more conventional charitable causes.

Yet, the impact of spontaneous generosity aimed at making people feel special proved to be significant. Thus, the Spark Generosity Movement was conceived, dedicated to normalizing the act of spreading generosity, joy, and kindness for no specific reason. This random generosity has reached individuals worldwide at precisely the moments they needed it most. Over the years, my digital gift card has been scanned countless times. While the majority of the stories remain anonymous, those who have chosen to share their experiences reveal that Spark Generosity has accompanied them on both their best and worst days, during moments of celebration or grief, on their first days of work and the first day of retirement. The recurring theme is evident: seemingly small acts of generosity possess the remarkable power to make a significant difference in the lives of others. Connect with me and join the generosity on Facebook:
https://www.facebook.com/DanielleLoras

RADICAL GENEROSITY

My Story

REBECCA MURTAGH

The world seemed like a mystery,
I struggled to find my place.
Until a secret was revealed to me,
That made sense of the human race.
We are not in competition.
There is no ultimate prize.
We are meant to make soul connections.
Made in a moment in one other's eyes.
We cannot erase what we see, think, or do.
Challenges and celebrations define me and you.
How we respond defines our path.
Every day we expand or contract.
Our years may be numbered, yet one thing is sure.
Human connections are timeless, unbreakable, and pure.
Quantum science calls it entanglement.
From which there is no escape.
We impact every soul and the universe.
With every action we take.
Far beyond our understanding.
Yet within our grasp.
Our influence is ever-expanding.
Every connection creates impact.
Now I'm on a mission to help others see,
Love and connections are our divine legacy.
AI may lead to human extinction.
Technology will dominate.
We must elevate humans,
Before it is too late.

Show Up Stand Up Speak Up

Life is an amazing adventure!

In addition to nature, art, music, and writing, I am passionate about helping others achieve their goals. After a near-fatal accident prevented finishing my bachelor's degree, I learned to pivot and innovate. Over the years, I developed a reputation for identifying emerging trends and creating forward-thinking strategies. As a futurist, I have reinvented myself and my businesses numerous times and helped countless executives, entrepreneurs, students, organizations, and professionals do the same.

I am a 2X award-winning CEO with over 30 years and 100,000 hours of real-world experience working with technology and collaborating with leaders from Fortune 500 to Silicon Valley, and beyond. As an internet pioneer in the age of digital transformation, I have been recognized by Inc. Magazine, Entrepreneur, Digital Future Times, CMO.com, Google Analytics, Yahoo Finance, NBC News, C-Suite Network, and numerous media outlets as a global thought-leader on tech, marketing, and the future of business. It has been an exciting journey. Years of research have revealed concerning trends in technology that threaten humanity. Once fears were confirmed in statements by tech leaders, I set out on a mission to educate, inform, and inspire a responsible, ethical balance between pursuit of exciting opportunities created by AI - and avoiding what experts call imminent threats that could diminish quality of life or lead to human extinction. I love technology. I love humans more.

Ascently Institute, is a 501(c)(3) nonprofit I started to educate, empower, and inspire individuals, students, parents, communities, and leaders to create a #HumanFirst culture that respects and protects human freedoms, privacy, commerce, and sovereignty of body, mind, and soul from threats of biological, psychological, or technological manipulation or extinction. I invite you to join me!   Connect@RebeccaMurtagh.com

HUMAN FIRST

My Story

CARMEL ECKER

"Dearest Carmel,
You are doing GREAT!
Love you XO
Melissa"

My eyes started to water as I looked at the note on my kitchen table.

That morning, I'd left my friend Melissa to leisurely pack up and head back to Ontario after an evening of reminiscing, giggling, and philosophizing on life into the wee hours of the morning. Something in our conversation had told her I needed to read those words. The reality is that I didn't FEEL like I was doing great. Things were certainly better than they had been immediately after my divorce 2 years earlier. I had a decent job, great friends, my 3-year-old son and I were settled into the condo I had bought, and I'd recently crossed off my bucket list goal of doing the BC Bike Race, a 7-day 300 km mountain bike race. But I wasn't excited about my future. I wasn't especially excited about my present either. I was mostly living the same day over and over and that day wasn't filled nearly enough with what I loved.

"You are doing GREAT!"

What would it take for me to live up to those words? I wish I could say that the answer came to me right away, but it took a few years for me to build the courage to even be honest with myself about what GREAT might look like. I was too consumed with what was realistic. What could I reasonably achieve? What would make me money and give me greater stability as a single parent?

It was all very practical and uninspiring. No wonder I kept spinning my wheels.

I finally got a glimpse of GREAT early last year. I decided to make mountain biking-my 27-year passion-the focus of my life. I didn't know exactly what this would look like, but I knew it would start with spending more time on the trails. So, I scheduled a mountain bike ride for noon 3-4 days a week and then I kept the appointment with myself. No excuses. By June, I had spent more time in the saddle than I had the entire year previous. I felt strong and fit. I was reengaging with the mountain biking community, finding new riding partners, attending events and coaching. I started dating someone who was as passionate about mountain biking as I was. I took on 2 mountain bike related book projects.

I began to feel truly alive and aligned for the first time in YEARS. And it all started with one simple decision to make my passion a priority. I still don't know where this is all leading, but after years of searching outside myself for the key to my future without much success, I've fully activated my internal compass and I've never been happier.

Show Up Stand Up Speak Up

"There's a fine line between bad ass and dumb ass. There's a fine line between bravery and stupidity. And it's not always easy to recognize where that line is, but you know when you cross it."
-Leo Houlding, British Rock Climber

If you've done any kind of "extreme" sports, you've felt the tension between fear and fun. You've lived in the space between "I've got this!" and "oh shit!" And there's one thing that impacts your success more than anything else: the conversation that's happening inside your head.

As a mountain bike coach, I've heard one thing over and over: "I know I can do this, but I just can't get over the mental piece." Yes, you need skills and experience, but the internal dialogue determines in a split second whether you say yes or no to what's in front of you.

So how do you take control of this dialogue and make the right decision, whether that's to go for it or take a pass for now? You build your mental muscles the same way you work your physical ones. Pro athletes have been doing this kind of thing for years because it's incredibly effective. Games and races have been won or lost according to whether an athlete could wrangle their nerves and emotions.

So how do you build your mental muscles? You do short exercises that shift you from fear to calm, so you can make the best decision for yourself, be that a "heck ya!" or a "not today."

If you'd like to learn how to manage your internal dialogue surrounding risk so you can safely move yourself to the next level, reach out: carmel@youroneamazinglife.com

RIDE HARD

My Story

WHITNEY KOBRIN

Between the ages of 15 and 30, I found myself relentlessly chasing after love. I cycled through a banquet of damaging patterns, pursuing men who offered me mere breadcrumbs of affection, trying to mold myself into whatever I thought would please my man, and jumping into passionate, fiery romances that flickered out just as fast as they ignited.

While nursing the wounds of yet another failed romance, a simple Google search led me to a Relationship and Femininity Coach who changed my life forever. As I devoured the new material, I was struck by a profound realization— What I thought I knew about relationships was ALL WRONG! By this time, my son was starting school and I wanted, more than ever, to have a stable family unit.

With the help of this coach, I had a breakthrough! I learned how to speak up and communicate my needs and boundaries. My natural feminine energy transformed from my weakness to my source of power. My biggest realization, though, was that I'd been seeking external validation to fill the gaping hole where my self-love should have been. "If *he* loves me, then I can feel loved." I wasn't a dumb person; I knew the concept of self-love. But I had never entirely loved and accepted myself. I wonder if you can relate to this.

Just as I started brimming with confidence, powerful feminine energy, and profound self-love, I met my husband – a testament to the power of self-love and personal growth in magnetizing love. Together, we navigated the complexities of career and family life, weaving dreams and aspirations into the fabric of our relationship. But fate had other plans, and with my beloved husband's untimely passing, our tragic love story was cut short. I'd finally found the loved I'd looked for, only to lose him. WTF? My world was shattered…

But this is a story of resilience. Grieving opened me up to even more healing, growth, and spiritual alignment. Eventually, out of the ashes, I started building the next phase of my life. Amidst the ruins of my shattered dreams, I discovered my true purpose – helping women navigate the tumultuous seas of modern dating and cultivating the love they desire. I am no longer the young, desperate, clueless version of myself. I have become the wise mentor that she wishes she had known.

Show Up Stand Up Speak Up

All the joys, sorrows, and lessons I've endured are now poured into my work as a Love Coach. You'll find me on the sidelines of modern dating apps, and Zoom rooms nationwide, cheering women on throughout their dating journey, helping them love themselves, speak up, set boundaries, and express their authentic self. I teach practical skills for the modern world, while also guiding and supporting their emotional journey. As if relationships weren't challenging enough already, modern technology, texting, and societal shifts have complicated things, but I believe love is still worth it! After helping hundreds of women aged 24 – 74 on their journey to love, I've learned a few things!

Love is often obscured by fear, expectation, misunderstanding, or disillusionment. Sometimes we simply need to remove these barriers to let the deeper connection shine. We are limited in how much we can love another person by how much we love ourselves. It's easy to find blame, but more effective to find accountability. Masculine and feminine energy attract each other like opposite poles of a magnet. Embrace this law of nature.

We are not naturally experts in love. We learn our habits from TV and movies that entertain us through comedy and tragedy, and from our families, (which all operate in varying degrees of dysfunction).

You can create a future unlike anything you've ever experienced before, so stop limiting your future vision to what you're experienced in your past.

It's kind of funny things work. What used to be my greatest weakness and source of pain, has now become my absolute superpower! I feel like I've been let in on the secret to real love, and the best part is sharing it with others. My dear reader, if you or someone you know have a desire for love and are struggling to get there, please reach out to me through my website, www.WhitneyKobrin.com.

I would love to hear from you!

217

LOVE FIRST

My Story

PAT ALVA-KRAKER

Amidst the intricate tapestry of my life's journey, I hold onto the belief that I'm not solely a human being, but a spiritual entity experiencing a unique existence. This belief intertwines threads of courage, generosity, self-discovery, humor and an enduring joy, weaving a beautiful mosaic that shapes my path. As a spiritual being, I've learned to embrace each present moment, acknowledging the intricate symphony of life's design. It's like a celestial dance guiding me, reminding me to release my grip on control and flow with the rhythm of life's journey, even when it takes unexpected turns.

Even in the ordinary moments of life, like the search for matching socks in the morning, I find humor. Those mundane situations hold a kind of wisdom, a reminder that even in the simplest corners of life, there's something to learn -- like the mystery of disappearing socks. Life invites us all to crossroads, often through challenges, urging us to reflect on our essence, direction and values. My moment came on February 20, 2023, when I faced the reality of a second battle with breast cancer.

I summoned courage from within, embarking on an unfamiliar journey. This time, I decided to shape the narrative, taking control of how I experience it. At my core, I believe in self-care. When I got the diagnosis, I made the choice to pause my business and focus on healing with tenderness. I become my own advocate, orchestrating a healing process with self-compassion. Navigating chemotherapy and surgeries was scary and stressful, I held onto the power of choice. I chose hope over despair, serenity over chaos, joy over sadness and gratitude over anguish. During those long chemotherapy sessions, there was time for reflection. I often asked myself "What truly matters?" The answer was clear: living in alignment with my core values, crafting a life that mirrors my authentic self.

In the infusion lab, where stories of fellow women intersect with mine, I see reflections of my own journey. These women have faced their fears, weathered storms, and emerged as pillars of strength. They remind me of the resilience within. And you, too, are part of this community of strong souls.

At the heart of my existence is a mission: to keep evolving into a more compassionate version of myself. If we all commit to this journey of self-improvement, aligning with the universal rhythm, we can weave a tapestry of kindness and progress across our shared planet. In the grand mosaic of life, I am but a single thread, working to radiate light within the intricate weave. My life, an ongoing masterpiece, continues to unfold – one conversation, one chapter at a time.

Show Up Stand Up Speak Up

Back in a cozy El Paso neighborhood, I was a pint-sized entrepreneur with mega dreams and wild imagination. While other kids played with toys, I was cooking up the grandest "Business" game ever. Time rolled on, and my passion grew stronger. Today, I'm steering the ship at MajesticCoachingGroup.com. I totally believe that leadership holds the key to a better world. For me, business isn't just about the numbers; it's about nurturing leaders who light up the universe. That's my driving force. Let's talk about Mindful Leadership – it's my jam. I've cooked up my own Mindful Leadership training program for companies and I've got a knack for turning teams into total rockstars.

Out there in the world, I'm just me – no masks. I've learned that authenticity creates real connections, unbreakable trust, and a lasting impact. Partner with me, and you get the real deal. Ladies in leadership, I've got your back. I've created a safe space for professionals and entrepreneurs to find their strength, resilience and authenticity. Oh, and I host kick-butt women's leadership retreats, too.

When I step up as a speaker, I'm all about shouting from the rooftops that Mindful Leadership is the secret salsa to success. After 25+ years in business, my golden rules are: 1. Define your success. 2. Keep growing 3. Have fun – if it's not fun, it's not worth it. From that El Paso kid ruling the "Business" game, my journey's led me to a place where my "why" drives me. I'm on a mission to shape leaders who radiate compassion, vision and positive change. Let's team up and build a world where leadership shines bright -- where organizations thrive and people truly soar!
pat@majesticcoachinggroup.com

BE BOLD

BRANDIE PHILLIPS

My Message to Women is...

Always remember that you are your first priority.

Show Up Stand Up Speak Up

APPRECIATE TIME

My Story

PEARL CHIARENZA

Embracing the SHERO Within

As a child, I embarked on a unique journey that traced a triangular path across the vast landscape of the United States. Born in California, my early years were marked by my father's service as a Marine during the Vietnam War. During his deployment, my family stayed with my Granny in upstate New York sharing laughter, warmth, and comfort.

When my father completed his service, we ventured to sunny Florida, creating memories that would linger in the recesses of my childhood. However, life's unpredictable nature led us back to California as I transitioned into adulthood. Little did I know that my childhood odyssey would later mirror my adult life in a peculiar way.

In California, fate intertwined our stories as I met my husband, and we embarked on a new chapter together. With his job leading us to Virginia and then back to sunny Florida adding another vertex to my life's triangle. Before our move to Virginia, an unexpected twist altered the course of our lives. We were offered witness protection due to our decision to testify against drug dealers in our neighborhood, who harbored a clandestine drug lab in their garage. The gravity of our choice was immense, yet we declined this extraordinary offer. Starting a family and remaining close to our extended family was a priority, and witness protection would have meant sacrificing these vital connections.

However, the most significant shift occurred when tragedy struck our family. In 2022, we faced the unimaginable—the loss of our beloved son, Matthew, at the tender age of 25. A car accident snatched him away, leaving an indelible void in our lives. The pain was palpable, and grief threatened to consume us. Yet, amid the darkness, I relied on my inner SHERO Matt had seen me become. Matthew's passing became a catalyst for change, a stark reminder of life's fragility. It was in this crucible of sorrow that I embraced the role of a SHERO even more determined to honor his memory by living life to the fullest.

When questioned about my seemingly unyielding determination, I share the secret – I am the SHERO of my own story. The loss of Matthew compelled me to reevaluate my priorities and embrace a life that celebrates every moment including the recent engagement of our son Nate. No longer burdened by guilt, I prioritize self-care, understanding that it enables me to be the best version of myself for those I love. The journey from a wandering child to a resilient adult, from a witness against crime to a grieving parent, has defined the tapestry of my life. Through it all, I've learned that embracing the SHERO within is not just a choice; it's a necessity. I've discovered the strength to navigate life's complexities, finding solace in the knowledge that our stories, no matter how tumultuous, can be rewritten with resilience and love.

Show Up Stand Up Speak Up

Hey Gorgeous!

I am always ready for a heart-to-heart chat. So, let me spill the tea on a journey that transformed my life—a journey to become the SHERO I was meant to be. I bet you can relate—those days of people-pleasing, putting everyone else first, and feeling drained. Sound familiar? But guess what? I decided to flip the script and put myself in the spotlight. It wasn't a walk in the park, but it was the glow-up I desperately needed. Now, I'm here, radiating strength, happiness, and authenticity.

Here's the inside scoop: I learned the magic of saying "No" to others and a big, resounding "Yes" to myself. It's like giving yourself permission to be the priority for a change. And girl, let me tell you about this game-changing life hack I came up with— a pocket pebble. Move it three times every time you say "No" and reclaim your time and energy. It's a total game-changer! As my journey continued, I morphed into a CEO Mom, running my home like a boss babe, and releasing myself from the chaos. I said "Yes" to the things that truly matter and embraced collaboration like never before. It's a whole new level of empowerment.

And now, I can proudly say I'm the SHERO of my own story—a fierce, radiant, and authentic version of myself. The journey wasn't a cakewalk, but girl, it was a glow-up for the books. Now, here's the exciting part—I want you to join me on this empowering adventure. It's time to say "Yes" to yourself and watch the magic happen.

I'm inviting you to kickstart your glow-up journey with the Glow-Up Challenge at https://www.wsliving.com/30-day-glow-up-challenge/. Trust me, this is where the magic begins. Imagine us, both on this journey, supporting each other every step of the way. Let's be the SHEROs we were meant to be—strong, happy, empowered, radiant, and oh-so-original. Ready to unleash your glow-up? I know you are! Join me, and let's make this transformational journey together.

STOP PLEASING

My Story

DR. PATRICIA 'PATTI' JO GROVER

Today, I write this after surviving a childhood that most people couldn't conceive, let alone believe, some even going as far to say was nonexistent. It affected my life well into adulthood, causing three failed marriages by age 29. It wasn't until after the third divorce that I decided to examine every aspect of the woman that I had become by dismantling all the puzzle pieces that had made me that woman.

At that time there really weren't any women motivational speakers or authors on the scene, they were all men. I had to take what I could learn from them and create something heart centered that would work for me. I spent a lot of time in both prayer and meditation to help me through this part of my journey to learn to Know, Like, Trust, and Ultimately Love Myself as I was putting myself back together. This was the period when I developed my Philosophy on Life being like a Jigsaw Puzzle.

Once I had picked myself up and put my pieces back together, and finally had learned to love myself, I met and married the love of my life. We were blessed to have lived an amazingly beautiful life together for 5 years when we had a severe motorcycle accident where I sustained a fractured skull, a brain bleed, and blew out my right eardrum giving me a Traumatic Brain Injury. I couldn't smell or taste things for the longest time, and had to have speech, physical, and occupational therapy. I would have panic attack just being a passenger in a car, and I never thought I'd ever be able to drive a vehicle by myself ever again. There is an entire month of my life that I'm unable to remember. He was there for me like a rock through it all and then 7 years later he was diagnosed with MLC which is non-curable and reoccurring. We got him into a Clinical Trial at MD Anderson in Houston, TX. We got him into remission, and then he was tragically & traumatically taken from me by the Powassan Virus. This time the ripple effect of losing him affected all 8 Dimensions of my life, my puzzle pieces had been dismantled for me.

Today, I'm also proud to share that after all this I've gotten my PhD in Entreprenology.

Show Up Stand Up Speak Up

Rise Above" the Challenges That Life Brings Your Way...

Dr. Patricia Jo Grover, The Goal Achievement Strategist, and The Queen of Re-Taking – Re- Shaping & Re-Making Lives, Businesses and Futures incites action with the platform that she specifically created around her proprietary "Conquering Skills Education" to Encourage, Educate, and Empower individuals to achieve more success and be able to "Rise Above" any Challenges they may have in any of the 8 Dimensions of Life.

She uses a heart – centered approach, that focuses on helping her clients have Mindset Shifts, create New Belief Windows, and find their Why & Purpose. Allowing them to Dream, Conquer Fears, and Create a Work/Life Balance so they can Have, Be, Do, and Earn more while they live their lives Purposefully, Joyfully, and Gratefully.

In her 38 years of Business Management & Ownership, she has recruited, trained, coached, consulted, taught, and mentored Thousands of Entrepreneurs, Ultrapreneurs, Corporate Employees, and Staff of her own businesses. The International University of Entreprenology from where Patricia received her PHD believe so much in what she is doing with her platform that they have chosen to be the sponsor of both of her TV Shows and Podcasts ("The Good Morning Risers Show" & "The Rise Above Show" with Patricia Jo Grover), as well as all of her events. patti@patriciajogrover.com

RISE ABOVE

ZOE MORRIS

My Message to Women is...

Whatever you go through in life,
don't let it define you or change who you are.

Show Up Stand Up Speak Up

LOVE ON

My Story

CATHERINE HOLT

What a ride life has been, filled with so many adventures, fascinating people, revered moments. Sometimes it felt like the house of horrors, other times like floating on clouds of sunshine.

All these experiences have shaped me into the determined, resilient woman I am today, and that, I celebrate (although I'm on a constant journey to give myself as much grace as I give others).

I was given a great foundation. My parents raised me to be what my Father called "an independent individual" who could flourish on my own, when needed. But like most girls growing up, confining social norms confused me. I had a thirst for knowledge, but felt pressured to ignore it to chase after the demure femme fatale persona. At home, I was encouraged to ask questions, to challenge boundaries. I learned to welcome change and the new opportunities and adventures that came with it.

I was fortunate to travel extensively and live abroad, though NYC is my happy place. Learning new cultures was sometimes embarrassing, like when I used foul language at a party in Brazil (I thought I was saying something totally acceptable). I learned cultural humility and honed an ability to see things using a different lens – to be a life-long and compassionate learner.

I have learned so many lessons along my labyrinthine path - many that seem to circle around fairness, especially for girls and women. When someone would say "nobody promised you things would be fair." I would always respond "but they should be".

My daughter had a life-altering stroke when she was 18. She went from being a nationally ranked equestrian with Olympic aspiration to a hemiplegic relearning how to walk. I drew inspiration from her tenacity to forge a new life. Accompanying her on her recovery journey and seeing how society often treats differences, elevated my quest for fairness.

I came to realize that it was the challenges I confronted that helped me evolve the most. They made me turn off autopilot and pay attention, learn, and change. But change isn't easy. It's scary and can make others uncomfortable, but without change we become extinct.

I have been fortunate to meet and know other women who gave me a hand up as they were climbing. I raise my homemade margarita to all those who unblocked the path before me and to those whose paths I will clear

Show Up Stand Up Speak Up

My mom used to say that no one gets out of life unscathed. It was how you reacted to hardships that showed your mettle. As with most, I have faced storms that have almost shipwrecked me. Fortunately, I had those in my life who valued the lessons of those storms, and how they led me to evolve. In the 70s, I remember the frustration of being considered second rate – I was a girl. I was encouraged to stay in my socially acceptable box in a supporting role. Tired of having my voice silenced and disregarded, I began delving into what makes a person stand out and someone others want to follow.

I am grateful to the women who shared their secrets to raising their voices despite their social confines. Voicing my opinions emboldened me, and others started viewing me as a leader. You notice I said others – because it took me a long time to recognize that I was. Through my global work with traditionally marginalized grassroots women, I witnessed many emerge as leaders, either to right unfairness or to survive. I learned from their struggles and sometimes life-threatening challenges. By challenging the status quo, they became changemakers.

I have guided many in recognizing the strength of their voices and strategies in shaping change. I have shared my experiences with women whether in the university classroom, political arena, or on the global stage. Leaders aren't "born" - I think all women have what it takes to be leaders. By embracing and nurturing your inner leadership, you can become an effective, authentic, and influential leader – changemaker. As a changemaker advocate, I am ready to support you in developing your leadership capabilities and accompanying you on your leadership journey. Where do you want to see change? Let's connect cathy@catherine-holt.com

229

EMBRACE LEADERSHIP

LISA MEITNER

Nuclear Physicist

BEULAH LOUISE HENRY

Inventor

My Story

NATALIE MCQUEEN

I've been reflecting on life lately, and it's like we're all artists with a blank canvas. Six years ago, I had a wake-up call—a near-death experience that shook me to my core. It made me reevaluate how I was living. It made me realize I now appreciated life and what I was surrounded by, as if my eyes and heart were taking snapshots of everything as if seeing them for the first time and appreciating them as fine art pieces that I want to cherish and put on display to see daily. I realized that those little things in my life are what made my life so significant and meaningful. I now look at each day as a blank canvas for my photography and plan out what I want to shoot and keep as my life's art today.

It's become my guiding principle, a reminder that we have the power to set intentions, focus on what truly matters, and attract positive energy into our lives.

Life is too short to be on autopilot, wasting precious time on things that don't bring real value. That wake-up call initiated my journey to craft and preserve the legacy I want to leave behind—a legacy of intention and purpose.

Today, I'm all about living in the present, cherishing meaningful moments like laughter, love, and family times. Daily expressions of gratitude have become my norm because none of us can predict what life may throw our way.

Stepping out of my comfort zone has been a transformative journey, but it's unlocking a world beyond my imagination. Life, I believe, is an opportunity to break free from monotony, to create our legacies, and to live with intention.

This exploration is not just about my journey—it's about shared experiences and inspiration. Let's embrace the analogy of life as a series of photographs. Each day offers a new opportunity to focus on what truly matters, to capture moments that define our narrative.

Here's to living with purpose and creating the chapters yet to be written!

Show Up Stand Up Speak Up

After almost five years of publishing other authors' books, I thought I was living a fulfilling career and making an impact as a publisher. I was helping others take their wisdom to the world as I sat in the background. Once I realized that my important legacy message needed to be heard by the world, I felt a new excitement and a little bit of fear, knowing I could not stay in the shadows anymore. My realization of the importance of living your life to the fullest and stepping out of your comfort zone to make an impact in the world in whatever way you are called to was so strong that it almost overrode the fear. This awareness led to the formation of my company, Gifts of Legacy. It is a company that continues to share and inspire others on how to leave an impactful legacy and how to write and record your legacy so generations can enjoy it.

I continually create innovative products that help me to share not only my voice but also the voice of the fantastic people I am surrounded by daily. I help inspire individuals on a daily journaling path through my product, My Talking Journal. I believe journaling is one of the most powerful things you can do when creating and leaving your legacy. My Talking Journal is a new way of using inspiring messages from creatives around the world to help you be your best and most creative self.

I would love nothing more than to help you create the legacy that you want to be remembered for so the world can continue to be inspired by you long after you are gone. www.GiftsOfLegacy.us

CREATE LEGACY

My Story

JOYCE INGRAM

I didn't fit in. When I started Grade 1 in the, predominantly white, small town my family had immigrated to, I spoke only Chinese. I had no knowledge of any English. I tried to fit in with the rest of the class, but it was a struggle and without a lot of help. I think this was the first time I felt like an outsider. I felt like I wasn't good enough.

All the way through high school, I recall being very accommodating to others. My mom thought I was gullible and that anyone could get me to do anything. But I wasn't gullible. I just wanted to be liked and accepted.

I can't remember a time when I didn't have self-esteem and body issues. I always felt self-conscious, like I wasn't "enough" in every way and didn't matter. Being introverted and shy, I always stayed in the background where it was generally safe. But I'd always had a gnawing feeling that I was meant to do more with my life. So, I attended the University of Life as a professional in the travel industry that I started to see myself in a new light. During that 25-year personal development program, I learned that I was more capable than I had previously thought, navigating through countries where I didn't know the language or customs. My natural curiosity was the key to fun and adventure over the years:

I flew to the top of Mount Fuji in what felt like a little tin can—a four-seater prop plane. I'll always remember the sense of freedom and exhilaration I felt as we ascended to the top of this iconic volcano.

I took in the New Zealand landscape hundreds of feet below me as the jet boat I was in sped along a cliffside river. Facing my fear of water after nearly drowning as a teenager, I went snorkeling off a boat in the middle of the ocean. Bobbing around in my life jacket, I came face to face with a barracuda, which was both exciting and nerve-wracking. Attending a retreat in my 30s, I invoked my inner trapeze artist and jumped off a platform 30 feet in the air. As I reached for the approaching trapeze bar, I remember thinking, "If I can do this, I can do anything!"

With each adventure, I got another glimpse of who I truly am and what I believe in. After all these experiences and more, I've realized I was able to adapt and make decisions quickly, challenge myself, take calculated risks, be adventurous and have fun. I felt empowered, more confident to take on more challenging jobs, tasks, and put myself out there in the world. What I've learned is even though it may be scary or risky, taking consistent actions over a long period of time builds self-belief and confidence. I no longer see what doesn't work as failure. I adjust and keep moving forward. And if I stay on the course long enough, I know I'll be able to help others along the way as well as myself.

Show Up Stand Up Speak Up

My journey to being a financial advisor started when I was turned down for a Mrs. Field's Cookie franchise at age 19. I had been visiting Hawaii when I first discovered the tasty opportunity, and I was sold on the idea of making my own business out of it. Sadly, I was turned down because they weren't operating in Canada yet. Instead of dampening my entrepreneurial spirit, the experience made me realize there was a part of me that didn't want a conventional 9-5 life. And even though I did 9-5 work through 40 years of living, including getting married and raising my son, that entrepreneurial spark stuck with me. I always had a side hustle.

Then, four years ago, I decided to take a financial mentorship program. I'd had financial challenges many years before and since then I had wanted to become more educated in this area. Plus, I was looking for a new business opportunity that would allow me to leave the corporate world. I soon realized most people didn't grow up learning how money and debt works or how to build wealth. I knew this was where I wanted to be, and my focus would be helping other women learn how to better manage their money and efficiently build wealth. The more I talked to other women, the more stories I heard about staying in bad relationships for financial reasons, fear of running out of money, embarrassment over not knowing how to budget, abandoning goals and dreams, settling. As an independent agent with World Financial Group, I can now help remove the real and perceived barriers that keep women and their families stuck.

I'm on a mission to help families navigate their financial roadmap. I take a holistic, nonjudgemental approach to help my clients, whether they need tax strategies, insurance, additional income, to get out of debt or to determine their financial independence number for retirement. Together, we design a plan for their future so they can make smarter financial decisions. I'm so excited I'm going to help 180 families within the next five years, providing financial literacy, mentoring new advisors, and empowering women and girls through financial education. If what I've shared resonates with you, please reach out at jingram12tapc@wfgmail.ca

235

SELF ACCEPTANCE

My Story

AMY JANECE

"You live loud," the artist said as she worked her tattoo needles into my arm. We had already spent more than 100 hours together over the past two decades. I had never even heard that phrase before. We were discussing how people show up in life. That phrase resonated, so it now lives on a sticky note on my computer monitor. It serves as a reminder that you should show up completely every day.

Have you ever shrunk for those around you because they thought you were "too much" or "not enough" of whatever they thought you should be? I have. It's freaking exhausting. Somewhere in my thirties I decided to just be me and let others fall where they may. Living loud means that you take life by the horns... Or ears, or whatever you can grab onto. Embrace every opportunity you can to experience life in the moment. (There is a huge difference between living and existing. *Choose* to live every day!)

Sometimes that means I'm riding a motorcycle, other times I might swim with sharks, jump out of a plane, or climb onto anything I can to get a different view. For you, that might look a lot different. Maybe it's yoga, hiking, or even base jumping. Whatever that is for you, realize that the more you say yes to the things you love to do or want to at least try to do, the more full you'll be.

When you show up authentically and fully, you give space for others around you to do the same. I think that's the most beautiful way to love someone - to accept you just as you are.

As a woman, you've probably been taught from an early age to be "the best" at everything you do and every role you play. That's just not possible, which is why insecurities and cattiness run rampant among women. Instead, be the best YOU that you can be. And surround yourself with women who are the best them that they can be. Together, we are a force of light and love and positivity for the world.

This life is short. Grab your rhino (or unicorn, or whatever) by the horns and say "YES!" to being the amazing woman you are.
Try something new,
Find a new view,
Be the best you,
And smile a little, too.

Show Up Stand Up Speak Up

Have you ever felt like you were hiding in plain sight?
Or even worse - they see you, but it seems like it doesn't go beyond the surface level? That was my life. After playing behind the scenes for two decades, I decided to step out from the shadows. I met a woman who typed in the elements, and I was typed as a Fire (fall colors). I didn't like the colors or identify with the characteristics of a Fire, so I set out to prove her wrong. I failed. Instead, my life changed by simply changing the colors I wore. Imagine your whole life changing in less than 6 months. Your income doubled, your relationships deepened with everyone around you, and even strangers treated you differently. That happened! I felt seen. The consultant said I had an eye for it and wanted to train me. After resisting for a year and a half, I gave in, if only so I didn't have to keep paying her to type my circle. The first time I publicly shared about this 3 people ran to sign up; and several other women shared that my words changed their lives.

That's when I realized this is my calling and purpose. I type in the elements using your eye/skin/hair color, natural body movement, shape of your facial features, and your core characteristics. We use the energy of colors within your palette to align your physical appearance with your message, and dress with intention to create the energy you want to put out and receive on any given day. I get to hold the mirror for you to see a glimpse of the beauty you possess. You are a masterpiece, and your clothes are merely the frame.
Are you ready to be seen? amy@embodyyourelement.com

LIVE LOUD

My Story

ALYSSEN NGUYEN

If I could drop everything right now, the dogs, the husband of 7 years, work, everything, I would be on the first flight out of here! To where, you might ask. Honestly, anywhere overseas, Japan, Italy or Paris would be nice. Traveling just excites me beyond anything else. I love meeting new people. I love learning about their lives, their upbringing, their culture, their traditions, their religion, their school, and their food, oh man, the food. Traveling brings new experiences, it offers new perspectives that expand my mind. The diversity, but also the friendliness, the excitement the locals have when talking about their country and their culture is amazing.

We have already done my dream trip and it was better than I could have ever imagined. We spent 2 weeks in French Polynesia from December 23, 2019, to January 8, 2020. We spent 4 days in Tahiti, 8 days in Mo'orea and 3 days in Bora Bora. It was wonderful. We met Katie Cleary and Paul de Gelder at the New Year's party the Hotel hosted for us in Mo'orea. We got tattoos done, we bought pearl necklaces, we swam with sharks and stingrays, did a 4x4 adventure ride up a big mountain, and went skydiving! We also met Bob and Jody, they were so much fun, they had won their trip to the casino! So far this has been one of the best vacations we have ever taken.

We also take a cruise once a year. For those of you that may fear the ocean, or drowning or water in general, I am telling you it is not that scary! I was terrified. My biggest fear is drowning, and the ocean scares me, I love the beach, but the wide-open ocean… oh no. However, I decided to finally go on a cruise back in 2016, once I got onboard it honestly was just like being on land. Unless you are staring at the ocean and thinking about impending doom, you don't even realize you are in the middle of the ocean. Ever since that cruise I was hooked. So far, we have been on 8 cruises, 2 with Norwegian Cruise Line, 5 with Royal Caribbean and 1 with Carnival. I do not plan to stop cruising anytime soon. Do not let your fears hold you back from living life. I have had a lot of bad experience in the water and that is why I fear drowning. But I love cruising, and there are tips and tricks for having a better experience on the ship if you are truly that concerned. My husband and I live by a philosophy of "I will try anything at least once." You will be surprised at what you end up enjoying.

Traveling is a way of life for me, it opens new worlds, gives me many memories and it brings me so much joy. I hope that all of you find something that brings you as much joy as traveling brings me.

Show Up Stand Up Speak Up

It all started when I lost myself. After terrible relationships in my late teens to early twenties, I no longer knew who I was. I was a big people pleaser and over-thinker. In relationships I tended to be obsessive, clingy, and desperate. Now, the others did lie, cheat, and manipulate me for years. It was devastating, exhausting, gut wrenching and emotionally and mentally debilitating. But I knew I had to change. I knew that the only way things were going to get better was if I sat down and did the work. IT WAS SO HARD! It's not easy blaming yourself for situations and taking responsibility for your part, especially in a relationship where most would have said it was their fault and not mine, that they needed to change and not me. See after relationship number 1, I told myself this would not happen again. However, I did not do any of the work, which led me to experience the same relationship again.

I was lost, I was broken, and I was alone. I did some deep, internal work. I had to learn who I was again, I had to learn to put myself first, I had to learn what I liked and what I didn't, what I would compromise and what I wouldn't, what I was looking for and what I was not looking for. This led me to learn and understand that self-care, self-love, and self-respect are so important.

The most important relationship you will ever have in life is the relationship you have with yourself. It is time to take care of you. It is time to learn to love you, the whole of you. It is time to show up as the real, raw, authentic you.
Self-care is not selfish, it is necessary. elevatedaspectscoaching@gmail.com

YOU CAN

My Story

CATHARINE O'LEARY

Do you ever get that nudge feeling like you're meant for something big? Dream of that swanky house or a cozy cabin retreat? That's the universe tapping you on the shoulder, saying, "Go on, make a difference – make a huge difference"! So, my start was a bit rough. Picture this: born dead. No pulse, no breath. My entrance was literally a fight for life.

Here's the scoop:
My parents, fresh in their love story and expecting me, hit a terrifying bump. My mom started hemorrhaging during a vacation. Imagine my dad, the calm businessman, turning into a stunt driver from a movie, racing to save her and me. By the time we hit the hospital, I was declared gone. But, guess what? We both pulled through. Me, with a slightly quirky arm as a souvenir, but hey, I was alive! Cut to my homecoming aligning with "a giant leap for mankind". Yep, the moon landing! Talk about grand entrances, right?

Fast forward through a childhood idolizing my globe-trotting dad, acing university, and diving into a corporate career that had me rubbing elbows with big names. I was living up to the expectations, or so I thought. But here's the kicker: I was miserable. My life was a cycle of drive, work, drive, sleep, repeat. Until my body yelled, "Enough!" leading to a wake-up call no one wants. My corporate career ended, my health tanked, and I faced the real cliff of depression and wondered what my purpose was. But I wasn't ready to bow out. So, I faced my demons, and asked myself, "What now?"

The answer wasn't in a job title or another person's dream. It was about finding joy in the journey, not just the destination. I discovered my passion for guiding entrepreneurs to their ideal clients, blending my expertise with genuine fulfillment.

Today, I'm not just surviving; I'm thriving. No more hiding. I celebrate life's moments, big and small, without needing to escape. My business isn't just a job; it's a mission to empower others to live their dreams fully. So, here's to great expectations, not as a burden but as a beacon guiding us to our true purpose. And guess what? You're capable of reaching them, too.

Show Up Stand Up Speak Up

Imagine standing at a crossroads. Behind you, a path littered with traditional methods and expectations. Ahead? A road less traveled, brimming with creativity, innovation, and the promise of true connection. That's where my journey with Ideal Client Academy begins.

I've walked the corporate tightrope, celebrated the highs, and wrestled with the lows. I've felt the exhilaration of success and the sting of misalignment. Through it all, a question nagged at me: "Is this as good as it gets?" The answer, I discovered, was a resounding "No."

I founded Ideal Client Academy with a vision to revolutionize how entrepreneurs attract, engage, and retain their best clients. No more faceless transactions or fleeting engagements. We're about building lasting relationships with curiosity, where clients aren't just numbers—they're the heart of the business. Our approach is different. We dive deep into the essence of what makes a business unique, then craft a client attraction system that resonates with authenticity and value. It's not just about being seen; it's about being seen for who you truly are and connecting with those who will cherish that authenticity.

This journey hasn't been just about business growth; it's been a transformation. I've learned that the key to attracting ideal clients isn't in the latest marketing gimmick—it's in standing confidently in your story, embracing your unique voice, and daring to do business differently. Ideal Client Academy is a testament to the power of authentic connection through curiosity in business. Here, we don't just chase success—we redefine it, together, on our own terms. Want to learn more? Go to www.quizformybiz.com to see what is stopping you from attracting more ideal clients right now!

ASK QUESTIONS

My Story

JO ANN GRAMLICH

While growing up a twin with five siblings, I instinctively knew that my path would be different from my family and friends and that it might lead me down a road of unconventional twists and turns that in the long run would allow me to fulfill my purpose and dreams.

I remember reading a quote from Dr. Wayne Dyer and he said, "Don't die with your music still in you." Basically, he was saying listen to your inner voice and avoid following the expectations of others. If you follow others and go with the crowd, your music will die within you. You will always be afraid of taking important risks that provide you with opportunities to grow as a person. If you don't listen to your inner voice, you may miss out on transforming your life for the better and inadvertently neglect helping others find their true calling or passion. Listening to the music within you lets you ignore what everyone else thinks you should be doing.

I know this feeling very well and I decided to pursue my passion instead of following the crowd. My inner voice was telling me to tap into my creative being and not settle for what might be considered good enough based on other people's standards. As it is said, "When you follow the crowd you lose yourself, but when you follow your soul, you will lose the crowd." I knew I had to spend a lot of time in silence and solitude to listen to my heart's desire. Passion for me was recognizing my own aspirations and understanding that even when I was pursuing my passion, I would be confronted with stumbling blocks and trials. The life lesson I've learned is to find your passion and listen to your own inner voice because it will enable you to move forward during difficult times and in directions you never thought were tangible or possible. Avoid negative distracting thoughts as you venture out on your journey and remember that obstacles are a part of life that help us discover more about ourselves. Your passion will not only lead you to make conscious decisions and significant life choices but may provide you with opportunities to develop relationships on a global scale with compassionate people who believe in you and your dreams.

Cultivating your passion may be one of the most important things you can do to identify your unique gifts. You may need to participate in activities of interest, network with like-minded people, engage in life-long learning, or pursue exciting adventures that inspire you to tap into your creative side. Creativity can become a big part of your nature and keep you balanced, grounded, and happy. We all need to strive to become better, so why not find your passion and make a grand mark on the world around you.

Show Up Stand Up Speak Up

I have worked as a children's speech-language pathologist for almost 30 years! My journey began when I graduated from high school, and I wasn't really sure what direction to take. I didn't go to college right away and worked in various business offices in downtown Buffalo, New York. While going through this experience, my brothers and sisters were having children and I quickly learned I really enjoyed interacting with them on a regular basis and the rest is history! Children have brought so much joy into my life and I feel I am naturally in tune with them. I never minimize the work of a child because they have so much to learn and at the same time are teaching me indirectly about myself. Not only do I develop special relationships with children, parents, and caregivers, but impact their lives in positive ways. My optimistic nature enables me to empower children to be confident in their own voice so they can be heard and recognized out in the world. It all begins with me, a.k.a. Miss JoJo, teaching and helping children to tap into their imaginations and skillful minds. My philosophy of making learning fun and educational will bring out the best in children and help them explore their own creative abilities during the early years and beyond. It's so exciting to see their eyes fill with wonder and curiosity. Such magical moments!! Mixing education with imagination is so rewarding!!

As a result of working with children daily, my business and books Talk, Play, And Read were inspired because of my personal passion for helping young children learn and achieve. My overall theme resonates a simple message for all parents and caregivers to understand. Simply put, talk, play, and read with your child every day starting as early as birth to ensure school success!! My books not only guide parents, caregivers, and educators, they also provide many stimulating activities and games that are developmentally appropriate and designed to help enhance children's language skills during the early years. In addition, I speak to help bring awareness of the importance of early intervention and language development for infants, toddlers, and preschoolers.
For more information about me and my resources, visit Talkplayandread.com. I would love it if you would take the time to tell me about you and your story as well! Thank you!! jojogr1020@yahoo.com

EMPOWER CHILDREN

My Story

DANIELLE COULTER

When I tell my story, I play the part of "Dan Can Shred." The part aligns with my ability to do adaptive snowboarding, and "shredding" is how we express our fun at the moment. My strength as a woman tells me never to say no to what I choose as a goal; besides, the adrenaline rush is incredible!

The other side of my story is acting, entertaining children, and enjoying my life along the journey. It took effort and time to become independent while enduring the issues surrounding Cerebral Palsy. Plus, my fierce determination to be the best I can be shines through, and I never let the inevitable temporary setbacks break my spirit!

I thought hard about being an inspiration to others and decided to create a website and book to tell my story. I designed my website to show I can help other people learn that they can do anything that they put their minds to, with or without a disability to overcome. On my website, I show how I am a woman who can snowboard with a disability. I wanted to write and show what I could do in pictures or videos while showing other people that they could live their dreams, and nothing should get in their way! The best way I believe I can influence others is to share my story with the world, and typing out my thoughts onto a website, on a piece of paper, or in a book is the best way to get my story out to the world.

Show Up Stand Up Speak Up

I was born with Cerebral Palsy. I know that I do stuff differently and more slowly than ordinary people, but that never stops me from being the woman I am today. Through a rigorous routine, I have adapted to my needs and accomplished whatever I choose to do.

I became the first adaptive snowboarder in the world by playing a video game, learning the skills, and through help from friends and family. Nothing is impossible once you put your mind to it. Now, I am racing all over Colorado, and people are amazed by seeing how I shred up and down the mountains. A crucial key is working out enough to build the endurance and strength for snowboarding.

I work through a lot of exercise, but my favorite workout is riding my horse, Jewel. My relationship with Jewel is an essential part of who I am. Whatever else I do; I make sure our relationship is good.

My other passion is acting. Performing for others or making bubbles for the kids is how I express my joy. I also love many forms of art. Writing is one art form I embrace because it is my way of communicating with others. I pray my writing helps you realize your dreams.

Whatever your passion is for life, always do it for yourself, and don't let anyone tell you that you can't. Even if you have more than one passion, go for it! You can do it all. danielle.p.coulter@gmail.com

GO TRAILBLAZE

My Story

CONNIE ZELLER

Have you ever felt that you were destined for greatness? Many of us have had that feeling and have pushed it down. Maybe it was the influence of our family and friends, or our community.

I've always known that I was destined to be powerful. Not in a Wonder Woman Superhero sort of way, but in a calm and quiet way. I have always been strong and haven't let my power be pushed down. I have been steadfast for things that I considered to be unjust. I've supported the underdog and the under-represented. When I was in grade school, I would call out bullies and challenge them to a fight. I would tell them to pick on someone their own size. The bullies didn't care about me. I wasn't in their sights. The world of kid justice isn't always fair, but it's often swift. When I challenged bullies to a fight, the answer was, "I don't fight girls". My response was always, "You won't fight me because you know that I will take you down". It only took a couple of fist fights (which I won) to earn a reputation for being a powerful girl and defending formerly bullied kids.

I grew into a powerful woman. When I saw inequities, I called them out. I never intended to cause trouble, but I also never turned a blind eye to those who experienced inequality and discrimination. I got into trouble many times and I got out of it too. I never regretted doing what I thought was right. Being a powerful woman has served me well.

Show Up Stand Up Speak Up

I am an accidental entrepreneur. I reached a glass ceiling and realized that I needed to take my talents and go. It was refreshing to work with colleagues in an environment where the mission statement and company values were more than a plaque in the office.

I had my dream job. I coordinated corporate training events across the U.S. and I was working for what I considered to be the best company in the world. I really thought that I would work with this wonderful company until retirement. It never occurred to me that the partners would want to retire before me. The company was sold to a venture capital group, and they did what they do best - trim fat. My office was shuttered.

I wasn't ready to retire, and I couldn't afford it. I applied for many jobs and came across a common problem, salaries weren't aligned with my experience. There was only one thing for me to do - manifest my dream job. I wrote down what I loved to do, not only what I enjoyed but also lit me up. Then, I wrote down my list of non-negotiables. When I finished, I realized that I had to create my own dream job. The focus of Salty Bee Events is supporting event hosts so that they are fully present for their attendees. I've never strayed from the company values of authenticity, integrity, and independence.

I support my clients by giving them the space they need to pour into their audience. A well-run event should make attendees excited for the next event. I've been asked why I named my business Salty Bee Events. It's in honor of my Salt Lake City heritage and a reminder that not all bees are sweet, a little salt goes a long way. connie@czellerevents.com

BE PRESENT

TAMMY WONG

Blessed am I that life wasn't always easy or perfect.

Growing up with critical parents who had demanding expectations and siblings who were always arguing was difficult, however; it was their expression of love.

Those experiences shaped me into a better, stronger woman today - more forgiving, compassionate and resilient. For that, I am most grateful.

I remember spending every day after school with my grandma. She didn't speak much English, wasn't the touchy-feely type, not a good housekeeper, and an average cook, but I adored her, and she made me feel loved.

'Por Por' as we called her, never had a job, but she raised 6 children, 18 grandchildren, and 25 great grandchildren.

She was an incredibly strong, and disciplined woman who I admired and respected.
I miss her deeply.

Show Up Stand Up Speak Up

My family has a slew of amazing women who are self-sufficient and self-made. Because of my upbringing, I am independent, entrepreneurial, and extremely curious. I am proud to be a daughter, sister, aunt, friend, mentor, and relationship builder.

We all can design our lives the way we want, and not the way it has occurred.

We can strive to pursue goals or choose mediocrity.

I believe we can each make a difference using our individual talents, sharing them with others while making an impact.

My fondest memories come from large family gatherings and traveling globally. Meeting fascinating people and listening to their stories allows for growth.

My journey continues by surrounding myself with like-minded thinkers who want to give back, help others and build a community.
tammyjowong7@gmail.com

HAVE FUN

KARLEE HAWES

My Message To Women is ...

Loving yourself doesn't mean loving every imperfection.
It means prioritizing yourself.
And loving yourself is a relationship you'll never regret.

Show Up Stand Up Speak Up

CHIN UP

TERA HAWES

My Message to Women is ...

In no uncertain terms, trust your gut.

Show Up Stand Up Speak Up

SLOW DOWN

DEB HAWES

My Message to Women is ...

Take the trip.

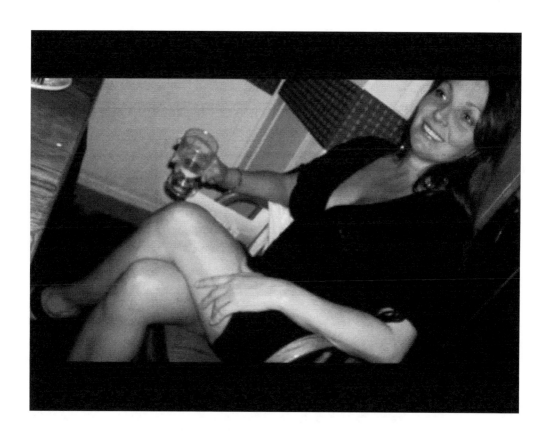

VEGAS BABY

DEB DRUMMOND

My Message to Women is ...

We are not equal until we are all equal.
We are not free until we are all free.

Show Up Stand Up Speak Up

SHE SAID

My Story

DEB BENSON

My life journey is much like a Lotus emerging gracefully from the muddy depths. With each unfolding petal, I discovered more and more about my true self.

I delved into various practices, such as; homeopathy, essential oils, seeking guidance from healers, spirit guides, and enlightened mentors. Through these endeavors, my inherent gifts began to manifest themselves. Some were already familiar to me, while others came as pleasant surprises. Reiki, Pet Reiki, Mediumship, Animal communications, and Channeled drawings, to name a few, surfaced as prominent aspects of my being.

My primary focus has been assisting those who were unable to help themselves find a starting point and connect, both humans and animals alike. Allow me to be your guide as you navigate through life's stages, exposing your new self.

Together, we will uncover your true self!

Show Up Stand Up Speak Up

As an empathic and compassionate energy healer I provide you with emotional support systems through challenging life stage changes; including, retirement living. Reiki restorative healing, chakra clearing and mediumship. I am here to assist you on your journey, resolve everyday challenges, promote a meditative lifestyle, mediate relationships, and convey messages from your pets and loved ones to balance understanding. I also personalize your essential oil blends and tailor them to promote self-esteem, healthy Chakra, balance, relaxation, and rejuvenation.

Together you and I can find pathways to a better healthier outlook in all stages of life. I discovered my calling while working in retail manufacturing, where I built and grew one of the very first premium brand pet food manufacturers. My team and I set the benchmark for high quality nutrition for specialty pet retailers throughout the province.

During this time, I networked with social service organizations in the province to leverage Vancouver's deep resource of inner-city residents. Over twenty-two years my team and I mentored healthy life choices and empathetic communications for clients, animals, and employees. debbie@harmonicwisdom.ca

REVEAL YOURSELF

JANE WAKELYN

My Message to Women is ...

In the symphony of your life, let your self-worth be the conductor,
not the applause of others.
Steer Your Course. You're the driver of your life's journey.
Navigate wisely, embrace every turn with purpose.

Show Up Stand Up Speak Up

PERSEVERE DARINGLY

My Story

LYZA ULRYCH

Growth. To me that's what it's all about. Healing myself and helping others. The older I become, the more I treasure emotional, mental, and physical peace. So many years of my life were spent consumed with the stress from childhood trauma and various self-destructive behaviours which kept that cycle going.

With God's help and a wonderful support system of therapists, family, and close friends, I have conquered the major personal issues and have been able to experience the joy of being a mother, and other meaningful aspects of this life.

These days when the journey gets challenging, just knowing that growth is the key brings increased strength. It keeps me focused forward in this world and able to fight the demons of fear, negativity, and impatience. A little fun thrown in here and there, and I am a very grateful woman.

Show Up Stand Up Speak Up

Aside from my purpose as a mother, the passion in my life comes from being a healer. That has manifested in doing massage, serving food at the restaurant I co-owned and named after my son, caring for elderly, and acting.

Acting has been my heart's desire since I was a child. I started training at university and continued with various coaches. I'm thankful to them all for what I have learned; first and foremost, Shea Hampton, who has been my teacher for many years. I have acted on stage, in film, and television. I enjoy embodying the character and touching people with various emotions.

Collaborating with other creatives on projects is one of my favourite aspects of the industry. It's exciting to be a part of this book alongside such talented and inspirational entrepreneurial women with Deb Drummond at the helm.

My Message to Women: One World, One People, Be Kind. lyzaulrych@gmail.com

DIG DEEP

My Story

MINDY SCHEIER

Mindy Scheier was born in Philadelphia, PA, but moved to New York City right after graduating from the University of Vermont with a design degree. Even from an early age, Mindy always dreamed of being a fashion designer, but she never wanted to think small. She had her sights set on becoming a global brand and worked in the fashion industry for over 25 years.

However, life had other plans for her. Mindy's middle child, Oliver, was born with a rare form of muscular dystrophy called Rigid Spine MD. As Mindy often says, "there is no rule book on being a parent, and most certainly no rule book on being a parent of a child with a disability." So, like many things in life, she learned with her husband Greg and their other two children, Stella and Beau by taking it one day at a time. Oliver's diagnosis opened Mindy's eyes to the incredible world of people with disabilities. She saw firsthand the challenges they face in finding stylish and functional clothing that meets their needs. This experience inspired her to pivot her career and make change happen in our world. In 2014, Mindy founded the Runway of Dreams Foundation, with the mission of making fashion more inclusive for people with disabilities. The foundation quickly gained recognition, partnering with major brands to develop adaptive clothing lines that prioritize both style and function. In 2019, Mindy founded GAMUT Management, a consulting agency that helps brands develop Adaptive products and services.

Mindy's personal story is a testament to the power of one person's passion to drive meaningful change in the world. It serves as an inspiration to all those who aspire to make a difference and create positive change in the world. Mindy's unwavering dedication to her mission reminds us that even in the face of adversity, we can achieve great things. Mindy's work is far from done, and she continues to inspire others to embrace inclusivity and celebrate diversity in all its forms. In a world where everyone feels seen and valued, Mindy's vision serves as a guiding light toward a brighter, more equitable future. Her personal story is a shining example of what can be achieved with passion, perseverance, and a deep commitment to making the world a better place.

Show Up Stand Up Speak Up

Mindy Scheier is a pioneering advocate for inclusive fashion, leading the charge to revolutionize the industry's approach to adaptive clothing. As the founder of the Runway of Dreams Foundation and GAMUT Management, her mission is clear: changing the fashion, beauty, and lifestyle industries to be inclusive of people with disabilities. This commitment stems from a deeply personal place, ignited by her son's experience with muscular dystrophy, which revealed the stark need for more accessible and stylish clothing options. Mindy's impact reaches far and wide, reshaping the fashion landscape to be more inclusive and diverse. Runway of Dreams Foundation empowers people with disabilities to have confidence and self-expression through fashion and beauty inclusion.

Meanwhile, GAMUT Management actively collaborates with brands to develop Adaptive products and services that prioritize the needs of people with disabilities. Her efforts have not only opened doors for individuals with disabilities to express themselves through clothing but have also challenged industry norms and standards. Beyond the runway, Mindy's vision extends to fostering a world where inclusivity is the norm, not the exception. She believes in empowering individuals with disabilities to feel confident and valued, recognizing that clothing is more than just fabric; it's a means of self-expression and identity. Her advocacy transcends fashion, beauty, and lifestyle industries, sparking conversations about accessibility, representation, and equality on a broader scale.

Mindy Scheier's work is a testament to the power of passion and perseverance in driving meaningful change. Through her tireless dedication, she continues to inspire others to embrace inclusivity and celebrate diversity in all its forms. Mindy's vision serves as a guiding light toward a brighter, more equitable future. For more information, go to www.gamutmanagement.com and www.runwayofdreams.org .

CULTURE SHIFTER

My Story

KATHY BUSHNELL

I was a skinny, seven-year-old when Mom and Dad moved our family from sunny California to New York. The plane landed at La Guardia Airport soon after a blizzard had engulfed the area. Dressed in a crop top, shorts, and sandals, I sank up to my knees in a freezing, unfamiliar substance at the bottom of the metal staircase. A feeling of helplessness threatened to overwhelm me, and several tears ran down my cheeks. Suddenly, I envisioned my mother's father, Grampy, playing a soothing melody on his violin - and the world did not feel so alarming, after all.

In the days that followed my brother, Alan, showed me how to throw a football, and flip baseball cards. At other times, I would ditch my tomboy persona, build a miniature pony out of snow, and "gallop" as a Princess through the wonderous lands of my imagination. Each day, I ate fruit-flavored Trix for breakfast, and was nicknamed "Cereal Pie" by my family. Meanwhile, my brother was enrolled in violin lessons, and I began studying classical piano. Soon, the four of us were having fun-filled "family orchestra" sessions in our living room – featuring Alan on violin, and Dad strumming his guitar. I would handle the piano parts, while Mom (who was blind) played her ukelele - and added some rousing Kazoo!

Once my brother started high school, I had to make my way alone to class - and quickly learned to be cognizant of my surroundings. However, on the occasions when I was verbally accosted by older kids (or propositioned by drunkards in the Subway), special thoughts of Grampy playing uplifting tunes gave me an inner strength to fend off any would-be-assailants. Alan and I spent many Sunday afternoons together in Washington Square Park, listening to well-known musicians jamming near the fountain. By then, Dad had taught me various chords on his guitar, and I secretly longed to "play a tune" with these legendary minstrels. Many new rock bands were arriving on the scene, as well. Listening to their music through the earphone of my transistor radio, inspired me to begin writing some songs of my own on piano and guitar. During these solo, pivotal moments of change, it felt as though my TRUE SELF was emerging!

Although my parents "tolerated" my passion for the rock music scene, I was determined to check out various bands in concert. So, I attended some Rolling Stones gigs at NYC's Academy of Music, and witnessed The Beatles performing at Shea Stadium. By that time, I had written more songs, and was hell-bent on hanging out with my favorite bands in person. After all, I wanted them to know the ways in which their music moved me - heart and soul. It was only after Alan and I had chatted with members of The Rolling Stones at a Manhattan nightclub several months later, that my family finally understood how passionate I was about sharing my songs with the world!

Show Up Stand Up Speak Up

During the "Summer of Love" in 1967, the music of the British Invasion lured me and another American young woman to the U.K. We formed many new friendships and had fallen in love with London. As the two of us sat in a jet bound for JFK at summer's end, my travel companion suggested that we rent a flat of our own in London the following Spring, on February 3, 1968. Her serendipitous brainstorm turned out to be a pivotal, life-changing moment for us both. Although it was a risky move, we believed in the power of our destiny, and relocated from N.Y.C. to London on that same date. After renting a flat of our own in Chelsea, we co-founded EMILY MUFF, the first female rock duo in Britain. Many unexpected challenges tested our resolve while navigating the choppy waters of the male-dominated world of rock. However, we stood our ground when confronted with unreasonable (or distasteful) demands. After all, the two of us were determined to succeed without compromising our principles. We persevered, and our pioneer female rock duo toured extensively throughout Great Britain - opening shows for the bands Family, Quintessence, and other rock icons. Emily Muff's final concert appearance to a sold-out crowd of over five thousand at London's Royal Albert Hall is a testament to its courage, tenacity, creativity, and philosophy of self-empowerment.

As co-founder of a trailblazing female rock duo that was instrumental in re-writing the history of women in British rock 'n' roll, I was in a unique position to share my story with the world. So, in addition to various public appearances and interviews, I published the book "Em and Moo: Legacy of a '60s Female Rock Duo." This behind-the-scenes, inspiring memoir continues to empower women to be bold, yet true to themselves while pursuing their dreams! Now that you know about me, I would enjoy hearing about YOU! Contact me at: www.kathybushnell.com

BE GUTSY

BEATA JIRAVA

My Message to Women is ...

Perseverance is the bedrock of success.
As a mentee, instill a resilient mindset –
view obstacles as steppingstones, not barriers.

Show Up Stand Up Speak Up

JUST PERSEVERE

DOROTHEA KORTHUIS

My Message to Women is ...

DAILY nourish your inner Love, Joy, Peace,
Kindness, Gentleness, Faithfulness,
Patience, Self-Control and Teachable spirit.
When you are squeezed, that's what will pour out.

Show Up Stand Up Speak Up

BE STRONG

AMY THURMAN

My Message to Women is ...

Polish the mirror to see what message your soul has for you.

Show Up Stand Up Speak Up

YOU'RE POWERFUL

ARLENE HACHE

My Message To Women is ...

Leadership requires a high degree of self-reflection
to hold compassion and make space
for others' perspectives, experiences, and passions.

Show Up Stand Up Speak Up

BE COURAGEOUS

My Story

JACKIE COTE

I was the ultimate "I got it!" girl. You know her. . . The one who has everything "under control", doesn't need help carrying her suitcase or opening doors, she fixes everything, and takes care of the world! After my mom passed at the age of 5, I was moved around quite a bit from sitter to sitter and house to house while dad took on the responsibility of raising the 6 of us and running his construction company eighty hours a week. As well, a couple years later he spent time creating a new relationship with who is now my stepmom of 40 plus years.

My hero showed me that we can do it all! So, I did! Learning early on in life that even when no one was around I could figure out how to make food, do the laundry, and make stuff happen for myself. I didn't need anyone to help me because I learned that I Got IT!! This created the fiercely independent and successful woman I am today. It also created a woman who didn't let people fully in. A woman who never fully loved or let herself be fully loved by another. A woman who desired words of affirmation from her hero that she never got, but never knew she needed.

Until the day I had to fly across the country to NJ, leave my life and husband for two months to care for my father with dementia and my stepmom in the hospital for 2 months. During this time with dad I got the solo time I never got with him my entire life while hearing him tell me how much he loved me, he was proud of me, and how beautiful and courageous I am. I cried for three days after we placed him into his assisted living as I slept alone at his house and realized I finally got what I yearned for after 5 decades.

After one of the hardest journeys of my life, at 51 I finally got the healing and closure that placed the last piece of the puzzle into my foundation of true love for self that I needed to become who God has always meant for me to be in this world. Now I get to help others discover the same.
True love begins with YOU!!
Much love,
Jackie

Show Up Stand Up Speak Up

I was 15 and started my first real job at the local NJ bakery and they threw me the keys and said "You are going to run the night shifts!". They saw my leadership skills and ability to motivate others at such a young age.

From that moment my personal journey of freedom and leading others began. Every place I worked at they handed me the keys. From that belief others had in me, I realized that I had a God given gift. I have a natural ability to see what others can't see in themselves and I hold that gift of belief up for them until they get there. Then I raise the level even higher so they can truly be who they are meant to be!

While doing this I got to travel the country and always find a way to live a life of freedom while making money doing it. After creating over 300 plus leaders in the restaurant biz, I finally decided at 48 years old that I was meant to do my own thing. That was when I became your Freedom Empowerment Mentor, and Jackie Cote Coaching was created. Now I am a full time RV nomad with my husband and 2 pups living my life on my terms, doing what I want, when I want, whenever I want, without having to ask for permission from anyone, including myself!

It's my mission to help as many of you Awaken, Empower and Own who you are unapologetically in this world and become the Freedom Creator you are meant to be. Let's chat and talk about what your vision of your freedom life looks like. Oh, and it doesn't have to be selling everything and living in an RV. www.jackiecotecoaching.com .

BE FREE

My Story

KASIA FRYKLUND

My life's journey has been deeply shaped by the influence of music, spirituality, and healing. Music has been in my life as long as I can remember; guiding me through a lot of ups and downs. It all began with a love for classical piano, a passion that eventually led me into the realm of electronic music production. Through music production, I discovered a platform to express my creativity and connect with other artists.

From navigating societal expectations to overcoming physical setbacks, music has always been my refuge. In my early childhood years, classical piano provided me with a means of solace and expression. This allowed me to convey emotions that words often failed to capture.

At the age of fourteen, I entered a model search competition which turned out to be a bittersweet experience. While it offered an escape from my small town in Saskatchewan, it also triggered issues with body image and self-esteem. Ironically, this ultimately propelled me further into my love for music as a means of coping and self-expression.

There is a certain magic in music, particularly when experienced in specific frequencies. I have always been a spiritual person, but it wasn't until years later I experienced my first sound bath. This is how I discovered sound healing with solfeggio frequencies and their therapeutic properties. One of my favourites, 174 Hz, is linked to physical healing, pain relief; reduces inflammation and discomfort. I often relied on this frequency and playing sound bowls daily during my recovery from a broken jaw. While some may view this approach as unconventional, it was remarkable how quickly I had recovered without bruising, surgery or swelling.

Show Up Stand Up Speak Up

All of my crystal bowls are tuned to 432 Hz which is said to align with the natural rhythm of the Earth and resonate closely with the frequency at which our bodies naturally vibrate. Sound healing with crystal bowls and other healing instruments tuned to 432 Hz has become a cornerstone of my creative process. Playing sound bowls and learning healing frequencies provided an avenue for my spirituality and music production to intersect.

As a sound healing practitioner both in my own practice at MYSTIC ARTS and at the DEN Meditation in Los Angeles, I have merged my musical background with spiritual practices. This has provided unique experiences for my clients. This work has deepened my understanding of the healing potential of music and reinforced my commitment to holistic well-being.

Through my music, I strive to offer listeners a transformative journey that extends far beyond mere entertainment. By sharing my vulnerabilities and experiences, I aspire to create genuine connections and authenticity in a world often plagued by conformity. It is a privilege to witness the profound impact music can have on the lives of others. I am dedicated to sharing its healing power with the world. kasia@zhirecords.com

LOVE YOURSELF

My Story

SANDRA VON HOLLEN

Embracing the art of gratitude has been nothing short of transformative in my life. Gratitude has emerged as a powerful teacher, guiding me through this beautiful story of life. Realizing that we have one chance to write our best life story, I embarked on this profound journey into gratitude, discovering its ability to elevate every aspect of life. Gratitude casts a perspective that shines a new light on all circumstances and experiences, turning the ordinary into the extraordinary.

A few years ago, I delved deep into practicing gratitude, the abundant rewards that have since unfolded in my life have been nothing short of miraculous. The simple yet profound act of daily gratitude journaling has been a beacon, attracting more blessings into my world, creating a positive feedback loop of appreciation.

One of the most impactful applications of gratitude has been in the realm of relationships. Rather than allowing minor irritations to overshadow the beauty of connection, I was able to redirect my focus. Specifically, in dealing with my husband's seemingly trivial habits, I consciously chose to list ten things that I was grateful for about him each day. From our adventurous back road drives, capturing perfect moments with our cameras, to his unwavering commitment to putting our family first, this practice became a transformative force. It not only flipped the switch on irritating moments but also elevated our relationship, steering it away from the slippery slope of negativity and resentment.

Recently, I faced the devastating loss of a dear friend, gratitude emerged as an unexpected companion. Instead of succumbing to the darkness of grief, I chose to celebrate the moments we shared and the deep love that defined our friendship. Reflecting on the chapters of our lives, I discovered an enduring sense of gratitude for the richness my "no matter what" friend brought to my journey.

My story is a testament to the life-altering power of gratitude. It has become a way of life, shaping my perspective, and infusing every chapter of my life with positivity. Through the eyes of gratitude, each experience, whether joyful or challenging, becomes an opportunity for growth and appreciation. As I continue to navigate this abundant life of existence, gratitude remains my steadfast companion, lighting the path to a life that is not just the best it can be but also filled with gratitude every step along the way.
In Gratitude, Sandra.

Show Up Stand Up Speak Up

Using Gratitude For The Best You

In the tapestry of my life, helping others has been my natural inclination. Strangers are drawn to me, freely sharing their troubles and triumphs. My children have always marveled at this innate character trait of mine. When I step into a store for a quick errand, it inevitably turns into a twenty-minute encounter as someone within the store is drawn to me, eager to share their story.

My children often suggest that helping others should be my profession, considering it's something I naturally engage in every day. As a family, we have embarked on various business ventures over the years. Each pivot brought us closer to a business that resonates with our true purpose. The Fall of 2023 marked another transformative period. Our business underwent a rebranding, emerging as "Ignite The Light".

My daughter and I have directed our focus towards helping others through gratitude, self-development, and wellness. We have finally reached a point where our hearts are in alignment with our daily endeavors. We are now dedicated to developing personal development courses and sharing our wellness line with a broader audience.

Our mission extends beyond business, it is about building a legacy by creating ripples of positive change throughout the community. We promote and collaborate with other likeminded business owners/ product makers to enhance our community. Together, we truly do make a ripple of impact and big a difference. We aim to help many others realize the dormant power within themselves, guiding them to find and shine their own light. Our message is clear: The Magic Sauce others seek to find, to become their best, is already embedded within them. I would love to connect with you and assist you with embarking on your journey to discover your own Magic Sauce. Reach out at ignite@ignitethelight.ca

BE GRATEFUL

DAPHNE WELLS

My Message to Women is ...

Lead your own life
Rewrite the rules of leadership
so you can sustainably do life and business your way.

Show Up Stand Up Speak Up

BE YOU

CHIQUINHA GONZAGA

Composer

MARGARET DUMONT

Comedienne

ANAGARIKA DHARMAPALA

Revivalist

AMRITA SHER-GIL

Painter

My Story

CARINA REEVES

Just one quick Live I said to myself.

It was the most gorgeous summer's day, late afternoon, with golden sunshine and my happy heart keeping me company on my way downtown. I was floating on air, (albeit a little late!) heading towards a first date with a man I was very excited to meet. It felt like I was surrounded by magic - I'd had a photo shoot that morning, so my hair and makeup were killer, my dress was adorable, I was teaching an energy workshop that weekend, I had money in my bank account, my kids were taken care of... in other words? Everything was good and ANYTHING was possible. I could feel it in my BONES, and so I did! I did a little Live, beaming my energy out onto Facebook, talking about energy, beliefs, and receiving from the Universe. Little did I know just how much Magic was brewing, as that date turned out to be the love of my life, my life partner, and now my relationship coaching business partner too.

Life has changed so much - I remember being 12 and walking in the neighbourhood with my oldest friend talking about boys. I remember saying to her, oh I'm never going to be with anyone, and part of me really believed it. I just couldn't imagine how I would be a fit for anyone. I was bullied at school, a head taller than everyone and a know-it-all, had glasses and frizzy hair, and *I played the cello*... I mean, hopeless weirdo, right?! But as I moved through life, from having wildly beautiful adventures like drinking champagne in a lavender field after performing in Sienna Italy, to the heartbreaking loneliness of postpartum depression, I learned that believing in MYSELF was the hardest part. That was the real mission, the real secret and WORK of being at peace and present to the wonders life has to offer.

What I realized was that when I wasn't believing in myself nobody could convince me that good things were possible for me... but once I did? That's when you get to dream big. That's when you get to go after what you want knowing you deserve it all, and that's when the magic starts to appear as though out of nowhere... but it was you. It was you all along.

Show Up Stand Up Speak Up

It's funny, how everything goes together when you look back.

I've been playing cello since I was 5, and I was a professional cellist until my late (very late) 30's when I had my daughter and then 18 months later my son. I've sold Girl Guide cookies, taught cello, played gigs, and been a telemarketer in my teens, and then slowly it was only cello by the time I finished my Masters in Boston and moved to Toronto to start freelancing. When I arrived, I sent out four resumés, and by the following week I had booked an orchestra gig and been invited to a sight reading party by a local composer. Well, that party led to a teaching position which I held for 10 years, and each concert led me to another, and then another, eventually including the Toronto Symphony, the Canadian Opera Company, and my beloved Kirby String Quartet which I co-founded.

My love affair with music and performing has never gone away, it's just changed form. Playing Beethoven and Brahms connects you to something more beautiful and bigger than yourself, and I think it's the same with relationships. As a relationship coach I help connect people's hearts with their souls, and I can see now how the discipline of learning a musical instrument is like the work of building relationships - both require presence, intention, awareness, inspiration, and craft. I love seeing over and over that a happy relationship is greater than the sum of its parts, just like music, and that it's the true love of our hearts that makes every sour note worth fixing. We are all meant to love, ourselves first and then each other, and that gives life the best soundtrack of all.
transform@carinareevescoaching.com

PURE PRESENCE

CHERYL BISHOP

My Message To Women is ...

Manifest your dreams from your visualizations.
Take action on ideas from the Holy Spirit.
Embrace your divine inspiration and intuition.

Show Up Stand Up Speak Up

TAKE ACTION

My Story

DESI BOLIN

Fragments of My Strength

I have always loved swimming, the sensation of gliding through the water, reading under the shade of a tree with a captivating story, the clatter of bowling pins as I aim for the perfect strike, and the exhilarating freedom of horseback riding.
But sometimes I struggle to find that joy.

3 years ago, I found myself wide awake in the still of the night, lost in my shattered dreams. Each moment felt heavier than the last, weighed down by the emptiness where hope once flourished. It was the hardest time of my life, grappling with the aftermath of a miscarriage while shouldering the responsibilities of supporting my family, managing a business, and wrestling with the relentless grip of depression.

Days turned into nights, a ceaseless cycle of tears and tasks. My business, once a beacon of ambition, now felt like an anchor dragging me into despair. Yet, amidst the chaos, I unearthed flickers of strength within.

My family became my sanctuary, their unwavering support a lifeline in my grief. Together, we navigated the sorrow, finding solace in each other's presence.

Within the confines of my business, I discovered a semblance of control. Pouring my heart and soul into every endeavor, I stitched together the fragments of my fractured spirit, weaving them into a tapestry of resilience.

Yet, the battle against depression raged on. It lurked in the shadows, whispering taunts and planting seeds of doubt. I fought fiercely and leaned on my loved ones for support. Through my vulnerability, I discovered a mountain of courage within.

Slowly, like a phoenix rising from the ashes, I began to rebuild myself. With each sunrise, I greeted the day with renewed determination, knowing that I had weathered the worst of the storm and emerged stronger than before.

The wounds have become scars, the experience etched into my being as reminders of the battles fought and the victories won. But they are no longer symbols of pain; they are emblems of resilience. I continue to surge forward, my heart heavy with loss and buoyed by hope, knowing that within me lay the strength to withstand any adversity that lay ahead.

Show Up Stand Up Speak Up

In a world where business success reigns supreme, I firmly believe in the importance of companies making a positive impact. As an entrepreneur deeply committed to this principle, I embarked on a journey to not only build a prosperous enterprise but also to leave a meaningful mark on society.

Driven by the conviction that businesses can be catalysts for change, I set out to establish a company that not only thrived financially but also contributed to societal betterment.

Along the way, I encountered like-minded leaders who shared my passion for effecting positive change. Together, we formed a close-knit team devoted to realizing our shared goal of running a purpose-driven business. We set out to make a positive impact on the world around us.

As our business expanded, so did our influence. Through innovative initiatives and collaborations with similarly aligned organizations, we addressed pressing social and environmental issues, leaving behind a lasting legacy of positive change.

However, our journey was not without its trials. We faced setbacks and challenges that tested our resolve, but we remained steadfast in our commitment. With each obstacle overcome, our belief in our mission only grew stronger, propelling us forward in our quest to create a better world through our business.

Ultimately, our story was not just one of business triumph but of making a meaningful difference in the world. It served as a testament to the potential impact of purpose-driven entrepreneurship and the transformative power of passion and dedication.

In an era defined by rapid technological advancement and unprecedented global challenges, my mission remains clear: to enable business leaders to operate at their fullest potential while simultaneously creating positive change in the world. Though the road may be challenging, the rewards are immeasurable, and there is nothing I would change about this fulfilling journey. desi@virtuallysourced.com

STAY RESILIENT

AME-LIA TAMBURRINI

My Message to Women is ...

In the darkest places are the most beautiful treasures.
Be courageous and go on a treasure hunt

Show Up Stand Up Speak Up

FIND JOY

My Story

CHRISTINA MICHAEL

In my recent reflections on what brings me joy, I've traced the roots of my current happiness back to early memories that laid its foundation. Despite life's challenges, the recurring theme in my life to date is a deep understanding—a certainty of who I am and where I'm meant to be, engaging in activities that align with my true self and validate my happiness.

Recalling my carefree, younger self with blonde hair, big brown eyes, and a free-spirit, I find that the joy experienced then still resonates within me today. Life's journey, marked by challenges and a lack of quality parenting, shaped my choices. However, a deeper connection with myself now allows me to find joy both in the present and upon reflection. At 19, a fortune cookie imparted the wisdom that "simplicity of character is the natural result of profound thought." This has become a guiding principle for me, emphasizing the joy found in simple, uncomplicated moments—those seat-of-the-soul (Gary Zukav: Seat of the Soul) experiences that bring out the best in me. While not inherently simple, I've developed a profound appreciation for simplicity, guided by the mantra "it doesn't have to be so hard" during troubled times Today, I am more centered and connected to myself than ever, focusing on harmony over balance, simplicity over complexity, and finding joy in the pursuit of happier-ness (thank you Oprah and Arthur Brooks: Build the Life You Want).

Understanding that happiness may be transient, I embrace the enduring feeling of joy, creating a vision through a gratitude board that enriches life in unexpected ways.

In the tapestry of my earliest memories, joy weaves through experiences such as snuggling with my Cookie Monster stuffed animal, dancing to 1970's TV jingles, and embracing the enchantment of first kisses. It extends to the liberty of growing up near the beach, personal triumphs, celebrating all things about my son and the harmonious connection with my partner and friends. Joy encompasses spontaneous adventures, the thrill of learning new things, and the conscious decision to continue to simplify life. It also finds expression in simple acts like making my bed, indulging in favourite candy and a good action movie. Through this mindful process, I unearth an abundance of joy, becoming a conduit for its expression.

I advocate for relishing the moment—capturing its essence and wholeheartedly embracing it. Let joy radiate and reverberate! Embody Joy! Speak Up

Show Up Stand Up Speak Up

Navigating the landscape of self-expression is a nuanced journey marked by the delicate dance between authenticity and potential consequences. As I reflect on my life's trajectory—from carefree childhood to ambitious adulthood, navigating pivotal moments in my 20s, 40s, and now in my 50s—I recognize that speaking up is a fundamental aspect of staying true to oneself. The fear of rejection and the desire to avoid unnecessary drama have, at times, led to self-imposed silence. However, I've learned that speaking up, when approached with careful consideration and intention, aligns me with my values and authentic self. It's a skill that requires finesse—a balance between assertiveness, understanding, and compassion. Through decades of self-discovery and reinvention, I've realized the importance of delving inward for answers, comprehending and honouring my beliefs and values. This internal clarity establishes boundaries that allow me to serve myself, loved ones, and professional relationships authentically. The essence of speaking up lies not only in the message but also in its delivery. It involves responding deliberately, not reacting impulsively. I've learned that I am accountable for expressing myself with respect and compassion, regardless of how my words are received. Expressing praise, gratitude, validation, or addressing issues with experience and support are equally crucial.

Life's lessons, including my missteps, have taught me the importance of vocalizing concerns when faced with situations that challenge my values and integrity or when confronted with wrong or unethical circumstances. Rooted in clarity, connected to our values, and guided by experiences, speaking up becomes a powerful tool. The key is to approach it thoughtfully, without judgment, fostering understanding. If you're intrigued by purposeful and confident self-expression, skillfully balancing response and reaction, and cultivating personal and professional growth with clear intention, I invite you to connect. Let's embark on an opportunity to get closer to yourself, where genuine expression is fostered with meticulous care and thoughtful consideration. Email: christina@fcegrp.com

295

EMBODY JOY

My Story

NICKI KEOHOHOU

Being raised in a large family, I learned many lessons as a middle child. I was known to be the mediator, it is almost as if it came naturally to me. It was fulfilling to inspire my loved ones to find common ground and support them to make progress with collaborative decisions. At one point I began to question my role in the family dynamics. I started to compare myself to my sisters and brother.

One day I had a conversation with my mother and mentioned to her that I felt different. I wasn't like my siblings. They were all A+ students and enthusiastically studied for hours after school. I told her I would rather be with friends, playing sports and meeting new people.

My Mother had the gift of communication and asked questions that brought out the best in others. One profound question that she posed to me was, "what do you feel are your gifts and talents?"

I said, my gifts and talents are with people. I understand people and easily build relationships. She responded, "then make that your life's work." That was the start of my personal and professional development journey and the reason I became a speaker, author and certified in coaching as well as emotional intelligence.

I now realize she was modeling coaching best practices while asking empowering questions, and most importantly, being present as I thoughtfully responded.

It's fascinating what can be caught versus what is simply taught. It is an honor to carry on her legacy and live the life I love!

Show Up Stand Up Speak Up

I discovered at a very young age to surround myself with people who championed me and my zest for life. I began my career as a teacher because I was passionate about building self-esteem in children. When I found direct selling, I realized I could reach more adults who could have a positive influence on future generations. My career evolved to impact more people as a VP of Sales and Marketing for a party plan company followed by becoming a President of an international MLM corporation.

All of this led me to one of my most significant professional roles, establishing the Direct Selling Women's Alliance (DSWA.org). For years, we traveled the world providing education that would support women with access to opportunities, income, and leadership.

The DSWA is a never been seen before collaborative community that serves all women in any direct sales company. Whether you're in the field or corporate, the DSWA has proven methods and training that enhance growth, retention, sales advancement and understanding. We pride ourselves on our established reputation in the industry, ability to stay current and forecast what the industry will need for sustainability. We also provide those solutions first to the market.

From your first 30 days to your years of success in direct sales, we have what you need for every part of your business. Our supportive community awaits to meet and greet you! DSWA is a global alliance that elevates the level of professionalism for women in Direct Sales. We give you more access, increased performance, the path to succeed, and the confidence to act! Our goals aren't met until yours are. https://dswa.org/

297

LOVE LIFE

My Story

MARILYN ANDERSON

I was a Manitoba prairie farm kid who spent hours outside with our collie dog in the garden months and winter months building snowmen on the lawn. We moved from farm to town life and then from the Prairies to the Okanagan Valley, before eventually settling into the Lower Mainland of British Columbia. Each of those new homes gave me lots of experience being 'the new kid' and learning how to fit in, make friends and belong.

Looking back, it's no wonder to me that my most insightful moments come through inquiry. I am genuinely fascinated by people and what makes them 'tick'. I spent many hours with my grandmothers, listening to their stories about the lives they had led and the life skills they had to share with me. In my first career (in Health Care), I had the opportunity to see people in many different situations and types of stress. That led me to go back to college to study business communications and a little bit about marketing, which opened doors into the world of business and the aspects of networking relationships upon which much of my career has been founded.

I love hearing people share their stories and insights from the lives they have experienced, and asking questions and listening carefully has opened many doors and led to many longstanding relationships.

When I want to think and reflect, I am happiest when I am on the move. A great walk is my "happy place", whether in a park, near to a waterway or beach, or on a trail through the forest. This is where I can explore and develop ideas, considering circumstances and creating strategies that can expand into plans and actions.

I am also comfortable in 'mobile meetings', with a colleague (and possibly their dog) who is like-minded about fresh air walkabouts, and I have taken sessions as a consultant in those circumstances, as well.
Every fall, as the season turns, I collect a variety of leaf trophies on my walks – those beautiful colored gifts falling from the trees. I add them, walk after walk, to a wooden salad bowl I cherish, and I call this my "Fall Salad".

What's one thing you do purposefully that makes YOU smile? Enjoy!

Show Up Stand Up Speak Up

RU Ready?

On November 5, 2011, Capilano University in North Vancouver, British Columbia, Canada hosted a TEDx event. It was a groundbreaking venture and an auspicious project, supported by Department heads and volunteers alike. At the invitation of a colleague and friend, Gerry Spitzner, I was recruited onto the Organization Team, headed by Patricia Lambert, and, as the saying goes, off to the races we went. This process took several months to put together—gathering talent and sponsors, technical support, and donors, among other things.

While I was no stranger to networking at that point in my Communications career, this was an incredible opportunity to stretch, develop and grow in new directions. I got to meet a variety of very interesting and accomplished people, learned a lot about organizing large-scale events, and was invited to prepare a TedTalk of my own, as a back-up for any speaker who was unable to participate on the Day!

As the date approached, I had the privilege of delivering my Ted Talk to one of the premiere Coaches in that arena. I remember the day as if it were yesterday, almost pinching myself to make sure it was real. He was in a classroom, waiting for me when I arrived at the College. Butterflies aflutter, I took off my jacket, introduced myself, and stood across a classroom table from him to deliver my speech. 18 minutes later, he was telling me how much he liked it, including my ending quote from Nadine Stair's "If I Had My Life to Live Over Again", which is all about cherishing the Moments in life! As things turned out, I didn't get to deliver my presentation on stage. I did, however, name a sailboat "Moments", and enjoyed every one! marilyn@marilynanderson.com

MOMENTS MATTER

WENDY BERGEN

How do you become unstoppable when facing adversity?

Wendy Bergen here, best-selling author of Getting Unstuck.

Now I have a deep desire to pass on to the world, and family a few things that might make a difference. I'm all about perception and turning our limiting barriers into clarity, freedom, and power.

My story begins with me being a very angry young woman. I had just left an abusive marriage and was working at the Sheriff's office. I didn't realize I was depressed and moody. A co-worker got angry with me and told me she couldn't stand me or my moods. She told me I complained about everything. She never knew if I was going to laugh, cry or be rude and she also threw in that nobody at work liked me, they just tolerated me. I was so hurt. However, I truly believe because she was so brutally honest she saved my life.

When I reached out to a counselor, at that moment I learned I was pushing people away. I also learned I was an amazing courageous woman. At age 25, I took a transformational course that altered my life. "Landmark Worldwide". I am the author of my story. I did not have to live my life from my past beliefs, I excitedly learned that I could create and invent a future worth living into, but how? The course is about the blind spots that keep me from living a fulfilled life. I continue to do their seminars and that is the source of my living a powerful life.

Show Up Stand Up Speak Up

Part of my journey is to keep discovering any disempowering conversations I have about myself, and the world in general. These conversations sabotage me and limit my ability to be free and powerful. Some of them are:

I'm not lovable,
What's the use,
Why bother,
that's not fair,
I'm not smart,
I'm a failure,
I'm not good enough.

When you start recognizing disempowering conversations you can now choose differently. I try to freely express my love by feeding my friends. What a hoot! I feel so loved and appreciated by hundreds if not thousands of people. I am so grateful for the life I live. When I look at my past it could have been so different if I had not started loving and trusting myself and others. You see, I had a violent upbringing. was sexually violated, beaten, and betrayed by some of my caregivers. But now I have been able to forgive them. My children and grandchildren are the reason that I smile, laugh, and cry. They are my happy place and my frustration. They are what make my heartbeat and sometimes break. My children and grandchildren are my everything. I reach out to you here to say that, I love you always and forever. https://thrivingatsixty.com/

RECLAIM YOU

My Story

CHERYL A. RAFTER

I always loved the beach at a young age since being born on the island. After moving away at 5yrs old to another province where there was no ocean, only lakes, I always had this longing to be at the water. I love the feel of the sand between my toes, the sound of the splashing waves, the birds flying overhead, breathing the saltwater air. Even now, I am grateful to live minutes from the ocean where at any given time I can be there.

I remember as a kid for our summer holidays we would always go see my grandma on the island. There was something about being at the beach that was magical, like I was in another world of peace and tranquility. Life at home wasn't the easiest, but when I was around water it was freedom from everyday life at home. It was always exciting to be able to see my other cousins, my aunt and uncle. We would always go to the beach; the best part was when the tide was out and I could walk for miles exploring. I loved looking for crabs under rocks, and starfish, seashells and to this day my favourite, sand dollars. I had a bag full of memories to take home with me. I was grateful to be at grandma's house where we got spoiled, ate good food, stayed up a little later, played in her big back yard, and, oh ya, her big hugs.

Enjoy life to the fullest, remember LIFE'S A BEACH TIME

Show Up Stand Up Speak Up

KEYS TO YOUR COMEBACK ... unlocking your true potential.

I remember becoming single in my 40's after 20 years and not knowing who I was, what I liked, or even what kind of shows I wanted to watch. Then in my 50's packing up my car and moving to another province, where I only knew one person, to start my life over. Now, here I am in my 60's starting another new chapter as a best-selling author.
I am living proof that if you are in action, trust the process, and follow your heart, you can do anything to live the dream life you deserve. When life sucks and we don't like where we are, at any given time we can come back from adversity to move in a new direction. There have been so many times throughout my adult life that I had to start over again. I wished that there was a Comeback Coach who could have supported me to move forward in a different direction.

After writing my story and becoming an international best-selling author, I realised the need for women to have the choice to see things from a different angle. I created this mastermind for women who want to get unstuck from whatever curve ball life has given them. My life journey experiences will help as I relate to different situations and can offer a new perspective. I would like to leave you with this thought, when you're feeling down, always reach out. It takes courage to come back. I'm here to be of service to you for your comeback to happen sooner, and in a healthier way. Please reach out. I am curious to find out what you're up to. cherylrafter.ignite@gmail.com

303

MOVE FORWARD

My Story

KIM JACOB

As I approach my 54th birthday, part of me still feels 24, while the other part realizes I couldn't have fit the countless gifts of love, learning, and joy I've experienced into just 24 years! I've had a very blessed life – from being born to a mother and father who loved me unconditionally, to building life-long friendships based on trust and mutual respect, to marrying a man who challenges me to be the best version of myself and raising two incredible boys together.

Then there are the opportunities I've had to see the diverse beauty and people of our world – living in Brazil for 11 years, Chile for 1 year, and many trips to Europe and across North America. Finally, my work experiences have allowed me to create, learn, make connections with people, and help make the world a better place.

My gratitude for all of this goes first to God, who has blessed me with more than I deserve, while carrying me through the darkest of times. Things I'm most proud of: raising two happy healthy brilliant boys; reconciling with my husband after a 5-year separation; speaking a second language fluently (Portuguese); and creating a business out of nothing while making a positive impact in the world.

What I'll leave behind: an example of loving others unconditionally, never giving up on your dreams and deepest desires, and connecting people for the purpose of making the world a happier place. Every chance I get, when I meet someone new, I look for others to connect them with, to help both get closer to reaching their personal and/or business goals.

I also look for the win-win in every situation. I believe that everyone deserves a second chance. We are all born with pure hearts, but the losses and traumas of life can derail us. This philosophy is what drew me to serve for two years on the board of a not-for-profit that uses the restorative justice process to bring healing to both victims and offenders in situations of crime and conflict. I often see those who have committed a crime as the first victim because 'hurt people, hurt people'. But if given the right love and support, most will feel remorse for the harm they caused and take steps toward turning their life around. I'm a person of faith and I believe that, even when we feel completely alone or abandoned, God is there. He loves us deeply and wants to see us achieve true happiness and peace. He's always there to help us on this journey if we let Him. When I faced the most difficult crisis in my life – a broken marriage and family – I learned to trust in His timing, not mine. So, when times get tough, believe your Higher Power is working for your good, and love unconditionally.

Show Up Stand Up Speak Up

Translation expert, language-accessibility advocate, and community builder

From a very young age, I've been fascinated with languages. I studied French, Spanish, and Italian throughout my school years and later lived in Chile to become fluent in Spanish. Upon returning home, it made total sense when I fell for a Brazilian, got married, and raised our two boys in a two-language home for the past 20 years.

My first career – fundraising and marketing for charities – was born out of my passion for making a difference in the world. I learned to give back watching my mother volunteer at soup kitchens, our schools, church, and community. While living in Brazil for 11 years, I embarked on a second career – translation. My love for editing and for language made this the perfect match. Returning to Vancouver, I was inspired to marry my multiple passions for wellness, language, and making a difference.

I launched my business, Arvorei Communications Group, to support impact-driven businesses – particularly those dedicated to the well-being of people and the planet – to reach new language audiences at home and abroad. I love supporting businesses trying to make a positive impact in the world – those with products and services that improve people's lives and those that take a person-first approach to doing business. I want to help them do even more good by removing language barriers for customers and employees.

My own mission to do good centers around supporting freelance translators across the globe. This industry can be very transactional and isolating, so I built a community of purpose-driven translators who meet monthly for business development talks and networking. The name 'arvorei' comes from the Portuguese word for 'tree'. But, as a verb, arvorei represents how we connect with people across cultures through language, much like trees connect and support each other through their branches and root systems.

https://www.linkedin.com/in/kimberlyjacob/

305

BELIEVE LOVE

LINDA NASU

My Message to Women is ...

Life is short and time passes quickly.
Remember to squeeze the juice out of life.
No regrets.

Show Up Stand Up Speak Up

SQUEEZE JUICE

My Story

ELIZABETH MANUEL

Although I love being on stage and out in the world, teaching and sharing the tremendous value of genuine sustainable happiness, at home, I enjoy a quiet meditative space. While I savor silence, I also value music! I have curated many playlists, with the deliberate intention of lifting my energy or vibration. I call them happiness inducing playlists and often sing out while doing the dishes!

If there is water, I will be in it! Swimming for me is a visceral response of joy and freedom, especially in deep lakes or oceans. For me it feels like being in the womb of mother earth, quiet and dark. Caveat* as long as I have my safety boat/board person beside me! For some reason, feeling vulnerable about becoming chopped up fish bait by the propellers of a speeding motorboat is not conducive to my peace of mind.

The library has been my best friend since I was a young child (especially as an introvert). I am an avid and voracious reader, both fiction and non-fiction. My friends all poke fun at me because I travel with at least five books in my suitcase... I like the feel of a physical book! I consider myself a life-long learner.

Feeling vulnerable after being assaulted. I spent a challenging and life affirming six years in my thirties dedicated to getting a black belt in Tae Kwon Do, while being a single parent. I gained a lot of inner strength and confidence as a result. In my forties I was drawn to explore the benefits of yoga, becoming a certified teacher, and going within to find peace of mind.

I am nourished by nature. In the summer you will find me in my flower gardens, along with my whimsical collection of garden frogs in yoga poses, and wonderful fence art! I'll let you in on my dirty secret: I feel nourished by the dirt on my bare hands and feet! Digging into earth and soil is primitive and soothing (the earth's magnetic energy is grounding and energizing for our saltwater bodies).

On pleasant days you will notice me pedal by on my spiffy green, seven gear, upright comfort bike, with my cute woven basket (with a huge smile on my face)! I enjoy all the river valley vista's and exploring my city's wonderful bike paths.

My beautiful dog takes me out for my daily walk, no matter the weather! I assign high priority to copious amounts of quality time with my husband, daughter and son in law, sharing meals and making memories. Choosing to make every precious day count!

Show Up Stand Up Speak Up

A low genetic set point for happiness, and series of unfortunate events led me to a fateful battle with my brain! Like the movie the Matrix I had to choose what would be my reality. Take the "blue pill" and live in depression or take the "red pill" and cultivate genuine happiness. I chose the red pill—to become my own happiness heroine.

I am devoted to educating others about the remarkable positive impact happiness has, both individually and collectively. Genuine happiness gives us a better narrative for our lives. Genuine happiness is not the outcome of achieving milestones or completing tasks. It's also not the result of acquiring things such as million-dollar homes, fancy cars, award winning dogs, lazy-boy furniture, or new socially approved hairstyles. Happiness is especially not automatically found by being "successful." Many of my clients are extremely wealthy by all external measures and they come to me because happiness eludes them.

As a Grief Therapist and happiness expert, I observe first-hand the reality that mood disorders like depression, anxiety, stress and unresolved grief are at an all-time high. And women are twice as likely as men to experience detrimental mental health issues, and chew on antidepressants and sleeping aids like gummy bears. This is why I teach my clients how to grow a happier brain. I bring them to a place where they find inner peace, hope and optimism for their future. I help them develop an infinite inner power source for resilience and well-being. And we are so interconnected in this world that attending to our own well-being has a ripple effect far beyond what we might believe.

I'm Elizabeth Manuel your guide to the science of happiness and I would love to connect and find out more about you and your happiness journey!
elizabeth@elizabethmanuel.com

LIVE HAPPY

My Story

CHRISTINA SOMMERS

Have you ever experienced a time when you woke up suddenly one day and wondered things like, "How did I get here?" and "Is this all there is to life?" Realizing you weren't living life; you were merely surviving each day.

I realized this was my story when I woke up one morning dreading going downstairs because I didn't know what I would find. Would my husband be there? If he was, would he be alive, and what kind of shape would he be in? At this time, I had the realization that God did not allow me to survive the head-on-collision I was involved in to live every day in hell.

In 2016, I was in a head-on collision that changed my life forever. About a year into the healing journey, I felt God impress upon my heart that I needed to share my story and that He was using my pain for His purpose. He would work all things out for the good of those who love Him. I was shocked at this idea; I wasn't a writer and thought that was the only way to share my story at the time.

Before I had a chance even to consider how this would work, my marriage became very volatile. I was doing all the things a good Christian wife should do. But the more I tried to make it work, the more I prayed, the more I tried to set boundaries, and the more things I tried, the worse the situation became. Finally, one day, I collapsed to my knees in tears, crying to God, "Why wouldn't He fix this? Why wouldn't He take the addiction from my husband? Why wouldn't He heal our marriage?" I knew He could, so why wasn't He? I heard in the depths of my spirit, "Yes, I can heal him, but I won't force him; it has to be his choice." This event was the first of the three signs I received, and it became undeniably clear it was time to start taking my life back.

When I finally got the courage to file for separation, I thought I would have the peace and joy I longed for as soon as he left. Surprise, that is not what happened. What happened instead, and I think honestly, is even better; it started me on my current journey. My discovery journey in finding who I am, my authentic self. It is a journey in finding holistic healing modalities including meditation, journaling, EFT tapping (Emotional Freedom Technique), movement, and, my favorite, Breathwork. There are so many more to explore. Each practice has a space and place; each person and circumstance is different, so that each tool will work differently at various times. Not only have I found the peace and joy I so longed for, but I can honestly say that I am Loving My Life Again.

Show Up Stand Up Speak Up

It became undeniably clear when God initially called me to share my story that it would involve the car accident, but that was not the focus as I initially thought. The main focus was to be what came next: the demise of my marriage and myself. He was calling me to share so much more; the car accident, though significant, was just a piece of the bigger picture. My calling is to help women in toxic marriages realize that is what it is and that there is nothing wrong with her. Walking with her while deciding, "What's the next best step?" No matter the decision, we will first start taking her life back by finding her authentic self and walking in it. This is a journey of transforming trauma into peace and joy. It is my passion that no one stays stuck. The healing process can be lonely, so I am creating a safe community space where you know you are not alone and are loved and supported just as you are. I am passionate about sharing the tools available, how to utilize them, how to become aware, and what to do once you become aware. I do this through my Podcast, "Loving Your Life Again," through Coaching and Breathwork, helping build a toolbox of resources, and being available for conversation and holding space.

The sharing of my story is using my story and the experiences I encountered and what I have done since; it is becoming a Coach and Breathwork Facilitator, and who knows what's coming next. I am here to support you while you work through whatever needs to be worked through or in whatever way you feel best supported. I will give tough love and tools that feel good. You have all the answers inside you; I can help you uncover them. https://reloadinchrist.com/

BREATHE DEEPLY

ANTJE SWART

My Message To Women is ...

Make your mind your best friend.
Me, myself, and I, always there when we need each other.

Show Up Stand Up Speak Up

GO FLY

My Story

CHRISTINE VON PANDER

It is with special thanks to Kelsey Carter, that I learned the following about myself, and my purpose for being. I am forever grateful.

When I started learning about Human Design and how learning about yourself using Human Design, could help you see your purpose and path more clearly than any other modality, it was like I was in a hot air balloon with all the weights being dropped in succession. Feeling lighter and lighter for each point found, and explored. At first it was overwhelming, there was sooooo much information. Then, as I started chunking away at it, more and more pieces of me, my life and my purpose made sense.

I am here to be a specific type of Entrepreneur. An entrepreneur who spreads inspiration and transformation like wildfire. A conduit of concepts and ideas that captivate the interest of everyone I encounter. My commitment to contributing to humanity's betterment is a driving force. Envisioning how my passion and enthusiasm for what moves me resonates with others, even if I'm not always aware of the profound impact I'm making.

When I see myself as a beacon of light, radiating trust, prosperity, and co-creation to those who share my ideals, it's easy to inspire others to pay attention to the valuable assets and opportunities that align with my vision. I can feel delight and excitement, as I pass on the flame of enthusiasm, igniting the passions of those who connect with me. Imagine a world where cooperation and collaboration are second nature. Envision individuals eagerly embracing my suggestions and contributing their insights to enhance our collective endeavours. Feeling the joy of setting an example that encourages others to rise above societal norms and embrace extraordinary possibilities. Making an impact as an entrepreneur who brings out the best in those around me.

I see businesses flourishing, individuals realizing their potential, and communities thriving because of my infectious enthusiasm and transformative influence. Every endeavour leads to opportunities that exceed our expectations. Feel the energy of passion and purpose flowing through my veins, fueling my dedication to this entrepreneurial path.

I let my authority guide me in forging meaningful connections and collaborations. Allowing myself to fully embrace my role as a torchbearer, spreading inspiration, prosperity, and transformation wherever I go. My future is aligning already. This journey is awe-inspiring, and my ability to ignite change is unparalleled. I promise to embrace each day with the same fervor and excitement that I use to inspire others. My calling is a gift to the world, and my journey as an entrepreneur will be an extraordinary adventure filled with growth, success, and fulfillment.

Show Up Stand Up Speak Up

I am a self-professed Shoe addict! And NO, I'm not looking for a cure. I love shoes. Specifically, I love how I feel when I am wearing a wonderful outfit, and my shoes are different and fun and level up the outfit.

There is something that happens when I put on a pair of shoes, I feel literally and figuratively uplifted. Polished and professional, elegant, and feminine. I love to embrace my feminine side and find occasions to dress up as often as possible. To that end I have a large group of amazing friends who know this about me, and make sure to invite me to anything that comes across their desk. I am forever grateful for these people. That is my playtime, my time to shine.

I look forward to meeting you someday at an event, hearing your story and enjoying time and space with you. https://www.linkedin.com/in/christinevonpander/

BE PRESENT

My Story

REBECCA HARRISON

Ways to Love Me ~

sit quietly to remind me that nothing else is required
no busy-ness
no cooking
no washing of socks or dishes
no repairing of hearts
or calming others stray and wild thoughts
no convincing
no soothing
holding all together
(though these are done with whole heart and tender hands)
only sit quietly
and breathe
and listen
to blood pulsing
breath sighing
and remember that this is enough
no more is required.

Show Up Stand Up Speak Up

A mom to two artistic young people, a best-selling author, world traveller and a soon-to-be executive coach.

My love for sharing stories started as a child and continued in University Theatre when I got my BFA and was writing and performing one woman shows.

I love to be creative, and my latest creations include my Family Tree book series, a children's book, and a screenplay in the works. I've been blessed to see many places in the world and my ultimate dream is to travel and write!

Because of a major life transition, I'm back in school and currently loving the Graduate Certificate Program in Executive Coaching at Royal Roads University. I am authentically fascinated by people and my SuperPower is connection.

I would love to learn more about you! If you are inspired to connect, you can find me at redheadrebecca@telus.net

SHARE STORIES

JACKIE MERCER

My Message to Women is ...

Don't let yourself be limited by other people's limited imaginations.

Show Up Stand Up Speak Up

STAY HOPEFUL

My Story

MAGGIE AHEARNE

My name is Maggie Ahearne, living in the charming city of Kilkenny, Ireland. As a true Aries, I embody the fiery spirit and unwavering passion for the things close to my heart. Fueled by the prospect of travel, I find immense joy in meticulously planning our next family adventure. With my children's adventurous spirits, each journey is an exhilarating quest for the next thrill.

Engaging with my local community invigorates me, and I eagerly lend my time and expertise to volunteer in areas where I can make a tangible impact. Finding solace and rejuvenation in mindfulness practices like meditation and yoga, along with indulging in a luxurious spa day, is my ultimate self-care ritual.

Yet, amidst the hustle and bustle of life, I harbor a dream of tranquility—a quaint cottage nestled along the rugged coastline of County Waterford, Ireland. There, I envision myself gazing out at the majestic waves, cradling a steaming cup of coffee, engrossed in a captivating book, all while a crackling fire warms the room. It's a vision of serenity and bliss that beckons me with its promise of quietude and natural beauty.

Show Up Stand Up Speak Up

After two decades in the corporate world, I found myself increasingly disheartened by the number of talented women and mothers forced to shelve their career aspirations to prioritize family responsibilities. It became evident to me that there's a pressing need for change in our approach to work-life balance and inclusivity. That's why I'm deeply committed to supporting organizations that recognize the value of fostering a more inclusive workplace culture. I advocate for flexibility in all its forms—whether it's remote work options, part-time schedules, or the implementation of a condensed workweek. No woman should feel compelled to sacrifice her career ambitions due to factors like embarking on a fertility journey, raising young children, caring for elderly parents, or simply preferring to avoid the confines of a traditional 40-hour office week. Furthermore, I champion female entrepreneurs by providing them with affordable, visually stunning, and highly functional websites tailored to their unique business needs. These websites not only streamline their operations but also authentically reflect their personality and brand identity. By empowering women to thrive in both their professional and personal pursuits, I aim to contribute to a more equitable and inclusive society.

I run a consultancy which specialises in providing expert guidance and support in the areas of web design, product management, remote working, and mentorship. I work with businesses and organisations of all sizes to help them achieve their goals and succeed in today's competitive marketplace. I'm eager to connect with fellow women who share my drive to empower others and create opportunities for all women to achieve their goals and live authentically. Please feel free to reach out to me at info@distributedproduct.com . Let's inspire and support each other on this journey towards fulfillment and success!

TRUST YOURSELF

My Story

GISELLE & GISSALA FU

They say good things come in twos, so here we are. Two little nuggets that grew up in a small city in the middle of Canada with big dreams and ambitious goals.

In 2014 we established ourselves in the Vancouver queer community with a desire to bring movement to the culture. So, aim for stars, we are ready for takeoff.

Show Up Stand Up Speak Up

Music has always been a natural yet significant part of our lives for as long as we can remember. If you ask us what kind of music we listened to in a specific period of our lives, we'd be able to tell you, song titles, artists, genres, and how it made us feel at the time.

Music was always there to guide us through the waves of our journey. Over the years, we've had the honour to bring happiness to so many people through the frequencies and melodies. In turn, It has brought us a vast amount of fulfillment.

Contact: Stay tuned with us Giselleandgissala@gmail.com

I CAN

My Story

SHAE LAMBA

As a woman who owns and operates a business in a traditionally male dominated industry, I have made it my personal mission to empower and uplift other women.

I find joy in supporting others, especially women and underrepresented groups whilst prioritizing diversity. This is my way of fostering a more inclusive community, where there are equal opportunities for everyone to have the chance to rise up in a supportive environment.

Show Up Stand Up Speak Up

Being a bar/business owner fuels my resiliency and determination in the face of setbacks and failures. Refusing to be discouraged by obstacles, setbacks, or naysayers, I draw strength from my passion to persevere and ultimately achieve my goals to build a successful business, as well as make a meaningful impact in the world.

I see adversities as opportunities for growth and innovation. My curious nature pushes me to think outside of the box, to experiment with new ideas, and seek creative solutions that influence positive changes to the hospitality industry.
l.shae@biminispub.ca

REACH BEYOND

My Story

ALLA KORNILOV

I find immense joy in life's simple pleasures, like sharing weekend morning coffee with my husband, Robin, and relishing in our conversations. My friends are my treasure, adding richness and warmth to my life through heartfelt conversations over coffee, lively gatherings, or spontaneous adventures. Nature is my sanctuary, whether I'm taking long walks on the beach or enjoying leisurely strolls in the park. Recently, I've discovered a newfound passion for painting, attending oil classes to express my creativity on canvas.

Family is at the core of my existence, and I cherish moments with my 89-year-old mother who inspires me with her resilience and positive outlook on life. I also share a special bond with my son, a talented chef, filled with sarcastic humor and delicious meals. My granddaughter, Mila, brings me immense pride and joy with every moment we spend together as she grows. Traveling with my husband is an adventure we both cherish, fostering humility and wonder as we explore new cultures.

Together with my friends and family we navigate life's journey, sharing experiences, dreams, and aspirations with love and an adventurous spirit.

Show Up Stand Up Speak Up

I've been on a beautiful journey as a makeup artist in Vancouver for over 25 years now. Picture this: lights, camera, action—I've worked my magic behind the scenes of your favorite TV shows like "The Good Doctor", "X-Files", "Battlestar Galactica", "Million Little Things", " Magicians", "The Man in the High Castle", "Untold Stories of the E.R.", "Supernatural", and contributed to blockbuster films like "Night at the Museum", "Godzilla", and "Man Of Steel".

But beyond the glitz and glamour, what truly lights up my world is the people with whom I get to work. From local talents to international stars, each face tells a story, and I'm honored to be a part of their narrative.

You might have caught glimpses of my work in People magazine or felt the inspiration from my makeup tips in Vancouver magazine. And let's not forget about the brides I've helped feel like queens on their special day—there's something magical about being a part of those moments.
Let me share a little secret with you: I believe makeup is more than just colors and brushes; it's about confidence, self-expression, and embracing your unique beauty. That's why I poured my heart and soul into creating "Secrets Of Makeup," a seminar where I spill all the celebrity secrets to help you feel like the best version of yourself, inside and out.

So, whether you're walking down the red carpet or strolling through everyday life, remember this: makeup is your ally, not your mask. Let's empower each other through beauty and celebrate what makes you, you. alla_kornilov@hotmail.com

LOVE YOURSELF

My Story

DR. THERESA ASHBY

The family has been a constant in my life! They make me laugh and encourage me to go after my dreams. The nieces and nephews see life with such fresh eyes that it reminds me not to let barriers get in the way of going after my dreams. Plus, there is nothing like spending time with friends, enjoying the storytelling and the sharing.

I can remember when I was younger, I loved to build things. I built a super-cool treehouse! It wasn't exactly up in the tree, rather more around the tree and on the ground. After all, I was only ten at the time. I just wanted a place to hide so I could read and create. To this day, I love reading. I devour the content of a new book every week.

I built my favorite thing when I was 12—a lectern. I am sure this is where I got my appetite for speaking from the stage. Of course, I had my two younger sisters and stuffed animals as my captive audience. I still enjoy sharing my experiences with audiences across the US.

Aww, and I love to travel. There is nothing like visiting different countries and learning about other people's perspectives—in fact, I have had the privilege of setting foot on six of the seven continents—Australia, here I come. Along with traveling, I love to jet ski, ride ATVs, and golf at home and while away. I'm a bit of an adrenaline junkie.

One of my early career experiences was as a volunteer and seasonal firefighter. I haven't exactly followed a direct career path. At one point, I was hired to be a part of the Helitack Crew—we were transported by helicopter to fight wildfires up and down the state of California.

During my service, I went on an emergency call, and we transported a patient to the emergency room. I stood in the lobby in my full turnout gear and felt this tugging on my pant leg. I looked down, and there was a little girl, about seven years old. When I said hello to her, she looked up at me with these big, brown, innocent eyes and asked, "Are you a girl?" I must have smiled from ear to ear when I said, "Yes."

She giggled and bashfully whispered, "I didn't know girls could be firefighters."
Of course, I was delighted and explained, "Girls can be anything they want to be."

Show Up Stand Up Speak Up

I enjoy spending my time helping people build a scalable business model that allows them to have the freedom to do the things they love. I seek to be a conduit for others, helping them build a business that generates significant revenue and allows them to create the lifestyle they deserve.

During my tenure as an executive, leading operations and multi-million-dollar projects, I focused on helping others be successful in their roles, driving business strategy, and maintaining fiscal accountability. I have always been able to see an organization's big picture and then put the operations into practice–that is why I am known as the "Stratologist." I have consulted companies from Fortune 500 to start-ups. I like meeting new people and listening to them share their life stories, business goals, and personal aspirations. I enjoy motivating and inspiring others through speaking, consulting, and coaching. I thrive when I can help others discover new concepts and methods of doing business and then help them figure out how to create great solutions. Ultimately, I love helping others succeed and create something unique.

Kaleidoscope Media Services is a full-service agency with a culture of service and gratitude. We help companies deliver an extraordinary client experience, leverage their intellectual capital, generate additional income, plus show clients how to use digital products for scalability and sustainability. In addition, we help our clients systematize and automate their business through our KMS Powered technology, helping eliminate the overwhelm, get time back in the day, and build a lifestyle business. Our agency supports our client's projects through the values of exceptional vision, innovation, creativity, and expertise. If you would like, let's grab a virtual coffee. Theresa@Kaleidoscopemediaservices.com

329

DO YOU

JODY MALEY

My Message To Women is ...

Authentic conversations lead to 'light-bulb' moments.
It's in those moments our vision is ignited,
our futures lifted, our dreams affirmed.

Show Up Stand Up Speak Up

SPEAK AUTHENTICALLY

My Story

MICHELLE JEWSBURY

When I was a young girl, I collected caterpillars in glass mason jars. Some of my caterpillars began to hang upside down from their twigs and spin cocoons, disappearing within their silk casings. I loved watching the process of metamorphosis. I'd run outside on our deck and open the tops of the mason jars to see the orange and black Monarchs fly into the blue sky. To see caterpillars transition to butterflies amazed me. It taught me to realize how resilient humans can be.

My daddy, a cheerful and hardworking man, served in the US Army for over 30 years. Our family moved many times during his enlistment, living in cities across Hawaii, Vermont, and Idaho. I attended roughly 7 schools during my childhood and learned very quickly how to make friends and stand out in a crowd. In Hawaii, I was a varsity cheerleader and then graduated High School in Idaho with Double Honors. Although I excelled in school, I never liked being forced to wake up at the crack of dawn, attend classes full of maddening students, and learn subjects that had nothing to do with how to live a successful life in the real world. So, I decided to move to Hollywood, CA and become a movie star instead of finishing college, thinking that was my way to success.

My dream of stardom was short lived when I met someone I fell in love with. Paul was a dreamy man with a gigantic vision for life and a work ethic to match. He reminded me daily, "you are the most beautiful woman I've ever known." He pursued me vigorously, sending me flowers and taking me to baseball games and concerts. Shortly after we began dating, I moved in with him 3 hours away from my friends and congregation.

In December 2012, Paul and I went to a New Year's party at a local hotel. About 2 hours into the evening, Paul said, "we are leaving now." I protested while walking with him outside the venue, then he turned, grabbed me by my throat, lifted me to the sky and slammed me down against a cement bench. Luckily, there were many people around to witness, and the police were immediately called. This was not the first or the last time violence happened in our relationship. I finally escaped in 2015.

Once I was away from his clutches, I began to reshape my life from being a victim to being a victor. In 2016, I wrote and performed a 65-min solo play about my involvement in domestic violence, in 2017 I started Unsilenced Voices, and in 2019 I published my first book entitled But I Love Him and began speaking and coaching worldwide. I choose to be resilient and continue listening to God's quiet voice leading me and allowing Him to transform my story for His glory.

Show Up Stand Up Speak Up

I believe abuse, trafficking, systemic racism, poverty, and other traumas will come to an end when we use our voices and tell our stories. Michelle Jewsbury Speaks, LLC. offers courses, speaking platforms, book collaborations and personalized coaching to assist survivors in speaking up and spreading their messages of hope and resiliency. I live by a bible verse from Ephesians 4:29, "Do not let any unwholesome talk come out of your mouths, but only what is helpful for building others up according to their needs, that it may benefit those who listen." Your story will always benefit people who listen.

We help clients get the exposure they desire, so that they can change the world. For more information about programs visit www.MichelleJewsbury.com

Through the nonprofit Unsilenced Voices, we work with over 1,500 people between 2 villages and a handful of brothels throughout Sierra Leone and have transformed thousands of lives through education and services. In 2022, we gifted $33,000 to survivors in the USA to use for rehabilitation, transportation, and childcare needs. In 2023, we traveled to Sierra Leone and built a cassava processing facility with The Fixers on BYU, to provide our communities with an economic vehicle for sustainability. Also in 2023, we published our curriculum, Graced for Prosperity, which leads participants through a journey of faith, finance, purpose, and success. Unsilenced Voices has worked in Ghana, Rwanda, Sierra Leone, and the USA. Our goal is to continue providing resources around the globe to end domestic violence, sexual abuse, and human trafficking. In the USA, we plan to build a day center with wrap around services aiding abuse survivors.

Globally we hope to bring even more awareness to these injustices through collaboration and co-creation with other countries, organizations, and people. For more information about Unsilenced Voices visit www.UnsilencedVoices.org

333

KEEP SWIMMING

My Story

JANE VANDERMEER

I knew that it was time to stop. I was exhausted. I felt like a salmon swimming upstream. The eternal optimist that I am, knew that it was time to take myself out of the equation. The empath in me forever wants to help. Finally, I realised that I needed to put myself first. So, I resigned from a well-paying job towards a future unknown. I knew that I needed some time off. The neck pain was constant. Two separate cancer scares, adrenal fatigue, unable to move my neck properly, and continual severe migraines finally floored me. I had a severely bulged disc in my lower back. I could barely walk. Even as I write this, it seems so obvious, but at the time, when I was in the situation, I was clouded in pain. Feeling the 'should' but not the 'stop' button was an unhelpful pattern I created.

The burn out of adrenal fatigue was looming. Yet the thing that broke the camel's back, so to speak, wasn't the health scares, or the peer bullying that comes with the fashion industry, but the client that pushed me to my edge. No matter how hard we tried, nothing made him happy. There was no time or space to reflect. The pressure never let up. So, I took myself out of the situation. I remember thinking a week or two of rest should do the trick. How wrong I was. My phone stayed on silent for 4 four months. I screened every single call. However, this epiphany was life- changing. I couldn't be more grateful for that time in my life.

A result of remaining within this state of 'doing' or continually stretched beyond okay, we defer our emotions. We ignore our red flags. We know it's harmful, but we push ahead anyway. We keep going. We keep pushing. I had the opportunity to listen to the 'whispers of my intuition'.

My body was screaming, "This is enough, and you need a break. You need to 'be' for a while. You need to heal". This unravelling gave me the time and space to 'unlearn' old behaviours. I did default back to workaholic behaviour. That is what we are taught to do isn't it? Work hard until we drop. To be honest, I didn't have many answers about moving forward. I questioned if there could be a different way to function, but I had no idea how. It was incredibly uncomfortable not having all the answers. However, it's in these moments that we create the space to allow the answers to surface.

I think that we are given the guidance we need at the time we need. We are given little drops of clarity. Usually not the whole picture, but moments of unique insight. At the time, I wanted answers, and reassurance to focus my energy.

Now my adrenals are happy, and no more cancer cells in sight. The stress in my life is viewed very differently, and that applies to my business- life too. Life is now magnificent.

Show Up Stand Up Speak Up

I am a highly respected trailblazer in the realm of personal style, renowned for my exceptional expertise and profound understanding of the "language of fashion" on an international scale. With qualifications in various facets of the fashion industry, including design, textiles, buying, consulting, and education, I have emerged as a leading authority in the field, earning admiration from industry professionals worldwide. My unparalleled insights into human behaviour and fashion have solidified my position as an influential figure in the industry. My remarkable ability to decode a person's character through their clothing choices enables me to provide tailored solutions that address the specific needs and aspirations of my clients. My influential presence extends beyond personal style, as I have been featured as one of the "10 Women Business Leaders to Watch Out for in 2023." "Best International Stylist of the Year 2023" and "Most trusted International Personal Stylist of 2023".

Clothing goes beyond superficiality. I emphasise that they serve as a powerful external manifestation of one's self-image, personal history, aspirations, and even limiting self-beliefs. Leveraging my extensive knowledge and experience, I inspire and empower individuals worldwide to embrace their personal style, utilising fashion as a transformative tool for creating authentic and confident self-presentations. As the visionary founder of Finesse Your Style, I have witnessed firsthand the transformative power of personal styling on a global scale. Providing tailored solutions to help them effectively communicate their message through their personal style, regardless of the international setting. Embarking on a style journey with me and Finesse Your Style means accessing the unparalleled expertise of an internationally renowned personal style specialist. Through my guidance, clients unlock the true potential of their personal style, self-discovery, empowerment, and professional growth. style@finesseyourstyle.com

335

BE MAGNIFICENT

My Story

ART FOR RESCUE

It's not often you come across something that resonates so strongly that you have an overwhelming desire to be a part of it. And when I heard about Destiny Rescue in 2020, I knew that I needed to find a way to not only support them, but to affect true and authentic change.

I was introduced to Destiny through a customer. They purchased one of my original paintings and immediately donated it to a charity fundraising auction. This act of selflessness inspired me greatly, so I needed to find out more. So, I bought a ticket to the auction, and immediately became a passionate advocate.

Destiny Rescue is a heart-led, soul driven Australian based charity with a global influence. They exist to eradicate sexual exploitation and sex trafficking of children globally, fuelled by a desire to end suffering, bringing joy and hope into the lives of those who have so terribly had it taken away from them. For anyone who has been through any situation that results in your power forcibly being taken from you, the impact is devastating. Your soul feels it. Deeply. Not just your body or mind. And no one, ever, deserves this way of living.

Fast forward to 2023, I am 51 years old, living on the Gold Coast, Australia finding myself sitting cross legged on my art studio floor, staring at my canvas, wondering how I can do more. So, I created the Art for Rescue movement, an authorised fundraiser for Destiny Rescue, that uses art and creativity to raise awareness and funds to support Destiny Rescue's mission.

At the heart of all our projects is the sharing of stories. Stories from rescued children. Stories of people who dedicate their life to changing other people's lives. Stories of people who have triumphed over adversity. And every story shared becomes the inspiration for a painting. Art speaks to people. Art creates change. We feel something when we view it. So, I am using this visual and visceral voice to create a point of connection for all communities to come together, to say enough is enough.

We will have the tough conversations. We will stand tall for those who have been unable, who deserve their journeys to be told. We will collectively create social and cultural change so children may live free, and with hope.
Join me. Today.

Show Up Stand Up Speak Up

I didn't think I would ever need to ask the question…how much is a person's life worth? And how do we value it? Is it a money thing? Is it an influence thing? Is it simply an energy exchange? I mean, my whole life I have always valued and respected those around me, and most certainly placed a significant value in being alive. And I have wanted to show others just how valuable they are. Yet, for some people this question, their lives, is literally valued based on a transaction.

"A raid by Destiny Rescue in South Asia rescues 36 people, including 29 children from an illegal brother where children were kept locked away. While a few were being sold for sex, most were being used as hostages to force their mothers into sex trafficking". Their value? Only as much as their captives deemed it to be. I have always been creative, driven and passionate. And it became extraordinarily clear to me that creating Art for Rescue means creating a way to bring value back to others. To use colour and creativity as the global voice to achieve this.

It takes $2000 (AUD) to rescue a person.
It takes $10,000 (AUD) to fund a raid to rescue multiple people at once.
It takes one person, then another, then another to decide to act. And act now. Just as I did.
I celebrate life. Art for Rescue is a way to celebrate the triumph, the hope, the joy that can be present on the other side of trauma. Paintings inspired by stories. Interviews sharing people's journey. Books celebrating strength and resilience.
Let's connect and chat! About you, about life, about creating a new beginning for someone. I'd love to. rescue@tracieeaton.com

INSPIRE CHANGE

MARIYA OKTYABRSKAYA
Tank Driver

SHAJARAT AL-DURR
Sultana

IDA PFEIFFER

Explorer

HANNAH SZENES

Paratrooper

LISA WILBER

I love surrounding myself with the things I love whether that be books, cats & dogs, friends, experiences and especially music.

Meeting new people, traveling, and experiencing new things is what I live for, and it gives me inspiration for all that I do.

I have gladly worn many hats in my personal and professional life. Personally, I'm a Mom, a daughter, a friend and a lover. Professionally I'm an entrepreneur, community play producer, social media digital creator, author, speaker, and I've even been a political candidate.

My interests are varied and continue to grow and expand.
I'm excited for each day and all that it brings.

Show Up Stand Up Speak Up

THE LADY WITH THE BLUE HAIR

If I had to pick a theme that is woven throughout my life, it would be that of personal responsibility. I teach it and I try my best to live it. I truly believe that every person should be fully prepared to accept full responsibility for themselves; financially and emotionally. I have too often seen friends and colleagues experience devastation, especially financially, after losing a spouse. It has become my mission to help people focus on preparing themselves for the fact that by the law of averages, every person will need to support themselves fully at some point in their lives.

As I recently turned 60, I was inspired to do something radically different. As it turned out, going "blue" ended up being my thing. I dyed my hair blue for the first time in 2021. I had never dyed my hair any color other than my natural color before that. It has been life changing! What started as a radical experiment, turned into a mission. A mission of saying yes more. A mission of helping more people take personal responsibility, especially financially. A mission of being authentic and helping others find their authentic self. A mission to simply BE. I'd love to continue the conversation with you and connect! If you feel inspired to reach out, you can contact me via text at 1.603.345.9466

TAKE RESPONSIBILITY

KATIE CHIN

My Message to Women is ...

Leap and the net will appear.

Show Up Stand Up Speak Up

DO IT

My Story

MARY WANDERI

I am Mary Wanderi, everyone calls me Mum as I am a mother to many! I love a good hearty laugh. The laugh is surrounded by REAL people, people who are happy, not because their lives are the best, but happy because they have realized that happiness is a GIFT that only they can give themselves. Only I can gift myself happiness.

A big laugh and a smile can reach people with what is inside me, because in life you can only give what is inside you. People may feel more confident when you approach them with a happy YOU that encourages them and eases them, making them comfortable around you.

Happiness exists when you search deep inside you and you tap into that happy corner, it eases the difficult situations you are going through. In life I have met so many people that have embraced happiness. I have supported many people who are on their deathbed, sick with HIV/Aids, Pneumonia, cancer, and many other things, and they are able to still have a smile on their face, they are able to face life's difficulties better.

Happiness is a choice. It is not about our external situations, it's a choice to not allow difficult things like poverty, and illness to take us down. It's about having resiliency. If you can choose to be happy during a difficult situation then you are very strong. It says a lot about people. It eases people, it makes people feel comfortable around you and it encourages them. For mums even in the hardest situation if they become so sad, they leave their children sad and if they can stay positive and happy they leave their children with that happiness.

I want to encourage people to fill their hearts with happiness so they have something to give. We cannot give from an empty plate. If we fill our plates then we can give from the overflow.

Show Up Stand Up Speak Up

Emerging from the destitution of the Kenyan slums, I navigated a challenging upbringing as one of eight children raised by a single mother entrenched in extreme poverty. The daily struggle for sustenance, witnessing pervasive poverty, and enduring days without food fueled a profound desire for change within me. Amidst the hardships, the intervention of compassionate social workers served as beacons of hope in my community. Their efforts to provide food, rescue children from abuse, and facilitate access to education inspired me to rise above my circumstances. Motivated by their angelic presence, I dedicated myself to academic excellence, securing scholarships that paved the way for higher education. My aspiration was clear – to become a social worker and contribute to the welfare of others. Embarking on my career, I specialized in children's social work, involving myself in orphanages, children's homes, and scholarship projects. An impactful realization occurred during visits to homes where mothers, afflicted by HIV/AIDS, faced the prospect of separation from their children. Moved by compassion, I initiated a holistic approach, providing food, medication, and emotional support to these mothers. Recognizing the potential for empowerment, I established a soup kitchen, gradually expanding to teach entrepreneurial skills.

The fruition of these efforts led to the creation of Living Positive 16 years ago. Centered around supporting individuals diagnosed with HIV/AIDS, the organization encompasses a Women's Economic Empowerment Program, Salama School in the slums, a community farm overseen by women, and a Psycho-social support group. Through the WEEP program, education initiatives, and sustainable farming, Living Positive has positively impacted over 1000 families, providing housing, ensuring children's safety and education, facilitating healthcare, fostering entrepreneurship, and distributing food. To further understand, contribute, or visit Living Positive in Kenya, please visit :
https://www.livingpositivekenya.or.ke/

345

BE HAPPY

My Story

RACHELLE ELIZABETH

It was Christmas Day 2020, when my entire life changed. I was taking a walk in the snow, when I was overwhelmed by the calling of a word, like a siren singing from the abyss, "Live". It was like a tidal wave had crashed into my subconscious mind. As I continued walking, I was elated with the visions and possibilities of what I could do with my life.

At the time I was making a living working for a corporate company. I made great money. I was on the rise amongst my peers, and my superiors were expecting big things from me. But everything changed with the pandemic. It was during those first months of lockdown, I came to the undeniable conclusion that the life I had been building towards, the top floor corner office, the power suits, a salaried lifestyle, would no longer come to fruition. However, this conclusion was simply the tip of the iceberg for where my mind went next.

I began asking myself, where did the vision for that particular future come from? Had I learned it? Was it what I really wanted? Or had I been denying my soul's calling in exchange for societal acceptance?

Up to this point in my life, I know in my heart, I had simply been existing, not living. The decisions I was going to make moving forward were going to be different… and they were. About 7 months later, I quit my job and began my personal pilgrimage to discover how to authentically live my most aligned life.

From being on the beach daily, to living in a glamping tent on a ten-acre goat farm in the mountains. Enjoying singing karaoke with locals at the bar, to experiencing an emotional breakdown in solitude under a Hunter's Moon high in the sky. After 8500 miles, I moved to a city simply on the gut feeling I was supposed to be there.

Each day challenged me to learn the differences between what I had been taught to want versus what I authentically desire for my life.

Living an aligned life is a learning that doesn't come with an instruction manual. It's felt through experiences: laughter, joy, tears, hurt, gratitude, and above all else: love. Love for the divine being you are and the light your soul illuminates from within. My hope for you, is you live authentically aligned too.

Show Up Stand Up Speak Up

To those who know me personally, I go by Rachelle. However, if you're amongst the neon light signs and Honky Tonks in Nashville, TN, I'm better known as Roxy the Karaoke Queen. The best Karaoke DJ on Broadway… and this is not your stereo-typical small town, dive bar karaoke. We turn the place into a full-blown club! Full of music, singing and dancing!

Each day I go into the Karaoke Bar, I meet all different people from all over the world. Most people I meet have a core desire to have fun! Now, singing songs is always easier in the car or shower, but in front of people can be intimidating and scary. That's where Roxy has your back. If you step on the karaoke stage and begin to talk badly about yourself, she will give you a look that will make you immediately forget your negative self-talk and tell you, "You are the star when you step up on that stage. Embrace the regal energy that you are and crush it!" For the length of your karaoke song, you feel like a true Rock Star! Roxy's there as your friendly secret weapon to having a blast!

How I became Roxy was the intersection of opportunity, previously acquired knowledge around business and branding, as well as a passion for people, performing, and karaoke. As the business and brand grows, I hope to inspire more people to have fun and enjoy more beautiful moments we can have in life. If you are in the Nashville area, I'd love the chance to connect with you. Please send a message of "262" to @roxythekaraokequeen

LIVE ALIGNED

My Story

KIM DECHAINE

It was a warm summer day. The red wagon's wheels were crunching the dirt beneath it as my husband pulled our two toddler daughters. I was walking behind, watching the three of them as if they were connected - they were one and I was separate. I felt as if I was watching them from above, as they moved forward in their lives – without me. A quiet peace washed over me, as it whispered the possibility of choices. I did not have to stay. Choosing to end my life was an option and that brought me solace.

The girls started fighting in the wagon and I was brought back to my painful reality. I was immobilized in a deep dark pit – a pit filled with despair, exhaustion, fatigue, guilt, pain, and anxiety. Attempts to climb out only led to falling deeper. I could not get out of bed. I would get my 3-year-old and 1-year-old food, put them in front of the TV and then escape back to bed until they called for me again. I prayed for a solution to alleviate the unbearable pain.

Every moment I chose to live was a conscious choice to move forward with a tiny baby step. My husband, medical doctor, naturopathic doctor, psychologist, psychiatrist, energy healers, were my support team and with their constant encouragement and assistance, I gradually began to emerge. As I started to feel better and stronger, I could focus more intently on my healing journey.

And I knew 6 years later that I had successfully risen out of the pit, when a pivotal moment occurred. Holding my 9-year-old daughter during a panic attack, a quiet, peaceful voice resonated within me.

"This is why you had to go through what you did—so you can help her, and others heal." The clarity reached my ears, mind, heart, and soul. It was a validation, my purpose revealed, that I had to feel and understand the pain, so I was able to help others through their struggles and heal like I had.

When I gaze at the red wagon now, I sit in profound gratitude for my life. My strong inner voice is a constant reminder of my purpose and reinforces the significance of my journey. The red wagon will always be a symbol of transformation, hope, and a life worth living.

Show Up Stand Up Speak Up

I was a teacher in my previous life – well that is half true. I was an elementary school teacher for 13 years and then burnt out. So even though I don't teach in the classroom anymore, I am a teacher at heart. It is my gift. And so, I continue to teach, but now to women in leadership roles.

I believe women are here to save the world and yes that includes you! You are probably laughing out loud right now and saying that is ridiculous Kim, I can barely make it through the day, let alone save the world. So many of us are feeling stuck in the hamster wheel of constantly doing more to prove our worth and make sure things are perfect. It often feels like nothing is ever good enough, and there simply isn't enough time in the day. Anxiety and stress levels are through the roof and when we do finally find a minute to relax, we feel guilty, and overthinking takes over. Sound familiar? Well, you are not alone. 43% of women are leaving their leadership roles due to burnout. I am here to change this. I created Inner Powered Leaders and the EmpowHER framework to teach, coach, and advise you and your team to reduce fatigue, burnout, stress, and get your mojo back and feel connected to your work again.

You can have it all – thrive in your leadership role AND follow a path paved with a calm mind, confidence, ease, energy, and clarity – and save the world on the side! I would love to meet you. Feel free to reach out and connect. We are in this together!
kim@innerpoweredleaders.com

BE YOU

IRENE BARLAS-RIMAR

My Message To Women is ...

Strive to be the best version of yourself, don't be afraid to stand out!
Do You with no apologies.

351

DO YOU

My Story

VERA MILAN GERVAIS

I am a mountain soul. When I'm in nature, and particularly when I'm in the mountains, I am whole. Complete. I know I'm insignificant compared to the majesty of the mountains, the world, and the Universe. At the same time, I know that I am part of everything ... Integral to life. I know I am here in this moment in time for a reason. I can embrace the power, strength, danger, and magnificence of the mountains as my Legacy. A legacy of love.

It's taken me decades to realize that love is the core of who I am. I was born with a physical handicap and labelled "defective" by the doctors. At school I was the "crippled girl", the "teacher's pet", the "brainiac".

Then I was a "teen" bride, a "divorcee", a "black sheep", and a "disowned" daughter. I was also an accountant, analyst, photographer, journalist, advertising agency executive, and strategic consultant. Then a "spoiled" wife, "working" mother, "award-winning" businesswoman and "seven-continent" world traveler. And now I'm a best-selling author, speaker, and workshop facilitator.
I am all of these. Yet I am much more. And so are you.

The labels used to describe us tell us what we can and can't do and do and don't deserve. Which means they affect our expectations and our lives.

My gift is curiosity, and as I started to explore the complex world of labels, I realized that our identities are not static. They are intended to evolve. That's how we grow.

But no matter who I become, the one thing that will always be integral to me is "love". And bubbling underneath love… "joy".

My Soul WORDZ. What are yours?

Show Up Stand Up Speak Up

I'm an adventurous introvert. It sounds like a contradiction, but it's who I am.
For years I hid behind one word. Being an "introvert" was an excuse to avoid uncomfortable situations. The truth is, I was afraid of being rejected. If I didn't try, I didn't have to take risks. I hid behind a label that allowed me to play small... and stay safe.

The place I didn't feel judged was outdoors, especially in the mountains. My scars didn't matter there. It was where I discovered fun and fulfillment. When I added "adventurous" to my identity, it changed my life. Since curiosity drives me, I dug into how a single word could make such an impact. Words are labels. The words we use to talk to and about ourselves are like clothing labels. They affect how we feel, and how we show up ... and that affects our actions, behaviors and choices ...the ABC's of identity. Which means we are our words.

I spent the first third of my life isolating myself ... dealing with my physical handicap and the limiting beliefs tied to it. The second third has been filled with love and adventure... my soul-mate Marcel and my two amazing children. The next third is about showing up fully. Giving back. Helping others come out of their shadows. The title of my book is The WORDZ We Wear: *How to show up with confidence and live the life you want.* I can't just SAY those words, I must LIVE them. Join me. I invite you along on your own journey to confidence and living purposefully. Living the life you choose ... filled with love and happiness. What words will give you permission to create the life you want? I'd love to know... vera@veragervais.com

BE ADVENTUROUS

My Story

MOLLY ANNE SUMMERS

Epigenetic Energy Healing has become a fundamental and vital tool in my Life Coaching Profession.

I had experiences throughout my life that led me to becoming and Epigenetics Healer. I was the only daughter of four children. I grew up in the 1970's and I clearly remember my mom saying… "as a girl, you will have to work twice as hard in life, to get half as far as your brothers." I resented this. Especially when I was grounded for 2 weeks the only time, I got a C instead of A's and B's. My brothers had C averages, and Mom didn't care!

I have had several ancestors visit me throughout my life. I feel their energy and hear their message. One day my maternal grandfather's spirit came to visit me. He raised my mom and her sisters because my grandmother was a nurse in WWII. (My grandfather had lost his leg in WWI and now raised his daughters.). His spirit's visit was a pivotal moment for me because of the message he shared with me. "Your mom is raising you with love, she has inherited emotional experiences through her side of the family where women were not able to shine or speak up. Your mom wants you to know you can move forward if you overcome these emotional blocks that you have inherited."

I came to Epigenetic energy healing during the pandemic. My position as client services in the film industry was eliminated because I worked closely with the actors, directors, and producers. I already had trained in life coaching. During the pandemic I was diagnosed with a rare form of Thyroid Cancer. (I feel this disease came from my trapped inherited blocks around feeling unheard and not speaking up.) Having received Epigenetic Energy Healing during this time, I knew it was my calling to be a practitioner. The healing I received brought me so much clarity and I truly believe that I found my voice and felt heard, and I am thriving.

Show Up Stand Up Speak Up

What sets me apart from many Life Coaches is that I am also an Energy Healer. I often can uncover where someone has emotional inherited blocks. I am an Advanced Certified Epigenetics Energy Healer.

Inherited emotional energy can present itself in many ways. We inherit fears, patterns and stories. These fears and patterns can create difficulty in many aspects of our life. We have difficulty in relationships, work, speaking or allowing ourselves to trust ourselves.

Within the DNA code is Epigenetics. Even though we can't change our DNA, such as the color of our eyes, we can remove blocks from our inherited Epigenetics. Have you had life experiences that are unexplainable? Do you continue to follow patterns in your daily life that really don't seem natural to you? I have had clients that grew up in other cultures. These women are from Iran and the Philippines. Not only do they struggle with independence because of cultural issues, they struggle with allowing themselves to be free of abuse and feeling guilty about being their true selves. We worked through how their culture influenced their tolerance of being treated abusively. I still noted that there was more than direct cultural influence inhibiting them. In both cases I discovered they had inherited fear and abandonment from their mother's side going back several generations. When we released these inherited trapped emotions, they now have the self-confidence to live their life in a way that is true to themselves. You can discover the mystery behind certain behaviors.

Contact me http://www.directionandhealingwithmollyanne.com/

LET GO

SARA MCNAY

My Message to Women is …

Wherever you are, start here.
You are strong. You are not alone.
Just keep going and stay open to opportunity.

Show Up Stand Up Speak Up

YOU CAN

JENNIFER MYERS

My Message to Women is ...

Embrace who you are. Because you are imperfectly perfect.

BACK YOURSELF

My Story

DARBY MILLS

Today I stood with my Father at the place my Mom will lay, for the rest of time. While hanging my head in thought, from the ground came a sparkle. As I took a second glance, there it was again. I reached down to uncover a glass bead buried just beneath my feet.

A worthless gem to most, and yet, as I removed the gem from the earth's clutch, it revealed to me my favorite pearlescent finish. It might as well have been a Diamond … I will treasure it as such. Like so many surreal events of that last week, my son was randomly taking pictures that day. Later that evening, he was showing me what he had captured. Miraculously he just happened to capture the moment of my discovery, on film.

What were the chances? I'm not sure, but I feel that she (my Mom) had a hand in this.

I so loved you, and I will miss you dearly. And now I have a Diamond from where you are, at "The Crooked Tree".

Show Up Stand Up Speak Up

I set out with some high school buds at 16 years old to take the stage for the first time. By 18, I was on the road singing in club bands across Western Canada. In 1980 I joined the Headpins and headed off across North America and Europe, sharing the stage with bands such as ZZ Top, Whitesnake, Eddie Money, KISS, Bret Michaels, Nazareth, Ritchie Blackmore, Quiet Riot, Loverboy and many more. 36 years later, in 2016, I redefined myself by starting again with the Darby Mills Project (DMP). Five years in, I released 2 new cd's, obtained a worldwide distribution deal, produced 4 new videos and collaborated for a wonderfully informative documentary produced for Telus On Demand.

Now in my 60's, I'm finding a love for those fabulous old songs from childhood and hope to be singing them for years still to come. This is what I'm doing now, a new band called Press Play, something just a little different than you may have seen of late. Some of the most talented players you can find, all right here in the Okanagan region of BC. So excited to be bringing songs to life from the 60's, 70's songs that will bring back memories long forgotten.

'PressPLay' is a must see for any who have lived through the best years of classic songs and writing. So, sit back, grab a glass of wine and let them take you there.
formusicpressplay@gmail.com

LIVE NOW

MICHELE HUMCHITT

My Message to Women is ...

Sometimes life doesn't give us choices
We have to find the strength
To get through the hardest moments

Show Up Stand Up Speak Up

JUST LOVE

JILL FAI

My Message to Women is ...

Love is like a boomerang, the further you throw it the more love returns.
Always Aspire to Inspire.

Show Up Stand Up Speak Up

MAKE MUSIC

My Story

DEB DRUMMOND

I'm happiest when surrounded by Art. Life has been life … no one escapes the unfolding of life. My heart's had many joys and holds truly phenomenal experiences, that's why I still love photo albums. Have you ever sat and gone through photo albums with your kids or by yourself? It's like looking at a carousel of why living is worthwhile. I've had those days when you don't remember who you are or why you are here. The days that survival washes over and your only Mission that day is one hour at a time.

I remember being almost 6 years old and standing on the sidewalk looking at the house I lived in and claiming that, when I got bigger, I had to make a better life for myself. As dramatic as that sounds, it's true. There have been too many people and things to list on how I went from a home of uncertainty to being the person I am today, accomplishing the level of achievements I have and having the incredible love and happiness I have with my children, my friends, and myself. I'm grateful for every coach, therapist, counselor, group, or expert that ever helped me. I'm grateful for the power of love to allow me to keep on keeping on. I'm grateful for "my peeps" who give me the allowance to let myself be seen and to stay real.

I am forever in debt to every musician that ever composed, sang, wrote, played, or created the one constant healer in my life … MUSIC. I can't explain the feeling I had taking out the first records I had and putting them on my record player. It was like the world stopped and nothing else mattered except the words in the song and the rhythm of the sound.

The life advice I gave to my beautiful daughter, Chloae, on her 16th birthday was the same advice I gave to my creative son, Ocean, on his 19th and it was this: Some days, the only good thing about that day is at some point it will end. My suggestion is go home, sit on your couch, pour yourself a glass of wine or better yet a shot of good whiskey, grab the album called <u>Pearl</u>, and let Janis Joplin take it from there.

And, by the way, that's the same advice I have for you.

Show Up Stand Up Speak Up

I was asked in school what did I want to be? When I asked what my choices were, I heard Teacher, Nurse, or Stewardess. I chose Stewardess. I never ended up being one, but I think my love for adventures is what made me answer the way I did. And an adventure it's been.

I was the neighborhood babysitter and by 8, I was helping my mom load up the car to go do her home parties. I got my first real job after school, working for a carpet cleaning company. They gave me a phone, a piece of paper with what to say, and a phone book. If I wanted to make a paycheque, I had to get people to agree to get their carpets cleaned because they only paid on commission. That was my first lesson in getting over fear and my first surprise in how much fun it was to meet new people, even if only on the phone. That was over 40 years ago, and I still do things that scare me and I still love meeting new people. It's been a career journey.

When I created Mission Accepted Media, it was because it was made clear to me, I was to create platforms for those creative, hope-based, fun, all-in, willing-to-help-others, determined, and fabulous entreprencurs to be seen and heard. Mission Accepted Media hosts an incredible podcast, including live podcasts on stage at events, and incredible anthologies that encourage the rise and celebration of entrepreneurship. We also have a Media School which teaches courses like: What's Your Media Score? What's Your True Avatar? and How to have the highest level of engagements using Summits, Stages, Books, TV, or Radio. So that's a bit about me. How about we grab a chat and learn a bit about you? Happy to connect! Deb@debdrummond.com

STAY GROOVY

My Story

SARAH SMITH

I knew from the earliest time I can remember that I cherished human connection above anything else in life.

I was raised in a church-going-farm-living family. My father played country guitar at all the local house parties. After a few adult beverages, he would gain the nickname Eeyore and people would start cheering him on to play some Johnny Cash or Kenny Rogers. His kind eyes and soft smile were infectious, and I was always so proud to be his daughter. To me, he was such a rock star! My mother was a little more proper, leading the church choir, quoting bible verses, and taking solos on Sundays. To me, she was my living hero, and I worshipped her! She also ran the youth choir, and of course, I was often nominated for solo performances (thanks Mom).

One of my life changing moments happened when I was five years old. A really interesting man in our church - a real life songwriter - wrote ME a song to sing. I remember the feeling standing by the altar, talking myself into not being nervous, gaining the courage to open my mouth and let those words sing! I remember the words and how they made me feel and I wanted to make sure I sang these words with truth. As a five-year-old, I still remember looking out at the congregation and feeling a sense of belonging. A sense that people were feeling my voice in their hearts. A feeling that I was and will never be alone. I felt connection.

There are times in my life that my heart has been closed off, in protection mode, scared and abandoned. I have lost love, I have abused my body and soul, I have sunk into the darkness and been lifted back into the light.

And through it all, I never lost sight of the absolute knowing that we are all going through this journey together and that no matter what, I will never be alone.
This feeling of connection - the same one I had at the young age of five years old - still makes me tick today and gets me out of bed in the morning.

I love you.
I love everyone.
I want to feel your heart and I want to cheer you on.

Show Up Stand Up Speak Up

Where do I go from here? What should I be when I grow up? What is my purpose? The ominous questions that go through all 17-year-old's mind when they're trying to figure out their purpose and passion in this life.

I knew I wanted to heal. I thought I wanted to be a doctor, but I didn't want to do all those years in school. Instead, I applied to Universities for the Kinesiology program. I got accepted to all five of the Universities I applied and decided to attend RMC - Royal Military College in Kingston, ON. I was now enlisted in The ARMY! It was there that I learned about my strength and resiliency. I learned self-discipline, time management, teamwork and camaraderie. I learned I could put my body through hell and still keep a strong mind and positive outlook. I dug deep into spirituality at this time, and started writing even more meaningful songs that became my therapeutic answers to life's questions. One fateful day, an officer that I trusted approached me and told me "Officer Cadet Smith - you're doing okay here in the military, but I have been hearing you sing and play your guitar and I really think you should follow your heart and just do music".
Um WAIT - do MUSIC?? Like you can make a living doing music?

Once I discovered this life hack, I immediately got an honourable discharge and joined a band a few weeks later. I've been making my living off music ever since. Fate. It's in the stars. And here I am, accepting this life mission, whatever is put in front of me, with a grateful and humble heart. Let's heal through music together! Share some musical inspiration or write a song with me sarah@sarahsmithmusic.com

SERVE WELL

My Story

RONA GOODMAN

I'm a doer maker, dream chaser, give not taker so take a chance on me! That's just a little play on words as I take a spin at Pat Benatar's song Heartbreaker. I don't know why it just popped into my brain as I'm writing this. I'm sitting in my "magical chair" in my studio where I write and compose songs and music. When it's quiet in the house and the dogs (two mini dachshunds) are not barking at the wind, my mind takes me to places imaginary and real.

Writing songs, playing guitar, and now composing music has always been my muse. Like a superhero it found and saved me at a very young age and led me on a life's journey in the crazy business they call music. Like time ticking it hasn't stopped. Sometimes I think, is it a blessing or a curse? Following your dreams when you don't get a degree at the end of the day can be a tough one. It's a school of hard knocks and you must have tough skin to survive!

As a female guitar player back in the day when women were not taken seriously or, may just have intimated a few along the way. I remember the first time I heard the band HEART. It changed my world, and I knew what I wanted to be! Nancy Wilson with her ovation guitar, well that was me! Next to my parents, they had so much influence in my life! I believe whatever we choose in our life, you must have the passion for it. The passion will drive you to where it's supposed to lead. Leading will encourage you to give back and giving back is the greatest gift of all.

Show Up Stand Up Speak Up

I'm a songwriter, music composer, musician (guitar), producer and a publicist.
I do what I do because I can't help myself, it's in my blood! I've been in the entertainment industry in many areas for over thirty years. I can look back with no regret because I went for it all. I always followed my heart. Some refer to me as Rona "Try" Goodman because I keep trying and don't give up! Trust me it's been a hellava ride with great joys, deep dark dives, and huge learning curves.

I'm grateful for all the opportunities given to me in my life. I've also worked very hard on every project! As a marketing and PR professional I was on the ground level in building a very successful music festival in Canada, worked on huge events that took the world stage, worked with the biggest music artists in entertainment and wrote songs with hit songwriters in Nashville.

I love to empower and encourage people especially young women who want to get in the business, learn an instrument or take on something big or small. You don't have to reach the summit to be successful. Looking back now I do realize it's the journey and not the destination. It's the small things in life like finding your passion, doing what you love and staying humble! Ronagoodman@shaw.ca

FINISH STRONG

My Story

JAN HOATH

When I was a little girl, I remember desperately wanting to be really great at something, "my thing". I moved a lot growing up. I tried new things in each new place I lived. My favorite color was rainbow. Passionate about life, I was ever craving to experience more in search of "my thing" in its full vibrancy.

Then life started happening for me in more profound ways. Severe depression as a teenager that led me to be an exchange student, a tragic death of a loved one that led me to start my business, a cancer scare with my then 6 week old son that led me to eat fruit loops just for the joy of it and I found myself on a spiritual path that awakened "my thing".

Words. Poetic words. Spoken. Written. Facilitating rainbows of my own directly from my soul. My rainbow gift to you. Love, Jan

There is a magic found when we learn to align in the now.

There is a wonder to witness when we stop fretting the how.

There is a beauty to behold when we pause to take in the reflection.

There is a freedom that arises when we let go of perfection.

There is a magnificence that takes over when we acknowledge the divine.

There is a brilliance that unfolds when we accept that all will be fine.

There is a humbling awakening when we give up doing it all on our own.

There is an awe-inspiring moment that shows up when we realize we are not alone.

There is a heartwarming sensation that comes over us when we truly trust.

There is a loving awareness that manifests when we see that our JOY is a must.

There is a kindness that comes when we revel in the art of forgiveness.

There is a compassion that surfaces when we can laugh at the mess.

There is a momentum that builds when we get that patience is power.

There is a light that shines when we can celebrate our darkest hour.

There is a radiance that sparkles when we own all our colors.

There is a liberation that comes when we appreciate the imperfections of our fathers and mothers.

There is a satisfaction that is realized when we dance in the expansion.

There is a fulfillment that flows when we acknowledge we will never be done.

All this to say and remind you anew

To enJOY the ride and just own you.

Show Up Stand Up Speak Up

Did you sign up for the kiddie ride of life or the full thrill adventure?

If you asked me what I wanted to be when I grew up, I would have said a roller coaster engineer. I loved the thrill of the twists, and turns, and the ups and downs. I loved it so much, my first summer job was at an amusement park. My passion showed as I received the "memory maker" award for having received the most guest comments that I made a positive impact on their visit.

I shifted that thrill to a more organic roller coaster: downhill skiing. I became a professional ski instructor, teaching in Aspen, Australia, and Jackson Hole for over a decade. My world opened up having followed my joy after graduating from university to ski instruction instead of following the conventional path. As I saw the outcome of living joy-led unfold in my life in the most magical ways, it became clear to me that my mission was to fulfill the vision of a Joy Led World, dropping the lie that you can "play only when the work is done". In my experience, it's better to play before, during, and after work for more effective and satisfying results! In 2008 I formally started my business as a roller coaster engineer, metaphorically speaking. My rides involve transformational retreat facilitation and coaching, guiding, and mentoring women leaders to stop sacrificing their joy for success and to start enJOYing the full thrill ride of life— only we finish on the up!

I help you own the metaphorical "roller coaster" thrill of life and leadership. Ready to find deep satisfaction within your soul? Ready to create an inspiring legacy? Ready to become radiantly revitalized and re-aligned? Let me guide you to your joy filled leadership!

www.JOYfilledLeader.com

JOY UP

My Story

JULIE BROWN

By the time my story is out in the world, I'll be on the doorstep of my 78th birthday! Hopefully I've accrued some wisdom along the way to share with you.

At 18 in Quebec, Canada I stood before forty Grade 2 munchkins praying I could teach them something valuable about life ... not just what was in my "teacher's manual". The decision to start the school day off singing a 'Beatles song' with my kids and having the whole class participate in creating gigantic murals with peanuts characters at the back of the classroom inspired not only the children but this teacher. Eventually, the principal asked me to teach 'art' to the whole school. We decorated the halls with murals after studying Picasso, van Gogh, and many other great artists. That inspired me to go back to school. I graduated with honours having both 'fine arts' and 'cinema' as my majors from Concordia university in Montréal. At this point I was doing voice overs for commercials as well as auditioning for roles in films. Never did I expect to meet the likes of Sophia Loren, American director/actor John Houston, Canadian filmmaker David Cronenberg and many other 'famous' people. Opportunities do knock on doors ... we just need to be ready to open them.

My soul craved a new direction other than teaching.It appeared the universe heard my call. A popular Montréal radio station was looking for audience members to fill in for their 'weather girl' while she was on vacation. A friend convinced me to audition. The morning host called and asked me to do an impromptu 'weather forecast'. Lacking confidence, I cheekily said it was 90 degrees, snowing, with a low of -10 expected that night'. I got the gig! I walked out of that CFCF studio on cloud 9, never expecting what was to happen next.

After hearing me on the air, the general manager of another radio station reached out and asked me to audition at an underground radio station called CHOM-FM. The producer there handed me some copy. I aced it and got the gig!!! The first few days I did 'weather' but by the end of the first week I was reading 'news' over the air. After a few weeks, I was asked by the program director if I could do an interview with singer/songwriter Joan Armatrading, who was in town. She was purported in various rock magazines as being a difficult interviewee, so the 'jocks' were reluctant to sit down with her. Despite her alleged reputation, I nervously jumped at the opportunity ("there are no problems, only opportunities" - John Kehoe 'mind power'). As it turned out, Joan Armatrading was totally engaging! We hugged before she left the building. I have consequently done easily over one thousand interviews during my 21 year radio broadcasting career including the likes of Leonard Cohen, Bob Hope, Shirley MacLaine, Anne Murray, copious authors, Neil Diamond, members of many bands including The Beach Boys, Barenaked Ladies, The Village People and many more.

Show Up Stand Up Speak Up

When you can clearly state your intention, in my opinion, you're more than halfway to achieving your goal. What I wanted more than anything else was to sing with a group who dug close, crunchy harmonies while performing jazz, blues and pop tunes. Music has always been a huge part of my life. Even as a very young child I loved 'performing' for family, and having an older brother who was a professional musician really helped! His Canadian group, The Rraftsmen, was much in demand on television, radio and stages across north America. In fact, they opened in Florida for the Smothers Brothers.

I learned so much from him throughout the years and we often sang together in close harmony. Today as I write this, I am living my dream and here's why. I hadn't sung professionally for many years, so I decided to join a choir. It was there I met Georgina Arntzen, an accomplished singer and musician. Never thinking 'G' would agree, I approached her about forming a group. (*show up stand up speak up!*) Much to my delight and amazement she agreed! The two of us later joined yet another choir and were very impressed with singer/actress Mary Ella Young. The rest is history!

Our Vancouver trio is called The Hot Mammas. We're entering our thirteenth year together, have recorded three cd's and are working on the fourth. Not only am I singing, which is my ultimate passion...I'm also writing original music. It truly is 'never too late' to pursue a new career direction and realize your goal or goals. Please check out our website and YouTube channel! www.thehotmammas.com

MUSIC HEALS

My Story

ANGELA CIEMNY

I am the best in my element. It's late morning and I'm outside on my patio with a coffee, the SoCal sun splashing my face with warmth. My mini-doodle Roxie Rose is running around looking for lizards. The kids are at school. Hubby is downstairs on calls. I thank God for mountain air. I make my smoothie. I think about my day and the freedom I have worked so hard for. I'm grateful I don't have to set an alarm anymore. It's funny when you stop to think about the things in life that make us happy. The things that truly matter are basic: Family, [real] friends, and simple moments like holding a newborn and watching her wrap her little hand around my pinky.

My priorities have shifted at each stage of life, pre-kids and pre-marriage life versus now, with three boys and a husband. I've learned that my soul is happier with each moment in time that I allow myself to take in life instead of life taking me in. It's easy to get that reversed. Every day we have a choice to make. We can choose happiness. It has been quite a journey so far discovering my passions and learning how to employ them daily, then creating and designing that life. It's not always what I thought it would look like. I've shed some tears, pushed through mental (and physical) boundaries, and ended up on the other side of adversity wondering how on earth I got through. My husband David pushed me off the Victoria Falls Bridge in Zimbabwe. Thank God I was attached to a bungee cord.

He dragged me kicking and screaming on a backpacking adventure around the world right after we got married. I had my third child naturally with no meds. I became Lady Gaga's personal assistant. These are all cherished chapters for me. I've had to learn to live an extraordinary life, not money-driven or success-driven, but happiness-driven. The more I think about simple things like an amazing meal or the smell of new leather in a car, the more I am convinced that if I am healthy, happy, and looking and feeling my best, nothing can hold me back. Every day I wake up I know it's a blessing and every second I live is a chance to create and design more personal happiness, and write another page in my book of life.

Show Up Stand Up Speak Up

I actually thought I would end up being a doctor. I've always had that inherent need to work on people. I had no compunction about tearing into cadavers in college to see what I could find. As the oldest child with three younger brothers, I grew up quickly taking care of all their cuts and broken bones. I knew marriage, kids and career were all inevitable, but I wanted my soul to be filled before I went down that road. I got out of the house fast and on my own and bought my first home at 22. I was always chasing freedom, but I realized it couldn't come from being a doctor. Through real estate development I discovered my passion for interior design, and the joy of colors, textures, shapes, art, hues, tints, and fabrics. These were all fuel for my creative soul. I would spend hours cutting out pictures from magazines of sofas, rooms, looks, fixtures, houses, patios, and color schemes.

As hubby, kiddos and the need for money all entered the picture, my soul became fed by love and a deeper purpose. I learned that happiness comes in small batches (sometimes only minutes) each day where we are undistracted and taking in life. The smell of rain on fresh sagebrush. The texture of a green lawn beneath your bare feet warmed by the morning sun. The hummingbird sucking on a flower. That song that plays at just the right moment to intersect your emotions at that time. I find happiness in the opportunity I have to help my business sisters level up their lives and finances. I celebrate them. I share them on social media. And I challenge you to do the same. Share your gifts. There is only one you. Let's connect! superiorspaces@mail.com

QUIT WAITING

RANDI LYNNE WEIDMAN

My Message To Women is ...

Allow your heart to break ... that's when it opens.

Show Up Stand Up Speak Up

EMBRACE PAIN

SANDRA TAIT HUMPHREY

My Message to Women is ...

Singing HU, this ancient name for God, during hard times, uplifts, purifies, and becomes a prayer of the highest order.

Show Up Stand Up Speak Up

CULTIVATE GRATITUDE

SAMAYA RYANE

My Message to Women is ...

Wishing you peace, a mind that is free, love of self, and a grateful heart.

Show Up Stand Up Speak Up

BREATHE DEEP

ROSALIND FRANKLIN
Biophysicist

GLADYS AYLWARD
Missionary

LA MAUPIN
Swordswoman

ALICE BROWN DAVIS
Chief

BRENDA SHELDRAKE

I've lived a life of helping and connecting with others. I'm happiest when I am meeting new people and making new connections. Like pieces of string in an intricately woven pattern each person who touches my life or I touch adds a new thread to the tapestry.

The tapestry started with a fourteen-year-old in a doctor's office alongside my family as a doctor said the words no child should hear, "We are here to help you understand that your mother is going to die. We can't tell you when and there isn't anything to be done. So, we want you to be prepared."

Unable to make sense of this crazy message and determined to fix it I formulated my plan. I would keep everything perfect, and mom wouldn't die. That began the journey of fixing and the life of a chameleon.

The years went by, and the little girl became a woman. But there was a problem, the life of a chameleon meant that I woke up with the realization that I had no idea who I really was. I could tell you about being a wife, sister, daughter but if you asked about my likes, my beliefs , and my goals, I'd freeze like a deer in headlights.

My quest for identity took me across the United States. I traveled with carnivals, meeting more people and touching more lives. The carnival allowed me to explore the joy of bringing smiles to people's faces. But the diversity meant I had to start to develop my own set of beliefs that worked for me.

I'm grateful for each person who touched my life and the lessons they left behind. They helped me become the caring, helpful person I am today. They helped me to know where you end and where I start and what was my problem and what wasn't.

The life advice I gave to my nieces was to travel, see the world but always have a home base. Know who you are and what you believe. And when life throws you curveballs in the brilliant advice of Dory from Finding Nemo "Just Keep Swimming." You matter! You are Gonna Make It! And that's my advice for you too!

Show Up Stand Up Speak Up

What do you want to be when you grow up? My teacher asked…

First answer, a truck driver just like my grandpa so I can see the world and sleep in a truck. A teacher so I can change the lives of lots and lots of kids. A carnival traveler, going places and bringing smiles to people's faces, seeing new cities, and never having to settle down. Never imagined I would become a drug addict dependent on substances to allow me to cope. From the hell of drug addiction to the freedom of the carnival life I moved like the chameleon I was. Seeking only freedom and the carefree life that would no longer necessitate hiding behind drugs. I traveled across Canada and the United States never stopping, never settling down.

Today I've left the carnival and the horrors of addiction behind and spend all my time connecting and sharing unconditional encouragement with early-stage entrepreneurs. The carnival life taught me the value of community and I've taken those lessons and used them to create the Building Better Business Relationships Community.

My mission is to help early-stage entrepreneurs, develop their passion, build their business, and increase their resilience. My heart breaks when an entrepreneur gives up on their dream and closes their doors. If you are letting that thought of giving up creep into your mind let's have a chat. My message to you: You're gonna make it! You can find me at https://www.bizleadsexpert.com

YOU MATTER

My Story

RHONDA GRANT

My road to enlightenment has been a lifelong journey. Early on, I noticed how my wishes to God materialized and believed this was the reality for everyone. I trusted it was how God worked because my grandma reinforced these ideas. As I grew, I knew things, and felt things, though sometimes these made me uncomfortable. I believed I was not old enough to process my abilities or profound feelings. When Grandma, passed, it left a void in my life. I did not know who to confide in anymore. I noticed people didn't believe these events I experienced or did not want to discuss them.

I encountered many odd mishaps that could have caused death. Well, at age five, one did cause death, and then being brought back from death. After major surgery at 21, I lay in my hospital bed in excruciating pain, day after day. My specialist entered my hospital room one morning. Hearing him enter, I opened my eyes and saw the panic on his face. He immediately barked orders to the nurses to get medicine. I was dying, and no one had realized I was, until that moment.

Other terrifying, yet enlightening, events occurred while driving. I spun out of control twice in freezing rain, once, missing a hydro pole, and another, sliding into oncoming traffic! Like a sudden silent movie, that last event peppered my brain with my life's history, all while I heard my vehicle smashing through guardrails, then crashing on its side in a swamp. Another, while driving on a busy major highway, the tractor-trailer in front of me lost its air brake, which then careened down the road, right at me. Thankfully, the air brake bounced in such a way, that I drove right over it. The force of this accident shook my transmission free, crushing me against the sunroof, and injuring my neck. I always seemed to be in a daze when these things happened to me. I don't ever recall thinking to myself – "why me?" At the time, I felt I was simply surviving my life.

Then, I was T-boned on my way home from work one day, remarkably altering my life and life's journey. Before this accident, I felt there just had to be more to life. This event shook my soul from my body, then gifted it back to me. Afterwards, I felt different. Reality, for me, was altered, I saw and heard things in a new way. This was the juncture when I graduated from my current state of being to becoming a *Seer*, a *Hearer*, and a *Feeler*, of energies in, and around, my body. I felt more "in tune". It was the moment of enlightenment where everything, everywhere, made sense. It granted me the ability to look back and realize that all these so-called "accidents" were rousing me from my lifelong trance. I saw the path that lay before me, had wisdom it had been created for me, and had been courting me my whole existence.

Show Up Stand Up Speak Up

Often, in our attempt to share our knowledge with someone, we are compelled to rush in, to show others we are an expert on a subject. However, it may mean we could be perceived as not appreciating another's gifts. I learned long ago to stay in my power, tread softly, take the temperature of the energy in the room, honor the one I am speaking with. I do this by the words I use, and the calm energy I portray. You could say it is the secret to my success.

Where you are right now is where you are meant to be, based on decisions you've made along your life's path. If you wish to be somewhere other than where you are right now, you must tap into the trueness of yourself. Ask your heart, higher consciousness, or gut, to provide you with your answers. Meditate to become intimate with who you are. Listen to the whispers that come to you and learn from them. Honor your being, your essence, your health, and your relationships. Rhonda Grant is a true renaissance woman. Co-Founder and CEO of Stand Fast Homes Ltd., and Grant's Marble Inc., she is an active leader and highly regarded as an award-winning real estate professional.

Abruptly, a near-death experience fractured her everyday routine, compelling Rhonda to author her book, Magical Forces Within: Extraordinary Discoveries in an Ordinary Life. This dynamic exploration of the metaphysical inspires her readers with real-life stories of transformation and enlightenment. Her book is an Amazon International #1 Best Seller in multiple categories, and an Amazon National Best-Selling Audiobook. Rhonda is a Radio Talk Show Host with her Podcast: The Rhonda Grant Show, on which she interviews people from all over the world. Rhonda organizes and hosts charity golf tournaments for Sandy Pines Wildlife Centre. rhondagrantauthor@gmail.com

BE LOVE

CAROL LANGE

My Message To Women is ...

Mindset is everything.

LET GO

My Story

RACHEL LEE

Arist, Designer & Brand Stylist

I'm in my happy place when I'm making things — whether it's a drawing to vent my emotions, a gift to express my love, or a crazy home improvement project that makes my space even more awesome.

But it's not just a skill. Having a spirit of creativity is the lifeline that helped me get through the darkest seasons of my life…

When I left an abusive relationship.
When I ran away from home.
When I walked away from my religion.
When I dug myself into debt.

Creativity allowed me to create hope in moments of despair, connections when I felt alone, and opportunities out of thin air — it allowed me to create a new life for myself, and I couldn't be more thankful.

For me, it's not about making art.

It's about seeing the world through the lens of curiosity, and giving yourself permission to believe that anything is possible.

I hope to leave a legacy where my work inspires people to embrace their difference, live their lives loudly, and say, "so what?" to all the haters who want you to be just like everyone else... because you're not!

Thank you to everyone who stuck around on this crazy journey — my family, friends, colleagues and of course... my cat! I wouldn't be here without your support and encouragement to chase my dreams... even if they're crazy ;)

Here's to the next chapter of our lives. Let's make it AWESOME!

Show Up Stand Up Speak Up

Growing up, I knew that I wanted to make things for a living — I just didn't know what that meant. All I knew was that I LOVED seeing the look on people's faces when I made something especially for them, and that was enough to get me studying in art school with a dream of becoming a designer. But when my dream finally came true... I realized that I wasn't happy, so I quit my job at the start of 2019 to start up my own branding agency — with ZERO business knowledge and a naive sense of optimism that it would somehow be easy to "do the thing I love for a living".
I couldn't have been more mistaken.

Even though I was in an industry that is all about showing your difference, I found myself caving in to the pressure of showing up just like everyone else, even when I knew that it wasn't me. It wasn't until 3 years in that I knew that something needed to change. I felt like I was lying to people about who I was, so I stopped censoring myself out of my own content and built a brand that CELEBRATED my difference instead. After this turning point, every single person I've connected with has told me that they remembered me because I stood out. Yes, the brand styling helped... but ultimately, it was because I was finally brave enough to stop trying to fit in and let the world SEE who I actually am.

Today, I help other brands go through that same transformation and develop a style that turns up the volume on all the awesome things that make you... YOU! If you'd like to connect with me, you can reach me at rachel@racheltylee.com :)

BE DIFFERENT

My Story

STEFANI SEEK

I love LOVE. I am a born romantic, a Pisces, and a sensitive soul. I remember looking up at the stars from the backseat car window, around age 8, on the way home from a family trip. I wondered what the love of my life was doing at that moment. Was he somewhere close by? Would I meet him soon or in an exotic location in my 20s? For better and sometimes for worse, I was born contemplating romantic love. I yearned for a boy…and later a man…to love me for me.

Fast-forward 35 years from that little girl's dreams, and I have now been married and divorced twice. Never In my romantic imaginings could I have fathomed that on the road to love, I would have experienced such a bumpy ride. Throughout the ups and downs, I happily welcomed three daughters into the world. Sophia, Lyla, and Camilla have all inspired me to look at my life from new perspectives because they are each so unique. I am thankful that I have always been surrounded by their precious love.

One of the mantras by which I now live my life, and remind my girls of when they feel stuck, is this: You can ALWAYS change your mind. We are creators. We can partner with God & the Universe to co-create a life that reflects our most authentic selves. We can alter our life's course by what we choose to think each day. Isn't that realization *exciting?!* I decided to love myself more, and my entire world opened up.

It turns out that boy I was dreaming of…the man I now call the love of my life…was indeed under the same starry sky. He was making music. He was imagining. We even met briefly as children in a youth choir without realizing it was "us" until we met 30 years later. We both had to go on adventures, experience love and heartbreak, and become conscious creators so we could find our way back to each other and kiss for the first time under the full moon of a cold, wintry night.

Thank goodness for the experiences of things that I didn't want in my life, because now, I am enjoying the knowing of what I DO want. Love yourself first, and true love will always find its way to you, in so many wonderful forms!

Show Up Stand Up Speak Up

Little did I know that when a sales career chose me right out of college, it would teach me so much about human connection and purpose. Sales is about matching someone's need with a service or a product that helps them be successful, find satisfaction or solve a problem. As I grew into an executive sales leader at several global organizations, my true passion welled up like a rising tide: listening to and empathizing with people, helping them feel better. In elevators, on airplanes, and at conferences, people—especially women—gravitated towards me to share a part of their life stories, wanting to be heard and seeking advice. The idea of writing a book had been bubbling up within me for decades, but I didn't know what story to tell. I finalized divorce #2 and downsized to a new home three weeks before the Covid-19 pandemic forced us all inside and into our minds to contemplate a new reality. I felt moved to write a book about life and love. Partner-less and very alone, I knew that I had learned some tough lessons that women could relate to and learn from.

For a year, while working an intense corporate job remotely, I wrote. I published "The Love Compass: A Girl's Guide to Finding Authentic Love" in October 2022, and it became my launching pad to helping women find connection, self-love, and renewed confidence. I finally found my own authentic voice. I quit corporate America to become a Certified Life Coach, while also launching my sales consulting firm. I help women who feel stuck get unstuck by re-discovering their inner voice. I help sales professionals & companies sell through authentic connection.
We all deserve abundance! www.stefaniseek.com

BE LOVE

KYRA WONG

My Message To Women is …

Follow your heart with faith, trust, and pixie dust.
Believe in your magic and shine like the star you are!

DREAM BIG

M. DEANNE MORRELL

My Message to Women is ...

Unleash the divine gifts within you.
Fiercely and fearlessly embrace your purpose
and boldly walk in your unstoppable, destined light.

Show Up Stand Up Speak Up

FAITH NOW

TRICIA PARIDO

My Message To Women is ...

Unleash the power within.
Reclaim your narrative, embrace authenticity, and thrive in your own light.

Show Up Stand Up Speak Up

LIVE AUTHENTICALLY

My Story

JANITRA ELLISON

As a child, my aspirations consisted of grand dreams involving a luxurious lifestyle complete with a mansion, private chef, vacations, and an unlimited supply of vanilla bean ice cream with caramel drizzle! Surprisingly, my childhood dream job was to become a high school history teacher. Years later, I graduated from Winston-Salem State University with a Bachelor's degree in History; only to discover the harsh reality that teachers are overworked and underpaid. God Bless the educators!

Who am I today? A Believer, divorced, super proud mom of Faith (15) and Ariel (11), incredibly embarrassed dog mom of Rosie (Bichon-frise/shih tzu), and determined entrepreneur. My current journey has been filled with peaks and valleys. Feelings of abandonment from my father in early years, a frustrating relationship with my mother at times, the destruction of my marriage mid 20's, homelessness, abuse, I mean the list goes on and on!

In everything I've experienced, it all worked out for my good in the end. Life is full of valuable lessons that are meant to allow us to, "Go, Grow, and Learn," in the words of my Grandmother Ollie. Forgiveness is especially important during this process. Forgiveness allows the opportunity to release pain, hurt, anger and resentment to elevate and grow.

There's no manual in life. We do the best we can with the circumstances we have. In many ways, our brains adapt to the trauma that life can bring by innately implementing "survival mode." I've learned to forgive myself for the things I felt were necessary to do while living in "survival mode." You see, the past is the past. What has happened is done. However, if we're blessed to wake up to see the beauty of a new day, there is a fresh start.

Our hardships tend to take us on a journey towards finding our passions. Our passions then prepare us for our purpose and calling in life. For me, my passion involves helping women, especially single mothers, escape a mindset of scarcity and hoist them into abundance. If I can make a positive impact on one woman, I've fulfilled my mission. In life, hardships produce discipline, but discipline brings forth success.

Show Up Stand Up Speak Up

Moms2tech Inc. was formed from an emotionally broken place during the height of the pandemic. At the time, I worked for a cybersecurity institute, in the admissions department. The more I learned about cybersecurity, it provided the understanding that a career in tech could provide job security and financial stability. I also yearned for supportive networks, who could empathize with my struggles and journey. During this time, I went through a divorce and realized I didn't understand anything about finances; including health insurance, life insurance, budgeting, wealth accumulation, credit management, you know ... name it! Moms2tech Inc., has now emerged as the phoenix from the ashes of my past tribulations, a catalyst now for positive change.

Recognizing the barriers that women, much like myself, face in securing financial stability and escaping the cycle of poverty; Moms2tech Inc. aims to bridge the gender digital divide and cultivate a community of female leaders in the digital age. Through our programs, resources, support, and educational opportunities, we believe that women can not only improve their own lives but also make a lasting impact on their families, communities, and the world at large.

To learn more about our mission and how you can get involved, please reach out to us at info@moms2techinc.org . Together, we can make great strides towards a more inclusive and vibrant tech industry. Remember, change is not in the masses but starts with one. If you change the course of one life, you begin to change the trajectory of a community.

PUSH FORWARD

DELMIRA AGUSTINI
Poet

ADA LOVELACE
Mathematician

TOMOE GOZEN

Samurai Warrior

BERTHE MORISOT

Impressionist

My Story

HEATHER TAYLOR

Stumbling about within this space of existence left to wonder of self realization, authenticity and a confirmation of worthiness, she lingers on a thought… "What if no one ever truly saw what I wrote?". She silently inquired, "Would I still write my book?". Although she found herself at a conscious pause, it wasn't to ponder the answer, but rather what did this truth mean to her, about her? A quick feeling of guilt came over Heather, as she began to evaluate her truth. The answer was No… She would not write the book. Suddenly a culminating moment within this space occurred. All the neglect, abuse, loss, horror, devastation; Mentally, emotionally, physically and spiritually, were building blocks to guide others through healing cycles of self discovery. If this book was never seen, what does that say for the purpose of such tragedy and darkness? What does that say about her?

A reflection of her sitting in the wheelchair in a temporary home trapped in a state she has never known.
Her caretaker/boyfriend had family over. People she had only recently met. They liked Heather, yet with two children, while bound by wheelchair, they instructed him to run as fast as he could. "They are not your children." "She is broken, do you really want this life?" They meant well in their own way. Heather being an unrealized empath found herself hiding out in the kitchen. All of a sudden, her right leg slipped off the silver footrest of her chair. Somehow the granite from the tile cut her foot, within an instant her foot was bleeding, and it triggered a petit mal seizure. While being held down in the chair, tears uncontrollably roll down her face, as she sees everyone staring helpless in awe, shock or maybe sorrow for him. She then looks at her two beautiful daughters. Heather had always been so strong or so everyone had thought. Now they see her in a state of complete weakness. What they don't know is, this is the moment that shifts the balance of darkness into light. Within the entirety of this moment while looking at her babies she told herself never again, this is not my life or purpose. I will find a way no matter what others say. A time of sheer humility offered a profound gift. A choice she had found herself facing was clear. Live a life she had been born to, sadness and suffering or make a difference and embrace the unknown light of love's abundant fruition, of the authentic purposeful higher self.

This memory was one of a thousand lifetimes worth. A situation that embodies vast diversity not because of the scenario, it was the drive for positive change no matter the challenge ahead. Jim Carrey once said; "It's not about having fear it is about how much fear you allow in today and it is not about having hope, but turning hope into faith."

Show Up Stand Up Speak Up

Heather Taylor, founder and CEO of Get Taylored!, is a beacon of resilience, unwavering dedication, and wisdom. Bridging ancient roots and progressive horizons, her journey brings to life the essence of unyielding determination. Her story begins with a decade-long quest from being bound by a wheelchair for 10 years to a walking wellness expert. However, this was not simply a journey of physical recovery. Heather's voyage took her deep into the caverns of introspection, shaping the crucible of her self-development path, and thus, catalyzing her life's mission: To Thrive, & To See Others Thrive.

With her unique blend of metaphysical expertise and tenacity, she has refined her methods, infusing 20 years of demonstrable experience into an empowering compass known as "The 5 Elements of You." Heather's approach balances the elemental dimensions of mind, emotions, body, spirit, and ether, fusing the microcosmos of individuals to the macrocosmos of communities. This equilibrium births infinite graces, giving rise to resilience, the kind that teaches us that "Life isn't about waiting for the storm to pass; it's about learning to dance in the rain." No stranger to hardships, Heather knows the power of emerging from adversity. Her contribution to this noble testament of influential women is more than an accolade. It's a testament to her life's work, a beacon of hope for those navigating their storms, and an invitation to dance in life's rain.

Join Heather's journey at www.gettaylored.love , immerse yourself in a loving community. Engage with the "5 Elements of You" and unleash your holistic potential. Herein lays the promise of a flourishing legacy, one stitch in the vibrant tapestry of 262 influential women. So, Rise, Thrive, Dance, and Get Taylored! Form Fit Yourself to Your Soul!

407

RISE THRIVE

My Story

ANDREA CRUZ HUDSON

As I sit here, reflecting on my journey, I can't help but feel a deep sense of gratitude and pride. My name is Andrea Cruz Hudson, from Colombia who dared to chase the American Dream. Life, in all its complexity, has taught me to savor every moment as if it were my last. I used to be a person consumed by fears and overthinking, which held me back from taking action. However, one decision—to move to the United States—transformed my life in ways I could never have imagined.

I am immensely grateful for the challenges that have shaped me, for my family and husband whose love makes me a better person every day, and for my mentors who have guided me. My journey from Colombia to the United States, from uncertainty to entrepreneurial success, is a testament to the power of perseverance, focus, and hard work. My story is a vivid reminder that with a clear vision and relentless pursuit, dreams do materialize.

Show Up Stand Up Speak Up

In Colombia, despite being a professional in International Business, I faced limited job opportunities that fell short of my aspirations. The decision to move was not easy; leaving behind my parents, sisters, nieces, and nephews was heart-wrenching. Adapting to a new country with its distinct language and traditions posed its own set of challenges. Thankfully, the support from my sister, her husband, and my nieces here in the U.S. made the transition bearable.

My initial days in America were marked by my beginnings, working in a restaurant and cleaning houses. These experiences, though tough, were invaluable. They taught me the importance of hard work and ignited a desire for more—a desire to not just survive but thrive. This realization led me to discover e-commerce, a field that captivated my interest and passion. I invested in myself, enrolling in courses, reading books, and watching videos to learn everything I could about e-commerce. It became not just a business for me but a passion that allowed me to work from home and build something of my own.

My mentors played a crucial role in my journey, teaching me that without action, success is unattainable. They taught me that making mistakes is not a setback but a step forward, as each mistake is a lesson in disguise. I learned that the only obstacle to success is oneself. With focus and hard work towards my goals, I've realized that anything is achievable. I am a woman who dared to dream and took bold steps to make it a reality.
Andreacruzch3001@gmail.com

LOVE LIFE

CARI HANSEN

My Message to Women is ...

Be authentic, Be humble, Be loyal, Be true, Be connected,
and be proud of you!

Show Up Stand Up Speak Up

EMPOWER OTHERS

JENNIFER BOND

My Message to Women is ...

You don't have to be ONE thing.
You can live an AND life.
Go live your ampersand!

Show Up Stand Up Speak Up

BE BOLD

My Story

AMINA MOHAMED

Hey there, I'm Amina, and here's a glimpse into who I am.

I came to Canada as a refugee, having come from Uganda as a three-year-old. Growing up in Canada gave me many gifts but also taught me how to be grateful for everything I have.

I am a photographer - not just by profession but also something I am deeply passionate about. I got my first camera from my dad when I was 10 years old, and then taught myself film and digital photography without formal education in photography. It's like discovering a secret garden within myself, bursting with colours and stories waiting to be told. I love wildlife, nature, and documentary/street photography, but I also love exploring what my camera can do and learning from others. I am also currently exploring encaustic photography, painting with wax on top of my photos.

My love of photography led me into Toronto's film & television industry. One of my most memorable movies was working on the set of American Psycho, in charge of the wardrobe department on set for a whopping 1,000 extras. Talk about a whirlwind of costumes and chaos! But hey, I thrive in the madness; every moment was an adventure.

I love listening to good music, whether jazz, R&B, African beats or the oldies essential - music is the ingredient for life's joy. Need I say more? Music is my trusty sidekick, always there to lift my spirits and soothe my soul.

Finally, I love to travel and explore different cultures, eat different foods, meet new people, and see what lies outside my front door.

So, there you have it—just a glimpse into the quirky, adventurous, and endlessly curious soul behind the lens.

Show Up Stand Up Speak Up

As a refugee, you never leave behind the home you once had - especially when it has been ripped away from you. Driven by a yearning to reconnect with my roots as a refugee from Uganda and working as a documentary producer, I embarked on a mission to capture the untold stories of exiled individuals reclaiming their stolen properties. Witnessing the stark realities of immense poverty and the systemic oppression faced by women and girls in Uganda left an indelible mark on my heart.

In 2018, I embarked on a remarkable journey, transitioning from the film and television industry after 15 incredible years to dive headfirst into starting a charity because the passion for photography continued to echo in my soul.

Due to what I saw in Uganda, women and girls denied education, forced into early marriages, and trapped in cycles of poverty ignited a fierce determination within me to effect change. I was inspired by the desire to empower young women aspiring to pursue careers in journalism and photography, hindered by limited skills and resources, and the vision for Cameras For Girls was born.

Five years later, the impact of Cameras For Girls resonates deeply within me. Through this initiative, I've had the privilege of transforming the lives of countless young women, providing them with technical skills, confidence and opportunities to thrive and, most importantly, get paid work in the male-dominated media industry. Today, these remarkable individuals are not just photographers or journalists but beacons of hope and inspiration, paving the way for a new generation of empowered women across Africa.

As I reflect on this journey, I am filled with gratitude for the opportunity to make a meaningful difference in the lives of others. amina@camerasforgirls.org

415

BE GRATEFUL

RAMIA MARIELLE EL AGAMY KHAN

My Message to Women is ...

In your pursuit of improvement,
remember to unlearn what you gained
from those who do not want you to succeed.

Show Up Stand Up Speak Up

YOU'RE ENOUGH

SUE COLEMAN

My Message to Women is ...

Discover your dreams at any age –
never too late to become who you're meant to be!

Show Up Stand Up Speak Up

AUTHENTICALLY YOU

My Story

LYDIA BURCHELL

That first step into nature is like stepping in to an altered reality.

Nature is art. The forest's magical flora and fauna, the ocean's mystical treasures, the sky filled with depths of unknown. My soul comes alive when it connects with nature and everything else just falls away.
Put a camera in my hands and I come alive with fascination and intrigue. Nature doesn't mess around, her passion, and fury, and love holds no bounds.

Imagine if everyone knew themselves as nature knows itself....

Nature gives birth, nurtures its saplings until just before they're ready, then releases them to their own path with a 'you are trusted to put all the best of you into creating your best life', to thrive, and contribute to the continuation of the species.

Now that's art, that's love!

Show Up Stand Up Speak Up

Our presence in the world shows up in how we define ourselves.

The face I show the world each day is one well-crafted from beliefs, experiences, and conditioning. Imagine if my influencers had known more about instilling a deep inner confidence. Would I have had to carry so much self-doubt?

My venture through life has certainly had its challenges, turmoil, and tragedies. I see now that each one brought me closer to a greater knowing of love, love from within.

Knowing love from within has become my greatest resource of power and strength. To know love, is to be love, is to share love. Love is one of the most powerful influencers in the world. Imagine filtering all your choices in life through love. What would that do to your relationships, health, wealth, happiness and wellbeing?

Having love as your power center, and as the foundation of your inner confidence is what I see as possible in women. Their hidden power is love.

Women's inner confidence empowered from love is my mission, my purpose, my passion. Lydia@lydiaburchell.com

BE LOVE

JANITRA & FAITH ELLISON

My Message To Women is ...

Your network impacts your net worth.
Find a tribe that motivates, and transform your life to elevate.

Show Up Stand Up Speak Up

HAVE FAITH

My Story

JANNINE MACKINNON

You'll often find me barefoot in the backyard tending to my herbs and vegetables, listening to the birds chirping, my husband doing yard work, and the kids playing in the background. It's my happy place, one I'm forever grateful to have. Growing up in apartments, boats, and low-income housing, I never had a yard, let alone a garden. I could only dream of having a space like this to grow up in, and I have it now because of a strong work ethic, taking leaps of faith, and holding the big vision. The three things that have guided me since I left home shortly after turning 16.

When you hold the big vision and trust yourself enough to do the big scary thing, no matter what it takes, you can move mountains. It's been a driving force in walking away and burning down past versions of myself. Even if it takes breaking up with boys I love, leaving stable jobs and established careers, moving away from friends and family, or ending long friendships with those I care about. Because I know the life I want to create, and I'm willing to do what it takes to build it. Not only is the destination worth it, but nothing can replace the journey of becoming, and all the beautiful lessons and gifts that come along with it.

And that's my message for you.
Trust yourself. Do what it takes, and move mountains.
I promise it's worth it.

Show Up Stand Up Speak Up

Promiscuity was familiar territory throughout my teens and 20s. Seeking comfort and validation in all the wrong places, pleasure and intimacy always had to do with someone else. Then I came crashing into motherhood and completely lost myself. With four years of back-to-back pregnancies and breastfeeding, it felt like my body wasn't my own. It was of service to others, an honourable service, but disconnecting, nonetheless.

As my daughter turned two, I set out on a path to reclaim my body as my own. What started out as personal discovery through a commitment to myself, turned into an awakening that had greater impact than I could've imagined. Through pursuing the taboo of sexuality, I was able to meet my deepest darkest shadows with love, understanding, and acceptance. I reclaimed my body, fun and playfulness reignited my marriage, and I became the present mom I knew I was meant to be.

Unapologetic Coaching was created in dedication to this potent work. There's something so magical about women coming back home to their body and connecting with their sexual life force energy. They become radiant, magnetic, in flow, and delighted with life, creating ripple effects throughout their families, and communities, changing the world one yoni breathwork session at a time. We work in service of amplifying this ripple effect through our podcast, downloadable meditations, breathwork, and pleasure practices, and an array of programs that can all be found at: www.JannineMacKinnon.com .

425

MOVE MOUNTAINS

CRISTINA BALHUI

My Message to Women is ...

Change is the only constant in our life and comes from within.
You are one decision away from a fantastic thriving life.

Show Up Stand Up Speak Up

TRUST YOURSELF

My Story

TEBELLO MOKHEMA

I am a black South African woman who enjoys public speaking and moderating large-scale global events/conferences. I am recently a crypto enthusiast and have a deep love for the game of golf. I also have six children in heaven who are my angels.

There was a period in my life where I looked forward to carrying and giving birth to my children. However, that was not to be.

In 2016 I fell pregnant with twins and was excited as I had already lost 4 children. I was ecstatic when I discovered that I was carrying twins. Unfortunately, I have one of those bodies that struggles with pregnancies, so at 22 weeks, my health took a dive as I experienced a stillbirth of one of the twins and the doctor had to perform an induced abortion, of both babies, for the sake of saving my life. Of all the losses of my children, this was the hardest to accept and embrace. I was already in my forties and was looking forward to being a mother to those two children.

After losing the twins, I needed to make sense of all the losses, and I searched for books that could help. On Kindle I was able to find one book 'Grieving the Child I Never Knew – A Devotional Companion for Comfort in the Loss of Your Unborn or Newly Born Child' by Kathe Wunnenberg. In the chapter 'Who Do You Say That I Am?' I found the answer I had been searching for, every time I lost a child. When asked how many children I have, my response is 'I have Six Children In Heaven'. Ever since reading the book and chapter, I learned to embrace and accept that the spirits of the children will forever be with and around me. I was reminded that we are spiritual beings having a human experience. I thank the higher power for allowing me to be a conduit for all the children – even for the shortest of periods.

Show Up Stand Up Speak Up

Following a career managing and leading departments in large organisations from electricity, banking, and aviation, I witnessed how hard it was for women to find their voice in these male-dominated industries. This led me to help a lot of people in their journey of personal and leadership development and become an advocate for the development of communities through empowerment of their women. In 2017 I received a call from a trusted mentor and friend, who asked if I would be keen to help establish an organisation called Female Wave of Change in my home country of South Africa. I immediately said yes!

The aspect that most attracted me is the fact that FWOC offers women from all walks of life a safe space where they can grow into Authentic Feminine Leaders who take responsibility for their future, the future of their community and of the world. Since I said yes, I have supported the expansion in South Africa and other countries in the continent, notably Kenya, Zimbabwe, Zambia, Namibia, Botswana and Nigeria and we now have representatives in over 40 countries across the world. I'll never tire of seeing the transformation of women to becoming active and vocal changemakers in their communities and countries. I've seen women start projects helping put an end to female genital mutilations, creating new female owned and led companies in the engineering and mining sectors and even simply learning to put themselves and their loved ones first.

In 2023, the Founder and then President of FWOC, Ingun Bol, inspired me to take bigger and bolder steps on my own leadership journey and invited me to take over her role as President of the organization. I wasn't sure it was the right time or that I was ready, but she saw something in me that drew me forward. That experience reminded me of how important it is for change-makers to have someone in their life that truly sees what they are capable of. I encourage all women to find that person. If you want something different for this world and would love the support of a team of change-makers around you, please reach out. I'd be honoured to stand with you. LinkedIn - https://www.linkedin.com/in/tebello-mokhema-8b547610

429

UNIQUE MASTERPIECE

My Story

DR. LISA TAN

Got rhythm?

When I was a kid, I moonwalked to Michael Jackson's vinyl records in my living room. I break danced and hip hopped my way across the floor with my sisters. No one taught me. My body instinctively grooved to the beat, especially my hip. My hip would sway, undulate, shimmy, and swirl in figure 8's. The funny thing was that I could not count music but that never stopped me. I danced like no one was watching until my first performance in high school. I choreographed my first ballet with zero ballet training. I then challenged myself to tap dance in college. My happy feet tapped to the rhythm of taiko drums without counting a beat. After I took my last bow on stage, I stopped dancing for 10 years and focused on shiny objects like a white-collar job and a white picket fence home. When I disconnected from dance and the rhythm of my soul, my life played out like a broken record on repeat. I completely lost myself and died inside.

It was not until the birth of my beautiful daughter, Skylar, that I rediscovered rhythm, the rhythm of my breath. My breath was my best girlfriend, and I escaped an emergency cesarean section and delivered vaginally. Rhythm continued to flow back into my life. When my insightful son, Styrling was about to make his debut, I reconnected to the rhythm in my hip. I twirled my hip as he spiraled out of my womb into my soulmate's arms. This inner rhythm continued to guide me when finances suddenly hit rock bottom. To cut the high living expenses in California, a friend taught me to homeschool my kids in Asia. Every cell in my body tingled and resonated with "Heck Yes"! We packed our bags and turned a crisis into the best year of living on the edge.

Most recently, my soulmate, Ocean, assisted and witnessed my very own rebirth. A double helix of golden light spiraled from my hip to my crown and beyond. This serpent-like energy awakened orgasmic bliss. In that moment, I was reborn to my true nature. I am Love. We are Love. Shakira's right. Our hips don't lie. We've all got rhythm- heart rhythm, circadian rhythm, seasonal rhythm, celestial rhythm, and soul rhythm. We just gotta tune in.

Keep dancing,

Show Up Stand Up Speak Up

Where is the richest place on Earth? Is it the United States or United Arab Emirates? Guess again. Drumroll… the graveyard. It's where books are never published, forgiveness never given, I love you's never said, and dreams never dreamt. Years ago, I was buried in my fears of the past and worries of the grave future. I was trapped in an endless, dreamless sleep.

One day, I was lucky enough to get a wakeup call. I got home after an exhausting work shift. My babysitter ran up to me in excitement and shouted that my little boy, Styrling, said mama for the first time. Silence. I tried to muster a fake smile but all I wanted was to crawl to bed. Not a single cell in my body was excited. I was completely dead inside. How can my babysitter be more excited than me?

Something had to change. I delved into neuroscience, quantum physics, and tantra to turn my burnout into bliss. I was finally able to wake up and feel alive. I dared to forgive and dream again. Right now, you are holding and reading the very book that did get published. Bliss is your birthright too, so I created SPARK, a revolutionary reboot for your mind, body, and spirit. Imagine waking up and jumping out of bed with excitement. Imagine loving who you see in the mirror again. Imagine showing up, standing up, and speaking up to your truth. I am here to spark your fire of desire in minutes a day. Spark new neuron connections. Spark wings that will carry you far as a queen bee. Honey, come fly and spark with me and other queen bees in our global hive. Tune in to https://www.drlisatan.com/

431

SPARK MAGIC

CELINE O'DONOVAN

My Message to Women is . . .

Life is always happening for you, to propel you on your soul's mission.

Show Up Stand Up Speak Up

RISE UP

My Story

MICHELLE GARDINER

I am standing on a stage, dressed in a very proper gray pencil dress and behind a lectern. As I look at the audience, and gaze at the huge stage, I feel a strong urge to kick my shoes off and to dance around that stage. What I see is a huge and epic space that has been completely overlooked and potentially wasted. This was a vision I had of myself while in meditation, many years ago.

So much of this vision is me in this world and how I navigate life.

I am a huge hearted, community minded, spirit fed, soul led woman, who is orchestrating life, love, learning and expansion. I am a dancer and yogini. Essentially, I love the way that energy flows through me and I believe that I am here to make the very best use of what I have been given in this lifetime. I love that we get to choose how we channel and use our energy. In a world where I give a lot and care immensely, I give myself movement and a deep connection to the human vessel that I call mine in this lifetime. The things that most people label self-care, I balk at, and instead call dance and movement my own.

Many years ago, I was inspired by Isadora Duncan, the creator of contemporary dance. She said "you were wild once, don't let them tame you". I believe that we are here to live fully in every way. That life is both creativity and an adventure, only limited by how open we are with it, from imagining the broadest vision to attending to the tiniest details with precision.

I believe that if life is a stage, the world is our dance floor, and we are constantly being presented with opportunities to step more and more deeply into this, and into ourselves. I also believe that we are constantly being given the opportunity by life itself to shy away and to take the unobtrusive path, or to take a deep breath and to dive boldly, stepping into new spaces.

On this, I love space, and I love beauty. I love what is possible when humans are present with one another in the same space, and I believe that this is where change is truly instigated. In the space between you and I, where we get to see the reflection of life and humanity itself.

Show Up Stand Up Speak Up

I am a believer of story, purpose, passion, and change. I lead a global platform for women leading change and impact, called The Aspire Series and founded a project called 55 FACES. The number 55 stands for "significant change aligned with soul purpose" and I have witnessed firsthand how this body of work has both created magic and become medicine over and over again. We all exist here as vessels filled with stories and we all hold the threads of change and impact for humanity. As women, WE are the gateway to this change and now is our time! I know that this work is what I am here for, and it uses me fully. I have a gift in seeing a person fully and in drawing the story from them, amplifying this, and crafting it in a way that the average person can articulate their experience in words. That they can see humanity in one another. I am primarily a social worker by background, with threads of child psychoanalytic psychotherapy, life coaching, yoga teaching, women's work, and narrative therapy woven in. I am based primarily between Australia (Sydney/Melbourne) and Bali, Indonesia.

I have two dreams for The Aspire Series and 55 FACES. The first is that every woman has the experience of feeling whole, expanded, and able to do whatever it is that she sets out to do in this world, and that she leads with a heart and soul resonance that is her truth. The second is that I would love to have a physical home for The Aspire Series where our women can drop in and know they too are home. Hello@theaspireseries.com

LOVE EXPANSIVELY

KRISTINA L.

My Message To Women is ...

Investing in yourself, loving and bettering yourself, and fully trusting yourself
is ALL you need.

Show Up Stand Up Speak Up

PRIORITIZE YOURSELF

JO BROMILOW

I would have not thought I would do most of my life journey on my own. As they say, God only gives you what you can handle. However, the best part of this journey is having people in your life that you can walk and run with. I would say I'm a loner and love my own company, but I have had for many years a wonderful group of friends, my "second family". I find it very hard to ask for help, I've always been too proud to ask.

I'm a mum of 23 years old twins. I didn't have a choice but was thrown into single parenthood.
It's made me strong, and earlier in life I always believed I had to fight for what I believed in. The best part is, I know I've been a good example to my children, and now it is coming back to me two-fold.

I recently lost my father to cancer and one thing my children have never in their lives is their own father, but having my father around the last three years was a blessing and a joy to watch the friendships bloom between dad and my son and daughter. My son spoke at his celebration of life party and the love and sentimental adoration he had for his grandfather shone through. He reminds me so much of my father, and how lucky I was to have my father around me and my mother and father to move in with me for his last years.

After my father passed, I have found a love of gardening, how I can potter in the garden and lose myself for hours planting my vegetables. Every morning I look forward to seeing how much my apple and Lebanese cucumbers, tomatoes and capsicum have grown.

Show Up Stand Up Speak Up

Jo's approach to life and business:
- Passion is key to success
- First impressions are not always correct
- Have faith in yourself and others
- Have trust and respect for others
'

Early in her career working for several companies she identified the need for small businesses to have access to qualified experts who could look after their bookkeeping and payroll needs without the cost of in-house resources. CHAMP Enterprises began from Jo's passion for business finances and a desire to help small to medium business. She qualified in Accounting with the National Institute of Accountants, and her company has gone from strength to strength.

Jo moved to the lower Blue Mountains in 2004, and immediately looked for ways to be involved with the local community. When her children were at childcare age, Jo took an interest in her local after school OOSH. She saw again a need for childcare centres/OOSH centres to have access to qualified and dedicated bookkeeping experts.Her close work with the centres and their committees evolved into the provision of financial management and compliance practices, providing a 'one stop shop' for both the centres and parents. Her increased involvement in the sector led to ongoing opportunities to 'give back'.Jo never takes anything for granted, has always believed in herself and trusted that the universe would provide (of course, with dedication and hard work): a rewarding career, a great life and family, together with the opportunity to share what she loves doing whilst helping small to medium businesses, just like hers. Jo@champenterprises.com.au

439

BE TENACIOUS

My Story

TRACIE EATON

I adore colour. The way it makes me feel at any given moment. The way the green grass sparkling with morning dew makes me feel alive. The way the orange flowers at the gate to the horse paddock on my childhood farm made me giggle every time I saw them jiggling in the breeze. The way the blue sky as I lay on the hill making cloud shapes helped me feel peaceful. And how, in every version of me during my life, colour and creating with it was the one constant helping me heal and walk through the many experiences of my life. I have 'Lavender' my pet cow to thank for my love of colour. Her beautiful chocolate eyes soothed my soul every day. And I am forever grateful for this memory.

Colour is like a shiny object to me. I see it's fabulousness everywhere. I need to touch it too, as though I will be able to absorb the fabulous energy it is omitting, and sprinkle some of that joy to others.

You see, I believe we have two choices in life, to live with gratitude and joy, seeing all the beauty around us. Or allow our fears, our challenges, our tough moments to define us, suffocating our ability to shine. And I absolutely choose joy. Let me be clear, this does not mean I have not had my share of experiences that have shaken me to the core. Yet, is it not these experiences, these moments that amplify the beauty of life. Of love. Of adventure. Of play. Of living with a sense of wonderment – just like we did as a child.

I always knew I wanted people to feel as I did. But how? My intuition was clear – paint. Prolifically. Paint all the moments in bold and unapologetic colour. Show people how you see the world. Connect them to themselves, to each other. Gift them unconditional love, joy and beauty.
Ah, yes, I know, this can perhaps feel somewhat flippant. Yet, if I may share one key learning from my time here, it's this. Please, embrace ALL the moments. They only happen once so experience them wholly. Cry deeply when you need to, grieve the hard times. Laugh out loud at your mistakes, celebrate the fabulous. And *be present*. Always.

All are life changing. All create a chapter of who you are.

Show Up Stand Up Speak Up

I have always been creative. So, when I was deciding what to do with my life, well, pick one. Brain surgeon, artist. Teacher, artist. Aerial photographer, artist. Occupational therapist, artist. Sales, artist. Colour psychology, artist. I may have spent many YEARS exploring other options, choosing to NOT hear my intuition. But eventually, my intuition stopped me in my tracks, and I consciously stepped into what I always was…an artist. And my medium? Colour and visual arts. Painting.

I was working in an executive sales job when it became abundantly clear one morning that it was time for me to take on the most fearful journey of my life! I had a deep-set belief that being an artist wasn't a 'real job', so I worked in as many plan B jobs as you could imagine. Becoming the artist I always was meant being vulnerable, being seen, being open. There is freedom in embracing your inner challenges, so I did. And here we are. And what an incredible journey. Using colour and paintings to lift someone's day. I am honoured and grateful every time I create an original painting that someone feel so strongly when they see it, they have tears of joy. I create to showcase the luxuriousness of life. To encourage exploring boundaries. To bring someone's vision to life, visually representing moments in time. To remind people of the feelings of joy and optimism. And to connect people together with intention, to change lives visually sharing inspirations and stories.

How can a painting reflect you? What colours work best for you? How can paintings create profound change? You know a bit about me. Let's chat about you. I'd love to connect! tracie@tracieeaton.com

441

PLAY OFTEN

THAYNE WESTERMAN

My Message to Women is ...

Imagine how different the world would be
if we all took care of ourselves, our personal health,
mind, body, and spirit.

Show Up Stand Up Speak Up

BE LOVE

My Story

NICOLENE PRINSLOO

I am a student of life. My joy comes from learning through theory and practice & then sharing the discoveries. My family lovingly listens to and supports my adventures. I hadn't always experienced bliss. Have you ever felt like everything is a battle? The good in my life and my successes came from dragging myself by the hair, kicking and screaming, with a boulder strapped to my chest. Somehow, there was always a knowing that it didn't have to be that way. Like a dim light flickering far away in the night. It didn't make sense that things had to be so difficult. It didn't make sense that the only way to get somewhere was to get away from something else. I'd had glimpses of peace, ease, and no limitation. In others and myself. I knew it was possible.

In my quest to figure out what was wrong with me and how to improve, I found many ways to do that, and I got better. Have you ever tried to manage yourself like that? It's exhausting. And things you try to overcome never seem to go away completely. It lurks beneath the surface. I've learned a simple truth since then: You can create what you'd love to have, or you can try and solve everything you think is wrong with you. But you can't do both. It's one or the other. You can't be half-pregnant. Creation or problem-solving.

You're not broken. There is nothing to fix. Putting all my focus, effort, and energy into creating what I would love to have instead of self-helping and trying to fix myself has not only led me here but also to myself. Nobody gets to where they are on their own. From a simple cup of coffee because I've been sitting at my desk for hours. To receiving kindness and grace in moments where I don't deserve it. To experts and coaches sharing their wisdom. You teach me life, and I am deeply grateful.

Show Up Stand Up Speak Up

I support people in creating coaching and consulting businesses they love. I'm grateful to have experienced what a profound impact a small shift in understanding could have from mentors who have the courage to bring their expertise and wisdom to the world. In all areas of my life, I have learned from those who have already achieved my goals.

Those who have gone before me, who tested things out, who got the bruises and then cared enough to find a way to share it with the rest of us. That is what fuels the fire of my dedication to serving people who serve other people.

Many people have transformational insights and messages to share, but they don't know how to connect with the people that they were called to serve. I love to empower these people with simple ways to get long-lasting results with ease. I'd love to learn more about and connect with you.
nicolene.j.prinsloo@gmail.com

HAVE FUN

My Story

NADINE KAREN THOMPSON

I appreciate the simple things of life; walking in the park, observing nature, picking beautiful flowers, pressing them in my journals, and hearing birds chatter with each other. I look around at nature and think it's a beautiful representation of a great creator. This makes me want to create exquisite paintings and drawings, but I am not good at drawing or painting or that's what I told myself for a long time. I didn't see myself as a creative person. I love writing poetry but didn't consider myself an artist. Since living here in China, I had the privilege to join various expatriate groups that focus on getting together and doing DIY projects such as soap making/candle making, paint and sip activities and vision board craft. It was then that I discovered that I possessed my own style of creativity. We are all creative in diverse ways and I watched canvases, bags and journals transformed into their own themes based on the innate style of the artist working on the project.

Now, I happily describe myself as an artist. I treasure my first ever painting on canvas, I look at the first journal wrapping that I did four years ago and the one I did recently, and I am proud to say that I have evolved as an artist. The truth is the limits we place on ourselves only exist in our minds and that is what I have learned by doing these art projects. I wished I had gleaned this realization as a child. Enjoying the freedom to create, make a mess and start again. Sometimes art becomes a conversation about perfection, but beauty is in the eye of the beholder.

When I wake up in the morning. I listen to hear the distinct voices of the birds singing. I note the sound of the wind, and even when there are the sounds of cars and other noise around somehow, I hear nature first. I was born and grew up in a rural part of Jamaica. My family's home was surrounded by nature. It resides deep within me, and I find affinity with it wherever I call home.

Nature has all the healing aspects to nurture us, especially when we become stressed and overwhelmed by our problems. Gathering inspiration from nature on canvases, camera lens, and DIY craft will truly transform our outlook.

Start your art journey today!

Show Up Stand Up Speak Up

Growing up, I had one dream and that was to be a published writer. I loved having a notebook that I would fill with poems and anecdotal stuff that I observed around me. As time passed, I understood that breaking into the world of writing was a huge deal. Getting published by a traditional publishing house was quite illusive, and unattainable for me. I pushed this dream to the back of my mind and got wrapped up in making a living. Throughout the years, I continued drafting my poems, and I also discovered the power of journaling.

At the start of the COVID 19 pandemic in China, I was strongly reminded of the fragility of life. The question came to me, 'What do you want to do with your life?' I knew instantly that it had to do with my writing. I was led to a great editor and got my first book of poems published. This book opened the doors to so many great opportunities. I have spoken at virtual summits, done virtual book tours, held workshops on journaling and dived deeper into the world of coaching.

I see so many women out there just like me, keeping their purpose buried deep within. I created my book coaching around this theme of helping women especially to uncover and bring to life that untold story. Stories are powerful! What is your book idea? What doors can your story open? How will your story heal you? What message will it uncover? How will your storytelling enhance your purpose? Let's explore these deep questions together! Join me at https://nadinethompson.podia.com/

LIVE ABUNDANTLY

DEENA KORDT

My Message To Women is ...

In every moment, cherish yourself.
Be kind, gentle and loving.
Be the best friend and ally you deserve.

Show Up Stand Up Speak Up

TRUST INSTINCT

ANGEL TUCCY

On more than one occasion, I've been told that my energy sparkles. I'm certain that came from my mom – one of the strongest, most courageous and loving women I know. I'm certain she doesn't even know how her decisions continue to impact me every day, and now I feel so blessed to be witnessing how my three wonderful adult children are finding their own way to brighten the world.

I believe one of my gifts is the gift of encouragement and helping people around me feel like they have permission to rise and sparkle. As a shy awkward kid growing up, my word would have been "shadow", because I was always hiding in the shadows – starting a new school every few years, never really feeling like I fit in. I was in my thirties before I finally stumbled into a career in broadcasting, where I got to do one of my most favorite things in the world; put a microphone in front of someone and give them the spotlight.

One of the best parts of my work, is that if fits ideally into my lifestyle. Everyone has a story, a message, or something they're passionate about, and every day, there are radio shows, magazines, journalists, and podcast hosts seeking stories to share. I simply play matchmaker and bring opportunities together.

When you share what you're most passionate about, your eyes light up and sparkle. If you have a chance to share your story a couple of times each week, it will remove the shadows of doubt and fear that creep in and make you want to hide. I get to match my clients up with guest interviews every week giving them an endless opportunity to sparkle even brighter.

I've learned from many occasions of pivoting shifting, and changing directions, that when you follow your heart, you'll never make a mistake.

Show Up Stand Up Speak Up

I was a shy introvert throughout my youth, probably because I was a Navy kid who changed schools and friends every few years. Barely graduating high school with tremendous stage fright, I eventually found comfort behind the microphone hosting a podcast.

Within 6 months, my show was discovered by a local radio station, and I became a local radio talk show host, broadcasting every day. I ended up with a 10-year career in broadcasting, hosting 2 daily talk shows, and syndicated across 28 stations. During that time, I hosted over 2500 shows and interviewed over 5,000 guests. I was getting to do what I loved and what I felt I was finally good at. Due to a format change at the station, and an abrupt release from my contracts, I chose to become a public speaker, and took my stage fright on the road, speaking on over 100 stages over the next 18 months.

When the pandemic struck, all my traveling ceased, and everything went virtual. I found myself sitting back in that familiar seat, speaking to a microphone, and hosting another daily show., but this time, from my house, rather than a radio studio. With my network and connections, I was constantly being approached with the request, "I need a guest", and I became the "Media Matchmaker" helping speakers find stages and podcast hosts find guests. An idea sparked to start an online community to bring those requests together, and today, that spark of an idea has grown to a network of over 32,000 people coming together to find guests and get booked. www.NeedaGuest.com

SPARKLE ON

My Story

VANDANA PURANIK

Imagine the thrill of standing on a precipice, not out of recklessness, but at the cusp of a transformative journey. That's where my story took root, on the verge of the unknown, poised to leap into boundless potential. It was in this moment, with the horizon stretched wide before me, that I found my calling: to guide audacious women who are restless outliers across the uncharted landscapes of their ambitions, towards a horizon where possibilities know no bounds. This purpose was born from an intimate epiphany, intertwined with my children's stories and a profound awakening.

Flashback to a pivotal moment when I sought a psychologist's expertise for my children, suspecting my son's mischief was rooted in sheer boredom. True to our hunch, he was a gifted mind yearning for more rigorous mental gymnastics. A relief washed over us, knowing we could quench his intellectual thirst with advanced studies. However, it was the revelation about my daughter that turned my world on its head. Also highly gifted, she was perfectly content in her bubble. When quizzed about our plans for her, we faltered, mistakenly equating her happiness with fulfillment. "That is exactly why you need to push for her and champion her cause. This is the exact reason girls get left behind. They find a way to make things work. They are diplomatic. They choose happiness, keeping the peace and making friends. You need to champion her cause because if you don't, who will?" the psychologist implored.

That was my moment of reckoning. It dawned on me that this wasn't just about my daughter—it was a clarion call for all women. A reminder of the dormant volcano of potential within us that often goes unnoticed or neglected. It spotlighted the imperative to be our own and each other's cheerleaders. In the entrepreneurial sphere and beyond, women are reservoirs of infinite potential that we often gloss over in our quest for contentment, oblivious to the power that lies within.

My odyssey since that epochal day has been a crusade to kindle a firestorm within women. Much like my daughter, many of us may bask in contentment, unaware of the giftedness that, if cultivated, can catapult us to stratospheric successes. My mission transcends mere business triumphs; it's about sparking an epiphany of our true essence and ensuring that every woman is bolstered to navigate her boundless potential. This is the crux of my journey—an odyssey of exploration, empowerment, and unbridled possibilities.

Show Up Stand Up Speak Up

I'm Vandana Puranik, a trailblazer in the entrepreneurial scene, passionately committed to lifting ambitious women entrepreneurs to heights beyond their imagination. My mission? To inject momentum into their ventures, shining a beacon of success and infinite possibilities. My path is one of shattering the status quo, kindling audacious dreams, and envisioning a realm where women lead in every domain.

Boasting over 25 years in marketing, innovation, and strategy, my knack for creative problem-solving sets me apart. I've written and championed this indispensable skill, turning turmoil into clarity and fostering steady business expansion. My approach melds bold thinking, relentless curiosity, and love for the unexpected. My varied career spans significant roles at sprawling multinationals to spirited startups. This reflects my undaunted dedication to surmounting industry-wide hurdles. As a USA Today & Wall Street Journal bestselling author and a worldwide speaker, I thrive on unconventional routes, guiding individuals and organizations through pivotal changes when old tactics fall short. Raised as a global citizen, my life is deeply influenced by a rich respect for diversity and insightful understanding of human psychology, shaped by my time across different countries. This worldly view and flexibility are key in reshaping my success strategy. My world outside work is filled with laughter, sports, cultural dives, reading, and cherished moments with my family. These experiences enrich my resolve and commitment.

At Active Ingredients Inc., I've developed a distinctive methodology for individuals to carve their paths to success. I'm devoted to mentoring and providing insights that bolster business acumen and personal growth. With new publications on the horizon, my role promises to light the way for educational and developmental leaps. I welcome connections to embark on transformative journeys brimming with boundless opportunities and unmatched success. If you're a woman entrepreneur who knows you're meant for more, reach out to me at https://www.linkedin.com/in/vandanapuranik

STAY CURIOUS

YVETTE DURAZO

I embraced motherhood at the age of 17, facing numerous challenges along the way. Despite the obstacles, my unwavering determination propelled me to pursue education relentlessly. At a pivotal point of my journey, I struggled with heath issues, while being a single mother, and dealing with an organization in where I couldn't see career advancement, that along my retirement funds looked not promising.

Recognizing that, as a Latina woman, I was adept at negotiating for others but often neglected myself, I decided to break this pattern. In my late 30s, I returned to school to pursue a master's degree in Negotiation, Conflict Resolution, and Peacebuilding. This transformative experience not only equipped me with invaluable skills for personal growth but also inspired me to establish a business, recognizing the scarcity of such teachings in traditional education.

Through this journey, I discovered the broader impact of negotiation skills, realizing that I could contribute to breaking the cycle of women not advocating for themselves in both life and career. Having grown up in two cultures, I intimately understand the challenges of cultural diversity, which can hinder women specially to learn conflict resolution and negotiation skills. This realization fueled my passion to guide others in turning challenges into opportunities and empower women to develop life-transforming leadership skills.

Show Up Stand Up Speak Up

Yvette Durazo, MA, PCC, the founder of a boutique firm Unitive Consulting. She serves as a factional Ombudsperson for organizations, providing training, mediation, and conflict resolutions services. Yvette, with a PCC coaching credential, holds a master's degree in Conflict Resolution and an undergraduate degree in International Business. A Professor at the University of California, Santa Cruz Silicon Valley Extension and UC Davis, she teaches Human Resources, Leadership Development, Mediation Skills, Negotiation and Conflict Management. Yvette's leadership includes coaching women in negotiation skills.

If my story resonates with you, I invite you to continue our conversation at ydurazo@unitiveconsulting.com. Together, let's inspire positive change and growth.

NEGOTIATE LIFE

LUCKY LAURIDSEN

My Message to Women is ...

Embrace Self-Compassion to unlock your inner strength,
nurture self-worth, wellbeing,
and elevate fulfillment and happiness in your life.

Show Up Stand Up Speak Up

LOVE YOURSELF

My Story

KELLY WAGNER

Aloha, I am Kelly, a divine spirit having a human experience. A woman of many roles—wife, mother, daughter, entrepreneur, psychic medium, and confidant—I am unequivocally committed to embracing life's opportunities and the power of saying "Yes." For much of my existence, I conformed to the expectations of others. However, amidst my journey of transformation, I unearthed my inner voice. I actually confronted the realization that I must cease surrendering my aspirations to fulfill someone else's dreams after dedicating 17 years to my family's company. This epiphany shook me to my core, igniting a profound exploration of the beckoning opportunities around me.

My extensive array of experiences, "mistakes," and unconventional education have sculpted the person I am today. From humble beginnings in family-run businesses to navigating the complexities of international corporations, I have cultivated a multifaceted skill set, fostering adaptability and empathy unparalleled by my peers. Since wholeheartedly embracing my true calling and path, my creativity has blossomed exponentially, unveiling a realm of boundless possibilities.

In 2021, my husband and I embarked on a monumental endeavor, acquiring Edge Magazine, a venerable print magazine devoted to holistic and spiritual discourse. Despite the magnitude of this leap of faith, every facet of this endeavor has seamlessly fallen into place. It felt not just right but divinely aligned.

Never did I envision myself as a Psychic Medium and a magazine publisher, disseminating over 100,000 magazine copies annually across North America, hosting a podcast—The Being Curious Show—ranked within the top 10 percent, and orchestrating events attended by thousands.

Yet, here I stand, embodying curiosity and wholeheartedly embracing opportunities as they manifest daily.
Mahalo

Kelly.

Show Up Stand Up Speak Up

Three years ago, I assumed the role as publisher for Edge Magazine and the Edge Network. Our platform stands as a comprehensive multimedia nexus, uniting holistic and alternative thought leaders with our community and sharing insights, wisdom, and offerings. Our objective is to cultivate a nurturing, safe space wherein individuals can undergo transformative journeys, dismantling entrenched norms and beliefs to construct something new and authentic, guided by the tools we provide and aligned with their optimal outcomes.

We are at the intersection of the enigmatic, supernatural, and paranormal-focused communities. Leveraging my corporate and marketing expertise, we're refining our media platform to function as an all-encompassing resource center and ecosystem. Here, those with inquisitive minds can access insights from esteemed thought leaders spanning diverse subjects alongside information on community gatherings, educational classes, immersive retreats, and thought-provoking experiences. Our platform facilitates connections among thought leaders, fostering fertile ground for partnerships and collaborations. It continues to grow, boasting over 40,000 monthly website views, 600 distribution points for our print magazine across North America, three dynamic podcasts, and a robust social media presence.

We meet everyone in our community through the lens of curiosity. Approaching life with curiosity affords us the flexibility to expand our consciousness, fostering receptivity and openness among individuals. Hence, the magazine's mantra, "What are you curious about?" resonates deeply with us. This sentiment echoes in our podcast, "The Being Curious Show," where an eclectic array of guests share their wisdom, inviting the curious to partake in the discourse.

The Edge Partner Directory (edgedirectory.net) boasts a diverse spectrum of specialists in print and online in unconventional fields and specialties, alongside innovative products and services. It nurtures a dynamic community of teachers and seekers alike.

Our mission is clear: to extend a supportive hand to those grappling with unanswered questions, dissatisfaction with their current circumstances, or a yearning to share their innate gifts. We strive to empower individuals to embrace their higher purpose in whatever form they find most fitting. Individually, I provide guidance and counsel as a psychic medium and intuitive business advisor. Curious about working together? I invite you to connect with me at **Kelly@edgemagazine.net.**

459

BE CURIOUS

My Story

MARIETJIE MACMILLAN

People matter to me! When I feel completely out of place, when I have lost my focus, my why, it typically is because I cannot serve people! Sometimes, and often, it is from the background, and I am okay with that. Serving people is exactly that, doing good without expecting a reward! Knowing I made a difference in someone's life, inspiring them to grow, beyond what they imagined they could do, is especially satisfying – life feels good!

My Message to Women is …
Everything around us tells us every day what beauty is or should be! But there is no one like you – be you, the unlimited version of you, because there is only one of you! Be unlimitedly Fabulous!

Show Up Stand Up Speak Up

When I was 15, choosing subjects, in South Africa, I was told that I cannot pick the subjects I wanted, as they were University level. We could not afford University, therefore, there was no point, and I was forced to pick non-university level subjects. I grew up incredibly poor, with most of my childhood and teenage years, many days going hungry as there simply wasn't food. I started working at age 13 at the grocery store packing groceries, I quit school at 17, my parents could not afford to keep me in school! But I didn't want to settle for what I was told; that I am only good for POVERTY, like all my family, living barely from paycheque to paycheque. I knew I could do more. I finished my grade 12 in English, taking distance courses. I immigrated to Canada, and I made a promise, I will be an example to my family! Show them that you can become more, you don't have to settle.

Not being materialistic, but out of encouragement. I worked hard, studied while working and obtained my Accounting Designation. I worked my way up to a CFO, even Acting-CFO for the Liquor board of British Columbia. Did it change who I am? NO! If I can do it, with determination, courage and despite being told NO several times and getting up after being knocked down – anyone can! Yes, YOU CAN! I am seeing the next generation taking that leap, getting an education, choosing to create a better life! I hear them say, we are encouraged because you did it. I achieved my purpose!

Don't stop at no, don't stop at what others think, but change the world for the better, even if that world especially if the world is around you!

EMBODY FABULOUSNESS

YAN-KAY CRYSTAL LOWE

My Message to Women is ...

Unabashedly embrace who you are.
Remember that there is someone out there
who can, and will,
benefit from your specific tenacity.

Show Up Stand Up Speak Up

KEEP GOING

Your Story

YOU

This chapter is waiting for your name at the top. It's waiting for your quote, for your bio at the bottom of the page, for your beautiful picture where you can't help but have the biggest smile. It is waiting for your story of success. It is here, a blank page waiting for you to tell us how you were able to understand your journey, expand your heart and brave your life.

We're waiting to read your pages of what dreams you have seen realized. We are waiting to read how you made changes, added, subtracted, altered, expanded after reading this book ….

Share what the moments, hours, days, or months have been like on your way to the place of where you want to be.

This page is being left for your journey, your experiences, your struggles, your aspirations, and your path to freedom … whatever that means to you.

These pages await your untold story. You will share how you were able to help yourself, your family, your friends, or your community because ONE DAY, you decided that if all these women in this book could do it, SO COULD YOU!
You realized when you finally made that decision, that deep-seated internal YES, somehow everything in your life got better. Doors opened, possibilities and opportunities became clear, the relationships in your life just got 100 percent better, you smile more, you walk differently, you feel lighter, and everyone notices that something is different about you.

Maybe this chapter is where you are going to write your advice to the next person you want life to bless, to feel the same freedom, to feel the same hope and to achieve the same things that will change their life, like yours has.

Let us be the first to say Congratulations. This page awaits your words and we all can't wait to read them VERY SOON.

YOU

ABOUT DEB DRUMMOND

Deb Drummond lives in beautiful Vancouver, Canada. She is the mother of her two favourite people: her daughter, Chloae, and her son, Ocean. With her new title of YaYa, she gets to add to that "favourite list" Brynlee and Kashton.

Deb is a pioneer in the world of entrepreneurship and was one of the first in her country to create companies in the health and wellness sector. To date, she has built 7 international companies and inspired thousands around the globe. Deb has been recognized in SUCCESS magazine 48 times, has been given numerous nominations, and has won numerous awards for her accolades in her personal and business achievements.

She is the Founder and Visionary behind the Show Up Stand Up Speak Up, Yes You! movement. This is a televised, heart-centered project with a reach of over 350 million designed to inspire women, and those that support women, to remember the solidarity of International Women's Day.

Deb's thirty-year deep dive of study and training in Top Performance has built her reputation in the field as a speaker, mastermind trainer and personal coach. She has inspired, educated, and motivated audiences of over 20 thousand to stand to their feet. In her private practice, Deb has personally worked with over 30 thousand clients, moving them to a higher state of optimal health and wealth.

A well-known radio host of the Mission Accepted podcast, Deb interviews dynamic Entrepreneurs, Ultrapreneurs, Creatives, and Media Professionals who share the guts and glory of entrepreneurship. Also, included in the weekly podcast is the "GenZ Is Us" show where Deb and Ocean interview other 'Momagers', 'Dadagers', and GenZ entrepreneurs that are creating successful & generational companies, experiences, and wealth. Deb is the founder of Mission Accepted Media where she creates anthologies and books about people and business. She is the creator of the ever so popular Top Performance Day Planner and Tracker.+
Deb loves music and is happiest when she is connecting people that she knows will benefit from meeting each other and, if you were to go to her home, you would be greeted with a table of "treats" that look like she took over Willy Wonka's candy shop!

Social media handles:
www.debdrummond.com
Deb@debdrummond.com
LI – https://www.linkedin.com/in/DebDrummond/
FB – https://www.facebook.com/deborahldrummond/
IG – @deborahldrummond; @debdrummond_official; @missionaccepted_media
YouTube – https://www.youtube.com/channel/UCsnh0BsWjHS1aba4cItw4rw
Media:
#1 International Best-Selling Author
Featured in 500+ Media houses & Magazines
As seen on Amazon, AppleTV, Roku

ABOUT MISSION ACCEPTED MEDIA

The name Mission Accepted took a lot of time for me to polish. It was essential to have a name that truly represented what needs to take place, both fundamentally and at the core of every person who decides to become a self-starter.

Entrepreneurship on every level captures the essence of anyone willing to "take on the mission" of creating a life by design. Whether it's the singer that is looking for their big break, the entrepreneur looking to make their mark in the marketplace, the actor waiting to be discovered, or the radio host who is building an audience, if you said "yes" to making your own way in your career, then you took on the mission.

Before one says yes to being an entrepreneur, there most likely have been a lot of conversations going on with other people, advisors, and close friends, and for sure in the confines of one's own mind. One must make the decision to say yes on the inside: in your heart, your brain, or both before the word YES comes out of your mouth and the excitement starts! We understand those moments so well!!

We wanted to create many platforms to offer what entrepreneurs need the most: the right kind of exposure. We wanted to celebrate that spirit of YES by assisting and creating an easier way to do that. Deborah Drummond, the owner of Mission Accepted, has been an entrepreneur for over 30 years and knows firsthand the behind-the-scenes work it takes to make it. It was her vision to offer a plethora of support through media opportunities to help current entrepreneurs set up for future success.

Deb was a pioneer in entrepreneurship, building her legacy before we had smartphones and social media. She understands the challenges that can be brought to all generations who want to "make their own mark", and her goal is to create a safe, successful place for all generations, even these new incredible GenZs, to land.

Mission Accepted Media is made available to anyone needing a place to get the word out about who they are, what they do, and what they need. It is also a place for everyone, entrepreneurs or not to come and be inspired by the stories, the climb, the diversity, and the unbelievable creativity that these crazy folks draw from to keep on keeping on.

Mission Accepted Media hosts an incredible podcast, including live podcasts on stage at events, or in the comforts of your home studio, aka your desk! We also publish collaboration anthologies of incredible books that encourage the rise and celebration of entrepreneurship.

Mission Accepted Media recognizes entrepreneurship shows up in many different ways, which is why we highlight Entrepreneurs, Ultrapraneurs, Creatives such as artists, singers, actors, and authors as well as self-started media like radio, podcasts, tv hosts, and print publications.

Please reach out to explore opportunities to be on the show as well if you'd like to be featured in one of the books or if you have an event and want live podcasts on-site.

May you keep your Mission alive, whatever that means to you!
Passion is the fuel to expansion and expansion is one of life's best gifts!

In good health and new friendships
Deb Drummond

OTHER PUBLICATIONS

Top Performance Success Tracker
This is the ultimate system for keeping track of all your contacts and follow-up steps. Designed and used by Deb Drummond.

Top Performance Success Planner
Designed to complement your Success Tracker, Deb has created a full-year day planning system, embedded with inspirational quotes from top leaders around the globe.

262 Project Journals
A selection of 9 different beautiful covers. These journals are for writing, gratitude, priorities, creative expression, or diary writing.

22 Women Ultrapreneurs & History-Making Couples Leaving Legacy in Network Marketing Tell All - International #1 Best Seller
An incredible collection of highly successful Direct Sales Professionals that have revealed never shared before Top Network Marketing Secrets.

All of these incredible books and more resources are available at
https://debdrummond.com/

THE CONTEMPORARY
AFRICAN KITCHEN

THE CONTEMPORARY
AFRICAN KITCHEN

HOME COOKING RECIPES FROM
THE LEADING CHEFS OF AFRICA

ALEXANDER SMALLS

WITH NINA ODURO

16

NORTHERN AFRICA

COUNTRIES OF AFRICA

Northern Africa
Algeria
Egypt
Libya
Mauritania
Morocco
Sahrawi Republic
Tunisia

Eastern Africa
Comoros
Djibouti
Eritrea
Ethiopia
Kenya
Madagascar
Mauritius
Rwanda
Seychelles
Somalia
South Sudan
Sudan
Tanzania
Uganda

Southern Africa
Angola
Botswana
Eswatini
Lesotho
Malawi
Mozambique
Namibia
South Africa
Zambia
Zimbabwe

Western Africa
Benin
Burkina Faso
Cabo Verde
Côte d'Ivoire
Gambia
Ghana
Guinea
Guinea-Bissau
Liberia
Mali
Niger
Nigeria
Senegal
Sierra Leone
Togo

Central Africa
Burundi
Cameroon
Central African Republic
Chad
Congo Republic
DR Congo
Equatorial Guinea
Gabon
São Tomé and Príncipe

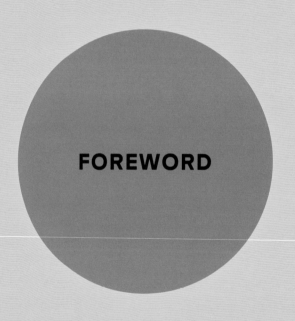

FOREWORD

As far back as I can remember, I knew I was different. I grew up in the American South surrounded by Negro people, sheltered in our respected communities, set apart from the heart of the city where White people, whom I'd encounter with caution in mostly public areas, appeared to flourish. Life seemed compartmentalized, tainted, and chained by a lack of freedom, a "privilege" that was held hostage for those who looked like me. This forced environment was due to an order of authority imposed by Whites, who, for some reason, seemed to own our very existence and control our fate, if not our destiny. This reality, one that suffocated us, was to most normal and unquestioned. Our customs, our daily activities, and all aspects of our lives were informed by *them*; we were strangers, out of place even in our homes. Our existence lacked context, origin, and depth.

I always felt my life only scratched the surface of what was within me, yet my family planted seeds of connection in a myriad of ways. As a child, sitting on a stack of pillows in my mother's kitchen, I claimed space at a table—a table that once belonged to my mother's mother—along with my father, sisters, and extended family. We ate from china that had survived grandparents, uncles, and aunts, filled with heritage dishes cooked from pots and pans passed down the generations. The understanding that there was a powerful language of shared currency, dignity, and pride, silently spoke what was unspoken: the customs, traditions, and treasured stories trapped within our beings

made it clear that we were more than the sum of our appearance. For generations, we had suppressed our origins and our sense of identity. But in these bowls, pots, and pans, simple and deeply layered dishes and sauces were brought to life in our beat-up ovens and on our worn-out stovetops.

And it was not only at our tables; through rituals, dance, and community gatherings that we all practiced, the ones we'd kept alive all these years, we lived our worth, respected and honored our own values, and recognized the depth of our connection to another world.

Now, centuries after the uprooting from Africa, from whence the brutal interruption of our organic lives dragged us and delivered us upon these shores in America, we recognize that we never stopped being African. We have carried the weight of our truth in our hearts, souls, and spirits.

Our culture has been kept alive in great part through our culinary currency and traditions. Our ancestors shared with us the stories of gardens, growings, and dishes that transcend time and place. Our pots overflow with history and remind us from whence we came. These dishes are kinship on a page. They bring us home, again and again.

I'm beyond proud to share with you this collection of dishes rooted in ancestral linkage, yet awakened with modern flair. May this exploration from the minds, hearts, and cultures of my African brothers and sisters fill you with pride, joy, respect, and recognition of the depth of our history as you relish them.

●

Alexander Smalls

INTRODUCTION

The Contemporary African Kitchen is a celebration of African food through taste and the tales of my travels and explorations, culminating in this collaboration of recipes, which shares and showcases more than 30 talented culinarians from all five regions of the continent—Northern Africa, Eastern Africa, Central Africa, Southern Africa, and Western Africa. The diverse library of recipes invites, intrigues, and instructs as it collectively shares Africa with you through the language of food and its creators.

Peanuts, okra, cornmeal (maize meal), Scotch bonnet peppers, and rice—all may be ubiquitous elements in many African dishes, but this is often where the similarities between regions end. Though you will certainly find some cross-regional dishes, Africa is a large and distinctly diverse continent, from which a virtually infinite number of plates and possibilities have sprung forth for centuries.

My passion for food, and the stories of my parents, my grandparents, and their parents before them, all led me to this very special part of the world. Made up of fifty-five countries, over 1.4 billion people, and more than 2,000 languages, it continues to give birth to ingredients and seasonings that dazzle and dance in my head and delight my palate. This book shares the coming of age of the legendary African kitchen, and considers the historical and current footprint of these five regions. It brings the conversation about this continent's cuisine into a contemporary, modern, and stunning realm, illustrated through a myriad of stories, images, and recipes, all of which highlight Africa's gifts to the world, through people and food.

Africa has always lured and fascinated me. Not only because it is the motherland from whence we all came, and from which so many were uprooted, but because today, going there, tasting all the continent has to offer, and meeting people who feel so much like family is a homecoming for so many of us. This is what I am sharing with you. Each culinarian—from a wide variety of backgrounds, and with a broad collective breadth of knowledge—shares their distinctive tales along with their recipes, drawing you in and allowing you to taste the flavors presented in the book as you read about them. You will be enveloped by the stories, all of which demonstrate that we are inextricably bound together, joined by a history that has brought forth a strength of spirit, ingenuity, and creativity, with a deep well of enriching ideas and relevant dishes to wrap yourself up in. Though this is by no means a comprehensive compilation of all the talent and dishes this continent offers, it provides a broad introduction, organized by region, to many unique and rich voices.

Today, I'm as at home in Ghana as I am in Kenya, as I am in Harlem, as I am in my native South Carolina. For this reason, it was my dream to bring together some of the most significant chefs and culinarians who are setting the new African table with a range of traditional dishes paired with some of their newest creations. From Mame Sow's Chicken Yassa and Couscous (page 212) and Mostafa Seif's Grilled Fish with Oil and Lemon (page 36), to Mogau Seshoene's Okra Stew (page 172)—and with so many in between—all are rooted in a continent that has given the world life in every sense of the word. Though dishes and ingredients may vary, the mainstays—warmth, vitality, rich aromas and flavors, and comfort—are the ever-present attributes of the African kitchen.

Africa is the birthplace and starting point of where we are today, and *The Contemporary African Kitchen* weaves a wondrous tale of flavors and colors, constructing its modern existence by collecting and sharing its historical roots.

Join me, as I invite you all to dive head first into the inspiring, thought-provoking, and delicious dishes presented here! I promise you will never be the same.

●

Alexander Smalls

**AFRICAN FOOD IS
A MOVEMENT**

"This is a movement," Alexander Smalls proclaimed as we talked about African food while sitting in Alkebulan, the African dining hall in Dubai he was invited to curate in 2021. The two-story building, filled with stalls featuring diverse African diaspora foods, was bustling with people at peak lunchtime. I watched them twirl, absorbing as many menus as they could, before committing to visiting the stalls that would bring satisfaction to their stomachs. I was in awe of the sight. A space, outside of Africa, where menus of Africa's most celebrated chefs are within reach, is scarce. Yet here, I felt the movement.

This movement has no leader, it has talent and treasures. The talent is unparalleled, from the chefs and caterers, home cooks, food bloggers, journalists, and restaurateurs, all in service to shaping the way African food is accessed and experienced. The treasures are voluminous, with ingredients, techniques, and traditions built over generations and generously shared with people and communities. Fueling this movement are the abundant voices from Africa and the diaspora, adding narratives that keep the flame burning for those that will come after us—for a legacy of African food that is rich, diverse, and nourishing for all—wIth Africans at the helm.

Legacy is to think beyond yourself. To imagine a world without your physical presence, yet enriched by your actions and impact. In any movement, legacy is the barometer of success. So when I asked the culinarians engaged in this movement about the legacy they hope to leave through their food, their words were resoundingly clear: African food must not only nourish palates, but be protected and serve its farmers and producers—a feat they all work daily to achieve. To this end, such esteemed voices in the African food movement as Selassie Atadika, Anto Cocagne, Michael Adé Elégbèdé, Coco Reinarhz, and Pierre Thiam share their thoughts and experiences throughout the book, interspersed among the recipes, stories, and insights of their fellow culinary contributors.

As I sat in conversation with Alexander, with Alkebulan's vibrant African art as our backdrop, he said, "I'm telling his story, and her story, until my last breath." With this I understood his legacy—creating spaces and opportunities that enable African diaspora food talent and treasures to be nurtured, valued, and celebrated globally. So, grab your plate, pan, or voice, and join this movement!

Nina Oduro

HOW TO USE
THIS BOOK

The culinarians who contributed their talent and time to this book had an idea in mind: they wanted to share their dishes as they considered how they could be presented by a host. Hosting is something I relish. I get great joy from collecting both diverse people and diverse dishes. I invite you to do the same as you dig into this book.

●

Start by perusing; let yourself travel through these different regions on an exploratory journey. Note recipes you may be familiar with and new ones you'd like to sample. Savor the stories. Some will draw you in because they may remind you of your own histories. Others will bring you into a realm that's enticing because it's new. Either way, I hope there will be many dishes that resonate with you, spark your desire, and become part of your own repertoire in time.

●

Though the recipes are presented as stand-alone dishes, the serving and pairing suggestions offered by the culinarians throughout, as well as the Directory of Chef Recipes on page 274, will allow you to create menus to share with your guests in your own home. Or as you consider your gatherings, you may want to do as I do and adapt your own menu based on the season, availability of ingredients, and the dishes you and your guests might enjoy most.

●

Another point of interest is that, as in other areas of the world, there are certain dishes that appear across regions. Throughout the book, for example, you will notice the presence of highly seasoned dishes served with starch—African cornmeal (maize meal)—known as *pap*, *ugali*, *nshima*, or *sadza*, depending on the area. These can be used interchangeably across regions, as you adopt and adapt dishes and create new pairings.

●

All the recipes within the book—though contributed by chefs and culinarians—are intended to be accessible for the home cook. While some ingredients may be new to you, all are easily resourced online; and where there may be a local or seasonal ingredient used, alternatives are given. In addition, all the recipes are accompanied by brand-new images created by Phaidon, based on the chefs' supplied recipes; all dishes depicted are Phaidon's own interpretation of these recipes.

NORTHERN AFRICA

Pigeon pie; mountains of couscous topped with grilled meats; rich stews; delicate pastries laced with honey, sprinkled with nuts, and dusted with cinnamon; sips of fresh mint tea: this is Northern Africa to me. Designs that dazzle and draw you in with bold colors, with a backdrop of African meeting French meeting Arabic meeting Spanish, and more, the northern part of the continent is blended and soaked in sweet, delightful, and intriguing influences. Magically mysterious, this region entices with aromas and patterns, in food, fragrance, and people.

I fell in love with North African food in the mid-1970s as a young opera singer studying in Paris and hanging out in the streets of Le Marais. At an evening gathering with friends who made up our global community of misfits, and limited by a tight budget, we were lucky to find an eatery that served excellent one-pot dishes for very low prices. My favorite was a big pot of couscous with grilled meats that was both affordable and otherworldly delicious. I became immediately obsessed, and recognized that I could eat the flavorful stew every day if I had to. Years later, I taught myself to make this amazing dish.

I have developed a love for North Africa that is rooted not only in fond memories of couscous and meats, but in kinship with my distant relatives of Nubia. While the pharaohs and pyramids of ancient Egypt were ingrained in my head as a result of dominant American narratives about the country, I had yet to explore the lands of my Black brothers and sisters in the southern part of the region— the Noba people of Nubia. It was when I encountered the work of Mohamed Kamal that the culinary traditions of Nubia came alive for me. The grains, fish, and dates on his plates were served with stories of rhythmic Nubian sounds and dances, much like that of my own Gullah Geechee heritage. This kinship is layered with our connected journeys of protecting and celebrating the foods of our forefathers. The celebration is felt in these pages, with Kamal's gold-powder-topped dessert dubbed "The Land of Gold" for the glamor and richness of Nubia (page 66).

I'm sure you will find many celebratory occasions at which to serve the numerous dishes in this chapter. From *foul*—Fava Bean Purée—brought to us from Egypt thanks to Mostafa Seif (page 50), to *molokheya*—jute mallow (a green vegetable that could be called spinach's North African cousin) and chicken stew, one of Egypt's most famous dishes, from Moustafa Elrefaey (page 26). And from Akram Cherif's Tunisian Brik with Egg and Tuna (page 42), a stuffed pastry street food that's been around for centuries, to Farida Zamradje's Moroccan dishes, including Slow-cooked Lamb Shoulder (page 18) with carrots, potatoes, and cumin—Northern Africa is waiting for you to discover all of its treasures!

SLOW-COOKED LAMB SHOULDER

FARIDA ZAMRADJE

PREPARATION TIME: 20 MINUTES
COOKING TIME: 8 HOURS
SERVES 2

1¾ oz (50 g) ground coriander
¼ cup (1¾ oz/50 g) butter, softened
1 tablespoon fine salt
3 lb 5 oz (1.5 kg) lamb shoulder
3 lb 5 oz (1.5 kg) onions,
  roughly chopped
9 oz (250 g) carrots,
  roughly chopped
9 oz (250 g) potatoes,
  roughly chopped
1 heaping tablespoon cumin seeds,
  ground in a mortar and pestle,
  to garnish
finishing salt, to garnish

If you're looking for the perfect dish for a gathering, you've come to the right place. In Morocco, lamb is a culinary icon that is common at celebrations and family gatherings. The key to this recipe is patience. While the difficult part is waiting eight hours to enjoy the lamb shoulder, you'll thank yourself when you achieve the final result. The aroma of spices and vegetables with the tender meat will embrace you so warmly that clearing your plate will be inevitable.

Preheat the oven to 140°F/60°C/Gas Mark ¼.

Combine the coriander, butter, and salt in a bowl. Brush the mixture over the lamb shoulder.

Place the onions in a pot and add the lamb shoulder on top. Add ⅓ cup (3½ fl oz/100 ml) of water, cover with a lid, and cook for 8 hours.

About 20 minutes before the end of the lamb cooking time, steam the carrots and potatoes in a steamer, or in a steaming basket set over a pan of simmering water, until tender.

Debone and shred the lamb shoulder into smaller chunks. Place the vegetables in the bottom of a tagine serving bowl, with the pieces of lamb shoulder on top. Garnish with the ground cumin seeds and finishing salt, and serve.

BEEF CHEEKS

MOHAMED KAMAL

PREPARATION TIME: 20 MINUTES
COOKING TIME: 1 HOUR 25 MINUTES
SERVES 4-6

2 lb 4 oz (1 kg) beef cheeks
½ cup (3½ fl oz/100 ml)
   corn oil, plus extra if needed
1⅜ cups (7 oz/200 g)
   medium-diced carrots
1¾ cups (10½ oz/300 g)
   medium-diced onions
1⅜ cups (7 oz/200 g)
   medium-diced celery
8¼ cups (68 fl oz/2 liters)
   vegetable stock
4 tablespoons ground cumin
4 tablespoons ground coriander
2 teaspoons ground black pepper
a pinch of salt

This dish and method of plating are inspired by a Nubian game from my childhood called ⲅⲉⲥⲉⲣ ⲕⲁⲇⲉⲅ (pronounced: Je-ser ka-deh), which literally translates as "throwing a bone." After the sun set, children would play with a bone, tossing it and forming teams to search for it in the dark night. The team that successfully found the bone emerged as the winner. This simple game reflects the ease and simplicity of life in Nubian villages.

In a large pot over high heat, sear the beef cheeks in the corn oil for about 3 minutes each side, until they achieve a nice color on both sides. Remove the beef from the pot and set aside.

In the same pot, over medium heat, sauté the diced vegetables for 3–5 minutes, adding a little more oil if needed.

Return the seared beef to the pot and deglaze it with the vegetable stock, scraping the base of the pot to incorporate any caramelized elements, then add the spices and seasoning. Cover the pot and let it simmer for 1 hour, then remove the beef from the pot again and set aside to rest.

Using a stick blender, blend the liquid to create a smooth sauce and reduce it over medium-high heat to your desired consistency. This might take anywhere from 7–15 minutes, but you are looking for a sauce that coats the spoon as you stir it through.

Serve the beef with the reduced sauce.

BEEF SHANK TAGINE

FARIDA ZAMRADJE

PREPARATION TIME: 15 MINUTES
COOKING TIME: 8 HOURS
SERVES 1

10½ oz (300 g) beef shank
2 cloves garlic, halved
4 tablespoons ground cumin
pinch of saffron threads
¼ preserved lemon
⅓ cup (3 fl oz/80 ml) olive oil
1 oz (30 g) smen mdeweb

When it comes to Moroccan food culture, the tagine is essential. The traditional cone-shaped clay pot is used for cooking beef shank and other meats and vegetables slowly—an early slow cooker that has been used by Moroccans for generations! Its magic lies in its shape, trapping steam and preserving moisture, ensuring that every ingredient is cooked to tender perfection.

Preheat the oven to 140°F/60°C/Gas Mark ¼.

Combine all the ingredients in a bowl except the beef shank.

Brush the beef shank all over with the mixture, then transfer to a tagine, cover the pot with parchment paper, and cook in the oven for 8 hours.

Transfer the beef shank to a serving plate and drizzle with some of the cooking juices.

ALEXANDRIAN LIVER

MOUSTAFA ELREFAEY

PREPARATION TIME: 15 MINUTES
COOKING TIME: 15 MINUTES
SERVES 2-4

2 cups (16 fl oz/475 ml) vegetable
  oil, for frying
1 lb 2 oz (500 g) beef liver,
  thinly sliced
3 large fresh red chili peppers,
  chopped
1 heaping tablespoon crushed garlic
1 teaspoon ground coriander
1 tablespoon salt
juice of 2 lemons, plus extra
  to serve
¼ cup (2 fl oz/60 ml) distilled
  vinegar

TO SERVE
Egyptian baladi or fino bread
arugula (rocket)

This classic recipe immediately transports you to the shores of Alexandria, as it is one of the city's most iconic street foods. This method, where beef liver is cooked in an abundance of oil and flavorful additions, differentiates it from any other liver recipe, and locals and foreigners alike are in love with its exceptional flavors.

Heat the oil in a deep skillet (frying pan) on high heat and drop in the liver slices. Cook the liver in the hot oil, being sure to coat each piece, stirring constantly with a spatula, for about 3 minutes, until the liver changes color and begins to stiffen.

Add 2 of the 3 chopped chili peppers with all the garlic, coriander, and salt, and stir well to evenly cook in the oil, for a further 3 minutes. As the mixture cooks, add the remaining chili pepper, the lemon juice, and the vinegar. Stir well, leaving to simmer for another minute or two. Scoop the liver and chilis into a bowl, being sure to squeeze out any excess oil against the side of the skillet.

Serve alongside Egyptian baladi or local fino bread with an extra squeeze of lemon juice, and fresh arugula (rocket).

JUTE MALLOW WITH CHICKEN

MOUSTAFA ELREFAEY

PREPARATION TIME: 30 MINUTES
COOKING TIME: 1 HOUR 45 MINUTES
SERVES 2-4

FOR THE CHICKEN AND BROTH
1 whole chicken, approximately
  2 lb 10 oz/1.2 kg
13-17 cups (100-135 fl oz/
  3-4 liters) cold water
1-3 bay leaves
2-3 cardamom pods
1-3 pieces mastic gum (plant resin)
1 onion, peeled
½ teaspoon whole peppercorns
handful chopped celery
handful chopped carrots
3 tablespoons ghee and oil
  mixed together
salt, to taste

FOR THE GARLIC TOPPING
2 tablespoons ghee or oil
2 teaspoons minced garlic
½ teaspoon ground coriander

FOR THE MOLOKHEYA
4½ cups (1 lb 2 oz/500 g) minced
  molokheya leaves (frozen works
  as well)

TO SERVE
cooked white rice

I love jute mallow (*molokheya*) because, to me, it's an essential home staple. When I was a child, we made it with succulent rabbit meat, and I've since tried it everywhere across Egypt—in Port Said and Alexandria, it is made with shrimp; in Cairo, it is made with pan-seared chicken. Each one is delicious, but the taste of our home-cooked rabbit version will always be my favorite.

Molokheya is a delicious national dish made with minced jute leaves, and it is loved across all of Egypt—from north to south! In several surrounding countries, *molokheya* leaves are left whole as they cook. In Egypt, they are minced, usually by hand, and many people spend long, laborious hours picking, cleaning, and mincing the leaves to enjoy their remarkable flavor and texture. Usually cooked in chicken or meat broth, the dish is topped with garlic fried in ghee and packed full of nutrients. Some people enjoy it alone as a soup, but it is traditionally enjoyed with white rice or bread.

When cooking the chicken, I suggest using aromatics such as cardamom, mastic, onion, peppercorns, celery, and carrots.

To prepare your chicken, remove any organs (if needed), excessive fatty tissue, and membranes, or ask your butcher to do this. I like to cut the chicken in half lengthwise to bring out the best flavors. Place the chicken in a deep pot with enough of the cold water to cover, and bring to a boil, then reduce the heat and let it simmer slowly with the bay leaves, cardamom, mastic, onion, peppercorns, celery, and carrots for about 1½ hours. Wait until at least 40 minutes into the cooking time to add salt to chicken (or 1 hour when adding it to meat); adding it prematurely slows down the cooking process and toughens the proteins. Once cooked through, remove the chicken from the broth and set aside. Strain the broth into a pan, ready to use for the molokheya. You will need 6¼ cups (50 fl oz/1.5 liters) of broth in total.

To make the garlic topping, add the ghee or oil to a small saucepan on medium heat and add the garlic. Cook for 3 minutes until fragrant and the garlic is starting to change color. Add the ground coriander and cook together for a minute or two until golden. Set aside.

Add the minced molokheya to the hot broth and cook on low heat, being sure not to boil the mixture (molokheya will lose its unique consistency if boiled, as the green particles will separate from the broth). Using a whisk, stir the broth and molokheya together for 1–2 minutes until consistent. Add the garlic-coriander mix to the molokheya, stirring through, and leave on the heat for a few more minutes for the flavors to enrich.

To prepare the chicken, heat the ghee and oil combination in a deep pan. Drop the chicken halves into the pan, skin-side down, and shallow fry on high heat for 2–3 minutes until golden, turning around and over at different intervals for a consistent golden color.

Serve the chicken alongside white rice and a bowl of hot molokheya.

ARGEEH

MOHAMED KAMAL

PREPARATION: 30 MINUTES, PLUS
 OVERNIGHT SOAKING
COOKING TIME: 1 HOUR 30 MINUTES
SERVES 6

FOR THE ARGEEH AND PEPPERS
¼ oz (10 g) dried fava (broad) beans
½ oz (15 g) dried chickpeas
¾ oz (20 g) whole wheat grain
¼ oz (10 g) dried green split peas
¼ oz (10 g) sorghum grain
¼ oz (10 g) dried corn
¼ oz (10 g) dried black-eyed peas
 (beans)
2 red peppers
¼ oz (10 g) garlic, finely chopped
1¾ oz (50 g) onion, finely chopped
¼ cup (¾ oz/20 g) ground coriander
4 teaspoons ground cumin
salt and pepper, to taste

FOR THE EGYPTIAN DOK'AA SPICE BLEND
2 teaspoons ground cumin
4½ teaspoons coriander seeds
2 teaspoons mustard seeds
1 teaspoon sea salt
1 tablespoon chopped peanuts
1 tablespoon white sesame seeds

FOR THE PIGEON
3 tablespoons ghee
scant 1 cup (7 oz/200 g) butter
2 sprigs each rosemary and thyme
6 pigeon legs
6 pigeon breasts

This dish symbolizes the essence of Nubian culture, and its deeply rooted historical story has been passed down through generations. Known as the Nubian Argeeh (ⲁⲣⲉⲉⲅ), it features seven grains. The number seven holds great importance for the Nubian people. Nubian traditions and rituals are intertwined with this number, such as blessing children for seven days and visiting graves for the same duration. After giving birth, Nubian women perform rituals involving seven types of incense and washing the newborn in the Nile on the seventh day. The Nubian groom visits his family on the seventh day after henna and the wedding, while we celebrate International Nubia Day on July 7 each year, honoring our history and culture.

The Argeeh dish was traditionally prepared by Nubian women to bring solace to people's hearts and as an offering to a higher power.

Soak each grain and bean in water separately overnight.

Preheat the oven to 400°F/200°C/Gas Mark 6.

Place the red peppers on a tray and roast in the oven for around 20 minutes until the skin has started to blister and char. Remove the peppers and place inside a plastic container; let cool, then peel the skin and remove the seeds by hand. Place the peppers in a baking tray and prepare a charcoal grill, if possible (or use a smoker). Add some oil to the charcoal to create smoke, then cover the tray with aluminum foil to prevent the smoke from escaping. Place over the charcoal and let sit for 20–30 minutes. This may seem like a complicated step, but the results are outstanding!

Cook each grain separately in a pan of boiling water: fava (broad) beans for 15–25 minutes; chickpeas for 20–30 minutes; wheat for 10–20 minutes; peas for 7–10 minutes; sorghum for 20–30 minutes; dried corn for 10–20 minutes; and black-eyed peas (beans) for up to 25 minutes.

In a pot on high heat, add the garlic and onion and sauté for 2–3 minutes. Add all the cooked grains and legumes, then add the coriander, cumin, and salt and pepper to taste. Add hot water, a ladleful at a time (similar to risotto), until it's fully cooked and becomes saucy, about 15–20 minutes. Meanwhile, blend the smoked red pepper quickly in a blender until you have a chunky, textured mix (it should not be a purée), then add to the pot.

For the Egyptian dok'aa spice blend, add all the ingredients to a pan over medium-high heat and toast until fragrant. Set aside.

Heat the ghee in a skillet (frying pan) over medium-high heat with the butter, rosemary, and thyme, add the pigeon legs and breasts, and cook for 2–3 minutes each side, until golden brown, basting with the melted butter as they cook.

Press the Egyptian dok'aa onto the breasts to form a crust.

Plate a circle of the Argeeh and red pepper on each plate, then top with one pigeon leg and one breast.

MOROCCAN PIGEON PIE

FARIDA ZAMRADJE

PREPARATION TIME: 45 MINUTES
COOKING TIME: 1 HOUR 15 MINUTES
SERVES 6

⅓ cup (3½ fl oz/100 ml) olive oil
10 pigeons (about 3 lb 5 oz/1.5 kg)
2 onions, chopped
1 bunch cilantro (coriander), finely chopped
1 bunch flat-leaf parsley, finely chopped
3 cloves garlic, diced
4 teaspoons ground ginger
pinch of saffron threads
1 tablespoon ras el hanout
2½ teaspoons grated nutmeg
8 eggs
4½ cups (1 lb 2 oz/500 g) slivered almonds
1 oz/30 g honey
3 tablespoons orange blossom water
2 teaspoons ground cinnamon, plus extra for sprinkling
12 sheets phyllo (filo) dough
3½ tablespoons (1¾ oz/50 g) butter, melted
salt and ground black pepper

If you treasure both sweet and savory dishes, the pigeon pie is a great marriage of the two. From the honey, sugar, cinnamon, and nutmeg to the pigeon wrapped in phyllo, the baked pie is a delight to eat. Though traditionally made with pigeon, you could substitute your favorite protein, from chicken to fish, if desired; the dish is receptive to alternatives and always emerges with a taste that graciously complements your preference.

Preheat the oven to 400°F/200°C/Gas Mark 6.

Heat the olive oil in a stovetop-safe casserole (or Dutch oven) on medium-high heat. Add the pigeons and brown on all sides for 10 minutes, then remove from the heat and season with salt and pepper. Add the onions and a pinch of salt to the casserole and cook for 4 minutes. Add the cilantro (coriander), parsley, garlic, ginger, saffron, ras el hanout, and nutmeg, then cook for 5 minutes. Add the pigeon and cover with water. Let cook, covered, for 20 minutes until bubbling.

Remove the pigeons, then let the sauce simmer on low heat for 20 minutes. Meanwhile, debone the pigeons, pulling the flesh with your fingers.

Break the eggs into the casserole and mix them into the pot (like scrambled eggs) to thicken the sauce.

Mix the slivered almonds, honey, orange blossom water, and cinnamon in a bowl.

Cut 6 of the phyllo (filo) sheets into 12 x 5-inch (12-cm) circles. Brush the round sheets with the butter along with your 6 large sheets.

Place 1 large sheet in the base of a small baking pan, then add 2 spoonfuls of pigeon meat. Cover with a round sheet and add 2 tablespoons of the casserole mixture. Cover with 1 more round sheet and add 2 tablespoons of the almond mixture.

To finish, fold the large sheet up and over the filling so the pie is entirely enclosed, then turn over the pastry, and set on a baking sheet. Repeat with the remaining ingredients, then bake in the oven for 10 minutes.

Place the pies (pastilla) on a board. Sprinkle with cinnamon, use a sieve to coat with confectioners' (icing) sugar, and serve.

SINGARY FISH

PREPARATION TIME: 15 MINUTES
COOKING TIME: 30 MINUTES
SERVES 2-4

FOR THE FISH PASTE
2 cups (8 oz/220 g) green bell
  peppers, roughly diced
1 cup (6 oz/175 g) roughly
  chopped onion
2 tablespoons minced garlic
⅓ cup (3½ fl oz/100 ml) vegetable oil
2 tablespoons chopped cilantro
  (coriander)
½ teaspoon ground coriander
1½ teaspoons salt
½ teaspoon ground black pepper
1 teaspoon ground turmeric
1 teaspoon ground cumin
juice of 2 lemons

FOR THE SINGARY
2-3 potatoes, sliced into ¼-inch
  (5-mm) rounds
3 bell peppers of different colors,
  sliced into rounds
2 onions, sliced into rings
1 large sea bass (or your preferred
  fish), cleaned, deboned, and
  butterflied (ask your fishmonger
  to do this)
1 tomato, sliced
2 cloves garlic, thinly sliced
2-3 chili peppers, sliced (optional)
1 lemon or lime, sliced
chopped dill
chopped cilantro (coriander)

Singary has a special place in my heart. I once entered a culinary competition in Italy in 2012, and I chose to invent a new dish derived from the old on a bed of delicious *freek* (page 52). I used the same spices and herbs we traditionally use on the fish but on butterflied shrimp (prawns), which I cooked casserole-style, so all the flavors merged together. I won the competition and it was an absolutely delicious dish that I'll never forget.

The seafood scene in Egypt is vast and diverse. While most parts of the region opt for grilled or fried fish, this particular recipe is a coastal favorite—classic singary fish. It is an extremely flavorful butterflied whole fish slathered in a special marinade packed with herbs and aromatics, then laid atop a selection of vegetables and baked in the oven. The recipe also works well with other kinds of seafood, such as shrimp (prawns). Serve with white rice.

Preheat the oven to 425°F/220°C/Gas Mark 7.

Place all the fish paste ingredients into a blender and blend to a paste. Set aside.

In a large, oven-safe dish, arrange the potatoes and half the bell pepper and onion slices on the bottom of the dish. These will protect the fish from burning and soak up all the flavor from the fish as it cooks.

Evenly spread 3–4 tablespoons of the fish paste over the arranged vegetables. Place the whole fish, skin-side down, over the vegetables. Slather the remaining paste over the open flesh of the fish with a spoon. Let the fish rest for about 5 minutes to soak up the flavors.

Top the fish with the remaining onion and bell pepper slices, and the tomato, garlic, and chili pepper slices, if using, lemon or lime slices, a sprinkle of dill, and cilantro (coriander).

Bake in the oven for 20–30 minutes, until cooked through. Enjoy hot from the oven.

STUFFED
SQUID

AKRAM CHERIF

PREPARATION TIME: 30 MINUTES
COOKING TIME: 1 HOUR
SERVES 10

10 squid (8 lb 13 oz/4 kg
  total weight)
5 cups (2 lb 4 oz/1 kg) long-
  grain rice
10 cups (2 lb 4 oz/1 kg)
  chopped onions
1 lb 2 oz (500 g) tomatoes, sliced
5½ oz/150 g minced garlic
2 cups (2½ oz/70 g) dried mint
1½ cups (3½ oz/100 g) minced
  parsley
3½ tablespoons ground cumin
¾ oz/20 g saffron threads
⅔ cup (5 fl oz/150 ml) olive oil
3½ tablespoons harissa
5½ oz (150 g) tomato paste (purée)
salt and pepper

Stuffed squid is my signature dish, and one of the most popular dishes at my restaurant. My clients, friends, and family come to the restaurant solely to order it and get their fix of delicious squid. They're always in luck because I catch the squid myself in Bizerta, Tunisia, where I live. I not only find pleasure in fishing for squid, but also in preparing it for people to enjoy. The dish originated in Sicily, Italy, and was brought to Bizerta by the Italians. To add a Tunisian flavor to the original recipe, I have added harissa and dried mint.

Wash the fresh squid, remove the tentacles and cut them into 1-inch (2.5-cm) slices, then season with 1 teaspoon of salt. Bring a large pan of water to a boil, add the tentacles, and boil for 15 minutes. Remove and set aside.

Meanwhile, wash the rice under cold running water, then add to a pan with 1¼ cups (10 fl oz/300 ml) of water, bring to a boil, and cook for 12 minutes. When almost done, remove it from the heat, then set aside.

In a bowl, mix the cooked rice, 7½ cups (1 lb 10 oz/750 g) of the onions, the tentacle slices, the fresh tomatoes, 3½ oz (100 g) garlic, the dried mint, parsley, cumin, saffron, 1 tablespoon fine salt, 2 tablespoons ground black pepper, and 3½ tablespoons (1¾ fl oz/50 ml) of the olive oil. Take the bodies of the squid and stuff them with the mixture, then close with a toothpick (or cocktail stick).

To prepare the sauce, add the remaining olive oil to a large, deep skillet (frying pan), then add the remaining garlic and onion and the stuffed squid. Fry for 5 minutes, then add the harissa, tomato paste (purée), and salt and pepper to taste, and pour water over until covered. Bring to a boil and cook for 35–40 minutes.

When ready, cut the squid into slices and pour over the tomato sauce. Serve hot.

GRILLED FISH
WITH OIL AND LEMON

PREPARATION TIME: 15 MINUTES
COOKING TIME: 15 MINUTES
SERVES 2

FOR THE MARINADE
⅓ cup (3½ fl oz/100 ml) olive oil
3 cloves garlic
1 tablespoon ground coriander
½ teaspoon salt
1 teaspoon ground black pepper
½ teaspoon ground cumin

FOR THE FISH
2 lb 4 oz (1 kg) whole sea bass

FOR THE SALSA
⅓ cup (3½ fl oz/100 ml) olive oil
3½ tablespoons lemon juice
¼ oz (7 g) fresh red chili pepper,
  finely chopped
¼ oz (7 g) cilantro (coriander)
  leaves
½ oz (15 g) scallions (spring
  onions), sliced
½ teaspoon (3 g) salt

I learned to make this dish while I was doing my military service in the Suez Governorate on the Red Sea. My superior in the army was from Alexandria and taught me how to cook it. In no time, I was making it for everyone in the army to enjoy. I would buy the Suez Canal tilapia from the fish market in Suez and cook it in the kitchen, which was very basic compared to the ones I use these days. Despite that, it had all the essentials I needed to make the dish. So, I would get straight to work grilling the fish.

Note: If you would like to try carving the cooked fish, do it as follows. Remove the fin bones. Separate the top fillet from the head and collar bone. Separate the top fillet from the tail. Separate the dorsal and belly halves of the top fillet. Remove the dorsal fillet half, then the belly fillet half. Lift the bone cage. Clean the bottom fillet halves, and serve each person a fish fillet. Alternatively, you can simply remove the skin and cut away the fillets.

Preheat a grill pan over high heat, or preheat the oven to 350°F/180°C/Gas Mark 4.

Mix all the marinade ingredients together in a bowl. Rub the marinade on the inside and outside of the fish.

Cook the fish in the grill pan on a medium heat for 7–8 minutes each side, or place on a baking pan (tray) and cook in the oven for 15 minutes until crispy on the outside.

Mix the salsa ingredients together in a bowl and scatter over the cooked fish straightaway.

Serve the fish whole on a large platter and carve it in front of guests (see headnote), if desired,

NUBIAN TILAPIA

MOHAMED KAMAL

PREPARATION: 20 MINUTES
COOKING TIME: 15 MINUTES
SERVES 2

FOR THE TAHINI SAUCE
1 oz (30 g) tahini
2 tablespoons white vinegar
3 g ground cumin
3 g ground coriander
salt and pepper, to taste

FOR THE TILAPIA FISH
oil of your choice
2 sprigs your preferred herb
1 clove garlic
1 tilapia fish fillet (28-35 oz/
   800 g-1 kg), or you could use a
   whole fish
ground cumin

FOR THE DILL OIL
3½ oz (100 g) dill, roughly chopped
generous ¾ cup (7 fl oz/200 ml)
   corn oil

The Nubians have a deep connection with the "feri" fish—Φιρρι in the Nubian language—also known as river tilapia. Though it's classified as tilapia, there's a distinct difference that you'll come to appreciate when you visit Nubia. In ancient Nubia, feri was considered the best fish, cherished by the Nubian people and playing a significant role in their lives. These river tilapia would grow to an impressive size, weighing tens of kilos and reaching over five feet (a meter and a half) in length. Nubian elders fondly recall their childhood days, before the flooding of most of the Nubian land due to the construction of the Aswan Dam. They vividly describe riding these fish on the Nile waters and racing with them. The influence of the feri fish extends beyond such playful memories. Watching the way it gracefully swims in the Nile waters, we have found inspiration for a dance among Nubian girls, where they mirror the fish's swaying movements amid the strong current passing through the Nubian gondolas. This fish has also left its mark on our homes, with our grandmothers engraving it as a symbol of good luck and blessings. While the tradition is now considered a mere superstition, the practice has become an inevitable part of our heritage, connecting us to the water of the Nile that sustained our livelihood for thousands of years.

To make the tahini sauce, combine all the ingredients in a bowl and mix thoroughly.

Heat the oil in a pan with your preferred choice of herbs and garlic until it reaches a temperature of 175°F/80°C. Gently place the tilapia in the heated oil and cook for 10–15 minutes, depending on the size of the fish.

To make the dill oil, mix the dill with the corn oil and heat the mixture until it reaches a temperature of 215°F/102°C. Once heated, strain the oil through a fine strainer to remove the solids.

Serve the fish on a platter, drizzled with the dill oil, and with the tahini sauce alongside.

EGYPTIAN OKRA STEW

MOSTAFA SEIF

PREPARATION TIME: 15 MINUTES
COOKING TIME: 15 MINUTES
SERVES 2

1½ tablespoons (¾ oz/20 g) butter
1½ tablespoons (¾ oz/20 g)
  chopped onion
1 clove garlic, minced
6 oz (180 g) dried okra
2 teaspoons (¼ oz/10 g) diced tomato
5 basil leaves, plus extra
  to garnish
½ cup (3½ oz/100 g) chicken
  or vegetable stock
9 oz (250 g) canned peeled tomatoes
2 g sliced fresh red chili pepper
  (optional)
1 teaspoon ground coriander
1 teaspoon ground cumin
juice of 1 lemon (optional)
salt, to taste
cilantro (coriander) leaves,
  to garnish
mint leaves, to garnish
parsley leaves, to garnish
1 arabesque tuile, to garnish
  (optional)
2 lemon wedges, to garnish

Some foods are as much for nourishment as they are a tool for showing off. When I was growing up, okra was an ingredient that fit this description. Traditionally, women would cook the okra, and when it was on the menu, you would see balconies lined with hanging okra. My mom was an active participant. After she washed her okra, she would dry it on the balcony where others in the neighborhood would see it abundantly displayed—lush and green. She would add her garlic and onions as well, and after they were dry and had been seen by enough eyes, it was time to cook okra stew, or *bamia* in Arabic.

This recipe uses only vegetables, but you can add lamb if desired.

In a medium pan on medium heat, melt the butter. Add the onion and fry for 1 minute. Add half the garlic, okra, diced tomato, and basil. Then add the stock and peeled tomatoes and cook for 10 minutes.

Using a mortar and pestle, crush the remaining garlic, the chili pepper (if using), ground coriander, cumin, lemon juice (if using), and salt to taste.

Add the crushed ingredients to the pan, mix together, then transfer to a deep bowl to serve. Garnish with cilantro (coriander), basil, mint, parsley, an arabesque tuile (if using), and lemon wedges on top.

41

BRIK WITH EGG
AND TUNA

AKRAM CHERIF

PREPARATION TIME: 10 MINUTES
COOKING TIME: 30 MINUTES
SERVES 4

4 medium potatoes
generous ¾ cup (7 fl oz/200 ml)
  olive oil
2 onions, finely chopped
3½ oz (100 g) canned tuna
1½ cups (3½ oz/100 g) minced parsley
4 sheets brik pastry
4 eggs
salt and pepper
lemon wedges, to serve

During Ramadan, the holy month for Muslims, we prepare and eat *brik*, a thin and brittle pastry, every day. It's easy to prepare, inexpensive, and I love eating it, especially with the unctuous yolk. It creates a sensory experience in my mouth that is worth every bite. The dish is undeniably a favorite in Tunisia, and a popular street food. Now, you also have the chance to eat this dish daily.

Bring a pan of water to a boil. Add the potatoes and cook for 20 minutes. Drain, then when they are cool enough to handle, remove the skin. Place them in a bowl and mash them, or pass them through a potato ricer, then add salt and pepper to taste. Let cool completely.

Heat 1 tablespoon of the oil in a pan. Add the onions and fry for 3 minutes on low heat until browning. Remove the onions from the pan and mix into the mashed potatoes, along with the tuna and minced parsley.

Lay the brik sheets in front of you on a work counter, put a small amount of the potato filling in a corner of each sheet, and make a hole in the center of each pile of filling. Break an egg into the hole, then fold the empty half of the pastry over the filling and seal the edges with a little water.

Heat the remaining olive oil in a pan. Add the briks and fry on medium heat for 2–3 minutes on each side until golden brown. Once browned, place them on paper towels to remove the excess oil. Serve hot with lemon wedges.

CLASSIC EGYPTIAN FALAFEL

MOUSTAFA ELREFAEY

PREPARATION TIME: 20 MINUTES,
   PLUS 6-8 HOURS SOAKING
COOKING TIME: 10 MINUTES
SERVES 4

5 cups (1 lb 2 oz/500 g) split fava (broad) beans
1 cup (4 oz/115 g) chopped Egyptian leeks (not green/spring onions)
1 yellow-skinned onion, roughly chopped
garlic, peeled, to taste
¼ cup (½ oz/15 g) cilantro (coriander) leaves
¼ cup (½ oz/15 g) parsley leaves
1 tablespoon minced dried coriander leaves
1 teaspoon salt
½ cup (4 oz/115 g) sesame seeds
1 tablespoon crushed coriander seeds
6¼ cups (50 fl oz/1.5 liters) vegetable oil

When I was a kid, I used to love going to this old shack where an elderly lady sat making fresh home-style *taameya* (falafel). I haven't had it for more than forty years, but I can still taste it like it was yesterday. Because of her, I can tell right away if the *taameya* will be good or bad, just by the smell.

Taameya is served all across the nation, seeping into neighboring countries to become a part of their breakfast traditions, too. In Egypt, you'll find it served in breakfast carts starting from the crack of dawn. What is distinct about Egyptian *taameya* is that it is made using dried split fava (broad) beans as the core ingredient. While making it with split beans is a longer process that requires several hours of soaking, the results are definitely worth the wait to get a light, crispy, green disk of vegan goodness. It's so irresistible that this recipe was recognized as the best falafel in a 2016 competition at London's Borough Market.

Enjoy with Egyptian baladi bread, traditional green salad, and tahina sauce.

Soak the split fava (broad) beans for 6–8 hours—the longer, the better. They should have the same bite as a raw fava bean. Note that you must change the soaking water often to prevent fermentation.

Place the leeks, onion, garlic, cilantro (coriander), and parsley in a food processor, and process until evenly chopped.

Add the presoaked split beans, and process until smooth, pausing occasionally to clean down the sides of the processor with a spatula. Add the dried coriander and salt, and blend again until incorporated. The dough should be slightly foamy, as a result of adding the salt in the final step. Scoop out the dough into a bowl.

In a separate bowl, mix together the sesame seeds and crushed coriander.

Fill a deep wok or skillet (frying pan) with the oil and heat until it reaches 350°F/175°C—you can also test the oil to see if it is ready by tossing in a few sesame seeds; when they rise to the surface, the oil is ready for frying.

Scoop about 1 tablespoon of dough into your hands (or use an ice cream scoop) and shape it into a disk. (Or you can form your dough into other shapes, including balls and sticks.) Sprinkle some sesame and coriander mix onto the disk, and carefully slip it into the oil. Cook for 2–3 minutes, until golden brown on the outside. Repeat in batches of a few at a time until you have used all the remaining dough, then serve warm.

MECHOUIA SALAD

AKRAM CHERIF

PREPARATION TIME: 30 MINUTES
COOKING TIME: 20 MINUTES
SERVES 6

6 green bell peppers
6 green or red chili peppers
2 tomatoes
6 eggs
1 onion, thinly sliced
6 cloves garlic, grated
2 teaspoons olive oil
4 teaspoons fine salt
2½ tablespoons ground black pepper
¾ oz (20 g) ground coriander
3 tablespoons caraway seeds
5½ oz (150 g) canned tuna

To me, no salad compares to mechouia salad. Translated from Arabic to English as "grilled salad," it is my favorite, especially during the summer. On a nice sunny day, I'll cook fish or meat over charcoal and use the same charcoal to prepare this salad. It's delicious, and saves time and money.

This dish comes from the Cap Bon region in Northeast Tunisia and can be traced back to the Andalus people who escaped from Spain to Tunisia in 1492. Selected as the third-best salad in the world by TasteAtlas in April 2023, it's a favorite of many locals and tourists.

Grill all the peppers on the stove top, holding them with tongs over the flame, while rotating every few minutes. The skin needs to be charred and the peppers soft. Do the same with the tomatoes and let them cool.

Boil the eggs in hot water for 12 minutes and set aside to cool.

Once all the vegetables are cool, remove the skin and seeds of the peppers and set aside. For the tomatoes, remove the skin and squeeze out any excess liquid. Cut the peppers and tomatoes into thin strips with a sharp knife, and place in a serving bowl. Add the onion to the bowl. Add the grated garlic, olive oil, salt, and spices (black pepper, coriander, and caraway). Mix well until everything is well combined.

Peel the eggs and cut into quarters.

Add tuna chunks and pieces of hard-boiled egg to the salad before serving.

PICKLED TOMATO SALAD

MOSTAFA SEIF

PREPARATION TIME: 15 MINUTES,
    PLUS 1 HOUR CHILLING
SERVES 4

10 tomatoes, cut into wedges
1 red onion, julienned
½ red chili pepper, sliced
    into rings
¼ oz (10 g) cilantro leaves
    (coriander)
¼ oz (10 g) mint leaves
¼ oz (10 g) thyme leaves
1½ tablespoons olive oil
1 teaspoon sea salt
2 teaspoons ground black pepper

If you could have tasted tomatoes in Egypt when I was growing up, you would have boasted about how delicious they were. Back then, you couldn't have convinced me that better tomatoes existed. That was twenty years ago, when my mother would make pickled tomato salad for me. Now, I enjoy the dish as much as I did all those years ago. It is a Mediterranean delight that is refreshing when the weather is warm. We eat it for breakfast, lunch, or dinner—so there is never a wrong time to enjoy it.

Add all the ingredients together in a bowl and leave in the refrigerator for 1 hour before serving.

FAVA BEAN PURÉE

MOSTAFA SEIF

PREPARATION TIME: 15 MINUTES, PLUS
  OVERNIGHT SOAKING
COOKING TIME: 30 MINUTES
SERVES 2

5½ cups (2 lb 4 oz/1 kg) dried fava
  (broad) beans
scant 1 cup (7 oz/200 g) tahini
⅔ cup (5 fl oz/150 ml) cold water
1 tablespoon ground coriander
2 teaspoons ground cumin
2 teaspoons sea salt

This recipe may remind you of hummus, and though it's created using the same process, instead of chickpeas I use fava (broad) beans. Fava beans, known as *foul*, are very popular in Egypt, and can also be used in place of chickpeas to make falafel. Once you try this dish, you too might opt to use these beans in your cooking.

You can serve it in a bowl as a dip with bread, falafel, or salad for lunch and dinner, or with eggs for breakfast.

Soak the fava (broad) beans in water overnight.

Bring a pot of water to a boil, add the fava beans and cook for 30 minutes.

When cooked, drain the fava beans and add to a food processor or blender. Slowly add the tahini and cold water while mixing. Then add the ground coriander, cumin, and salt. You'll know it's ready when all the ingredients are well mixed together. Serve.

51

SIDES

FREEK

PREPARATION TIME: 15 MINUTES, PLUS
  3 HOURS SOAKING
COOKING TIME: 40 MINUTES
SERVES 2

2½ cups (1 lb 2 oz/500 g) freek
3½ tablespoons (1¾ oz/50 g) butter
1½ cups (8 oz/225 g) minced onion
2 cloves garlic, minced
1 tablespoon ground coriander
1 tablespoon ground cumin
¼ cup (1¾ oz/50 g) tomato paste
  (purée)
5¾ cups (46 fl oz/1.4 liters)
  beef stock
2½ teaspoons fine salt
3 teaspoons ground black pepper

Fridays were the best days when I was young. It was the first day of our weekend and my family would usually spend it at my grandmother's house in Qena Governorate in Upper Egypt in the south of the country. It was on these Fridays that she would cook *freek*, a green wheat dish. I would eat with the whole family, enjoying each bite. I hope this dish reminds you of good times with friends and family, or helps you create new memories.

This recipe requires a tagine—a pot used for slow cooking with a conical top used in Northern Africa and the Middle East. You can add chicken or beef to this dish.

Soak the freek in cold water for 3 hours,

After 3 hours, preheat the oven to 350°F/180°C/Gas Mark 4. If you are using a tagine, make sure it can also be used on the stove. Put it in the oven to heat up.

Drain the freek and set aside.

Get your tagine out of the oven, then put the butter inside to melt. Alternatively, melt the butter in an oven-safe lidded pan.

Place the tagine or pan on medium heat and add the onion and garlic and sweat for 1 minute until golden. Add the coriander, cumin, and tomato paste (purée) and stir to combine. Leave to cook for 4 minutes.

Add the freek and toast for 3 minutes until heated through. Add the stock, salt, and pepper, cover the tagine, and bring to a boil. Once the stock has boiled, transfer the pot to the oven and cook until the freek has soaked up all the stock, approximately 20 minutes. Uncover the pot and continue to cook the freek for another 10 minutes. Serve it in the tagine.

SAVORY RICE PUDDING

MOUSTAFA ELREFAEY

PREPARATION TIME: 10 MINUTES
COOKING TIME: 45 MINUTES
SERVES 2

1½ cups (12 fl oz/350 ml) whole
  (full-fat) milk
1½ cups (9 oz/250 g) medium-
  grain rice
4 tablespoons heavy (double)
  cream or keshta
¼ cup (2¼ oz/60 g) ghee
generous sprinkle of salt

I've always adored savory rice pudding (*roz mo'ammar*)—the thought of it tickles my palate right away! It was something I'd eat at any time of day—breakfast, lunch, or dinner. My grandmother used to make it plain with ghee and milk, and we would eat it for lunch with vegetable stew and goose or duck on the side. Then, for dinner, we would make it with honey for dessert—or at breakfast, we'd add sugar to the rice and milk, and it would be delicious! As I've gotten older, I've tried every possible *roz mo'ammar* variation in Egypt.

In colloquial Egyptian, *mo'ammar* means to "be filled" with something. Indeed, this rice dish is full of milk, heavy (double) cream or *keshta*, and clarified butter, and is one of the most highly appreciated rice dishes across the nation. *Keshta* is the layer of very thick cream skimmed off the top of fresh cow's milk after it has been boiled and cooled—this method of separating the *keshta* from the milk is common practice in rural homes all across Egypt, where milk is taken straight from the cow to the stove.

Some regions take this dish a step further by stuffing meat, duck, pigeon, raisins, or even boiled eggs with the rice. Others even make it with eels! In this particular version, I make the classic recipe, which is lightly seasoned and served warm alongside other Egyptian dishes of your choice.

Preheat the oven to 400°F/200°C/Gas Mark 6.

Heat the milk in a pan on medium heat.

Mix the rice, cream, and ghee together in an oven-safe dish. Pour the hot milk over the rice mixture, along with a generous sprinkle of salt, and stir to combine.

Bake in the oven for 30–45 minutes until golden on top (if you like, you can turn the broiler/grill on for the last 5 minutes for a perfect golden finish on the surface).

Remove from the oven and cover the dish with a lid or some aluminum foil for a few minutes to prevent the surface from drying out. Enjoy warm.

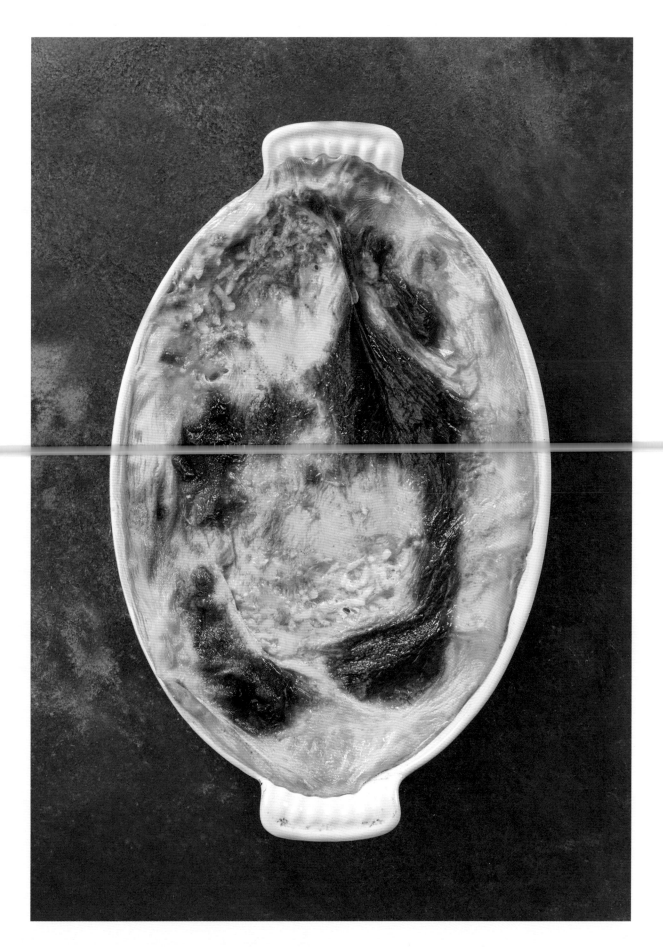

SUN
BREAD

PREPARATION TIME: 30 MINUTES,
    PLUS 6-24 HOURS FOR LEVAIN
    FERMENTATION, AND 3-24 HOURS
    RESTING
COOKING TIME: 30 MINUTES
SERVES 6

FOR THE LEVAIN
1⅝ cups (7½ oz/215 g) T65 flour
½ oz (12 g) T130 flour
⅝ cup (4¾ fl oz/140 ml) water
¾ oz (20 g) starter (you can buy
    this from a supermarket, if you
    don't have any)

FOR THE FINAL DOUGH
10 cups (42 oz/1.2 kg) T65 flour
½ cup (2¼ oz/60 g) T130 flour
1 oz (25 g) salt
1 cup (5½ oz/160 g) dried figs,
    chopped

This sun bread, or *eish shamsi*, recipe is older than me. At my restaurant, Khufu's in Cairo, the levain recipe we use for the dough is over one hundred years old. It's a treasured inheritance that one of our chefs received from his great-grandmother. Starter recipes like levain are commonly passed down from generation to generation in Upper Egypt, where sun bread is very popular. As time passes, each generation feeds it—ensuring it is eaten—and honors those we've received it from.

Mix the levain ingredients in a bowl, cover, and leave for at least 6 or up to 24 hours. The longer you leave it, the better, but no more than 24 hours.

In a large bowl, mix 3⅓ cups (27 fl oz/800 ml) of water with the levain and the remaining dough flours and salt, and mix until the dough comes together. Knead the dough for 10 minutes. Add the dried figs and knead for 1 minute.

Roll the dough into a ball, and let rest at room temperature, covered, for 40 minutes. Next, stretch the dough by hand, roll into a ball and let rest again, covered, for 40 minutes. Repeat the stretch and roll, then let it rest for another 40 minutes.

After this, stretch and roll again, then cut the dough into 1 lb 5 oz/ 600 g pieces. Roll each one into a ball and let it rest in the sun, without covering, or in a proofer, for 1 hour until it doubles in size and the top becomes hard. Alternatively, you can store it in the refrigerator for 1 day.

Preheat the oven to 475°F/250°C/Gas Mark 9. Place a lidded cast-iron pot in the oven and leave for 15 minutes.

Place the dough on parchment paper, then add to the pot with 3 ice cubes, cover with the lid and bake for 30 minutes. To serve, cut into slices or 4 triangles and place in a breadbasket.

M'ENCHA

PREPARATION TIME: 15 MINUTES,
   PLUS 1 HOUR RESTING
COOKING TIME: 25-30 MINUTES
MAKES 8

FOR THE STUFFING
vegetable oil, for frying
4½ cups (1 lb 2 oz/500 g) almonds,
   blanched
1¼ cups (9 oz/250 g)
   granulated sugar
¼ teaspoon gum arabic powder
3 tablespoons (1½ oz/40 g) butter
2 tablespoons orange blossom water

FOR THE PASTRY
4 large sheets of phyllo (filo)
   pastry
1 egg, beaten
7 tablespoons (3½ oz/100 g) butter,
   melted

FOR THE DECORATION
generous 1 cup (9 oz/250 g) orange
   blossom honey
toasted slivered almonds, chopped
cinnamon ice cream, to serve

M'encha means snake in Arabic and it's no surprise that this dish bears such a name because of its pastry coils that lay flat, wrapped in a beautiful spiral. The dish invites guests to join in a communal experience, as they break off pieces until the spiral vanishes and the plate is empty. It's so satisfying to watch as the spiral disappears, one coil at a time.

Heat a little oil in a pan, then add half the almonds and fry for 3–4 minutes. Transfer them to some paper towels to soak up any excess oil, then grind the fried almonds with half the sugar and set aside.

Grind the remaining blanched almonds with the remaining sugar to create a smooth paste. Mix the 2 pastes together, along with the gum arabic, butter, and orange blossom water until fully combined. Let the paste sit for 1 hour, then mold the mixture into ¾-inch (2-cm) balls.

Preheat the oven to 375°F/190°C/Gas Mark 5. Line a sheet pan (baking tray) with parchment (baking) paper.

On a work surface, cut 1 phyllo (filo) sheet in half and turn the 2 pieces lengthwise. On the edge of the phyllo sheets, place the small almond balls and roll the sheets into a tube. Take one end of the rolled sheets and begin turning it in a circular motion, until you have made a spiral. Seal the end with the egg wash. Repeat this for the remaining phyllo sheets.

Place the spirals on the lined sheet pan. Brush each with the butter and bake for 20–25 minutes, until golden.

While still warm, generously pour the orange blossom honey on top and decorate with the almonds. Serve with cinnamon ice cream.

STRAWBERRY YOGURT DESSERT

FARIDA ZAMRADJE

PREPARATION TIME: 20 MINUTES,
    PLUS OVERNIGHT FERMENTATION
COOKING TIME: 15 MINUTES
SERVES 4

FOR THE YOGURT
4¼ cups (34 fl oz/1 liter) whole
    (full-fat) milk
¾ cup (5½ oz/150 g) superfine
    (caster) sugar
2 cups (16 oz/440 g) plain yogurt
2 drops orange blossom water
2¼ cups (9 oz/250 g) strawberries

FOR THE CRUMBLE
½ cup (3½ oz/100 g) sunflower oil
½ cup (3½ oz/100 g) superfine
    (caster) sugar
10½ tablespoons (5½ oz/150 g)
    butter
¾ cup (2¾ oz/80 g) ground almonds
6½ tablespoons sesame seeds
2 teaspoons ground cinnamon
5 cups (1 lb 9 oz/700 g)
    all-purpose (plain) flour
⅛ oz (5 g) yeast
1¾ teaspoons baking powder
2 teaspoons (¼ oz/10 g)
    salted butter
mint leaves, to garnish

When it's strawberry season in Morocco, you can bet this dessert is on the menu. It shows up in myriad forms—with whole or sliced strawberries, blended, or artfully crafted in a dish. Most of the work in this recipe is in the preparation, but once you've got the ingredients ready, the strawberries take center stage as you combine them with the yogurt and indulge.

To make the yogurt, put half of the milk with the sugar in a pan and bring to a boil.

In a bowl, mix the remaining milk with the yogurt and orange blossom water. Pour the hot milk into the cold milk mixture, whisking until smooth. Place the mixture in a sterilized airtight container and leave at room temperature to ferment overnight.

The following day, preheat the oven to 350°F/180°C/Gas Mark 4. Place the yogurt in the refrigerator. Wash and slice the strawberries, then set aside.

In a bowl, combine all the crumble ingredients (be sure not to overmix). Place the mixture in a sheet pan (baking tray) and bake for 12 minutes.

To assemble, pour the yogurt mixture into a serving bowl. In the center, place the crumble and then arrange the strawberries around it. Garnish with mint leaves and serve.

WHITE PORRIDGE

MOHAMED KAMAL

PREPARATION TIME: 10 MINUTES
COOKING TIME: 30 MINUTES
SERVES 10

3½ cups (1 lb 2 oz/500 g)
   all-purpose (plain) flour
pinch of salt
1¼ cups (10 fl oz/300 ml)
   black molasses
generous ⅓ cup (3½ oz/100 g) ghee

Nolo madeed (ⲛⲚⲟⲩⲗⲟⲩ-ⲛ ⲙⲁⲁⲓ̄ⲁ in the Nubian language), or white porridge, is a popular dish in Nubian culture and heritage. The day before a wedding, Nubians celebrate *Nolo* or the "white day." The bride and groom, along with their relatives, neighbors, and friends, gather at the Nile River for a joyous procession with customary Nubian dancing and singing (known as *arageed*), accompanied by dancers carrying a large plate known as *sahan fallah* (ⲥⲁϩⲁⲛ ⲫⲁⲗⲁⲁϩ). Inside the plate are portions of *madeed*, some with black molasses and others with milk. As Nubians dance and sing their way to the Nile, they believe there are angels residing within the waters who will bless and provide nourishment for the newlyweds. They joyfully toss the food into the Nile as part of the ritual, and afterward, the groom and bride wash their faces with the sacred waters. Whatever food remains is shared among the children. These customs and traditions have been cherished by the Nubians for countless years and continue to be upheld to this very day, serving as a testament to their enduring heritage and beliefs.

The porridge should ideally by stirred using the traditional Nubian cooking tool known as a "niper" (ⲛⲓⲃⲉⲣ), which is made of wood or ivory.

In a medium pot, add ⅔ cup (5 fl oz/150 ml) of water and half the flour. Mix over medium heat, then, as it heats up, gradually add another ⅔ cup (5 fl oz/150 ml) of water, the remaining flour, and the salt.

Continue to cook and stir the mixture for up to 15 minutes, using a wooden spoon (or niper, if you have one), until the mixture reaches a porridge-like consistency.

Meanwhile, heat the molasses and ghee gently in a pan until warmed through, then pour as much as desired over the cooked porridge, and enjoy.

TUNISIAN MINI DONUTS

AKRAM CHERIF

PREPARATION TIME: 20 MINUTES,
  PLUS 45 MINUTES RESTING
COOKING TIME: 10 MINUTES
SERVES 6

6 cups (2 lb 12 oz/1.2 kg)
  granulated sugar
scant ⅓ cup (2¾ oz/75 g)
  vanilla sugar
4 eggs
8⅓ cups (2 lb 4 oz/1 kg)
  all-purpose (plain) flour
1½ oz (40 g) baking powder
½ cup (4¼ fl oz/125 ml) whole
  (full-fat) milk
½ cup (4¼ fl oz/125 ml)
  vegetable oil
juice of ½ lemon
4¼ cups (34 fl oz/1 liter)
  sunflower oil, for frying

As a child, I was my mother's helper when it came to making these mini donuts. I would make sure I was right next to her as she made the dish because it was my favorite. My moment came when it was time to form the rings. I would use a cup to make perfect circles. Finally, when the donuts were ready, I had the privilege of tasting them first!

This dessert is a traditional Tunisian pastry. It's very easy to prepare, and delicious with a cup of mint tea or Turkish coffee.

In a bowl, mix three-quarters of the granulated sugar with the vanilla sugar and eggs. Add the flour and baking powder and stir to combine.

In a separate bowl, combine the milk and oil, then pour it into the bowl with the flour and sugar. Work the dough well and let it rest for 45 minutes, until risen.

Prepare a syrup by mixing the remaining granulated sugar, ⅓ cup (3½ fl oz/ 100 ml) of water, and the lemon juice in a pan, then bring to a boil, remove from the heat, and let cool.

In a skillet (frying pan), heat the oil to 350°F/180°C.

Cut 4-inch (10-cm) rings from the dough (you could use a cookie cutter, cup, or small glass). Fry the dough rings for 7 minutes until golden. Soak them in the syrup, then serve hot or cold.

LAND
OF GOLD

PREPARATION TIME: 1 HOUR,
  PLUS 1 HOUR RESTING
COOKING TIME: 20 MINUTES
SERVES 20

FOR THE DOUGH
5 cups (1 lb 9 oz/700 g) all-
  purpose (plain) white flour
6 cups (1 lb 14 oz/850 g) whole
  wheat (wholemeal) flour
pinch of salt
8¼ cups (68 fl oz/2 liters)
  warm water

FOR COOKING
2 tablespoons (1 oz/30 g) clarified
  butter (ghee)
2 teaspoons corn oil
4¼ cups (34 fl oz/1 liter) whole
  (full-fat) milk
½ cup (3½ oz/100 g) granulated
  sugar

As a child, I eagerly awaited wedding events because I could follow my grandma around, assisting in the preparation and enjoying this delightful homemade vermicelli dish, locally named *sheerya* or *makrota*. I named this plate NOB-N IPKI or "Land of Gold" because in the Nubian language, "nub" translates to gold, which is significant due to the presence of the largest gold mines in the region. The finishing touch of this plate is the edible golden powder, adding a touch of glamour to the dish.

In Nubian culture, for many years and continuing to this day, this dish has been a cherished breakfast served to all wedding guests. The tradition involves all the women in the village coming together in the wedding house to prepare it with love and care. This recipe holds a special place in my heart.

For the dough, combine all the dry ingredients in a bowl and gradually add the warm water, kneading until you have achieved a thick consistency, similar to pasta dough. Let the dough rest, covered, for 45–60 minutes.

Next, using a pasta machine, shape the dough into thin strands resembling vermicelli (known as sheerya or makrota). You will need to run the dough several times through the pasta machine, working from the largest to the smallest setting, then use the machine to cut it into strands. If making the vermicelli by hand, you will need to roll out the dough and cut the strands using a sharp knife—the strands should be 12 inches (30 cm) long and about 2.3 mm in diameter (just slightly thicker than an average toothpick). Hang the shaped strands on a palm tree, or a rope in the sun, or somewhere warm indoors, to dry and preserve them. Once fully dried, break the strands into smaller pieces.

To cook, in a pan on medium heat, toast some of the dried sheerya/makrota in the ghee and corn oil until they turn golden and release their flavors. Then, add the remaining strands to the pan along with 1 cup (8 fl oz/250 ml) of water and half the milk, then add the sugar. Cook the mixture while continuously stirring.

Gradually add another 1 cup (8 fl oz/250 ml) of water and the rest of the milk at intervals to create a thick, sauce-like consistency (you may not need all of it). Once the sauce has thickened to your desired consistency, your dish is ready to eat.

PIERRE
THIAM

Early in my career, as a
young cook in New York City, the
food capital of the world, I realized that
the food I grew up eating and loving was
absent from that world. I worked in American,
Italian, and French restaurants, and New York had
Indian, Chinese, Mexican, and Vietnamese outlets,
and although I appreciated those cuisines, I wanted
the food of my origins to be represented. It soon
became my source of inspiration and my life's
mission to introduce it to the world. Over the years,
I've opened several restaurants, written cookbooks,
and started an African food brand, with a mission
to open a global market for resilient, underutilized,
and nutritious crops grown by smallholder farmers
in Africa. It all sprang from a desire to belong.
I wanted to be a voice for my food culture.
My legacy to the world: A culinary
ambassador and an advocate for
the smallholder farming
communities in Africa.

EASTERN AFRICA

My adventure to Eastern Africa took me first to the hustle and bustle of Nairobi, Kenya. There, I was immediately struck by the physical characteristics of the people, from the height to the kind smiles, paired with lyrical grace. The city itself seemed frightfully busy and crowded; traffic jams and overfull minivans and buses lined the highways as everyone appeared to be going somewhere fast.

When it came to the food, what struck me initially was the prevalence of Indian influences. Indian spices were infused in almost every dish we tried. But then there were "old familiars" too—and different takes on their preparation. Okra is one example: At an outdoor restaurant with Kenyan friends, where food was prepared over an open fire, I consumed a serious amount of fried okra, prepared similarly to my home style, but instead of being coated with flour or fine cornmeal (maize meal), it was crispy fried and tossed with chilies and peppers.

While in Nairobi I learned about the beaches in Mombasa, Kenya's second largest city after Nairobi, which sits on the coast along the Indian Ocean. I planned to take a week to explore the place where influences from Africans and Arabs intertwine through language, architecture, and of course, food. I shared my plan with my good friend and host Shamim Ehsani, and he suggested I go north of Mombasa to the oldest Swahili town in East Africa, Lamu. Years before, a good friend of mine in New York had told me of the magical village lost in time on the beautiful beaches of Kenya near Somalia, and the thought of going there consumed me.

The flight to paradise was a bit of a journey. First was the flight on a small plane from Kenya to Manda Island. Then there was a short walk from the airport to a motorboat sent by the Majlis Hotel. And finally, Lamu! Breathtaking and exotic, I was immediately enamored. I wasted no time making plans to experience the cultural wonders, especially the food. Beyond sight and touch, I explored through smell: waves of aromatic rice dishes, curries, and other distinct aromas of Swahili culinary specialties greeted me. And this was on top of the colorful and textured array of fresh fruits, and the plethora of grilled fish and seafood. My favorites were the famous crab soup with ginger, a traditional dish in Lamu, and the delicious sautéed octopus with hummus, as well as cherry tomatoes with spices and chilies.

The meats were also varied in both type and spice, and served with a great choice of vegetables. There was a lot of goat and chicken, including grilled goat ribs and whole goat, as well as chicken dishes and accompanying vegetables—including pumpkin, sweet potatoes, and collard greens (spring greens), all found in diverse combinations throughout Eastern Africa.

This section includes dishes such as Zein Abdallah's Chicken Biryani with coconut rice and topped with bananas (page 76); Rubia Zablon's beautiful garam masala and tamarind-spiced Fried Whole Fish (page 82); while Sophia Teshome shares a recipe made with an Ethiopian collard green called gomen— her Gomen Ricotta Rotolos with Tomato Sugo (page 86), which highlights the Italian influence in the country's food.

Your adventure in Eastern Africa awaits— enjoy!

FRIED GOAT WITH UGALI

RUBIA ZABLON

PREPARATION TIME: 20 MINUTES
COOKING TIME: 1 HOUR 40 MINUTES
SERVES 6

2 tablespoons vegetable oil
2 lb 4 oz (1 kg) goat meat,
  cut into large pieces
1 red onion, diced
1 teaspoon minced garlic
1 teaspoon minced fresh root ginger
½ tablespoon salt
1 bunch cilantro (coriander),
  chopped
1 teaspoon cumin seeds, crushed
3 tomatoes, diced
2 red bell peppers, diced
2 green bell peppers, diced

FOR THE UGALI
2 cups (8 oz/225 g) fine white
  cornmeal (maize meal)
salt, to taste

Being part of a religiously diverse family means that there are many sacred celebrations and observations. My fondest memories are of when we put religious differences aside and participated in observances for both Muslims and Christians. For instance, when the Muslim side of my family is fasting, the Christian side participates as well. The fasting culminates at the end in a celebratory feast for everyone. We celebrate by cooking two goats: one for us and the other for our neighbors. May you unite with others with this recipe!

This dish is commonly called "goat wet fry" because of the moistness of the meat. It is a popular dish in most local restaurants and can be served with rice, steamed bananas, plantains, potatoes, or cornmeal (maize meal) polenta (*ugali*). I learned how to make *ugali* by tag teaming with my grandmother while she prepared the dish. I would join her in the kitchen and she would put me to work. While talking, she would take on her part of the team effort: boiling the water and mixing the flour. Then she would call me to help with stirring. I would jump up and dive in as if she were my coach on a football field! Using my strength, I would stir and stir while she guided my strokes. Within minutes, we would be done.

In a large, heavy pan on medium heat, add the oil. Working in batches, add the goat and brown on all sides for 10 minutes. Return all the goat to the pan, cover, reduce the heat to low, and cook for 15 minutes.

Add the onion, mix well, and cover. Let cook for 5 more minutes, then add the garlic, ginger, and salt, and mix well. Cover the goat again and cook for another 15 minutes.

Add the chopped coriander, crushed cumin seeds, and diced tomatoes and mix well. Cover the goat and let simmer for a further 15 minutes on low heat. Check and stir occasionally, to ensure it does not burn.

Increase the heat to medium, add 2 cups (16 fl oz/475 ml) of water and bring to a boil. Reduce the heat to low again, then let your goat simmer, partially covered, for 15–30 minutes, until tender. You may need to top up with water occasionally.

Finally, add the peppers, cover, and simmer for another 10 minutes. The end result should be tender pieces of goat, in a thick, flavorful sauce. Set aside to rest until ready to serve.

While the goat is cooking, make the ugali. Fill a small, deep pot with 1 cup (8 fl oz/240 ml) of water and bring to a boil. Add salt to taste (I suggest a pinch of salt because you want the water to be salty, but not as salty as pasta water). Keep another cup of water beside the stove. Gradually add the cornmeal (maize meal), stirring constantly with a wooden spoon for 5 minutes. Add more water as needed so the cornmeal forms a semi-solid texture.

Turn the heat down and keep kneading with the spoon for about 10 minutes until the water starts to dry out. When it is nice and thick, it is ready to be served alongside the goat.

RUBIA ZABLON

GRILLED GOAT RIBS

PREPARATION TIME: 15 MINUTES,
  PLUS OVERNIGHT MARINATING
COOKING TIME: 1 HOUR 5 MINUTES
SERVES 4-6

FOR THE MARINADE
2 tablespoons ginger-garlic paste
1 tablespoon dark soy sauce
1 tablespoon dried chili flakes
1 tablespoon chopped rosemary
  leaves

FOR THE GOAT RIBS
3 lb 5 oz (1.5 kg) rack of
  goat ribs

Barbecue meats are a staple in Kenya, and part of the food culture that I grew up on. They're called *nyama choma* in Swahili, which translates to "meat barbecue." One of my favorites is goat, or *mbuzi choma*. There is just something about barbecued goat that I love—the smell as it grills over fire is unlike any other meat. It is easily found on the streets in Kenya, where it is cooked right in front of you. Enjoy this recipe with family and friends, because *nyama choma* is best with conversation.

Enjoy with *Ugali* (page 72) and potatoes with Collard Greens (page 90).

In a mixing bowl, add all the marinade ingredients and blend everything together. Coat the goat ribs in the marinade and set aside to marinate for at least 3 hours, or ideally overnight.

When you're ready to cook, preheat a barbecue—ideally coal—and grill the ribs for 10 minutes.

Wrap the ribs in foil and move to one side of the grill, away from the direct heat of the coals. Leave to slow cook for at least 45 minutes, then unwrap the foil and return the ribs to the grill for another 10 minutes before serving.

CHICKEN BIRYANI

ZEIN ABDALLAH

PREPARATION TIME: 20 MINUTES
COOKING TIME: 1 HOUR
SERVES 6

FOR THE RICE
2½ cups (1 lb 2 oz/500 g) basmati
    rice, washed and rinsed
3 cardamom pods
1 cinnamon stick
7¼ oz (205 g) canned coconut cream
1 tablespoon ghee
1 cup (5½ oz/150 g) raisins

FOR THE CHICKEN
¼ cup (2 fl oz/60 ml) vegetable oil
    or sunflower oil
4 whole cloves
2 bay leaves
1 teaspoon cumin seeds
½ teaspoon black peppercorns
3 cardamom pods
1 cinnamon stick
1 tablespoon ground turmeric
1 tablespoon paprika
1 tablespoon garam masala
2 lb 4 oz (1 kg) chicken, cut into
    6-8 pieces
1 teaspoon ginger paste
1 teaspoon garlic paste
2 finely grated carrots (for
    thickness and sweetness)
2 chicken bouillon (stock) cubes
3 tablespoons tomato paste (purée)
½ cup (4 fl oz/120 ml) plain yogurt
salt, to taste

TO SERVE
3 onions, julienned, fried until
    crispy
6 hard-boiled eggs, halved
6 ripe bananas, peeled and halved
    on the diagonal
cilantro (coriander), to garnish

When I was growing up, every time my mom made chicken biryani, everyone would gather for a plate. She would make it for special occasions, like Eid, and served it on a big silver platter called a *saniya*. As soon as it was time to eat, we would dive into the plate with our hands. After the meal, the tasty aroma of the dish would be on my skin, and no matter the number of times I washed my hands, it wouldn't leave, and I was happy to remember the dish. Here I'm sharing my own recipe, filled with my mom's bold and rich flavors— one that will surely make you want to dig in with your hands!

This popular dish comes from the Swahili people who reside on the East African coast, from Uganda to Kenya, and including Tanzania. Their Arab influences are evident throughout the food and culture in the region and show up deliciously in this dish.

My mom served this dish with yogurt curd, cabbage salad, and blended green chili on the side.

Fill a pot with 3 cups (25 fl oz/750 ml) of water and bring to a boil over medium–high heat. Add a drizzle of oil, then add the rice, cardamom pods, and cinnamon stick, and cook for 8–10 minutes, until the water is almost gone and the rice is almost dry.

Reduce the heat to low and stir in the coconut cream. After 2 minutes, add the ghee and raisins (set aside a few to garnish), then cover and steam on low heat for 15 minutes.

For the chicken, place a medium pot over medium heat and add the oil. Add all the whole spices (whole cloves, bay leaves, cumin seeds, black peppercorns, cardamom pods, and cinnamon stick) and cook for a little less than 1 minute, until fragrant. Add the ground spices (turmeric, paprika, and garam masala), then add the chicken pieces and stir to seal for about 5 minutes.

Add the ginger and garlic pastes followed by the grated carrots, and keep stirring gently. Add the chicken stock cubes and continue to stir until the flavors combine. Then add the tomato paste (purée) and 1 cup (8 fl oz/240 ml) of water and let it come to a boil.

Add salt to taste, then reduce the heat to low. Add the plain yogurt and stir, then let simmer for 25 minutes (the gravy has to be thick and rich and the chicken soft), or until the chicken is cooked through.

Plate the chicken on top of the rice, and sprinkle over the crispy onions. Serve with boiled eggs, and banana, and garnish with cilantro (coriander) and the reserved raisins.

CHICKEN PILAU

RUBIA ZABLON

PREPARATION TIME: 20 MINUTES, PLUS
   30 MINUTES MARINATING
COOKING TIME: 1 HOUR
SERVES 6

FOR THE PILAU MASALA
6 whole cloves
1 cardamom pod, split open
1½ tablespoons black peppercorns,
   crushed
4 cinnamon sticks
2 tablespoons cumin seeds, crushed

FOR THE CHICKEN
½ teaspoon salt
½ teaspoon ground black pepper
1 teaspoon minced garlic
1 tablespoon dark soy sauce
1 whole chicken, jointed

FOR THE RICE
4 tablespoons vegetable oil
1 large onion, julienned
2 tablespoons ginger-garlic paste
4 potatoes, diced
2½ cups (1 lb 2 oz/500 g)
   basmati rice
salt and pepper, to taste

TO SERVE
Kenyan Salsa (kachumbari, page 92)
4 ripe bananas (optional)

I don't think there has ever been a gathering in my family without chicken pilau (*pilau ya kuku* in Swahili). Growing up, everyone in my family anticipated this spiced rice dish well before arriving at my grandmother's house in Mombasa, Kenya, to make memories with our grandparents, aunts, uncles, and cousins at the beautiful city on the coast. We would even call each other to chat about my grandmother's famous chicken pilau! Upon arriving, we would roll up our sleeves and start pitching in, from cutting the onions to preparing the chicken. Once ready, my grandmother served it on one plate and we would all dig in. This recipe gives you the chance to make unforgettable memories with your own family.

Preheat the oven to 350°F/180°C/Gas Mark 4.

Place all the pilau masala spices in a small pan on low heat and dry-toast them for 2–3 minutes until fragrant. Leave them to cool for a couple of minutes, then place them in a grinder and grind to a powder. The pilau masala will make more than needed in this recipe; store the remainder in a sterilized airtight glass jar for up to 3 months.

For the chicken, mix together the salt, pepper, garlic, and soy sauce in a bowl. Rub the marinade over the chicken pieces and set aside to marinate for 30 minutes. Then place the chicken in a large roasting tray and cook for 25 minutes. Set aside.

In a medium pot on low heat, heat the oil, then add the onion, and cook for 5 minutes until browned. The darker the onion, the better; the deep brown color of the onion will enhance the color of the final dish. Add the ginger-garlic paste, 3 tablespoons of the pilau masala, and the diced potatoes. Cook for a few minutes to ensure the spices are mixed, then add the roasted chicken and 4 cups (32 fl oz/950 ml) of water. Bring to a boil, then add the basmati rice and salt and pepper to taste. Simmer on low heat until cooked, about 20 minutes.

Serve the chicken pilau with kachumbari and ripe banana on the side, if using.

BEEF
PILAU

ZEIN ABDALLAH

PREPARATION TIME: 20 MINUTES
COOKING TIME: 45 MINUTES
SERVES 4-6

FOR UNCLE RICHARD'S CHILI SAMBAL
1 large Spanish onion, roughly
   chopped
1 garlic bulb
½ bunch cilantro (coriander)
½ bunch parsley
4-oz (120-g) piece fresh root ginger
9 oz (250 g) yellow habanero
   peppers, deseeded
⅓ cup (3½ fl oz/100 ml) olive oil
salt and pepper, to taste

FOR THE BEEF PILAU
⅓ cup (3½ fl oz/100 ml) vegetable oil
½ teaspoon black peppercorns
6 cardamom pods
2 cinnamon sticks
4 cloves
3 bay leaves
1 tablespoon cumin seeds
3 onions, julienned
1 lb 14 oz (850 g) beef fillet,
   cubed
1½ tablespoons ginger-garlic paste
5 potatoes, peeled and cubed
2 chicken bouillon (stock) cubes
2¼ cups (1 lb/450 g) basmati rice,
   washed and rinsed
salt, to taste

TO SERVE
red chili pepper, chopped, to taste
plain yogurt
cilantro (coriander), to garnish

Pilau was always one of my favorite homemade meals; the aroma alone leaves me feeling hungry. Growing up, we usually had pilau on Fridays after prayer. As soon as prayers were over, we would go home and feast with family and friends, and this dish was always on the menu. My mom would serve it in many different ways, adding banana or gravy and chapati on the side. It's a great meal for sharing with others, so get ready for everyone to ask you for the recipe.

Uncle Richard has known me throughout my life. He has a warm heart, a generous soul, and fantastic hospitality skills. His main loves are chilies and cooking, and he was excited to share this recipe with you all.

To make Uncle Richard's chili sambal, blend all the ingredients together in a blender or food processor, then put in a pot on medium heat, bring just to a boil, and let simmer for 30–35 minutes.

Meanwhile, to make the beef pilau, place a medium–large stockpot on medium heat and add the vegetable oil. Put in all the whole spices (black peppercorns, cardamom pods, cinnamon sticks, cloves, bay leaves, cumin seeds) and fry for less than 1 minute until fragrant. Add the onions, then sauté for 6–8 minutes until almost golden brown. Add the beef and stir for about 5 minutes to seal.

Continuing to stir, add the ginger-garlic paste, followed by the potatoes. Add the chicken bouillon (stock) cubes and continue to stir for 5 minutes until the flavors combine. Pour in 3 cups (25 fl oz/ 750 ml) of water and let it come to a boil.

Add salt to taste (remember that chicken bouillon cubes are already salty). Then add the basmati rice and stir gently to avoid breaking the rice and potatoes. Cook for 8–10 minutes until almost dry, then cover and steam on low heat for about 15 minutes.

Serve with the chili sambal, chopped chili (if using), and yogurt, and garnish with cilantro (coriander).

FRIED
WHOLE FISH

RUBIA ZABLON

PREPARATION TIME: 15 MINUTES,
   PLUS 30 MINUTES MARINATING
COOKING TIME: 30 MINUTES
SERVES 2

FOR THE FISH
½ teaspoon salt
3 tablespoons vegetable oil
juice of 2 lemons
3 cloves garlic, crushed
1 whole tilapia fish (cleaned,
   gutted, and scales removed)
1¼ cups (10 fl oz/300 ml)
   vegetable oil

FOR THE SAUCE
1 onion, chopped or sliced
2 red or green bell peppers,
   chopped or sliced
1½ teaspoons garlic paste
1 tablespoon tomato paste (purée)
1 cup (7 oz/200 g) chopped tomatoes
1½ cups (12 fl oz/350 ml)
   coconut milk
2-3 teaspoons garam masala
   or curry powder
1 tablespoon tamarind paste
   or lemon juice
½ bunch cilantro (coriander),
   chopped
salt and pepper, to taste

Growing up in Mombasa, Kenya, on the coast of the Indian Ocean, seafood was abundant and fresh fish was sold on the streets. One of the errands my mom would send me on was to buy fish. After finding a vendor, I would select one and ask them to cook it. While waiting for it to cook, I would get any other items my mom asked for and head back to the vendor to pick up the fish. The only hard part about the journey was going home with the delicious-smelling fish without taking a bite. Serve with *Ugali* (page 72) and vegetables.

In a large mixing bowl, add the salt, vegetable oil, lemon juice, and crushed garlic, and submerge the whole fish in the marinade. Leave it for at least 30 minutes.

Heat the oil in a skillet (frying pan) to a high temperature, then reduce the heat, add the fish, and fry gently for 15 minutes, flipping it halfway through, until golden brown.

Reduce the heat to medium and add the onion and peppers. Sauté for 2 minutes until the onion is translucent. Add 1 teaspoon of the garlic paste and the tablespoon of tomato paste (purée), and sauté for another 1–2 minutes. Add the tomatoes, coconut milk, garam masala, tamarind paste or lemon juice, and salt and pepper. Bring to a boil, then reduce the heat to low and simmer for 6–8 minutes. Finally, add the chopped cilantro (coriander).

Place the fish on a serving plate covered with the sauce, and serve with ugali and vegetables on the side, if you wish.

ROASTED PUMPKIN
AND SWEET POTATO SOUP

ZEIN ABDALLAH

PREPARATION TIME: 15 MINUTES
COOKING TIME: 45 MINUTES
SERVES 10

2 lb 4 oz (1 kg) pumpkin, peeled,
 deseeded, and chopped
1 lb 14 oz (850 g) sweet potatoes,
 peeled and chopped
1 onion, roughly chopped
3 cloves garlic, roughly chopped
2 sprigs thyme, leaves picked
1 teaspoon ground cumin
3-4 tablespoons olive oil
honey, for drizzling
2 tablespoons (1 oz/25 g) butter
generous ¾ cup (7 fl oz/200 ml)
 heavy (double) cream
4 cups (32 fl oz/950 ml)
 chicken stock
1 teaspoon plain yogurt,
 for drizzling
2 teaspoons chopped chives,
 to garnish
salt and pepper, to taste
bread, to serve

Uganda is known for its rich and organic fruits and starchy root vegetables. With almost every local dish, steamed pumpkin and sweet potatoes are provided as side dishes—and my family's kitchen is no exception! My mom's version of this was pumpkin and sweet potato in coconut cream, and that filling and delicious dish inspired this recipe. While contemplating how to make a lighter version of my mom's combination of the two vegetables, I created this soup, and it was met with great success: when I first served it at a gathering, everyone loved it. Here is your chance to have everyone at your gathering asking for seconds. This is great served with garlic bread or crusty bread on the side.

Preheat the oven to 350°F/180°C/Gas Mark 4.

Place the pumpkin, sweet potatoes, onion, garlic, thyme, cumin, and oil in a baking pan and mix together with your hands. Drizzle honey on top.

Roast the vegetables in the oven for about 20–25 minutes, until golden brown.

Place a pan on medium heat, add 1 tablespoon (½ oz/15 g) of the butter, then transfer the roasted ingredients to the pan and sauté for 5 minutes. Add the cream and chicken stock and let simmer for 10 minutes.

Using a blender, purée the soup until smooth and season with salt and pepper to taste. Reheat the soup until hot and add the remaining 1 tablespoon (½ oz/10 g) of butter. Ladle into a bowl, drizzle with the yogurt, and garnish with chopped chives. Serve with your choice of bread alongside.

GOMEN RICOTTA ROTOLOS WITH TOMATO SUGO

SOPHIA TESHOME

PREPARATION TIME: 20 MINUTES
COOKING TIME: 1 HOUR 10 MINUTES
SERVES 6 (2 ROLLS PER SERVING)

FOR THE LASAGNA ROTOLOS
2 tablespoons olive oil
8 lasagna sheets
½ tablespoon grated Parmesan cheese, plus extra to serve

FOR THE KOSTA GOMEN MIXTURE
1 tablespoon olive oil
3 tablespoons (1½ oz/40 g) diced red onion
1 tablespoon garlic purée
½ tablespoon red chili flakes
4 cups (5 oz/145 g) chopped kosta gomen (Ethiopian collard greens)

FOR THE RICOTTA FILLING MIXTURE
scant 2 cups (15 oz/425 g) ricotta cheese
1 teaspoon salt
1 teaspoon ground black pepper
1 egg
2 tablespoons grated Parmesan or Grana Padano cheese
½ tablespoon finely chopped basil
3 teaspoons finely chopped parsley

FOR THE TOMATO SUGO
2 tablespoons olive oil
⅓ cup (2½ oz/70 g) finely diced red onion
1 tablespoon garlic purée
3 cups (1 lb 5 oz/600 g) chopped tomatoes
1 cup (8 fl oz/240 ml) tomato paste (purée)
1 tablespoon finely chopped basil
½ tablespoon finely chopped oregano
¼ teaspoon ground nutmeg
⅛ teaspoon ground cinnamon
⅓ cup (3½ fl oz/100 ml) heavy (double) cream
1 teaspoon granulated sugar
¼ cup (¾ oz/20 g) grated Parmesan cheese
salt and ground black pepper

The cornerstone of my signature style of cuisine is combining flavors and ingredients from Ethiopia with other cultural foods that we love so much, such as Italian. This recipe is an Ethiopian and Italian fusion. Rotolos are a beautiful way to replicate lasagna-like dishes, exposing the colorful cross-section of the layers.

Kosta gomen, a kind of Ethiopian collard green (spring green), is a commonly used ingredient in every Ethiopian household. Traditionally chopped and sautéed with garlic, ginger, spices, and oil, it also makes an excellent filling for stuffed pastas—just as you would use spinach. The rotolos are baked with a sautéed *gomen* mixture, ricotta, and a creamy tomato sauce we call *sugo* (the Italian word for "sauce") to create a beautiful and delicious dish.

Bring a pan of water to a boil and add the olive oil, so the lasagna sheets do not stick together. Boil the lasagna sheets according to the package directions. Lay flat on a large platter to cool.

For the kosta gomen mixture, add the olive oil to a medium saucepan on medium–high heat. Add the diced red onion and sauté for 3 minutes. Add the garlic purée and red chili flakes and sauté for 30 seconds. Add the kosta gomen and cook for 2 minutes until completely wilted down. Remove from the heat and strain, then squeeze all the liquid out of the gomen mixture and set aside.

For the ricotta filling, add the ricotta to a bowl and add the salt, pepper, egg, Parmesan, basil, and parsley. Mix well until smooth.

For the tomato sugo, add the olive oil to a saucepan on medium–high heat. Add the red onion and sauté for 5 minutes, then add the garlic purée and sauté for 30 seconds. Add the chopped tomatoes and cook until soft and broken down, about 10 minutes.

Add the tomato paste (purée) and 1½ cups (12 fl oz/350 ml) of water and bring to a gentle boil. Add the basil, oregano, 1½ teaspoons of salt, ½ teaspoon of pepper, the nutmeg, cinnamon, cream, and sugar and let the sauce simmer for 5 minutes. Add the grated Parmesan. Let cool slightly, then transfer the tomato sugo to a blender and blend until smooth. Return to the pan, bring to a boil, and simmer for 5 minutes. Season to taste.

Preheat the oven to 375°F/190°C/Gas Mark 5. To assemble, lay the cooked lasagna sheets down on a cutting board with the edges overlapping to create one large rectangle-shaped lasagna sheet. Spread the ricotta filling evenly over the entire surface, then spread with the gomen filling. Starting at the long edge of the sheets, gently roll into one long roll. Slice into 12 × 1-inch (2.5-cm) lasagna rolls.

Spoon the tomato sugo onto the bottom of a 9 × 13-inch (23 × 33-cm) baking dish to evenly cover with about 1 inch (2.5 cm) of sauce. Save about 1 cup (8 fl oz/240 ml) of the sauce for the top.

Place each roll on top of the sauce, with crosswise sections facing up. Top each roll with a spoonful of sauce and the grated Parmesan. Bake in the oven, uncovered, for 30 minutes until the sauce is bubbling and the top of each roll is browned. Serve the rotolos on a bed of sauce, and finish with more grated Parmesan.

GREEN GRAMS WITH CHAPATI

RUBIA ZABLON

PREPARATION TIME: 30 MINUTES
COOKING TIME: 1 HOUR 30 MINUTES
SERVES 6

FOR THE GREEN GRAMS
2 cups (14 oz/400 g) dried green
  grams (mung beans)
6 tablespoons vegetable oil
¾ teaspoon mustard seeds
½ teaspoon cumin seeds
5 curry leaves (optional)
1 onion, finely chopped
1 tomato, finely chopped
¼ teaspoon ground turmeric
½ teaspoon ground cumin
½ teaspoon ground coriander
½ teaspoon garam masala
1 teaspoon chili powder,
  or to taste
salt, to taste
1 teaspoon chopped cilantro
  (coriander) leaves, to serve

FOR THE CHAPATIS
2 cups (10 oz/280 g) all-purpose
  (plain) flour, sifted, plus extra
  for dusting
½ teaspoon salt
1 tablespoon vegetable oil or ghee,
  plus extra for greasing and
  frying

Green grams is one meal I could eat daily. Growing up, we used to have an extended family get-together at least once a year, when my whole family would visit our grandparents and spend time with them. Green grams, also known as mung beans or *ndengu* in Swahili, was the meal everyone wanted to eat, and we would have it in different ways—curried, in coconut, with potatoes, or with carrots, and often with well-layered, soft chapatis.

My mom used to make the best chapatis. She worked during the week, so on weekends, she would devote time to making them for the family. The lead-up to the weekend was filled with excited anticipation. As soon as it was Saturday, it was chapati time! My mom would put her energy into making the most delicious chapatis, and as soon as she was done, my siblings and I would already be seated awaiting our portions. The aroma of the buttery bread on my plate was irresistible. I would take one and break it in half, watching the layers slowly pull apart like the inside of a croissant. To me, this is what made my mom's chapati the best. This chapati recipe is best cooked in a *tawa* (thick pan used for cooking chapatis).

Bring a large pot of water to a boil, add the green grams, and cook on low-medium heat for 1 hour, or until tender. Drain and set aside.

Heat 3 tablespoons oil in a pan on medium heat, then add the mustard seeds, cumin seeds, and curry leaves, if using, and cook for 2 minutes, or until they splutter (open).

In another pan, heat the remaining oil over medium heat and sauté the chopped onion for 3 minutes. Add the precooked spices and fry for 1 minute, then add the chopped tomato, turmeric, cumin, ground coriander, garam masala, and chili powder. Cook all the ingredients for 2 minutes over medium heat.

Drain the boiled green grams and add to the pan with 1 cup (8 fl oz/240 ml) of water and ½ teaspoon salt. Cover and bring to a boil, before lowering the heat and simmering for about 25 minutes, stirring occasionally.

Meanwhile, make the chapatis. In a mixing bowl, add the flour and salt, then add the oil or ghee and mix well. Next, add water as needed to make a dough that is elastic but not sticky. Let rest for 10 minutes.

Knead the dough on a lightly floured work surface for 5–10 minutes, until smooth and stretchy. Divide into 6 medium balls. With a rolling pin, roll each ball into a small circle, then brush with a little oil. Fold in half, brush with oil again, and fold into a triangle shape. Next, on a floured surface, roll each one out into a large circle.

Preheat a tawa (or skillet/heavy frying pan) on medium heat and grease with oil. Put the dough in the tawa and brush with oil. Cook on both sides for 3 minutes until small brown spots emerge.

Once the green grams are ready (they should be soft but not mushy), add chopped cilantro (coriander) leaves and serve with the chapatis alongside.

COLLARD GREENS

RUBIA ZABLON

PREPARATION TIME: 10 MINUTES
COOKING TIME: 15 MINUTES
SERVES: 4

1 tablespoon vegetable oil
½ onion, finely diced
1 tomato, diced
1 bunch collard greens (spring
    greens), chopped or sliced
salt, to taste
ground cumin, to taste

The garden of my childhood home provided us with healthy vegetables typically found in Kenyan cuisine, while also helping my mom save money. But the work wasn't all on her; we each got the chance to participate via our vegetable choices! Before cooking the main dish, she would ask my siblings and me which vegetable we wanted to pair with it. Then she'd send us into the garden to harvest. One of our favorites was *sukuma wiki*, or collard greens (spring greens). We would pick them, wash them, and assist in the preparation of this much-loved vegetable. Even if you can't get the ingredients from your own garden, you'll find this easy-to-prepare side dish is simple to cook and goes with many main dishes.

In a medium pan on medium heat, add the oil. Add the onion and sauté until translucent; this should take about 3 minutes. Add the tomato and sauté for 2 minutes until softened.

Next, add the collard greens (spring greens). Cover with a lid, and turn down the heat (you can add a splash of water to help with steaming). Let the greens steam for about 1–2 minutes, giving them a good stir so they don't burn. Cook for a further 5 minutes, then season with salt and cumin to taste, and serve.

KENYAN SALSA

RUBIA ZABLON

PREPARATION TIME: 10 MINUTES
SERVES 2

½ onion, sliced or diced
1 large tomato, sliced or diced
2 tablespoons chopped cilantro
  (coriander)
juice of 1 lemon
ground cumin, to taste
chili flakes, to taste
1 avocado, diced (optional)
1 mango, diced (optional)
salt and pepper, to taste

One of my favorite things is to go for barbecue—*nyama choma*—from a roadside vendor, where you select your meat and watch as it's cooked. This is one of the best places to experience the Kenyan salsa, or *kachumbari*. While the salsa is a side dish discreetly placed on your plate, it is a key part of the *nyama choma* experience. At these spots, the salsa gets a ceremonious presentation: a server comes to the table and makes it fresh, right in front of your eyes. Once they're done, all that is left to do is grab some meat with a bit of the salsa and some cornmeal (maize meal) polenta and enjoy. Try this live salsa production as you serve the *kachumburi* to wow your guests.

Serve with proteins like Fried Whole Fish (page 82) and *Ugali* (page 72).

In a bowl, combine the onion, tomato, and cilantro (coriander), then add the lemon juice. Season with salt, pepper, cumin, and chili flakes. Mix and adjust the seasoning as needed. Add avocado or ripe mango, if you like, to enhance the flavors.

CRACKED BULGUR WHEAT SALAD

SOPHIA TESHOME

PREPARATION TIME: 5 MINUTES
COOKING TIME: 15 MINUTES
SERVES 4-6

1¼ cups (7½ oz/215 g) cracked
  bulgur wheat
2 cups (16 fl oz/475 ml) hot
  vegetable bouillon broth (stock)
1½ cups (7 oz/200 g) finely diced
  carrots
⅓ cup (1½ oz/45 g) raisins
2½ tablespoons olive oil
1 tablespoon finely chopped basil
½ tablespoon finely chopped parsley
3 tablespoons fresh lime juice

The taste of *kinche*, or cracked bulgur wheat, takes me back to my mom's kitchen, where on weekends or for special brunches she would make a spread of classic breakfast dishes like *tibs* (stir-fried meat and vegetables) and *quanta firfir* (a soft, slightly crunchy dish of torn pieces of *injera* [sour fermented flatbread] in a spicy tomato-berber-onion sauce and mixed with dried Ethiopian spiced beef jerky). These were usually paired with *kinche* that was perfectly fluffy, with a slightly chewy texture and often bathed in high-quality, spiced clarified Ethiopian butter.

Kinche is one of my favorite Ethiopian dishes and is usually pre-pared as a nutritious buttery grain porridge served hot with *injera*. While it is never prepared as a salad in Ethiopia, I enjoy eating it as a cold salad, as in this recipe, with some olive oil, a tang of acidity from lime juice, and some contrasting crunchy veggies and fresh herbs. Together they create a delicious and healthy vegan side dish. This recipe pairs well with roasted chicken, grilled fish, or steak.

Add the bulgur wheat to a small pot with the hot vegetable broth and carrots. Bring to a gentle boil and then cover and simmer for 12 minutes, until all the liquid is cooked out and the bulgur can be fluffed with a fork. Add all the remaining ingredients and mix well.

Serve in a bowl or on a platter. It can be served warm, but it's best served slightly chilled.

SINAFICH DEVILED EGGS

SOPHIA TESHOME

PREPARATION TIME: 10 MINUTES, PLUS UP TO 1 HOUR SOAKING
COOKING TIME: 15 MINUTES
SERVES 14

FOR THE DEVILED EGGS
- 7 excellent-quality organic eggs (Ethiopian, if possible!)
- 3 tablespoons mayonnaise
- ⅛ teaspoon salt
- ⅛ teaspoon ground black pepper
- ½ teaspoon mitmita spice, to garnish
- ½ teaspoon finely chopped cilantro (coriander) leaves, to garnish

FOR THE SINAFICH MUSTARD
- 3 tablespoons black mustard seeds
- 1 tablespoon peeled and sliced fresh root ginger
- 1 tablespoon sliced garlic
- ¾ cup (6 fl oz/180 ml) distilled water
- ½ teaspoon salt

Anyone who knows me knows I am a big fan of organic Ethiopian eggs. Their delicious taste takes me back to my childhood. While visiting my grandparents' dairy farm, we would have fresh eggs and milk for breakfast. It also reminds me of my travels through rural Ethiopia, where it is common to find these tasty eggs.

In Ethiopia, you can ask for two types of eggs—*ye ferenji enqulal* (foreign) or *ye habesha enqulal* (local). The local eggs are from an organic breed that is smaller, usually grown on small farms, and they have a distinct bright yellow or orange yolk. In my opinion, they are much tastier, even if they are slightly more expensive than foreign eggs. Due to the high cost of production, they have become increasingly hard to find, as small-scale farmers find them difficult to produce. I make hard-boiled organic eggs regularly as a snack, just because the local eggs are so perfect.

This dish incorporates one of my favorite American appetizers with classic Ethiopian flavors and ingredients, such as ground black mustard seed made into a very spicy mustard paste with water called *sinafich*, along with cilantro (coriander) leaf, mitmita spice, and turmeric. It's an easy and fun dish to serve to guests and a perfect marriage of my roots in both Ethiopia and the United States.

Place the eggs in a large pot and cover them with water. Bring to a rolling boil and immediately cover the pot with a lid and remove from the heat. Leave the eggs to continue cooking off the heat with the lid closed for 12 minutes. After 12 minutes, remove the hard-boiled eggs from the pot, rinse with cold water, peel the eggs, and let cool.

For the sinafich mustard, grind the black mustard seeds until they become a fine powder and set aside.

Place the ginger and garlic into a ½ cup (4 fl oz/120 ml) of the distilled water and leave for at least 30 minutes and up to 1 hour.

Strain the ginger and garlic from the water, reserving the water. Combine the ginger-garlic water with the black mustard seed powder and add the salt. Then, beat with a spoon. The goal is to infuse the water for the sinafich with ginger and garlic flavor, but you don't want the pieces of garlic and ginger to end up in the final product. Continue to add the remaining ¼ cup (2 fl oz/60 ml) of distilled water as needed, and continue to beat with a spoon until you get a mustard paste that is slightly watery but still slightly thick and very spicy from the mustard seeds.

To assemble the deviled eggs, slice each egg lengthwise and place the halves on a plate. Scoop out the cooked yolks into a bowl. Add the mayonnaise, 2 tablespoons of sinafich mustard, salt, and black pepper, and mash with a fork until smooth. (You can store any leftover mustard in an airtight container in the refrigerator for up to 1 week.)

Add the yolk mixture to a piping bag, or a resealable storage bag with the corner cut off, and gently pipe the mixture back into the cooked egg white halves. Garnish each deviled egg with a sprinkle of mitmita spice and finely chopped cilantro (coriander) leaves.

CHAPATI
WITH OMELET

ZEIN ABDALLAH

PREPARATION TIME: 15 MINUTES
COOKING TIME: 5 MINUTES
MAKES 8

24 eggs
8 chapatis
salt

FOR EACH "ROLEX"
¼ cup (¾ oz/20 g) julienned
   white cabbage
¼ cup (¾ oz/20 g) julienned carrots
1 tablespoon (¼ oz/10 g) julienned
   bell peppers
1 tablespoon (¼ oz/10 g) julienned
   red onion
10g tomato slices
3 tablespoons (¾ oz/20 g)
   grated cheese
1½ tablespoons Sriracha-mayonnaise
¾ oz (20 g) cooked chicken
   or beef strips

An omelet wrapped with a chapati is called a "rolex" in Uganda (for "rolled eggs"). Growing up, it was the easiest, cheapest yet most delicious meal I could make while in school. I remember a rolex street vendor in Wandegeya, a town next to my university, who could customize it to my liking, adding beef, chicken, extra vegetables, and ground (minced) meat. His ingredient list was extensive and, my goodness, his rolexes tasted like no other.

Originating from the Busoga region of Uganda, rolex, or chapati with omelet, was considered to be the "poor man's food" before it became popular among students and bachelors in Kampala. The dish is quick to prepare and can be served at any time of the day, from breakfast to lunch, as a main meal or snack. On the streets of Kampala, it was always available. You can adjust the omelet ingredients to your own liking, and once you add the chapati, you'll be transported to Uganda!

Pair with salad or coleslaw and enjoy.

In a bowl, add 3 eggs, a pinch of salt, all the vegetables (cabbage, carrots, bell peppers, red onion, and tomato), and beat. Place a pan on medium heat, add the egg mixture, and fry for 2–3 minutes, then add the grated cheese and remove from the heat.

Place the omelet on a chapati while still hot. Spread with the Sriracha-mayonnaise, then add the vegetables, chicken or beef strips, and tomato slices. Roll the chapati and cut in half to serve.

Repeat with the remaining eggs and chapatis.

CHOCOLATE CAKE

PREPARATION TIME: 10 MINUTES
COOKING TIME: 40 MINUTES
SERVES 12

FOR THE FROSTING
2 cups (17 fl oz/500 ml)
  whipping cream
1 cup (4 oz/115 g) confectioners'
  (icing) sugar
generous 1 cup (9 oz/250 g) full-
  fat cream cheese

FOR THE CAKE
9 oz (250 g) dark chocolate
strawberries, to garnish
generous 1¾ cups (9 oz/250 g) all-
  purpose (plain) flour or cake flour
¾ cup (5½ oz/150 g) superfine
  (caster) sugar
5 eggs
½ cup (4 fl oz/120 ml) vegetable oil
1 teaspoon vanilla extract
pinch of salt
1 teaspoon baking powder
1 teaspoon baking soda (bicarbonate
  of soda)
⅓ cup (3½ fl oz/100 ml) whole
  (full-fat) milk
¼ cup (1 oz/30 g) unsweetened dark
  cocoa powder
cream, chocolate sauce, or custard,
  to serve

When I was growing up, watching my mom bake was one of my favorite pastimes, especially when she made anything chocolate. I come from a large family, so people were always in and out of our house. Yet my mom made the effort to spend personal time with us. One of those times was when she was making her special chocolate cake. She would wake up around five o'clock in the morning to start prepping. I would help her as soon as I smelled her cooking. The kitchen and the whole house would smell like heaven. The aromas of this cake still catapult me back to that time.

My version of chocolate cake is not typically Ugandan, but it's part of my Ugandan story. It's simple to make and has a real depth of flavor. I recommend enjoying it with Ugandan coffee, tea, or hot chocolate.

For the frosting, pour the cream and confectioners' (icing) sugar into the bowl of a stand mixer with the paddle attachment or balloon whisk, then mix to combine. Add the cream cheese and mix until smooth. Set aside in the fridge.

For the cake, use a round mold to shave or shape the chocolate into a decoration of your choice. Wash and cut the strawberries into your desired shapes for garnish.

Preheat the oven to 350°F/180°C/Gas Mark 4. Put the flour, superfine (caster) sugar, eggs, vegetable oil, vanilla extract, salt, baking powder, baking soda (bicarbonate of soda), milk, and cocoa powder together in the mixer, then mix to combine. Pour your cake mix into a 14-inch (35-cm) round cake pan (tin) and bake in the oven for 35–40 minutes, until risen and a skewer inserted into the center comes out clean.

Using a piping bag with a 1M tip, or a palette knife, add the frosting to the top of the cake. You may not need it all, so keep any leftover in the fridge for another cake.

Add the chocolate shavings and strawberries to the top of the cake in a design of your choice.

Portion the cake into equal slices and serve with cream, chocolate sauce or custard.

COOKIE BANANA PUDDING

SOPHIA TESHOME

PREPARATION TIME: 30 MINUTES,
    PLUS 1–1½ HOURS CHILLING
COOKING TIME: 15 MINUTES
SERVES 4

FOR THE VANILLA PUDDING
2¼ cups (18 fl oz/550 ml) whole
    (full-fat) milk
6 tablespoons cornstarch (cornflour)
1 cup (7 oz/200 g) granulated sugar
½ teaspoon salt
1½ tablespoons (¾ oz/20 g) butter
2 teaspoons vanilla extract

FOR THE WHIPPED CREAM
1½ cups (12 fl oz/350 ml) very cold
    heavy (whipping) cream
3 tablespoons confectioners'
    (icing) sugar
1½ teaspoons vanilla extract

TO ASSEMBLE
15 cream-filled wafer or sandwich
    cookies (I use Abu Walad),
    crushed
6 small or 3 large bananas,
    thinly sliced
mint sprigs, to garnish

I use Abu Walad cookies in this dish, which remind me of some of my first visits to Ethiopia as a young girl. They are golden and crispy on the outside, creamy on the inside, and they were a special treat that I was rarely allowed to eat, since I come from a family of very healthy eaters. Desserts were not something we indulged in regularly, as my mom typically serves fresh fruit at home. This recipe is exciting because we usually eat these cookies by themselves, and I have never seen them used in a dessert. Combining the classic American Southern dish of layered banana pudding with cookies is a contemporary spin on two sweet treats that I love so much. The slight hint of fresh mint leaf combines so perfectly with the slightly sweet whipped cream and vanilla pudding, and the creaminess and distinct taste of the sliced bananas.

To make the vanilla pudding, heat the milk to a low boil in a saucepan. Mix the cornstarch (cornflour), sugar, and salt in a bowl. Add a ½ cup (4 fl oz/120 ml) of the cornstarch mixture at a time into the hot milk over low heat and whisk until smooth. Continue adding until all the cornstarch-sugar mixture is added to the milk and the milk mixture has slightly thickened. Add the butter and vanilla and whisk until combined. Transfer to a bowl and place in the refrigerator to cool for 1 hour or in the freezer for 20 minutes.

To make the whipped cream, whip the cold cream, confectioners' (icing) sugar, and vanilla extract in a stand mixer fitted with the whisk attachment on medium speed for 2–3 minutes, or whip by hand with a whisk in a very cold metal or glass bowl for 10 minutes until fluffy. If using a stand mixer, watch it closely to make sure you don't overwhip it into butter.

Let the whipped cream cool in the refrigerator for 15 minutes.

To assemble, in 4 individual serving jars, layer the ingredients in 2–3 layers in the following order: crushed cookies, vanilla pudding, banana slices, then whipped cream, until your jars are filled, ending with whipped cream on top, then add mint to garnish each jar.

For best results, let sit in the refrigerator for at least 30 minutes, or up to an hour, to let all the flavors combine properly. This is great to make ahead of time and will keep in the refrigerator for up to 24 hours. Wait until you are about to serve before topping the last layer with the whipped cream and the mint garnish.

BERBERE ORANGE MARGARITA WITH GOJAM HONEY

SOPHIA TESHOME

PREPARATION TIME: 10 MINUTES
SERVES 4

FOR THE SPICY BERBERE SIMPLE SYRUP
½ cup (4 oz/115 g) honey
¼ teaspoon berbere (mix of dried
  spices available in specialty
  shops and online)
⅛ teaspoon ground cinnamon

FOR THE COCKTAIL*
16 shots fresh orange juice
4 shots good-quality tequila
4 shots Cointreau
1 tablespoon berbere, for the
  glass rim
2 tablespoons granulated sugar,
  for the glass rim
2 slices orange, cut into 4 half-
  moons, to garnish
12 slices jalapeño, to garnish
  (3 for each drink)

* Shots are measured as 1.25 fl oz
  (37 ml)

This spiced-up cocktail is Ethiopian pride in a cup. It's sweetened with pure Gojam honey—an extra special honey that I traveled all the way to Bahir Dar in Gojam, Ethiopia, to get my hands on. The city of Gojam is known for some of the best honey in the country, so I make sure to stock up whenever I visit. The smooth and golden pure honey comes from farms near the source of the Nile River on Lake Tana. With its slightly thick consistency and not-too-cloying profile, it pairs nicely with this modern African version of the classic tequila-based margarita cocktail.

Along with the honey, the drink also includes berbere, the Ethiopian dark and earthy spice. This, added to the freshly squeezed orange juice, tequila, Cointreau, and jalapeño, means the aromas and colors of this drink are fun and pretty, and provide a conversation starter at any gathering. So get your glasses and your cocktail shaker ready, and get your party started!

For the spicy berbere simple syrup, mix the honey, berbere, and cinnamon with ½ cup (4 fl oz/120 ml) of water in a small pan and heat on low until just warmed through. Set aside to cool.

To make the cocktail, pour the orange juice, tequila, Cointreau, and 4 shots of the spicy berbere simple syrup into a shaker and shake well. (Leftover simple syrup will keep in the refrigerator for 3 weeks.)

Prepare the berbere sugar for rimming the glasses by combining the berbere and sugar on a small plate. Run a slice of orange around the rim of each glass and dip the glass rims into the berbere sugar mix to coat well. Add crushed ice to each of the 4 glasses.

Pour the drink from the shaker over the ice, add the slices of jalapeño on top, and a slice of orange on the rim to garnish. Enjoy!

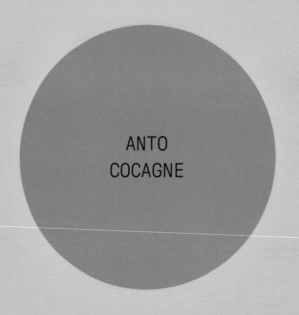

ANTO
COCAGNE

I wish, through my cuisine, to give back to my African brothers the desire to value our products and not to underestimate them. I would like our cooking to be taught in our training centers. I would like to raise awareness so that our African presidents are so proud of the cooks of their countries that they rely on them to make state dinners. I would like African women to stop being afraid of their dreams and to dare to claim chef positions in the kitchen, to dare to think big, and to realize that their dreams can be compatible with family life.

CENTRAL AFRICA

The countries that make up Central Africa span a variety of geographically delightful places. There are broad plateaus, smooth in the center and undulating around the perimeter, and the basin of the Congo River, which is joined to the Atlantic Ocean by a narrow pathway that crosses a series of ridges running parallel to the coast. Rich in number and diversity of flora and fauna, grasslands make up most of Central Africa, starting south of the Sahara and the Sahel and ending north of the continent's southern tip.

The bounty of the rainforest, farmlands, and the many lakes and rivers serves as a vast resource for feeding the people of the region. Readily available foods include bushmeat, chicken, cassava and cassava greens (leaves), oranges, pineapples, plantains, and bananas, and here you will find a number of exciting dishes from our culinary experts that are the perfect examples of the region's offerings. Several are reminiscent of my childhood, especially those made with black-eyed peas (beans), chicken gizzards, smothered fish, and seasoned goat. I'm sure that you will enjoy learning more, not only about the rich culture of this region, but also about how to prepare and share—as I do—these dishes in your home for family and friends.

Having followed chef Dieuveil Malonga's career for years, his talent and culinary excellence had captured me, and I invited him for lunch while he was visiting the United States. He was turning the fine-dining world of Paris upside down by curating dishes that had the spirit and flavors of his homeland in the Republic of Congo. We ate seared snapper with crab meat gravy, black rice, and roasted yams with green salad, which I prepared, as we talked like old friends, connecting over stories of building pathways for Africa's chefs.

After years of cooking abroad in Michelin-starred restaurants, Malonga had decided to return home to his beloved continent of Africa, and dedicate his life to raising the profile of African cuisine. Our meeting energized me, as I could see the passion emanating from him as he gave me a unique insight into Central Africa. Though we were born and raised on two continents, and had a gap in our ages that could have further separated us, there we were, breaking bread as colleagues—both champions of our ancestral culinary traditions and advocates of creativity.

Malonga and other culinarians in the region are helping to put Central Africa on the map. Dishes like Malonga's own Peanut Sauce Stew (page 114), inspired by his grandmother, will take you on an unforgettable journey to the Republic of Congo, while Forster Oben Oru and Agatha Achindu, both from Cameroon, will treat you to their respective recipes for Cocoyam Dumplings (pages 128 and 124).

Again, I invite you to make your own discoveries of Central Africa by trying these dishes, and then perhaps adapting them—as needed—to create your own personal journey and family favorites.

GOAT MEAT PEPPER SOUP

AGATHA ACHINDU

PREPARATION TIME: 20 MINUTES
COOKING TIME: 1 HOUR 30 MINUTES
SERVES 4

2-lb (900-g) bone-on goat meat
  with skin
½ teaspoon sea salt, or to taste
2 chicken bouillon (stock) cubes
5 cloves garlic
1-inch (2.5-cm) piece fresh root
  ginger, peeled and grated
  (about 1 teaspoon)
1 yellow onion
2 country onions (rondelles)
2 bush peppers
15 white peppercorns
1 pebé (calabash nutmeg), peeled
1-2 scotch bonnet peppers

TO SERVE
2 scallions (spring onions), sliced
3 sprigs basil, thinly sliced
bread or boiled plantains (optional)

As a child growing up in the southern region of Cameroon, I always thought of goat meat pepper soup as a "happy food." No matter the occasion, a big pot of pepper soup was on the menu. When someone had a baby, pepper soup was present at the "born house" celebration. Even at ordinary late-night gatherings, aunties would roll in a big pot of steaming soup. When I became an adult, I realized why the dish was ever-present. The myth that pepper soup helps reduce the effects of alcohol has been passed down for generations, so we seldom gather without pepper soup when libations are provided. The spiciness supposedly counteracts the effects of the alcohol, and even clears sinuses. And this brothy soup is truly a palate cleanser. The taste is incredible, especially the flavor imparted by the meat bones; it takes me back to my childhood, when my nose would run from the heat, yet I couldn't resist another spoonful.

In a large pot, add the goat meat, 15 cups (120 fl oz/3.5 liters) of water, salt, and bouillon (stock) cubes.

Put the garlic, ginger, onions, bush peppers, white pepper, peeled pebé, and scotch bonnet into a blender and blend until completely smooth. Pour the blended ingredients into the large pot with the meat and bring to a boil on high heat. Reduce the heat to medium and cook for about 1 hour (up to 30 minutes more, if needed) until the goat meat is tender.

Taste, and add more seasoning as needed. To finish, add the sliced scallions (spring onions) and basil, and continue cooking for 2 minutes. Remove from the heat and enjoy warm on its own or with a slice of bread or boiled plantains.

GRILLED CHICKEN AND
BASIL BUTTERFLIES

ARNAUD GWAGA

PREPARATION TIME: 20 MINUTES,
  PLUS 24 HOURS MARINATING
COOKING TIME: 20 MINUTES
SERVES: 2-3

3 cups (2¾ oz/75 g) basil leaves
3½ oz (100 g) cloves garlic
4¼ cups (34 fl oz/1 liter)
  white vinegar
5 tablespoons mustard
2 tablespoons garam masala
4 tablespoons olive oil
4 butterflied chicken legs or thighs

I started grilling in 2020, and I found it a form of therapy, something for me to focus on. My wife, Ninette, encouraged me to try various meats and marinade ingredients, and we started to invite family and friends to try our recipes. We once offered them chicken breasts with our homemade basil dressing, only to realize that chicken breasts tend to dry out on the grill. Ninette suggested we switch to butterflied chicken legs, and the result was exactly how we'd imagined it: tender and juicy.

Seeing people try our food gave me the confidence I needed to work harder for my young family, and we held the first Meat Gala in Bujumbura in 2021 for around fifty people.

Grind the basil leaves in a mortar and pestle with the garlic.

Place the vinegar into a large airtight container. Add the mustard, along with the ground basil and garlic, the garam masala, and olive oil. Mix everything together.

Add the chicken, seal the container, and store for 24 hours in the refrigerator.

Heat a grill or barbecue to 350°F/175°C. Put the chicken on the grill, and flip every 3 minutes until each side has a nice golden crust and the chicken is cooked through. Remove from the grill and let rest for about 5 minutes before serving.

PEANUT SAUCE STEW

PREPARATION TIME: 20 MINUTES
COOKING TIME: 50 MINUTES
SERVES 4

¼ cup (2 fl oz/60 ml) organic
   red palm oil
1 lb 12 oz (800 g) smoked beef,
   cubed
2 onions, diced
4 cloves garlic, crushed
scant 1 cup (4¼ oz/120 g) tomato
   paste (purée)
10½ oz (300 g) canned chopped
   tomatoes
⅛ oz (5 g) grated fresh root ginger
1 teaspoon red pepper flakes
scant ½ cup (3½ oz/100 g) natural
   peanut butter
salt, to taste

I learned this recipe from my grandmother when I was young. It has been passed down through generations among the Bakongo people of the Republic of Congo. Standing next to my grandmother in Linzolo Village, I felt proud and privileged to receive a lesson that no formal education could provide. Step by step, she guided me with precision, from cleaning the smoked fish to mixing the gooey peanut butter into the sauce. With this lesson, and many others that followed, my passion for cooking was ignited.

Serve with rice or fufu (pounded cassava) or fried plantains.

Heat a medium, heavy saucepan with the palm oil. Add the beef and sear on medium-high heat for 4–5 minutes on both sides until golden brown, then remove from the pan and set aside.

Turn the heat to medium–low and add the onions, then sauté for 6 minutes until golden brown. Add the garlic, while stirring constantly, and cook for about 30 seconds until fragrant. Add the tomato paste (purée), continuing to stir, and cook for about 3 minutes until the paste darkens slightly. Mix in the chopped tomatoes, ginger, red pepper flakes, and 1 cup (8 fl oz/240 ml) of water, and season with salt.

Return the beef to the saucepan and bring to a boil over high heat. Reduce the heat to low, cover, and simmer for 20 minutes. Take about 1¼ cups (10 fl oz/300 ml) of the sauce and place in a bowl with the peanut butter, then mix thoroughly. Pour the mixture back into the sauce and simmer, uncovered, for 10 more minutes, until the beef pieces are tender. Serve warm.

BEEF AND STOCKFISH
BITTERLEAF PEANUT SAUCE

AGATHA ACHINDU

PREPARATION TIME: 20 MINUTES, PLUS
  3-4 HOURS SOAKING
COOKING TIME: 1 HOUR 20 MINUTES
SERVES 6

FOR THE MEAT AND FISH
2 × 4-oz (115-g) pieces stockfish
8 oz (225 g) kanda (burnt cow
  skins), cut into 2-inch
  (5-cm) pieces
1 lb (450 g) oxtail, cut into
  2-inch (5-cm) chunks
½ teaspoon salt, or to taste
2 chicken bouillon (stock) cubes
1 small onion, chopped
1 teaspoon grated fresh root ginger
2 cloves garlic, minced
4 oz (115 g) smoked kuta
  or barracuda fish

FOR THE NDOLE
3 cups (1 lb/450 g) peeled
  raw peanuts
6 cloves garlic, minced
1-2 cups (8-16 fl oz/240-475 ml)
  olive oil
1 large yellow onion, diced
1-2 scotch bonnet peppers, chopped
1 teaspoon sea salt, or to taste
2 bouillon (stock) cubes (I use
  Maggi or Better Than Bouillon)
½ cup dried crayfish, crushed
1 lb (450 g) washed bitter leaf
  (ndole)

Bitterleaf peanut sauce is called *ndole* in Cameroon and is one of the most celebrated dishes. Growing up, this dish was for special occasions such as weddings, holidays, or visiting guests, since it was a bit on the costly side. As kids, we would always look forward to guests coming over for dinner, knowing Mami might make *ndole*. One of the first dishes I made in my own home when I moved to the United States was *ndole*; I would make it every other week, and it is still one of my favorite foods. Now, even my American-born-and-raised kids and friends love it, too!

This recipe includes burnt cow skins, a popular delicacy also known as cow hide. In Cameroon and a lot of other countries around the world, when cows are slaughtered, their skin is not just made into leather, but also consumed for its richness and nutrition. The skin is roasted over a wood fire and scraped with a knife to remove the fur until all traces of it are gone and you are left with a smooth, dried, smoky cow skin that tastes absolutely delicious. I like to serve this with rice, miondo (grated fermented cassava steamed in banana leaves), plantains, dodo (fried sweet plantains), fufu corn (cornmeal dough), cassava, water fufu, or garri (grated cassava).

Soak the stockfish in water for 3–4 hours.

Start by cooking the meats and fish. In a medium pot, add the kanda, oxtail, salt, bouillon (stock) cubes, onion, ginger, garlic, and 5–6 cups (40–50 fl oz/1.2–1.5 liters) of water, enough to cover the meat. Bring to a boil and cook for about 30–45 minutes until tender.

Meanwhile, bring another medium pot of water to a boil. Add the stockfish and boil, covered, for 30 minutes. Strain and discard the cooking liquid, then add the stockfish and kuta to the meat pot and continue cooking for 25 minutes until the fish is tender. Remove from the heat, pass through a sieve and save 3 cups (25 fl oz/750 ml) of the broth with the meat and fish. Freeze any excess broth for another recipe.

While the meat is cooking, in another medium pot, bring the raw peanuts with 4 cups (32 fl oz/950 ml) of water to a boil and cook for 20 minutes, or until soft. Drain and discard the water. Let the peanuts cool. Place the peanuts in a food processor or blender with the garlic and pulse/blend with 1½ cups (12 fl oz/350 ml) of water until you have a fine-grained consistency.

Pour ½–1 cup (4–8 fl oz/120–240 ml) of the oil into a large pot over medium–high heat until hot. Add the diced onion and sauté for 5 minutes, or until translucent. Then add the blended peanuts and stir frequently to prevent them burning for 5 minutes.

Add the reserved broth, with the chili, salt and bouillon cubes, and mix well. Bring to a boil, then cook for 10 minutes, stirring frequently to prevent burning. Add the crayfish, reserved meats and fish, and mix well. Stir in the washed bitter leaves (make sure any excess water is squeezed out) and mix very well. Cover and continue cooking for a few minutes. Add ½–1 cup (4–8 fl oz/120–240 ml) of the oil, cover, and cook for 2 minutes. Remove from the heat and serve.

EGUSI
PUDDING

FORSTER OBEN ORU

PREPARATION TIME: 30 MINUTES
COOKING TIME: 40 MINUTES
SERVES 4-6

7 oz (200 g) pork meat, cut into
  small chunks
4½ cups (1 lb 2 oz/500 g)
  egusi seeds
4 teaspoons ground black peppercorns
7 oz (200 g) dried tilapia
4-6 plantain leaves
salt

When I was growing up, egusi pudding—made from egusi, a protein-rich seed—was usually served during marriages and parties, and provided for leaders in the community such as chiefs, mayors, ministers, and doctors. Traditionally in Cameroon, the pudding was cooked by women, who offered it to men they held in high esteem. It is often called "the bundle of joy" because the dish is the only traditional meal that cuts across all the tribes in the country, and it is served when people are celebrating. I love the dish with boiled cocoyam or plantains.

Bring 2 cups (17 fl oz/500 ml) of water to a boil in a pan, add a little salt, and cook the pork for 10 minutes.

Soak the egusi seeds in water for 1 minute, then peel and let dry. Grind the egusi to a powder using a mortar and pestle or spice grinder, then add enough water to form a paste. Add 4 teaspoons salt, pepper, dried fish, and cooked pork meat and mix together with a spatula.

Portion the mixture into small batches, about 3½ oz (100 g) each, and wrap each batch in a plantain leaf, tied firmly with cooking twine or rope to form a bundle.

Bring a medium pot of water to a boil, place the bundles into the boiling water, and cover. Let cook for 30 minutes, or until the cooked bundles are solid and fragrant; they should smell similar to baked pumpkin. Serve alone or with boiled cocoyam or plantains.

Φ

A groundbreaking collection of 120 home cooking recipes and stories of heritage and legacy from the very heart of the food movement in Africa, curated by legendary chef and restaurateur Alexander Smalls.

With contributions by: Zein Abdallah, Agatha Achindu, Eric Adjepong, Selassie Atadika, Ikenna Akwuebue BobManuel, Clara Kapelembe Bwali, Akram Cherif, Anto Cocagne, Agness Colley, Michael Adé Elegbédé, Moustafa Elrefaey, Arnaud Gwaga, Mohamed Kamal, Kudakwashe Makoni, Mwaka Mwimbu, Forster Oben Oru, Joseph Dieuveil Malonga, O'miel Moundounga, Odoom, Thabo Phake, Coco Reinarhz, Mostafa Seif, Mogau Seshoene, Sinoyolo Sifo, Mame Sow, Sophia Teshome, Pierre Thiam, Rõze Traore, Matse Uwatse, Alfonso Videira, Nana Araba Wilmot, Rubia Zablon, Farida Zamradje

ERU
SOUP

PREPARATION TIME: 20 MINUTES
COOKING TIME: 30 MINUTES
SERVES 4-6

1 lb 2 oz (500 g) eru leaves
3½ oz (100 g) beef without fat,
  diced
3½ oz (100 g) dried fish (tilapia)
3½ oz (100 g) cow skin (kanda),
  cleaned and soaked (ask your
  butcher to do this)
3½ oz (100 g) dried crayfish
3½ cups (10½ oz/300 g)
  chopped spinach
4 teaspoons fine salt
¼ oz (10 g) fresh habanero chili
  (whole or ground, depending
  on how you like it)
3 bouillon (stock) cubes (I use
  Maggi)
1¼ cups (10 fl oz/300 ml) red palm
  oil
fufu (pounded cassava), to serve
  (optional)

Mom would always cook eru soup, especially on Sundays or for meetings and gatherings. The dish is a special delicacy for the Bayangi people in Cameroon. It signifies union, so when we come together the dish is present. Eru is a green leafy vegetable, used to make a delicious soup that cuts across the cultural boundaries of Cameroon, as it can be found in various regions. In Bayangi Land, it is served as an accompaniment with fermented cassava, which is later dried and cooked. Its starch is used to make fufu (a pounded cassava dish) or garri (grated cassava), which is fermented, dried, then fried with red palm oil. It is known as a food that holds the stomach, since it takes a long time to digest.

Create a small bundle of the eru leaves in your fist and place them on a cutting (chopping) board, then thinly slice (chiffonade).
   Into a medium pot on low heat, add the beef and 2 cups (17 fl oz/ 500 ml) of water and cook the meat until tender, about 13 minutes. Then add the dried fish, softened cow skin, and crayfish and let cook for 2 minutes. Add the spinach to the pot. Let it cook for 2 minutes, then add the eru. Use a wooden spatula and stir to incorporate the mixture. Add the salt, chili pepper, and bouillon (stock) cubes. Keep stirring for 5 minutes, then finally add the red palm oil and cook for 8 minutes, making sure the green leaves of the eru don't turn brown. Serve in a bowl with fufu.

CAPTAIN'S BROTH

PREPARATION TIME: 15 MINUTES
COOKING TIME: 20 MINUTES
SERVES: 2

1 lb/450 g fresh white fish fillets
   (about 5 pieces)
1 teaspoon chopped fresh root ginger
1 teaspoon chopped garlic
2 tomatoes, cut into quarters
2 okra, sliced into rounds
1 onion, finely chopped
2 fresh green chili peppers
pinch of mufira (country onion)
¾ cup (3½ oz/100 g) chopped sorrel
salt and pepper, to taste
parsley, to garnish, if desired

Gabon is renowned for its delicious broths, whether prepared with fresh or smoked fish. What makes these dishes special is the exceptional quality and judicious choice of the fish pieces used. For this recipe, I have opted for a perfect captain's fish fillet. The natural gelatin present in this piece acts as a binder and gives the dish its characteristic consistency. Additionally, selected local spices add a unique and exceptional flavor to this magnificent broth. Every bite tells the captivating story of the Atlantic Ocean and the picturesque beaches of Mayumba.

When you taste this typically Gabonese dish, your palate will dance to the rhythm of the exquisite aromas that emerge.

Carefully place all the ingredients in a saucepan, followed by 1¾ cups (14½ fl oz/430 ml) of water. Cover and cook over low–medium heat for 20 minutes.

Serve this succulent broth in individual bowls and savor each mouthful.

COCOYAM DUMPLINGS

AGATHA ACHINDU

PREPARATION TIME: 40 MINUTES
COOKING TIME: 1 HOUR
SERVES 6

6 large white and red cocoyams (macabo)
4 bunches cocoyam leaves or turnip greens
2 teaspoons salt
1 scotch bonnet pepper (optional)
3 cloves garlic, peeled
1-inch (2.5-cm) piece fresh root ginger, peeled
1 large tomato
1 onion
1 lb (450 g) smoked fish (strong canda/kuta), broken into chunks
1 cup ground crayfish
2 chicken bouillon (stock) cubes
2 teaspoons ground country onions (rondelles)
½ teaspoon powdered njanga leaves (optional)
1 cup (8 fl oz/240 ml) palm oil

When I was young, my mami told me that every time I felt sick, she would use *ekwang* or cocoyam (macabo) dumplings to assess the seriousness of the situation. If I turned down *ekwang,* it was time to head to the hospital. Throughout my childhood, I only turned it down three times. It is a delicacy that is essentially love personified. To cook *ekwang* for someone is to love them deeply. Every step in making this dish is a gift of love, and when you eat it, you can taste the love that goes into creating it. It is my all-time favorite food.

This recipe includes njanga leaves, which taste like smoked crayfish. In the past, people in the village would add them to mimic the taste of crayfish, which was much more expensive. Today, we add it even though crayfish is more accessible.

Peel the cocoyams with a knife or vegetable peeler and wash under running water until the water runs clear. Cocoyams can make you itchy, so wear gloves as you do this. Use a hand grater or food processor to grate or purée the cocoyams. Add 1 teaspoon of salt to the cocoyam purée and set aside.

Tear the leaves into wrappable, palm-size pieces and wash. Scoop about 1 tablespoon of the grated cocoyams and place horizontally along the leaf, then wrap it tightly into a cylinder shape, so it doesn't loosen while cooking. Place in a large pot with the seam-side down, making sure you leave tiny spaces in between the wraps so water can easily penetrate. Repeat the process until all the batter is used. In the meantime, bring 6 cups (48 fl oz/1.4 liters) of water to a boil in a kettle or another pot.

Place the scotch bonnet pepper, garlic, ginger, tomato, and onion in a blender. Blend and set aside.

In the ekwang pot, add the fish, crayfish, the remaining salt, bouillon (stock) cubes, country onions, and njanga leaves. Place the pot on the stove on high heat and cover for 5 minutes (this is important to create steam in the pot when you add water). After 5 minutes, pour in about 4 cups (32 fl oz/950 ml) of the boiling water, and the spice blend, and bring to a boil. Reduce the heat to medium–high and cook for 30 minutes. Halfway through, remove the lid, then using oven mitts (gloves), hold the pot with both handles, and shake very gently. Avoid stirring until the ekwang wraps are completely set.

After the 30 minutes' cooking time, stir gently by pushing a wooden spoon to the bottom of the pot and shake to loosen any bits that are stuck. Add the palm oil, 2 cups (16 fl oz/450 ml) or more of the boiled water, and continue cooking for 30 more minutes. Check every 5–10 minutes to make sure it isn't burning, gently passing your wooden spoon along the bottom of the pot to loosen any bits that are stuck there. Reduce the heat if needed. Taste and adjust the seasoning, and serve warm.

BLACK-EYED PEAS
IN PLANTAIN LEAVES

PREPARATION TIME: 40 MINUTES,
   PLUS 12 HOURS SOAKING
COOKING TIME: 30 MINUTES
SERVES 4

3 cups (1 lb 2 oz/500 g) black-eyed
   peas (beans)
¼ oz (10 g) habanero chili
2 teaspoons (¼ oz/10 g) fine salt
½ cup (3½ fl oz/100 ml) red palm oil
⅓ cup (1 oz/25 g) shredded soft
   fresh cocoyam leaves
4 plantain leaves
fried plantains or boiled potatoes,
   to serve

As a child, my grandmother used to cook black-eyed peas (beans) in cocoyam leaves, or koki beans as we call it in Cameroon. She made this dish often because it could be easily served to our big family. One bundle of koki beans could serve four children, which made cooking for us easier on her. In other parts of Africa, such as Nigeria, this dish is called *moin moin* and is made from a slightly different recipe but results in a similar taste.

Soak the black-eyed peas (beans) in water for 12 hours.

Drain the peas (beans) and crush them between your palms to remove the skin, then wash and rinse in fresh water. Put the black-eyed peas and the fresh pepper into a blender and process until they become a paste.

Into a mixing bowl, add the salt, red palm oil, shredded cocoyam leaves, and the black-eyed pea paste, then mix together to get a nice consistency.

Wash and dry the plantain leaves under the sun or by using the blue flame of a gas cooker (make sure not to burn the leaves; they should be flexible and elastic). Then place a leaf in the palm of your hand, creating a dish-like form out of each leaf. Using a medium ladle, scoop some of the mixture and place it inside the leaf. Then, wrap the leaf around the mixture (making sure to enclose the mixture fully inside). Next, use cooking twine or rope to tie the leaf like a bundle (this will secure the mixture in the leaf). Repeat for each leaf.

Bring a large pan of water to a boil, put each bundle in the water, and let them cook for 30 minutes, while checking from time to time to make sure the water has not dried up. When ready, the mixture becomes solid inside the leaves, and the aroma of the dish starts to emerge.

Take them out of the pot, let cool, and serve with the sliced fried plantains or boiled potatoes.

VEGAN COCOYAM DUMPLINGS

PREPARATION TIME: 40 MINUTES
COOKING TIME: 25 MINUTES
SERVES 5

1 lb 2 oz (500 g) cocoyams
½ cup (3½ fl oz/100 ml) red palm oil
2 teaspoons (¼ oz/10 g) fine salt
1 tablespoon (¼ oz/10 g)
   black peppercorns
5½ oz (150 g) soft fresh
   cocoyam leaves

When I was growing up in Cameroon, children were given cocoyam dumplings or *ekwang* to eat because they were easy to chew—and kids loved them because they were delicious! Parents also found the dish favorable because it was inexpensive to make. This dish is best enjoyed during the cocoyam season, when fresh new cocoyams are brought from the farm. In Cameroon, August through September is the ideal time, when they still have all their freshness.

I have now introduced the dish to my young daughter, who loves it. It's the first Cameroonian dish that I have introduced to her that she has embraced without hesitation. I enjoy making it for her, as I want her to learn about and eat more dishes from the place where I grew up.

Note: The most important part of this dish is in the base of the pan, as this is where all the ingredients will be after cooking.

Peel and wash the cocoyams. Then grate them using a fine grater (care should be taken with fingers when grating). Transfer the paste to a bowl and add half of the red palm oil, salt, and black peppercorns, and mix all together. Set aside.

Wash the cocoyam leaves and tear them into 1½-inch (4-cm) squares. With a spoon, scoop a small quantity of the cocoyam mixture and place it at the edge of the leaf, then roll as if you were rolling pastry dough. Continue the process while you layer them in a pot like the foundation of a house, and make sure the center of the pot is left empty.

Add the remaining red palm oil and 2 cups (17 fl oz/500 ml) of water to the center of the pot, then let it cook for 25 minutes, stirring gently every 10 minutes. When ready, the starch of the cocoyam will have set and the cocoyam leaves will have become more brown than green. If it does start to burn, reduce the heat.

Remove from the pan and serve at room temperature.

CRAB MEAT

PREPARATION TIME: 10 MINUTES
COOKING TIME: 15 MINUTES
SERVES: 2

5 oz (150 g) white crab meat
½ cup (3½ fl oz/100 ml) oil
1 teaspoon minced ginger
1 teaspoon minced garlic
1 teaspoon grated onion
2 tablespoons lime juice
1 teaspoon mufira (country onion)
½ teaspoon crushed fresh bird pepper
1 tablespoon butter
3 sprigs parsley, chopped
salt and pepper, to taste

Crab, a delicious crustacean native to the coastal waters of Libreville, more precisely in the Cape area, offers a unique characteristic: its taste varies, depending on where it comes from, as the influence of its marine environment is reflected in its flavor.

This dish is often appreciated after a day of fishing. We wait patiently for dinner to be ready, and this constitutes a delicious starter with appetizing aromas.

Place all the ingredients except the parsley in a saucepan and cook for 15 minutes over low heat until the crab has absorbed most of the liquid and you have a thick, dry, yet creamy consistency.

Around 30 seconds before the end of cooking, add the chopped parsley and stir.

Arrange on serving plates and enjoy.

KOKI CORN

PREPARATION TIME: 40 MINUTES
COOKING TIME: 30 MINUTES
SERVES 4–6

6 cups (2 lb 4 oz/1 kg) dried corn
   (maize)
2 teaspoons (¼ oz/10 g) fine salt
¼ oz (10 g) habanero chili, finely
   chopped
1 tablespoon red palm oil
⅛ oz (5 g) finely shredded cocoyam
   leaves
5 plantain leaves

I love making meals with fresh ingredients, and during the corn season in Cameroon, I make koki corn, a traditional corn-based pudding dish. Most tribes eat it as a snack in various forms—from roasted with plums, to boiled. This vegan dish is simple and quick to make, making it perfect for the busy home cook.

Blend the dried corn to a powder. Add the salt, chili, red palm oil, 2 teaspoons of water, and shredded cocoyam leaves and mix all together in a bowl.

Place a plantain leaf in the palm of your hand, and scoop a table-spoon of the mixture into the leaf. Repeat for each plantain leaf. Fold the leaves to cover the filling, and tie them with cooking twine or string to secure.

Bring a pot of water to a boil, and place the bundles in the pot. Let them cook for 30 minutes until the corn has firmed up. When ready, serve warm.

SALADE
ST. FABIEN

ARNAUD GWAGA

PREPARATION TIME: 10 MINUTES
SERVES: 4

6 tomatoes, diced
2 avocados, diced
1 cucumber, diced
5 carrots, diced
¾ cup (3½ oz/100g) pitted green
  olives
4 teaspoons lime juice
1 teaspoon Dijon mustard
salt and pepper

We love to cook for friends and family, and often have people over to our home. This salad was inspired by Fabien, who has worked with us for nine years. He is incredibly creative and prepares amazing-tasting salads—we loved this one so much we named it Salade St. Fabien.

Combine the diced tomatoes, avocados, cucumber, and carrots with the olives and mix everything together with a spoon.

In a small jar, mix the lime juice with the Dijon mustard and some salt and pepper. Toss the dressing through the salad mix, stir, and serve.

PUFF PUFF

AGATHA ACHINDU

PREPARATION TIME: 15 MINUTES,
  PLUS 3 HOURS PROVING
COOKING TIME: 10 MINUTES
SERVES 6

2½ cups (20 fl oz/600 ml) warm water
1½ teaspoons dried (active dry)
  yeast
½ cup (3½ oz/100 g) granulated
  sugar
½ teaspoon sea salt
3 cups (14 oz/400 g) all-purpose
  (plain) flour
4 cups (32 fl oz/950 ml) vegetable
  oil, for deep-frying

There is no gathering without puff puff in Cameroon. Growing up, the smell of puff puff cooking would wake my family up for breakfast. Some days we would have it as a snack with tea or hot chocolate, on other days Mami would serve it with *pap*, made from fermented corn. Sometimes, on my way home from school, the smell of puff puff would welcome me as I walked through the door because it was on the menu for dinner with beans. And at celebrations like birthdays, puff puff was also there to welcome everyone.

In a small bowl, mix 1 cup (8 fl oz/240 ml) of the warm water, the yeast, and 1 tablespoon of the sugar. Allow to prove and let rise for 5 minutes.

In a large bowl, mix the remaining 1½ cups (12 fl oz/350 ml) of warm water, the salt, and the remaining sugar until it dissolves, then add the proved yeast mixture and mix well. Next, add the flour and mix until the mixture is lump-free. Cover tightly and set aside in a warm place for 3 hours.

Heat the oil in a deep pot (my favorite is a cast-iron Dutch oven) on medium–high heat to 350°F/180°C. If you don't have a kitchen thermometer, drop a piece of the batter into the oil, and if it rises to the top, the oil is ready; if it sticks to the bottom, it's not hot enough yet. When the oil is ready, use a tablespoon to scoop and drop batter into the oil. Fry in batches until golden brown, about 2–3 minutes per side. Use a frying spoon to lift the pieces of puff puff out of the oil into a large bowl lined with paper towels, and repeat until done. Serve warm.

JUNE
PLUM JUICE

PREPARATION TIME: 10 MINUTES
SERVES 6

500g (1lb 2oz) June plums
⅔ cup (5 oz/150 g) granulated sugar
1¾ oz (50 g) fresh root ginger,
  roughly chopped

When in season, this fruit—a close cousin to the mango—can be found almost everywhere, especially in small stands along the roadside. I used to buy it after school, and it came with a pinch of salt and chili pepper; it was the perfect inexpensive snack!

This fruit has so many properties, and is rich in several vitamins. In my restaurant, I advocate health through the plate. So that is why I make this juice. It's so refreshing (great for hot weather), but what's more, it reminds me of my high school years.

Wash and peel the June plums (or you could try it with the skin). Remove the pit (stone) and dice the flesh.

Add the plums, sugar, ginger, and 6¼ cups (50 fl oz/1.5 liters) of water to a blender, and blend everything together. You may need to do this in two batches.

Strain the juice through cheesecloth or muslin, then transfer to a sterilized bottle and chill in the refrigerator. Once cold, it's ready to taste and enjoy.

COCO
REINARHZ

I want to make sure that in African cooking schools, we teach more and more about African foods. For so long, culinary education in Africa has centered European cuisine. We must center our foods in our curricula to document our culinary traditions, innovations, and techniques. This will help the next generation of culinary leaders build on our rich recipes and narratives. It is the only way that our diverse cuisines will be recognized worldwide and in Africa. As we say in Africa, it's time the Lion starts to tell the stories.

SOUTHERN AFRICA

As in other parts of the continent, spices dance deliciously through the air as we enter the kitchens of Southern Africa—cinnamon, cardamom, and ground coriander, to name just a few. Chilies, pickled fish, and stews are also popular. Of course, as in other areas, there is some overlap of dishes throughout the region. For example, chakalaka, a vegetable dish made of onions, tomatoes, peppers, carrots, beans, and spices, can be found in variations throughout Southern Africa. Traditionally served with *pap* (called *nshima* in Zambia, *ugali* in Kenya, and *sadza* in Zimbabwe), chakalaka can be just as at home at a South African braai as it is on tables in Zimbabwe and Zambia.

I remember the swell of anticipation and excitement while curating my first trip to South Africa. The occasion was born from a late-night, post-dinner conversation with my dear friend Vicki; we were trying to think of the most exceptional trip we might take for her birthday. It was then that the idea of going on safari, traveling throughout South Africa on the Rovos Rail (the Orient Express of Africa), making our way through the wine villages of Franschhoek on horseback, plus visiting amazing restaurants, cafes, museums, and art galleries seduced us into a plan for a marathon of wonder and adventure. Our intention was to fly into Johannesburg and spend a week touring the sites, including Robben Island and all things Mandela, and the cafes, restaurants, outdoor markets, and boutiques around Joburg. The idea grew into the adventure of a lifetime. We brought all our dreams to fruition and realized our wishes through a two-week extravaganza of breathtaking excursions.

Aside from the brilliant cinematic beauty of South Africa, I wasted no time delving into the unique foods and flavors of this amazing country. From Joburg and Pretoria to Kruger National Park, Cape Town, and beyond, I ate between borders and cities, country settings, and seashores. I savored plates of fresh fish that offered a delightful array of regional flavors. They were also infused with other influences—such as Indian and Asian—in cities like Durban and the surrounding Garden District; the food was its own character! And central to the production were the culinary talents who brought joy and a sense of creativity to the Southern African kitchen.

There are so many dishes to peruse in this section—from Thabo Phake's version of South African Braai (page 144), to Kudakwashe Makoni's Biltong with Chili Tomato Sauce and Sadza (page 148), Mwaka Mwiimbu's Garden Eggs from Zambia (page 176), and so much more. Start your Southern African feast with your eyes and find your inspiration.

SOUTH AFRICAN BRAAI

THABO PHAKE

PREPARATION TIME: 20 MINUTES,
  PLUS OVERNIGHT MARINATING
COOKING TIME: 55 MINUTES
SERVES 4-6

FOR THE MONKEY GLAND SAUCE
5 tablespoons olive oil
1 large onion, grated
5 cloves garlic, finely chopped
1 tablespoon ground coriander
3 bay leaves
2 tablespoons brown sugar
1 tablespoon smoked paprika
2 ripe tomatoes, grated
1 tablespoon tomato paste (purée)
¼ cup (2 fl oz/60 ml) Worcestershire
  sauce
3½ tablespoons (2 fl oz/50 ml)
  balsamic vinegar
1 cup (8 fl oz/240 ml) barbecue
  sauce (use your favorite)
5 tablespoons apricot jam
salt and pepper, to taste

FOR THE MEAT
2 lb 4 oz (1 kg) lamb chops
2 lb 4 oz (1 kg) chicken wings

Beyond rugby, we had braai! This dish brought all of us Black and White kids together in South Africa. The name itself tells a story: it's from the Dutch colonizers, and it means "to grill meat on an open fire." The dish has traveled through history, from colonization through Apartheid, and into the Rainbow Nation. Today it is recognized as one of South Africa's best-loved party dishes. A braai generally includes a variety of grilled meats, as well as a delicious sweet and smoky sauce that we call monkey gland sauce, which, I must say right away, does not include any monkey glands. It usually includes marinated lamb chops and chicken wings, and is commonly served with Grilled Butter Corn (page 182), *Pap* (page 186), and Chakalaka (page 184).

For the monkey gland sauce, put the oil in a large pot over medium–high heat. Add the onion and cook for 5–7 minutes, to give it some color. As soon as it's brown, add the garlic and cook for 3 minutes.

Once the garlic and onions are brown and sweated off, add the coriander, bay leaves, brown sugar, smoked paprika, grated tomatoes, and tomato paste (purée). Let it cook for 3 minutes and then stir in the Worcestershire sauce, generous ¾ cup (7 fl oz/200 ml) of water, and the balsamic vinegar to deglaze, then let simmer for 5 minutes.

Add the barbecue sauce and apricot jam and let simmer for a further 5 minutes. Finally, add salt to balance off the sweetness.

To prepare the meat, marinate the lamb chops and chicken overnight in half of the monkey gland sauce.

Preheat a barbecue grill or braai to high (425°F/220°C).

Bring the marinated meat to room temperature 20 minutes before cooking. Season with salt and black pepper.

Grill the lamb chops for 4 minutes on each side, then place the lamb on the side of the grill or braai where the heat is lower for 5 minutes. About 30 seconds before removing the lamb from the grill/braai, glaze it with a little of the remaining monkey gland sauce and place it on a tray.

Lower the heat to 350°F/180°C, add the chicken wings and cook for 8 minutes on each side, or until browned and cooked through.

Drizzle the remaining monkey gland sauce on top of the meat and serve hot.

MEAT AND GREENS
STIR-FRY

KUDAKWASHE MAKONI

PREPARATION TIME: 15 MINUTES
COOKING TIME: 30 MINUTES
SERVES 6

9 oz (250 g) chicken gizzards, cleaned
9 oz (250 g) beef fillet, cut into strips (I love using offcuts, including the fat)
¼ cup (2 fl oz/60 ml) vegetable oil, plus extra if needed
9 oz (250 g) boerewors (a substitute could be beef sausage or bratwurst), cut into bite-size pieces
9 oz (250 g) chicken livers
1 large yellow onion, diced
2 large tomatoes, diced
1 tablespoon beef stock powder
1 teaspoon red pepper flakes
1 teaspoon paprika
1 teaspoon curry powder
1 cup (2 oz/60 g) chopped collard or mustard greens (spring greens or mustard leaves)
1 cup (2 oz/60 g) chopped kale or rape greens (leaves)
salt and pepper, to taste
sliced fresh chilies or hot sauce, to serve

In the last decade, an assorted meat and greens stir-fry, known as *gango*, has become very popular in Zimbabwe. It is often cooked over an open-flame fire or on a braai (barbecue) stand. The word *gango* means a pan-like utensil used for dry-roasting items like peanuts and corn kernels. The dish is made of different kinds of meat and leafy vegetables, such as collard, mustard, or rape greens (spring greens and mustard or rape leaves); your taste buds, budget, mood, and maybe even the time of day determine the ingredients you will use to make *gango*. I have this dish in the afternoon when I'm feeling homesick or celebratory and I have a little extra to spend. The beauty of the dish is in its simplicity, like other Zimbabwean dishes.

This recipe includes a popular sausage called boerewors, which originated in South Africa. Serve with *Sadza* (page 148) or plain steamed rice.

Prepare the gizzards by washing them in cold running water and using a sharp-pointed knife to peel off the yellowish skin (most store-bought gizzards come with the skin off). Bring a pan of water to a boil and boil the gizzards for 10 minutes until they are tender and can be pierced with a fork. Cut the meats accordingly.

In a wok, large cast-iron pan, or—if you're lucky enough to have one—an authentic gango pan from Zimbabwe, fry the beef in the oil over high heat for 5–7 minutes until browned. Add the gizzards and boerewors and fry for 5 minutes until browned.

Add more oil if necessary and add the chicken livers. Fry for 3 minutes until browned. Then add the onion and tomatoes and stir-fry for 1 minute (and not 1 second more). Add the stock powder and spices and stir-fry until fragrant and the curry powder is cooked through, about 5 minutes; don't worry if there is caking on the bottom of the pan, just scrape it into the ingredients.

Add all the greens (leaves) and stir-fry for 4–5 minutes until wilted. Keep your eye on them and don't let them release too much liquid or brown too quickly; you want them to remain as vibrantly green as possible. Season with salt and pepper according to taste, then add fresh chilies or hot sauce on top.

BILTONG WITH CHILI TOMATO SAUCE AND SADZA

KUDAKWASHE MAKONI

PREPARATION TIME: 20 MINUTES
COOKING TIME: 15 MINUTES
SERVES 4

FOR THE SADZA
3 cups (12 oz/350 g) fine cornmeal (maize meal)
scant 3 cups (24 fl oz/700 ml) boiling water
⅓ cup (3½ fl oz/100 ml) fermented milk or amasi (substitute with buttermilk or kefir)
salt, to taste

FOR THE BILTONG
6 tablespoons vegetable oil
1 onion, diced
1 teaspoon minced garlic
1 × 14 oz (400 g) can chopped tomatoes
2 red chilies, chopped
⅓ cup (2½ fl oz/80 ml) vegetable or chicken stock (or water)
1 lb 5 oz (600 g) biltong, cut into strips (if the butcher has already cut it, choose pieces with a little fat on them)
salt and pepper, to taste

Biltong is one of my favorite things. It is a popular South African dish made with a variety of dried, cured meats, from beef to game. It can be eaten on its own or, as we do in Zimbabwe, you can make a stew out of it. Peanut butter sauce or tomato sauce are great with biltong. My grandmother used to make my uncle a special tomato, onion, and chili sauce called *sumu*. Here, I bring together all of these familiar flavors and memories into one dish.

This recipe includes *amasi*, a fermented milk used to make *sadza*, or Zimbabwean cornmeal (maize meal) polenta. The name comes from the Zulu, Xhosa, and Ndebele languages of South Africa. Ndebele is also spoken in Zimbabwe.

For the sadza, add 1½ cups (5½ oz/150 g) of the cornmeal (maize meal) to a large pot with just enough cold water to make a smooth paste. Place the pot on medium–high heat, and while stirring, slowly add the boiling water. Stirring evenly and constantly, to prevent the cornmeal from settling and hardening at the bottom of the pan, allow the mixture to boil on medium–high heat for about 10 minutes. Then add extra cornmeal, ½ cup (2 oz/50 g) at a time, and stir the sadza until it reaches a smooth yet thick texture.

After the sadza reaches the desired thickness and texture and is well mixed, take it off the heat and cover, then let it set for 2 minutes; it will harden a little bit more. At this stage add the sour/fermented milk and whisk until you get a creamy version of what you reached earlier. (It will sort of resemble very lumpy cottage cheese.) Season according to taste.

While your sadza is simmering, you can make the biltong stew. In a saucepan on high heat, add the oil and sauté the onion and garlic for 3 minutes until translucent. Lower the heat to medium, then add the tomatoes and chilies, and let it simmer for 6 minutes until the tomatoes have softened. Pour in your stock, mix, and simmer for around 7 minutes, until you have a thick sauce. Remove from the stove and set aside. Place the biltong in the "stew," with salt and pepper to taste, and let it steep for about 10 minutes.

To plate, place a large heap of sadza in the middle of each plate, top with the biltong, and spoon some tomato and chili stew on top.

BEEF
TROTTERS

PREPARATION TIME: 10 MINUTES
COOKING TIME: 8 HOURS
SERVES 6-8

2 cow legs, cut into pieces by
   your butcher
3 tablespoons vegetable oil
salt

FOR THE GRAVY
1 tablespoon vegetable oil
2 tomatoes, roughly chopped
2 yellow onions, roughly chopped
2 tablespoons tomato paste (purée)
2 tablespoons paprika
2 tablespoons beef stock powder
salt, to taste

In the average Zambian home, it is almost mandatory for one to know how to cook on a brazier—a small metal charcoal stove. This is something I found odd growing up, especially because we had a stove. I remember the very first time I cooked on a brazier with my mother in her village, we made beef trotters. Cooking this way is not easy, and I struggled, but it was so much fun because she shared her story of how she learned to do it; ironically, her first meal on a brazier was beef trotters too, so it was more like a rite of passage at this point.

Beef trotters take a long time and need to be treated with utmost care, but my mum taught me well. Fast forward to my university days. I was craving beef trotters so much and missing home. I did not have access to a brazier, so I figured I should try the recipe on a stovetop and it worked—now I find the stovetop a much easier way to prepare this beautiful dish.

Serve hot with *Nshima* (page 166) and enjoy.

Season the cow leg pieces with a little salt. Heat the vegetable oil in a large nonstick pot on medium heat and throw in the cow legs. Fry for about 5 minutes, then add enough water to cover the hooves completely. Cook the hooves on the stovetop on medium–high heat for the first 1 hour, then reduce the heat to low for the final 7 hours. Make sure to stir occasionally to ensure nothing sticks to the bottom of the pot. Add more water occasionally. Alternatively, you can cook your beef trotters in a slow cooker for 4–5 hours on high heat.

About 20 minutes before you are ready to serve, prepare your gravy by coating a pan with the oil. Place on medium heat, add the tomatoes and onions, and fry for 5 minutes. Add the tomato paste (purée) and paprika and fry for 2 minutes until the tomato is cooked.

Pour the gravy over the beef trotters. Dilute the beef stock powder with 1 cup (8 fl oz/240 ml) of water and pour over the beef trotters. Let simmer on medium heat for about 10 minutes. Season to taste, and serve.

ORANGE MUSHROOMS WITH MEATBALLS

CLARA KAPELEMBE BWALI

PREPARATION TIME: 20 MINUTES,
   PLUS 1 HOUR 20 MINUTES SOAKING
   AND FREEZING
COOKING TIME: 50 MINUTES
SERVES 6

FOR THE MUSHROOMS
2 lb 4 oz (1 kg) orange and red
   chitondo mushrooms (you could
   also use oyster mushrooms)
½ cup (4 oz/115 g) chopped onion
1 cup (7 oz/200 g) cubed tomatoes
3 tablespoons vegetable oil
salt

FOR THE MEATBALLS
2 lb 4 oz (1 kg) ground
   (minced) beef
3 cloves garlic
1 teaspoon ground black pepper
2 tablespoons vegetable oil
1 fresh red chili, chopped
   (optional)

FOR THE GRAVY
3 tablespoons vegetable oil
1 onion, diced
4 cloves garlic, finely diced
2 cups grated tomatoes
2 tablespoons tomato paste (purée)
1 teaspoon tomato sauce
leftover juices from cooked
   meatballs
chopped herbs, such as basil
   and parsley, to taste

Orange mushrooms are a rainy season bliss in Zambia. When it comes, it feels like the earth is raining mushrooms. These mushrooms are locally called *chitondo*.

I despised mushrooms as a child. However, as an adult, raising my own children, I find it important to introduce them to the dishes I grew up eating. I've since become a mushroom lover, and this dish is one of my favorite ways to enjoy the seasonal mushroom that Zambia gifts us with every year.

Serve warm with *Nshima* (page 166).

Soak the mushrooms in salted water for at least 20 minutes.

For the meatballs, mix all the ingredients in a medium-size bowl. Form the mixture into meatballs (about 1½ inches/4 cm in diameter), place on a tray, and freeze for 1 hour (so they don't break apart when cooking).

Preheat the oven to 350°F/180°C/Gas Mark 4.

Place the meatballs on a baking sheet (tray) and cook for 20 minutes until all pinkness is gone, then set aside, reserving any cooking juices.

Drain and rinse the mushrooms, then add to a medium pot over medium heat. Add salt to taste. Do not add any extra water, as mushrooms release their own water. Cook for 5 minutes. Drain some of the water released but don't drain completely. Add the onion, tomatoes, and oil, and simmer, covered, for 10 minutes.

To make the gravy, heat the oil in a medium pan over medium heat. Add the onion and garlic and cook for 3 minutes. Then add the grated tomatoes, tomato paste and sauce, juices, herbs, and meatballs, and simmer over low heat for 10 minutes.

Place the orange mushrooms on a plate next to the meatballs in the gravy and serve warm.

BEEF STEW AND SOUTH AFRICAN DUMPLINGS

SINOYOLO SIFO

PREPARATION TIME: 30 MINUTES,
  PLUS 1 HOUR RISING
COOKING TIME: 1 HOUR 50 MINUTES
SERVES 6-8

FOR THE STEW
2 lb 12 oz (1.2 kg) stewing beef
1 tablespoon all-purpose
  (plain) flour
3 tablespoons canola (rapeseed) oil
  or olive oil, or more if needed
1 large red onion, chopped
2 tablespoons crushed garlic
2 tablespoons barbecue spice
1 tablespoon garlic powder
1 tablespoon mild masala powder
1 teaspoon ground turmeric
2 teaspoons paprika
2 tablespoons barbecue sauce
1 tablespoon tomato paste (purée)
2 cups (17 fl oz/500 ml) concentrated
  beef stock
3 large potatoes, peeled and cut
  into small cubes
2 large carrots, peeled and chopped
salt and pepper, to taste

FOR THE DUMPLINGS
4 cups (1 lb 4 oz/560 g)
  all-purpose (plain) flour
2½ teaspoons (1 envelope/¼ oz/10 g)
  instant (easy-blend) yeast
4 tablespoons granulated sugar
pinch of salt
3 tablespoons (1½ oz/40 g) butter
1¼ cups (10 fl oz/300 ml)
  lukewarm water
1 cup (5 oz/140 g) peeled and
  grated carrots
oil, for greasing

This beef stew brings back so many childhood memories. My father owned butcheries and farms, so we would have meat frequently. It is a common recipe in my culture in the Eastern Cape of South Africa, where it is made for the most traditional of cultural gatherings, such as weddings, funerals, and *emgidini*, a Xhosa rite of passage celebration marking the transition from boyhood to manhood. The stew is hearty and spicy, and is best served with *idombolo* (South African dumplings) or basmati rice. I make *idombolo* for my wife whenever she is craving a nice traditional meal. While the process of making them is simple, the dish takes time to prepare and cook, but it's worth the wait. I also include carrots—a small twist to this classic dish.

For the dumplings, in a large bowl, sift together the flour, yeast, sugar, and salt, then whisk to combine. Rub the butter into the flour with your fingertips until you have a crumbly texture. Slowly stir in the lukewarm water. Knead the dough until it is smooth and elastic and doesn't stick to your hands. Add the grated carrots and knead into the dough.

Grease a large bowl with a little oil and place the dough in it. Cover with plastic wrap (clingfilm) or a lid, and leave in a warm place to rise for 1 hour until doubed in size.

While the dough is rising, make the stew. In a large bowl, add the beef and flour. Mix well to ensure the flour coats the beef. In a large pot, heat the oil on medium heat. Add the beef and cook until golden brown, about 5 minutes on each side. Remove the beef and set it aside.

To the same saucepan, add the onion. Sauté for 4–5 minutes, or until the onion is translucent (add more oil if needed). Stir in the garlic, barbecue spice, garlic powder, masala powder, turmeric, paprika, and barbecue sauce. Return the beef to the pot. Add the tomato paste (purée) and beef stock, and season with salt and pepper. Cover with a lid and simmer for 1 hour on low–medium heat, stirring occasionally, and adding a small amount of water as needed.

Once the dough has risen, break off palm-sized pieces and set aside.

When the stew has been cooking for 1 hour, add the potatoes and carrots, and mix well. Season with salt and pepper, to taste. Add the pieces of dough to the pot, on top of the stew, cover with a lid and simmer over low–medium heat for 40 minutes, or until the veggies are cooked through and the idombolo are "puffy," and when a skewer inserted into them comes out clean. Serve warm.

155

BEEF AND CABBAGE STEW

THABO PHAKE

PREPARATION TIME: 20 MINUTES
COOKING TIME: 5 HOURS
SERVES 6

3 lb 5 oz (1.5 kg) stewing beef
    (use any beef cut good for
    braising, with bones and fat,
    such as oxtail)
olive, canola (rapeseed), or
    grapeseed oil, for frying
2 large onions, thinly sliced
    or diced
1 head cabbage (no more than 4 lb
    8 oz/2 kg), thinly sliced
5 cloves garlic, finely diced
3 tablespoons curry powder
3 tablespoons chili flakes
1 tablespoon tomato paste (purée)
3 large potatoes, peeled and cut
    into 1½-inch (4-cm) cubes
8¼ cups (68 fl oz/2 liters)
    beef stock
salt and pepper, to taste

My grandmother, Elizabeth, was known for expressing love through her hands, and this recipe is love personified. With those hands, she blessed me with cooking lessons, and this beef and cabbage stew was my first creation. Elizabeth was known for this recipe, which she would make and share with our community in Johannesburg's Vosloorus township. She taught me that this dish is all about the "Maillard reaction," without ever actually using the term. This occurs when the amino acids and reduced sugars in food are heated to create a browning on the surface that results in the flavor. Now, I use my own hands to express my love for her as I caramelize the ingredients to their richest brown. With her recipe in your hands, you can serve love as well. Serve warm with *Pap* (page 186) or Dumplings (page 154).

Place the beef on wax (greaseproof) paper. Dab it dry to allow the searing process to occur more easily, and season it with salt and pepper.

In a large, stovetop-safe casserole or pot, add just enough oil to allow the meat to sear. Add the meat and sear on high heat for 8–10 minutes until browned. Remove the meat and set aside.

In the same pot, add the onions and cabbage. Allow them to sweat off and start to brown (add more oil if needed) for 5–7 minutes.

Move the onions and cabbage to one side and create a kind of well in the pot, so the garlic can caramelize. Add the garlic and cook for 3 minutes. Once caramelized, add the curry powder and chili flakes, stir it all together, and allow the mixture to cook for 2 minutes. If the cabbage and onions have soaked up the oil, add 1 more tablespoon of oil.

Move all the ingredients aside again to create a well and add the tomato paste (purée), then stir. Let cook for at least 1 minute.

Add the cut potatoes to the pot, then season the mixture again with a generous amount of salt and pepper. Let cook for 4 minutes, then add the beef, and 2 cups (17 fl oz/500 ml) of the stock to deglaze, using a wooden spoon to scrape the bottom of the pot, so all the caramelized flavors are mixed within.

Reduce the heat to low so it simmers or cooks slowly, then add the remaining stock, cover the pot, and let cook for 4 hours.

Open the pot, and if there's still too much liquid floating above your stew, allow it to reduce at high heat for 20–30 minutes, until it's at the consistency you want. The key to remember is that it shouldn't be a thick stew, but it also shouldn't be watery. You are looking for a silky, creamy, rich stew consistency. The cabbage and meat should melt in your mouth. Serve hot with dumplings.

GOAT AND CHICKEN GIZZARDS PITHIVIER

ALFONSO VIDEIRA

PREPARATION TIME: 30 MINUTES,
   PLUS UP TO 48 HOURS MARINATING
COOKING TIME: 1 HOUR
SERVES 2

10½ oz (300 g) goat meat
7 oz (200 g) chicken gizzards,
   cut into thin slices
2 cups (17 fl oz/500 ml) soy sauce
½ red or green cabbage, shredded
butter, for frying
1 onion, finely chopped
1 bunch parsley, finely chopped
2 × 13 oz (375 g) all-butter puff
   pastry (store-bought)
all-purpose (plain flour),
   for dusting
2 egg yolks, beaten
salt and pepper

I was introduced to the pithivier (a stuffed pie of the French Wellington variety) when I began working as a young chef in the Michelin-starred restaurant Bruneau, in Brussels, Belgium. By the time I started at Nyurah Restaurant in Kigali, Rwanda, I had forgotten all about the delicacy until I was challenged to reimagine the visual presentation of goat meat. Alongside the executive chef, we created a recipe using a zero-waste approach: we used goat bones to make a jus, and the leftover greens were used to make a green oil. The result was simply astonishing.

Marinate the goat meat and chicken gizzards in seasoned soy sauce in the refrigerator for 24 hours. The meat must be entirely covered. (You could marinate for 48 hours, if desired, so the meat will be even more tender.)

Blanch half of the cabbage in salted boiling water for 2 minutes, then set aside. Dry it a little so it won't release too much water when wrapped in puff pastry, otherwise your pastry will be soggy. Cook the remaining cabbage in a skillet (frying pan) with a little butter, and a tablespoon each of the finely chopped onion and parsley. Season to taste and set aside.

Grind (mince) or very finely chop the marinated goat meat. Combine with the chicken gizzards and cabbages, and season with salt and pepper.

Heat the soy sauce used for the marinade in a pan over medium heat, then sauté the finely chopped onion until soft. Add the goat meat and chicken gizzards mixture and cook until browned and cooked through. Set aside to cool.

Roll out the puff pastry sheets on a floured surface. Cut one pastry sheet into a 10-inch/26-cm round and another into a 9-inch/23-cm round. Place the larger round on a baking pan (tray) lined with parchment paper.

Spread the cooked filling mixture evenly over the 10-inch/26-cm pastry round, leaving a border. Top with the smaller pastry round and press the edges to seal. Brush the pastry with beaten egg yolks.

Preheat the oven to 400°F/200°C/Gas Mark 6. Score radial arcs into the pastry, working from the center outward, being careful not to cut all the way through. Brush with egg wash.

Bake the pithivier until golden brown, about 40–45 minutes. Allow it to cool slightly before serving.

PERI-PERI CHICKEN GIZZARDS

PREPARATION TIME: 20 MINUTES
COOKING TIME: 20 MINUTES
SERVES 2

FOR THE CHICKEN GIZZARDS
1 lb 2 oz (500 g) chicken gizzards
juice of ½ lemon
¼ teaspoon onion powder
¼ teaspoon garlic powder
2 tablespoons vegetable oil
3½ tablespoons (1¾ oz/50 g) diced
   tricolor bell peppers
¾ cup (2¼ oz/60 g) chopped scallions
   (spring onions), white part only
salt and pepper, to taste
2 lemon wedges, to serve
micro herbs, to serve

FOR DREDGING
⅓ cup (1¾ oz/50 g) all-purpose
   (plain) flour
¾ cup (1¾ oz/50 g) fine bread crumbs
2 teaspoons smoked paprika
1 teaspoon ground black pepper
vegetable oil, for deep-frying
salt, to taste

FOR THE PERI-PERI SAUCE
6 fresh red chilies
1 onion, chopped
generous ¾ cup (7 fl oz/200 ml)
   peri-peri sauce or hot sauce
juice of 1 lemon
¼ teaspoon ground cumin
½ teaspoon granulated sugar
1 teaspoon paprika

As a child, I wasn't allowed to eat peri-peri chicken gizzards, known locally as *Zvikanganwahama ne Mhiripiri*. I was also not allowed to eat chicken livers, hearts, intestines, feet, necks, and heads. My mom kept a small pot of gizzards anytime we slaughtered chickens, and she would make the delicacy for only herself, my aunt, and my grandmother. The Shona (Zimbabwean language) name for a gizzard is *chikanganwahama*, which translates to "forget your relatives," so I am totally convinced that the adults used that as the reason not to share the delicacy with us. Now that there is no one standing in my way of enjoying the dish, I love preparing it for myself and others. As for kids, I'll let you decide if they get a plate. Serve with bread, *Sadza* (page 148), or plain steamed rice.

Prepare the gizzards by washing them in cold running water, and using a sharp-pointed knife to peel off the yellowish skin (most store-bought gizzards come with the skin off).

Bring a pan of salted water to a boil, add the lemon juice, onion powder, garlic powder, gizzards, salt, and pepper, and boil for 5–7 minutes until the gizzards are tender.

For dredging, in a large bowl combine the flour, bread crumbs, salt, paprika, and black pepper. Throw in the boiled gizzards, then mix and evenly coat. Heat 2 cups (16 fl oz/475 ml) of oil in a skillet (frying pan) to 375°F/190°C, and deep-fry your gizzards for 4–6 minutes, or until golden brown. Drain on a paper towel.

Put all the peri-peri sauce ingredients into a blender and mix until you get a smooth, runny paste. Season to taste.

In a medium pan on high heat, drizzle the oil. Add the bell peppers and scallions (spring onions) and sauté for 2 minutes, or until the scallions are translucent. Pour all your blender contents into the pan, bring to a boil, and simmer over medium heat for about 5 minutes, stirring frequently, until reduced. Add the gizzards to the peri-peri sauce and toss evenly to coat. Serve with the lemon wedges and micro herbs.

SWEET POTATOES WITH CHICKEN AND VEGETABLES

CLARA KAPELEMBE BWALI

PREPARATION TIME: 20 MINUTES,
  PLUS OVERNIGHT MARINATING
COOKING TIME: 35 MINUTES
SERVES 6

FOR THE CHICKEN
¼ cup (2 fl oz/60 ml) peri-peri
  sauce (page 160)
2 tablespoons ginger-garlic paste
juice of ½ lemon
¼ cup (2 fl oz/60 ml) vegetable oil
6 skin-on chicken leg quarters

FOR THE SWEET POTATOES
4 sweet potatoes, peeled
¼ cup (2¼ oz/60 g) butter
4 cloves garlic, crushed

FOR THE VEGETABLES
7 oz (200 g) green beans, trimmed
9 oz (250 g) carrots, sliced
2 tablespoons (1 oz/30 g)
  unsalted butter
2 tablespoons mixed herbs
  of your choice

Sweet potato season is a special time in Zambia. They are locally called *ifyumbu* or *kandolo*, and we usually enjoy them boiled or cooked in peanut butter. Zambia is blessed with different types of sweet potatoes: yellow, orange, purple, white, and red. My favorite is the yellow one. Its sweetness is unmatched. This dish is a little outside the usual way of enjoying sweet potatoes, which is typically eaten in the morning with tea or cooked in peanut butter.

In a medium bowl, mix the peri-peri sauce, ginger-garlic paste, lemon juice, and oil. Set aside a little of the marinade for basting, then coat the chicken skin with the remaining marinade, cover, and put it into the refrigerator overnight.

On the following day, preheat a barbecue grill to medium–high heat.

Place the chicken on the grill and cook for 25 minutes, occasionally brushing with leftover marinade, until it is cooked and golden brown.

Meanwhile, to cook the sweet potatoes, bring a medium pot of water to a boil, and boil the potatoes for 15 minutes. Once cooked, drain and let cool completely.

Melt the butter in a medium pan on medium heat and add the cooled sweet potatoes. Add the garlic and cook for 10 minutes, turning the sweet potatoes regularly, until they have a beautiful brown coating.

Meanwhile, bring a pan of salted water to a boil. Add the green beans and carrots and boil for 5 minutes. Meanwhile, prepare a bowl of ice water. When the beans and carrots are done, put them straight into the ice bath for 5 minutes.

In a clean, medium pan on medium heat, add the butter. Once melted, add the vegetables and mixed herbs. Cook for 3 minutes until well combined and heated through.

When everything is ready, place the warm chicken, sweet potatoes, and vegetables on a serving platter.

BUKA FISH
WITH RAPE

CLARA KAPELEMBE BWALI

PREPARATION TIME: 10 MINUTES,
  PLUS OVERNIGHT MARINATING
COOK TIME: 25 MINUTES
SERVES 6

FOR THE BUKA FISH
pinch of salt
¼ cup (2 fl oz/60 ml) lemon juice
6 cloves garlic, crushed
12 buka fish (you could also use
  mackerel), gutted and cleaned
  by your fishmonger
cooking oil, for deep-frying
lemon wedges, to serve

FOR THE RAPE
¼ cup (2 fl oz/60 ml) vegetable oil
¼ cup (2 oz/55 g) diced onion
1 cup (7 oz/200 g) diced tomato
pinch of salt
3 cups (1 lb 2 oz/500 g) rape (can
  be substituted with collard
  greens/spring greens)

This dish is reserved for memorable occasions, so when I had it as a child, I knew it was special. I remember that buka fish was served when my uncle returned to Zambia after years of living abroad. It was the first time I'd met him, and when he unapologetically devoured the buka fish, it was telling of how much he'd missed it.

Buka fish is found in the deep waters of Zambia's Lake Tanganyika. It is seasonal and can be prepared and eaten in a variety of ways: fresh, dried, fried, or boiled. This dish is paired with the popular leafy green vegetable, part of the kale family, called rape, or *rapu*, as we say in Zambia.

You can serve this dish with *Nshima* (page 166).

Combine the salt, lemon juice, and fresh garlic in a container. Add the fish, cover, and leave to marinate overnight in the refrigerator.

Pat the fish dry to remove any excess marinade, then, in a medium pot, add enough oil to submerge the fish fully. Heat the oil to 350°F/180°C. Alternatively, place a wooden spoon in the oil to check if it's ready. If the oil makes bubbles around the spoon, it is hot enough.

Place the fish in the oil and deep-fry for 5 minutes, or until crisp and golden brown. You may need to do this in batches.

Remove the fish from the oil and drain away any excess oil on paper towels.

For the rape, heat the oil in a medium pan on medium heat. Add the onion and tomato and cook for 6 minutes until combined and broken down. Add the salt, then add the rape and mix well. Cook for 5 minutes, then remove from the heat to avoid overcooking (if overcooked, the rape will lose its rich green color).

Place the buka fish and rape next to each other on a plate and serve warm with lemon wedges alongside.

KAPENTA WITH CHINESE CABBAGE AND NSHIMA

CLARA KAPELEMBE BWALI

PREPARATION TIME: 20 MINUTES, PLUS
  30 MINUTES DRYING
COOKING TIME: 40 MINUTES
SERVES 6

FOR THE KAPENTA
pinch of salt
2 lb 4 oz (1 kg) large, fresh
  kapenta (or substitute with your
  sardine of choice), gutted and
  cleaned by your fishmonger
1 cup (8 fl oz/240 ml) vegetable oil
1 teaspoon finely chopped fresh
  root ginger
1 onion, cubed
1 teaspoon crushed garlic
1 cup (7 oz/200 g) diced tomato
1 teaspoon ground turmeric

FOR THE CHINESE CABBAGE
¼ cup (2 fl oz/60 ml) vegetable oil
¼ cup (2 oz/55 g) diced onion
1 cup (7 oz/200 g) diced tomato
pinch of salt
3 cups (6 oz/180 g) shredded
  Chinese cabbage

FOR THE NSHIMA
about 5 cups (20 oz/570 g) fine
  cornmeal (maize meal)
1 cup (8 fl oz/240 ml) cold water
2 cups (16 fl oz/475 ml)
  boiling water

As a child, I didn't find *kapenta* (Zambian sardines) delightful, but as I grew up, I began to enjoy them, and when I moved to South Africa for university, I suddenly found myself craving *kapenta* after years of despising the dish. They weren't easy to find, so when I finally came across them in the market, I took them home and began cooking. From that moment on, I found myself loving *kapenta*, and over time it has become a dish that I find immense joy in cooking and eating.

Kapenta, or Tanganyika sardines, originate from Lake Tanganyika in Zambia, and they are only available seasonally, therefore finding and enjoying them is always a treat.

You can serve this dish with *nshima*—cornmeal (maize meal) polenta—a staple in Zambia. We enjoy it regularly for lunch or dinner and serve it with a choice of vegetables and protein. I was ten years old the first time I cooked *nshima*. I arrived home from school and my mom told me it was my turn to cook it. As the firstborn in my family, she insisted that it was important for me to know how. She trusted that I could make it on my own after seeing her make it many times. I picked up the *umwinko* (similar to a wooden spoon, used to cook *nshima*) and began cooking and stirring. Despite the effort, my first time was not the best, yet we served it to my dad, who had only a bite. That encouraged me to get better as I practiced to make delicious *nshima* that my dad would eat every bite of.

Rub the salt into the outside and cavities of the kapenta, then set aside to dry out for at least 30 minutes.

In a medium pan on medium heat, add the oil. Add the kapenta to the pan and fry for 8 minutes until crispy, or until it looks golden brown. Set aside the kapenta and reserve the oil.

Add 3 tablespoons of the reserved oil to a medium pan. Over medium heat, fry the ginger, onion, and garlic for about 3 minutes, or until it becomes fragrant. Then add the tomato and turmeric and let simmer over low heat for 10 minutes. Add the kapenta and cook for just 5 minutes so the kapenta doesn't get soggy. You don't want it to lose its crispiness.

For the Chinese cabbage, add the oil to a medium pan. Place on medium heat and add the onion and tomato, then fry for 5 minutes. Season with the salt. Cook for 3 minutes more, until the tomatoes are soft and combined. Add the Chinese cabbage, then mix with all ingredients in the pan. Cook for 5 minutes, then remove from the heat immediately to avoid overcooking.

Meanwhile, for the nshima, put 2 cups (8 oz/225 g) of the cornmeal (maize meal) in a medium pot, then add the cold water and mix. Add the boiling water, then place on medium heat and simmer for 15 minutes. Then, start adding ½ cup (2 oz/55 g) of cornmeal gradually at 2-minute intervals. Between each addition, mix carefully with a wooden spoon. Once the mixture goes from soft to stiff, stop adding the meal. Set aside for 5 minutes.

Place the kapenta and Chinese cabbage next to each other on a plate and add the nshima on the side.

SWAHILI PLATE

ALFONSO VIDEIRA

PREPARATION TIME: 20 MINUTES,
    PLUS 2 HOURS MARINATING
COOKING TIME: 30 MINUTES
SERVES 2

1 whole tilapia fish, scales removed
    and cleaned (ask your fishmonger
    to do this)
juice of 2 lemons
2 cloves garlic, chopped
⅓ cup (3½ fl oz/100 ml) vegetable oil
2 onions, chopped
3½ oz/100 g tomatoes, chopped
1¾ oz/50 g okra, chopped
5 garden eggs (African eggplant),
    chopped
1 bunch pumpkin leaves, chopped
1 cup (8 fl oz/250 ml) oil (optional)
salt and pepper

I've been eating tilapia since birth. The nostalgia of enjoying it grilled in sauce, cooked in banana leaves, served with fufu (cassava flour) and greens like pondu or pounded cassava leaves takes me back to my childhood. In Angola, it is common to eat tilapia with a fresh lemon fennel salad. However, in East Africa, the salad can be replaced with *Ugali* (page 72), while in West Africa, attieke, ground couscous-like cassava, is a great substitute. Whatever you pair the tilapia with, it's bound to tantalize the tastebuds.

In a medium pan, marinate the fish in the lemon juice, garlic, salt, and pepper for at least 2 hours, covered, in the refrigerator.

In a medium pan, heat some vegetable oil and cook half the onions until soft, about 5 minutes, then add the tomatoes, and stir. Add the okra and garden eggs, then cook for another 10 minutes, stirring slowly until done. Add salt to taste.

In a hot pan, add vegetable oil and the remaining chopped onion and cook for 5 minutes. Stir, then add the chopped pumpkin leaves to the pan and cook at medium heat for 10 minutes. Add salt to taste.

In the meantime, cook the fish. The fish can be pan-fried in the oil, or baked in the oven at 400°F/200°C/Gas Mark 6, for 6 minutes each side.

Serve the fish with the vegetables.

ZANZIBAR CURRY

ALFONSO VIDEIRA

PREPARATION TIME: 30 MINUTES
COOKING TIME: 35 MINUTES
SERVES 2

2 tablespoons cayenne pepper
2 tablespoons curry powder
⅓ cup (3½ fl oz/100 ml) vegetable
  oil, plus extra for the cabbage
3 tablespoons garlic paste
4¼ oz/120 g onions, diced
1 lb/450 g tomatoes, cubed
6¾ oz/190 g zucchini (courgette),
  cubed
3½ oz/100 g carrots, cubed
5 oz/140 g eggplant (aubergine),
  cubed
3½ oz/100 g green pepper, cubed
1 cup (8 fl oz/250 ml) coconut cream
1¾ oz/50 g shredded green cabbage
1¾ oz/50 g shredded red cabbage
salt and pepper, to taste

On my first trip to Stone Town, Zanzibar, I experienced a culinary delight that would forever influence my perspective on flavor. Despite my initial indifference to coconut, I found myself ordering a second serving of the dish in a quest to unravel its intricate flavor profile. Upon arriving in Tanzania, I never imagined becoming a fervent fan of coconut-infused cuisine. However, my encounter with this dish was a revelation. Its harmonious blend of flavors compelled me to replicate it at the Rivertrees Country Inn, where I promptly added it to our à la carte menu. Now, we proudly present this Tanzanian safari on a platter, served within a coconut shell, inviting our guests to embark on their own journey of flavor discovery.

Heat a skillet (frying pan) on medium-high heat and toast the cayenne pepper and curry powder for 2 minutes.

Add the vegetable oil, garlic paste, and onions. Stir to combine, then add the chopped tomatoes, stir again, and cook for 10 minutes, or until well cooked.

Add all the remaining vegetables, stirring constantly. Reduce the heat to medium and allow the vegetables to cook well, about 5 minutes. Reduce the heat to low and cook until the liquid is reduced, then add the coconut cream and cook for 15 minutes.

Meanwhile, cook the cabbage in a skillet (frying pan) in a couple of tablespoons of oil until wilted.

Add salt and pepper to taste, and serve the curry on a bed of cabbage.

OKRA STEW

PREPARATION TIME: 10 MINUTES
COOKING TIME: 40 MINUTES
SERVES 4-6

2 tablespoons olive oil
1 onion, chopped
½ red bell pepper, chopped
1 teaspoon minced garlic
2 bird's eye chilies, finely chopped
2 tomatoes, grated
4 cups (10 oz/280 g) chopped okra
½ teaspoon baking soda (bicarbonate of soda)
salt and pepper

Okra stew is a simple dish from the Bapedi people in Limpopo, South Africa. Similar versions can be found in most Southern African countries, including Zimbabwe and Zambia, where okra is easily sourced and has been enjoyed for generations. This stew uses simple ingredients and can be enjoyed with any starch of choice, but the most popular is *Pap* (page 186) or *Sadza* (page 148), both dishes made with cornmeal (maize meal) that are common in Southern Africa. This dish always makes me think of moments in my grandmother's kitchen. Like many of her dishes, it's simple yet very nutritious. Okra's unique texture can take some getting used to, but it's delicious and adds interesting texture to a meal.

In a medium saucepan, heat the oil. Add the onion and fry for 1 minute on medium heat. Add the chopped bell pepper and garlic, then cook for 5 minutes to soften. Add the chilies, ¼ cup (2 fl oz/60 ml) of water, and the grated tomatoes, then simmer for 15 minutes.

Add the okra and baking soda (bicarbonate of soda) and cook for 10–12 minutes, mashing lightly with a wooden spoon as it cooks. Add ¼ cup (2 fl oz/60 ml) of water and season with salt and pepper. Simmer for another 5–10 minutes, until the okra has a sticky consistency. Serve warm with pap or sadza.

CHIKANDA
FRIED RICE

MWAKA MWIIMBU

PREPARATION TIME: 20 MINUTES
COOKING TIME: 40 MINUTES
SERVES 10–12

2 cups (7 oz/200 g) finely
   pounded peanuts
2 teaspoons salt
1 teaspoon chili powder (optional)
1 cup (3½ oz/100 g) pounded chikanda
4 teaspoons baking soda (bicarbonate
   of soda)
3 tablespoons (1½ oz/40 g) butter
1 carrot, diced
1 yellow onion, diced
1 red bell pepper, diced
1 yellow bell pepper, diced
2 cloves garlic
2 teaspoons paprika
2 cups (14 oz/400 g) cooked rice
   (preferably day-old rice)
3 tablespoons chutney
1 tablespoon soy sauce
olive oil
salt and pepper
chopped parsley, to garnish

Chikanda, also known as African polony, is a Zambian favorite and often classified as a street food. Many people eat *chikanda* plain with a toothpick (or cocktail stick) while sitting and chatting with friends over a cold beer. Another way it can be enjoyed is combined with fried rice. This Zambian delicacy is made from dried orchid tubers pounded into a fine powder. It is usually prepared over a charcoal fire, however, in this case, I'm sharing my home-kitchen recipe, where we love to simplify things but keep the natural and authentic flavors.

While there is no substitution for *chikanda*, if you do not have access to it, I suggest using another plant-based protein alternative, such as tofu. If using tofu, make sure you break it up into small to medium pieces.

Preheat the oven to 350°F/180°C/Gas Mark 4.

Begin by boiling 3 cups (25 fl oz/750 ml) of water in a pan and stirring in the pounded peanuts, continuing to stir. Once it returns to a boil, add the salt and chili powder, if using, and continue to stir. Slowly, emphasis on slowly, stir in the pounded chikanda, being sure to add it bit by bit.

After adding your chikanda, you'll notice it starts to thicken. At this point, add 1 teaspoon of the baking soda (bicarbonate of soda) and vigorously stir; this ensures the baking soda breaks down and loses its bitterness.

After about 3 minutes, in a separate bowl, mix 2 teaspoons of baking soda with ½ cup (4 fl oz/120 ml) of water and pour it into the chikanda mixture. Continue to mix the chikanda until the texture changes completely. You are looking for a thick, lumpy, and paste-like consistency.

Transfer the chikanda to a baking pan (tray). To smooth the chikanda, dip a wooden spoon in a water mixture (water and 1 teaspoon baking soda) and pat the chikanda until smooth. Put it into the oven and bake for about 20 minutes. To know if the chikanda is cooked, poke it with a knife or toothpick (cocktail stick). If it comes out clean, then it's ready. Once ready, remove it from the oven and let cool.

Heat 2 tablespoons of butter in a pan over medium–high heat until melted. Add the carrot, onion, bell peppers, and garlic to your pan and season with the paprika and a generous pinch of salt and pepper. Sauté for about 5 minutes, or until the onion and carrot are soft.

While the vegetables are cooking, slice the chikanda into small, bite-sized cubes; these should be slightly bigger than your vegetables. Set aside (make sure you leave some to snack on later!).

Add the remaining 1 tablespoon (½ oz/15 g) of the butter to the pan and stir until melted. Add the rice, chutney, and soy sauce and stir until combined. Continue sautéing for an additional 3 minutes to fry the rice. Then add the chikanda and stir to combine for another 2 minutes.

Remove from the heat and stir in the olive oil until combined. Taste and season with extra salt and pepper, if needed.

Garnish with fresh parsley and serve warm.

GARDEN EGGS

PREPARATION TIME: 10 MINUTES
COOKING TIME: 20 MINUTES
SERVES 4

3 tablespoons olive oil
14 oz (400 g) garden eggs (African
    eggplant), trimmed and quartered
½ teaspoon paprika
1 teaspoon garlic and chili salt
¼ teaspoon ground black pepper
2 cloves garlic, diced
1 red onion, sliced
1 red bell pepper, sliced
1 yellow bell pepper, sliced
1 green bell pepper, sliced
2 tablespoons mild peach chutney
2 tablespoons ketchup

Garden eggs, also known as the African eggplant, are from the wider eggplant (aubergine) family and called *impwa* in Zambia's Bemba language. They are round and typically white in color and have a bitter taste. Zambians have a love-hate relationship with *impwa,* but those who get it, get it. I disliked garden eggs as a child and even went as far as calling them "the devil's fruit," but as the years went on and I perfected my craft, they became one of my favorite things to eat. They do have a bitter side, but this recipe can change that perspective.

Heat the oil in a large pan on medium heat and sauté the garden eggs for 5 minutes.

Season with paprika, garlic and chili salt, and pepper, and fry the garden eggs for another 5 minutes. You will notice them start to become tender.

Add the garlic and onion to the pan and sauté for about 3 minutes. Next, add the red, yellow, and green peppers and cook for another 3 minutes. Add the sauces (chutney and ketchup) and fry for about 5 minutes. Serve warm.

PEANUT BUTTER
RICE BALLS AND PUMPKIN MASH
WITH SPICY RELISH

KUDAKWASHE MAKONI

PREPARATION TIME: 20 MINUTES
COOKING TIME: 1 HOUR
SERVES 4–6

FOR THE PEANUT BUTTER RICE
1 cup (7 oz/200 g) long-grain rice
   (like jasmine rice)
3 tablespoons peanut butter
⅓ cup (3½ fl oz/100 ml) chicken
   or vegetable stock

FOR THE PUMPKIN MASH
1 pumpkin, peeled and cubed (or
   substitute with butternut squash)
1 tablespoon (½ oz/15 g) butter
1 teaspoon brown sugar
¼ cup (2 fl oz/60 ml) heavy (double)
   cream; half-and-half (single
   cream) or chicken or vegetable
   stock can also be used
salt and pepper, to taste

FOR THE SPICY RELISH
3 tablespoons vegetable oil
1 large yellow onion, finely diced
2 cloves garlic, minced
½ cup (1½ oz/45 g) shredded
   white cabbage
½ cup (2 oz/50 g) julienned carrots
1 teaspoon curry powder
½ teaspoon dried mixed herbs
2 bird's eye chilies, finely chopped
   (with seeds)
2 large tomatoes, chopped
   (or 1 × 14-oz/400-g can
   chopped tomatoes)
salt and pepper, to taste

TO GARNISH
red chili oil
sour cream (optional)
micro herbs

This dish conjures up memories of my grandmother. Peanut butter is one of the most widely used ingredients in Zimbabwean cuisine, and is found in everything from breakfast to supper dishes. This is my take on two popular dishes in Zimbabwe—*mupunga unedovi* (peanut butter rice) and *nhopi* (pumpkin mash). Traditionally, these meals are not served together, but as I re-imagine Zimbabwean cuisine for a global palate, I have brought them together using peanut butter as a unifying ingredient, because traditionally *nhopi* is made with peanut butter. You can enjoy the rice in a different way the next morning by serving it cold with a cup of hot tea.

To make the peanut butter rice, bring a pan of water to a boil, then cook the rice according to the packaging instructions. Once the rice has cooked for the time specified, add another ½ cup (4 fl oz/120 ml) of water and cook on low heat for another 10 minutes so it is slightly overcooked and pliable (though not glutinous). Take off the heat and set aside.

Whisk the peanut butter and half the stock in a saucepan on medium heat and bring to a gentle simmer. Cook for 15–20 minutes. If this "peanut sauce" is too thick, loosen it with more of the remaining stock until it is very runny. Gently mix in the rice and make sure every grain is coated in the peanut sauce.

Using a flat, wide wooden spoon, over medium-low heat, begin pounding the peanut rice, attempting to mash as much of it as possible until it sticks to the spoon and is easy to mold. Do not overmash, as you want some little bits of grain in the rice. Once it's ready, take it off the heat and set aside. Wait for it to be cool enough to handle, then mold it into a ball.

To make the pumpkin mash, bring a pan of salted water to a boil. Boil the pumpkin for 10–12 minutes, or until you can mash it cleanly with a fork. Drain, then add the butter, sugar, and cream or half and half, then mix until you get a smooth and thick texture. Season according to taste.

To make the spicy relish, heat the vegetable oil in a pan on medium heat. Add the onion, garlic, cabbage, and carrots and sauté for 7 minutes until translucent and tender. Add the curry powder, herbs, and chilies and continue sautéing until fragrant. Add the tomatoes and let simmer for 10 minutes until cooked and the liquid has reduced. Season according to taste.

To serve, place the pumpkin mash at the bottom of a bowl, followed by the spicy relish in the center, then top with the rice ball. Drizzle with chili oil and sour cream, if using, then top with micro herbs.

MASHED POTATOES AND SPINACH

PREPARATION TIME: 15 MINUTES
COOKING TIME: 30 MINUTES
SERVES 4-6

4 large potatoes, peeled
1 bunch (1 lb 2 oz/500 g) spinach,
  destalked and finely chopped
2 tablespoons olive oil
1 large yellow onion, chopped
3 tablespoons (¼ oz/10 g)
  chopped thyme
3 tablespoons (¼ oz/10 g)
  chopped rosemary
1 tablespoon chicken rub spice
1 tablespoon ginger-garlic paste
2 tablespoons (1 oz/25 g) butter
⅔ cup (5 fl oz/150 ml) heavy
  (double) cream
salt and pepper, to taste

Mashed potatoes and spinach are called *imifino nama zambane* in the language of isiXhosa. Growing up, I used to help in my father's garden, which enabled me to understand fresh produce. Hence, this recipe takes me back to my childhood. The combination of spinach and potatoes is common among South African cultures, especially during potato harvesting season. It reminds me of my school vacations when my cousins used to visit. We would have this meal with crumbled *Pap* (page 186) or *uphuthu*, a crumbly maize porridge, after a full day of chores.

In a medium pot, cover the potatoes with water and bring to a boil. Cook for 25–30 minutes, or until the potatoes are cooked through. Remove the potatoes and set aside.

In another pot, add the spinach and 1 cup (8 fl oz/240 ml) of water, then bring to a boil. Simmer for 5 minutes until the spinach is wilted, then remove and set aside.

In a large pan, heat the oil over medium heat. Add the onion and sauté for 4–5 minutes until translucent. Add the thyme, rosemary, chicken rub, ginger-garlic paste, then stir. Return the cooked spinach to the pan and stir. Cook for 5–6 minutes, stirring occasionally.

In a separate pot, combine the cooked potatoes, butter, and cream. Mash until the potatoes are smooth and creamy. Stir in the cooked spinach and mix well. Season with salt and pepper to taste. Serve warm.

GRILLED
BUTTER CORN

THABO PHAKE

PREPARATION TIME: 10 MINUTES
COOKING TIME: 30 MINUTES
SERVES 8

4 corn cobs, halved
MSG or dashi powder, to season
1 garlic bulb
1 lb 2 oz (500 g) salted butter,
  melted
1 sprig thyme

Grilled corn is a popular delicacy in South Africa. It's often served as a side dish for South African Braai (page 144), however it is also a common street food. I always loved buying it on the side of the road from street vendors, who would grill the corn fresh and have it ready for purchase. As it's an affordable source of carbohydrates, it's common to see workers grab an ear on street corners to help them get through long days.

Preheat the oven to 300°F/150°C/Gas Mark 2.

Lay the corn in a baking dish and season with MSG or dashi powder. Cut the garlic bulb in half widthwise and place one half, cut side down, in the pan as an aromatic. Mince the remaining garlic and rub over the corn, then add the butter and thyme to the pan. Slowly bake the corn, submerged in the butter, in the oven for 15 minutes on each side.

As soon as your corn is cooked, let it cool down in the refrigerator, then finish it off on a barbecue grill and serve with South African braai.

SPICY
CHAKALAKA

SINOYOLO SIFO

PREPARATION TIME: 15 MINUTES
COOKING TIME: 35 MINUTES
SERVES 6-8

4 tablespoons canola (rapeseed) oil
1 large red onion, chopped
1 large green bell pepper, diced
2 tablespoons crushed garlic
2 tablespoons mild curry powder
1 teaspoon ground cumin
1 tablespoon tomato paste (purée)
1 tablespoon paprika
2 green chilies, chopped
5 carrots, grated
1 × 14-oz (400-g) can baked beans
1 × 7-oz (200-g) can green peas
⅓ cup (¾ oz/20 g) chopped cilantro
   (coriander)
1 tablespoon harissa sauce or paste
1 tablespoon sweet chili sauce
salt and pepper, to taste

This is a very popular vegetable side dish served with South African Braai (page 144), *Pap* (page 186), bread, stew (page 154), or curries. I learned how to make chakalaka from my mother when I was a teenager. It is said to have originated from South African townships and is a spiced-up version of the English baked beans. This recipe reminds me so much of home, as we used to have it very often; it was the only spicy dish I could tolerate when I was a teenager. I just love how simple and easy it is to make. Serve with *pap* and meat.

In a large pan, heat the oil on medium heat. Add the onion and green bell pepper. Sauté for 5–6 minutes until the onion is translucent. Stir in the garlic, curry powder, cumin, tomato paste (purée), and paprika. Add the chilies and carrots, then stir to combine. Cook for another 15 minutes, or until the carrots are soft.

Stir in the baked beans, peas, cilantro (coriander), harissa sauce, and sweet chili sauce, then season with salt and pepper. Simmer for 10–15 minutes and serve.

WILD GREENS AND CHEESE PAP

THABO PHAKE

PREPARATION TIME: 15 MINUTES
COOKING TIME: 30 MINUTES
SERVES 4-6

olive oil, for frying
2 cups (3½ oz/100 g) wild spinach
  greens (leaves) or collard greens
  (spring greens), finely shredded
1 tablespoon granulated sugar
3 cups (25 fl oz/750 ml) boiling
  water
2 cups (8 oz/225 g) fine cornmeal
  (maize meal)
1 cup (3½ oz/100 g) grated wagashi
  cheese or Parmesan/Gouda cheese

Corn is an affordable staple ingredient in South Africa. We grow it in the mountains of Kwazulu Natal, where everything—from the livestock to the crops—is sustainable. The rainy climate there is great for crops like corn. The local name for this dish is *pap*. I have added a twist with wild spinach (*morogo*) and a local Ghanaian cheese called *wagashi* that I was introduced to through my travels. The cheese makes the dish creamier and earthier with a hint of tanginess. Serve in a big bowl with beef stew (page 156).

Heat a drizzle of oil in a large pot and sauté the greens for 5 minutes on high heat. Once the greens have sweated, reduce the heat to medium, and add the sugar to help retain the green color of the leaves.

Add the boiling water to the pot with the greens. Add half the cornmeal (maize meal) and cover. Reduce the heat to medium–low and let cook for 8–10 minutes. Resist the urge to stir.

Remove the lid, then stir vigorously for 1 minute, to incorporate any remaining cornmeal into the water. Repeatedly mash the pap against the side of the saucepan for about 2 minutes to get rid of any lumps.

Gradually add the remaining maize meal, stir vigorously, and mash again. Reduce the heat to the lowest setting and add the lid. Let the pap steam for another 10–15 minutes. Remove the lid and stir. If the pap is a bit too dry, add a little more water and stir again. To finish, stir in the grated cheese. Serve hot.

SOUTH AFRICAN CORN BREAD

THABO PHAKE

PREPARATION TIME: 20 MINUTES,
  PLUS 50 MINUTES PROVING
  AND RESTING
COOKING TIME: 25 MINUTES
SERVES 8

2¼ cups (9 oz/250 g) fine cornmeal
  (maize meal)
scant ¾ cup (5½ oz/150 g) cold
  butter, unsalted
2 cups (10 oz/280 g) self-rising
  (self-raising) flour
½ cup (3½ oz/100 g) chopped
  corn kernels
1 egg, beaten
1 cup (8 fl oz/250 ml) milk
scant 1 cup (3½ oz/100 g) grated
  Gouda cheese

In my hometown in the northwest region of Pietermaritzburg, in the mountains of KwaZulu-Natal, South Africa, corn is an essential vegetable that plays a pivotal role in people's daily lives. It is called *insinkwa sombila* in Zulu. We grow corn for two reasons: for our own nourishment and to feed the cattle. As a child, I would wake up in the morning and go to work on the farm. Before leaving, I would collect some ears of corn and grind them for cow feeding. I would also take some of the whole corn cobs for roasting and boiling for the local taxi drivers.

This dish celebrates what it means to be African in the south of Africa, with elements drawn from the greater African diaspora; the ingredients, techniques, and process all have links to African American use of corn. For me, this dish says, "I'm African regardless of geography."

Preheat the oven to 400°F/200°C/Gas Mark 6. Line a 10-inch/25-cm round baking tray with parchment (baking) paper.

In a food processor, combine the cornmeal (maize meal), butter, flour, and chopped corn, and pulse.

In a separate bowl, combine the beaten egg and milk, then stir through the cheese. Add to the dry ingredients in the food processor and mix well. Take the mixture out of the processor and, using your hands, knead so it comes together.

Mold the bread dough into a circle and place on the lined, round tray. Allow it to prove for 30 minutes, then bake in the oven for 25 minutes. After baking, let it rest for 20 minutes and then serve.

PEANUT BUTTER
PORRIDGE WITH FRUIT

CLARA KAPELEMBE BWALI

PREPARATION TIME: 10 MINUTES
COOKING TIME: 45 MINUTES
SERVES 6

2 cups (8 oz/225 g) cornmeal
  (maize meal)
pinch of salt
2 tablespoons granulated sugar
  (or honey)
1 cup (3½ oz/100 g) finely pounded
  peanuts
1 cup (8 fl oz/240 ml) boiling water
1 tablespoon smooth, unsalted
  peanut butter
1 tablespoon cashew nut butter
  (optional)

TO SERVE
¼ cup (1½ oz/40 g) halved
  strawberries
¼ cup (1 oz/30 g) mulberries
¼ cup (1½ oz/40 g) blueberries
¼ cup (1½ oz/40 g) toasted cashew
  nuts or peanuts
honey, for drizzling

When I was growing up, peanut butter was always around me, and my mom made it from scratch. She would buy fresh peanuts, pound them, and make fresh peanut butter. The long process was worth it because the whole family would enjoy it, even my baby siblings—in Zambia, babies are fed peanut butter porridge in infancy. Although not typically eaten as a dessert, I made this version to enjoy after a meal.

Add the maize meal, salt, sugar, and peanuts to a medium pot. Add enough water to make a paste, then pour in the boiling water. Mix over medium heat until the mixture is combined and it starts to boil.

Cook for 30 minutes, then add the peanut butter and cashew butter, if using. Simmer for 10 more minutes.

Top with the fruit and nuts and serve with honey for drizzling.

LEMON BUTTER
MILLET PORRIDGE

KUDAKWASHE MAKONI

PREPARATION TIME: 15 MINUTES
COOKING TIME: 15 MINUTES
SERVES 2

2½ cups (5½ oz/150 g) millet meal
   (finger millet is best), or more
   if needed
1¾ cups (14 fl oz/400 ml) boiling
   water, or more if needed
3½ tablespoons (2 fl oz/50 ml)
   whole (full-fat) milk
juice of 1 large lemon (about
   3-4 tablespoons/2 fl oz/50-60 ml)
   or 3 tablespoons bottled
   lemon juice
2 tablespoons brown sugar
   (you can substitute with honey)
3½ tablespoons (1¾ oz/50 g)
   unsalted butter
pinch of salt

TO SERVE
2 teaspoons (¼ oz/10 g) butter
brown sugar, to taste
candied or dried citrus segments
   (lemon, orange, and grapefruit)
honey, for drizzling

On many of my holiday and weekend mornings as a child, we were fed porridge, mostly made from cornmeal (maize meal). Millet is grown abundantly in Zimbabwe and, though it is one of the country's indigenous grains, we did not eat it frequently. On rare occasions when we went to the village, we would have *sadza* made with *zviyo* (millet). As a grownup, I have come to love millet meal used in *sadza* and porridge because of its health benefits. This reimagined version is how, with a sweet tooth, I eat millet porridge in my home today.

Pour the millet meal into a small pot on medium–high heat. Add just enough cold water to make a paste, then add the boiling water and stir until it comes to a boil (don't stop stirring, because you don't want it to have little lumps).

Once it starts to boil, add the milk and continue stirring. Then cover the pot, reduce the heat to low, and let it simmer for about 7 minutes. If it seems too thick, add more boiling water. If it seems too thin, make a paste with some more millet meal in a separate bowl then pour it into the pot.

Add the lemon juice, sugar, butter, and salt. Whisk or stir it in, then let simmer for another 2–3 minutes.

Pour into bowls, top each with a spoon of butter, sprinkle some extra sugar and candied or dried citrus segments on top, and drizzle over some honey.

CANDIED
SWEET POTATO

PREPARATION TIME: 15 MINUTES,
  PLUS 10 MINUTES SOAKING
COOKING TIME: 30 MINUTES
SERVES 4

1 lb 9 oz (700 g) sweet potatoes,
  peeled and cut into medium-
  large chunks
1 teaspoon salt
2½ cups (1 lb 4 oz/550 g)
  peanut butter
3 tablespoons hot water

Sweet potato is one of the best kinds of potato out there—I absolutely love it. I am not a huge fan of peanut butter, but when I tried candied sweet potato (*sashilad kandolo*) for the first time, I was in dessert heaven—one of my friends brought it for lunch in school, and I wondered how anyone could make a beautiful sweet potato dish with peanut butter. My friend offered me some of the dessert and I said no with so much vigor, but little did I know I would end up eating this dessert often; since then, my mother and I have eaten it at least twice a week.

Sweet potato is a staple in many Zambian households. *Sashilad kandolo* is often enjoyed during teatime, or as we like to say, at "16:00." It is a sweet and slightly salty dessert that's perfect during the winter because of the warmth it brings, but you can enjoy it at any time of the day or year. The peanut butter turns into a beautiful nutty caramel and coats the sweet potato creating a delicious candied sweet potato. The potato (*kandolo*) will have a fluffy texture inside, surrounded by the smooth, creamy, caramel-like texture of the peanut butter.

Soak the sweet potatoes in water for about 10 minutes. After soaking, drain, and transfer the potatoes to a saucepan, then add the salt and 2 cups (16 fl oz/475 ml) of water. Boil on medium heat for 20 minutes, or until the sweet potatoes slightly soften.

In a separate saucepan on low heat, mix the peanut butter with the hot water, and stir with a spoon. This will soften it and make it more pourable. Once the peanut butter paste loosens, transfer your sweet potatoes to the pan with the peanut butter sauce and reduce the heat. Cook for 5–10 minutes until the peanut butter cooks into a thick, smooth, and caramel-like sauce.

Once the peanut butter turns a golden brown color, your sashilad kandolo is ready. Transfer to a bowl and serve immediately.

195

DESSERTS

ZAMBIAN DONUTS

PREPARATION TIME: 20 MINUTES
COOKING TIME: 15 MINUTES
MAKES 8-10

2 cups (10 oz/280 g) cake flour
2 teaspoons baking powder
¼ cup (1¾ oz/50 g) granulated sugar
2 eggs
1½ cups (12 fl oz/350 ml) whole (full-fat) milk
3 cups (25 fl oz/750 ml) vegetable oil

Every time my mom went into the kitchen and brought out the flour, my dad and I knew what was about to happen. We would go the whole afternoon singing a *chitumbuwa* song until she was done. *Chitumbuwa* is a Zambian deep-fried donut found on every street corner and loved by many people in the country. It's crispy and golden on the outside, yet light and fluffy on the inside. *Vitumbuwa* (plural) are often eaten as a snack, and I loved them growing up. If you're looking for a classic Zambian sweet treat, this is it!

Mix all the dry ingredients (flour, baking powder, and sugar) in a medium bowl. Once the dry ingredients are in the bowl, add the eggs and 1 cup (8 fl oz/240 ml) of the milk and mix until incorporated. Next, add the remaining ½ cup (4 fl oz/120 ml) of the milk and mix well. Make sure all the bubbles and lumps disappear.

In a large pan on high heat, heat the vegetable oil to 350°F/180°C. Alternatively, to check if the oil is ready, dip the end of a wooden spoon in it; if bubbles form, then the oil is hot enough. Use a large spoon or ice cream scoop to scoop the batter and place it into the hot oil; you can fry a few at a time, but don't overcrowd the pan. Deep-fry for 7 minutes, or until a nice golden brown. The donuts should flip on their own as they cook, but there is no harm in flipping them when they turn golden brown on one side. The batter may sink to the bottom but once it starts to cook it will rise. Repeat this for the remaining batter.

Once cooked, remove and place each donut in a bowl lined with paper towels so the oil can be drained. Serve with a hot beverage of your choice.

CHOCOLATE CARAMEL
ICE CREAM

SINOYOLO SIFO

PREPARATION TIME: 15 MINUTES,
  PLUS OVERNIGHT FREEZING
SERVES 6-8

2 cups (17 fl oz/500 ml)
  whipping cream
1 × 13½-oz (385-g) can sweetened
  condensed milk
1 teaspoon vanilla extract
1 cup (6 oz/175 g) caramel chocolate
  chips, plus extra to garnish
1 cup (6 oz/175 g) milk chocolate
  chips, plus extra to garnish
¼ cup (2 fl oz/60 ml) chocolate
  sauce
¼ cup (2 fl oz/60 ml) caramel sauce

We used to have ice cream after every big celebratory meal, such as birthday parties or Christmas gatherings with my siblings, so this recipe reminds me of home. I remember I would feel so good after eating ice cream that I would always look forward to it. Though the ice cream was store-bought when I was younger, I learned how to make it, and this recipe brings me back to those good times with family. The recipe is easy and no ice cream machine is required, though it must be prepared a day before serving.

In a large bowl, whip the cream with a balloon whisk until stiff peaks form. Fold in the condensed milk, vanilla extract, caramel chocolate chips, and milk chocolate chips with a spoon. Transfer the mixture to a freezer-safe container.

Sprinkle with extra chocolate chips on top and drizzle with the chocolate and caramel sauces. Cover with plastic wrap (clingfilm), close the lid, and freeze overnight.

FERMENTED
MAIZE DRINK

MWAKA MWIIMBU

PREPARATION TIME: 30 MINUTES,
    PLUS 3 HOURS SOAKING AND 24 HOURS
    FERMENTATION
COOKING TIME: 40 MINUTES
SERVES 6-8

5 dried munkoyo roots
3 cups masembe (crushed dried
  maize meal)
sugar or honey, to serve

When I was younger, my sisters, my mother, and so many other people would chase me around the house, trying to get me to eat a decent meal. Eventually they gave up and let me eat whatever I wanted, whenever I wanted. Once, I went to the village to visit my grandmother, and she brought out a calabash with *chibwantu*, or fermented maize drink. I was intrigued and asked her what was inside the calabash; she laughed and told me to taste. The moment I tasted the drink I knew I had found something I would love forever. I drank the whole calabash and went straight to sleep because it was so filling. From then on, I requested it every day. Now, whenever I go home for events and family gatherings, I take at least five bottles of *chibwantu*.

Chibwantu is a traditional drink common among the Tonga people of Zambia. There are similar drinks to this known as *munkoyo* (a more alcoholic version) and *tobwa*. It is made with crushed dried maize, also known as grits, and the Rhynchosia root, also known as *munkoyo* root in Zambia. It can be taken without a sweetener and has a fermented, slightly sour taste. Sugar and honey are often added to enhance its flavor. As much as it is a traditional Tonga drink, many people enjoy the flavors of *chibwantu*. It is a very filling drink and can even be classified as a meal on its own. *Chibwantu* is my favorite thing about my Tonga culture; it is a drink that brings people together and creates long-lasting bonds.

Add the munkoyo roots to a medium bowl and soak in warm water for about 3 hours. The water will turn a light brown color; you should reserve the liquid as this is what you will use to give the chibwantu its unique flavor.

Thoroughly wash the masembe by placing it in cold water for about 2 minutes. Repeat this step until the water stops being cloudy.

Put about 3½–4 cups (28 fl oz/830 ml–32 fl oz/950 ml) of water in a pot and bring to a boil. When it starts boiling, add the masembe and stir continuously with a wooden spoon for 5–7 minutes, until it starts to thicken and form a porridge. Once it does so, let the masembe cook for about 30 minutes or until completely soft. Then leave it to cool for at least 30 minutes, stirring occasionally.

Mix the cool masembe porridge with all the munkoyo water and roots. Make sure you break down the lumps in the water until it is mixed well. Let it rest, covered or sealed, for about 1 day for light fermentation to take place.

When it has fermented, remove the munkoyo roots. Alternatively, you can leave the munkoyo roots for about 4 hours. Serve with sugar or honey to taste.

BAOBAB
SMOOTHIE

MWAKA MWIIMBU

PREPARATION TIME: 10 MINUTES,
   PLUS 1 HOUR CHILLING
COOKING TIME: 5 MINUTES
SERVES 4–6

4 baobab fruit pods (or 1 cup
   baobab fruit powder)
16½ cups (135 fl oz/4 liters) whole
   (full-fat) milk or water
sugar or sweetener of your choice,
   to taste

My older sister used to make this for me all the time, before she got married—but she made sure I learned how to make it for myself, and I've been grateful ever since, as I've been able to continue enjoying this healthy and delicious drink. This smoothie is my favorite because it is rich in nutrients. It is made with the fruit of the baobab tree, called *mabuyu*, which has a tangy flavor that I love.

Smash the baobab fruit pods, releasing the powder and the seeds. Separate the seeds and powder from the casing and place them in a medium bowl, then set aside.

In a pan, bring the milk or water to a slight simmer. Add the baobab seeds and powder to the simmering milk. Stir the mixture until the powder separates from the seeds. The seeds will look black once the powder dissolves into the milk. The baobab-milk mixture might look a little curdled, but that's okay. Add sugar or a sweetener of your choice, and let it simmer for about 3 minutes.

Once all the seeds are visible, remove the pan from the stove and strain the seeds, saving all the liquid. Leave the liquid to cool down, then refrigerate for about 1 hour or until cold, and serve.

TAMARIND JUICE

MWAKA MWIIMBU

PREPARATION TIME: 20 MINUTES
SERVES 4

3 cups fresh tamarind pods
5 cups (40 fl oz/1.2 liters)
  warm water
1 small thumb-sized piece
  of fresh root ginger
granulated sugar or honey,
  to taste

The very first time I saw a tamarind pod, I didn't know it was something you could eat, until I watched my dad crack it open and toss the tamarind flesh into his mouth. He is obsessed with wild fruits, so eating tamarind straight from the pod was not strange to him. When he chewed on the flesh, I noticed him pout his lips and twitch his eye. I laughed, assuming it was not pleasant to eat. He told me to try it and I said no, but he insisted, saying it was delicious. Like him, I pouted my lips and twitched my eyes because it was so sour and tart, but it was delicious. From then on, I ate tamarind straight from the pod. One day, my sister attempted to make a drink out of the tamarind but failed. Years later, I decided to try different recipes until I came up with the perfect one—and this is it!

Tamarind, also called *kawawasha* by the Bemba-speaking people of Zambia, is a seasonal fruit that has a date-like texture with a very sour and tangy flavor. The fruit is named *kawawasha* because of its unique tangy flavor that is believed to have healing and cleansing effects; *kuwasha* means to wash or to clean, hence the loose meaning "it cleanses."

Kawawasha juice, also known as *tangawizi*, is a sweet and tangy juice with multiple health benefits, including maintaining a healthy blood pressure. The juice has a smooth texture, similar to guava juice, and is perfect for any time of the day. This drink is easy to make in bulk and can be shared over family dinners or simply on a hot Sunday afternoon.

Break the tamarind pods and remove all the flesh and pulp. Place the pulp in a large bowl and pour the warm water over the tamarind. Let the tamarind sit in the water for 10 minutes, or until soft. Transfer the softened pulp and water to a blender with your fresh ginger.

On the lowest setting, blend your tamarind and ginger for 15–20 seconds until you have a liquid consistency. You can add more water to the blender to get your desired consistency. The juice will be a dark, cloudy, brown color. Using a sieve, strain the tamarind juice into a jar leaving out all the broken seeds and unwanted pulp. Sweeten the juice to taste and serve with ice.

SELASSIE
ATADIKA

What I want to leave behind is that I was somebody who created opportunities for smallholder farmers and for producers of indigenous ingredients and products to make a livelihood for themselves and their communities. It's about creating ways that are accessible and approachable for people to continue to have indigenous foods. My chocolates and truffles are a gateway for people to want to learn more about the continent and about our cuisines. To want to learn the difference between West African and East African foods, for example, and to say that was a really interesting ingredient, or want to know more about the fermentation process that's being used.

WESTERN AFRICA

On my first trip to Western Africa, I landed in Accra, Ghana, and immediately felt a sense of familiarity and kinship; the sights and smells, the mannerisms of the people all reminded me of my own people, the Gullah Geechee of my childhood. The Gullah Geechee are descendants of Africans who were enslaved along the lower Atlantic coast of the United States. Despite being so often separated from loved ones, and scattered across North and South Carolina, they retained distinctive elements of their heritage: foods, music, art, and language. This translation of tradition is the one that raised me—and continues to influence me. It was also the one that enveloped me when I arrived in West Africa.

In Ghana, I was surrounded by voices that carried the flow and rhythmic sway of my grand elders, who sang every word they shared, like a chorus engaged in familial banter that demonstrated both strength of independence and unity. The sights—such as the loud pops of color proudly displayed and worn in full dress—were presented by the crowds of people as they strolled by, exuding a free-spirited confidence with every step. "Wow," I thought, "I'm home!" I knew that right there I had found a sense of belonging that I would never lose again. I was proud.

On a mission to trace my own African American heritage and identity through the lens of cooking techniques, ingredients, and flavors, I had come to West Africa to discover the foundation of who I was, through the foodways of the familiar: recipes passed down from generation to generation, connecting the dots, one collard green (spring green) at a time. The seeds of my beginnings were inextricably woven into my present.

My carefully planned trip included stops in Accra, Lagos, and Dakar. "Follow the food" was my mantra and guide, and I quickly discovered that, much like in my own culture, rice is king. Rice is perhaps the strongest, most important existing connection between the African and American continents, and now, in West Africa, I could see the prevalence of this imperative ingredient. In fact, it's the center of a friendly yet charged battle to create the best version—especially in the case of West Africa's jollof rice, which is cooked in a flavorful tomato sauce.

In West Africa, while hosted in homes of new and old friends, savoring even more from restaurants, food stands, and markets, I began to put the flavor puzzle together. The story through food unfolded as I discovered the great many similarities between what I had grown up with and what I was finding there. The fulfillment of connecting my story to a bigger, more fascinating engagement was just the tip of my journey. Familiar phrases, old folk sayings, and words not born of English that existed in the turn of a phrase being spoken, all resonated with me—I was finding clarity, as well as my identity.

It's thrilling to share these places, recipes, and culinary interpretations with you—you will notice the prevalence of some ingredients (lots of rice), but also the unique flavors that different countries and chefs bring to their dishes. Nana Araba Wilmot, from Ghana, shares her Arancini with Peanut Butter Soup (page 218), Agness Colley, from Togo, shares Scallops with Hibiscus Sauce (page 224), and Mame Sow, from Senegal, showcases her Chicken Yassa and Couscous (page 212)—and these dishes are just a small sampling of the rest of the West African fare shared here! Start your trip and enjoy—as always—the journey through this collection of dishes.

GRILLED STEAK SKEWERS

ERIC ADJEPONG

PREPARATION TIME: 30 MINUTES,
PLUS 1 HOUR MARINATING AND
OVERNIGHT SOAKING IF USING
WOODEN SKEWERS
COOKING TIME: 5-8 MINUTES
SERVES 4-6

5 cloves garlic, peeled
2 thumb-sized pieces fresh root
  ginger, peeled and chopped
4 tablespoons high-quality extra
  virgin olive oil
2 lb (900 g) sirloin (rump) steak
1 tablespoon kosher salt
2 teaspoons all-purpose seasoning
  blend
¾ cup (2¾ oz/80 g) suya, plus more
  to taste
⅓ cup (2½ fl oz/80 ml) neutral oil,
  plus more as needed
2 red onions, diced
2 red bell peppers, seeded and cut
  into large dice
2 yellow bell peppers, seeded and
  cut into large dice
sea salt, to serve

Along most roadsides in Ghana, it's common to smell the smoke from a charcoal grill cooking up local favorites, the distinct aroma of spices and aromatics in the air. *Chichinga* (meat kebabs) is on the list of beloved Ghanaian street foods. The combination of the suya, a spicy spice blend used to marinate meat in West Africa, and char, creates a wonderful earthy flavor with a bit of sweetness from the grilled onions and peppers. Serve alone or with jollof and a salad.

If using wooden skewers, soak the skewers in water overnight.

Place the garlic, ginger, and olive oil in a blender and blend until smooth. Place the steak on a cutting (chopping) board and cover with a layer of plastic wrap (clingfilm). Using a meat tenderizer (or a rolling pin), pound the meat to ¼-inch (5-mm) thickness. Cut the steak into 1-inch (2.5-cm) cubes, then transfer to a large bowl. Combine the salt, blended garlic mix, and all-purpose seasoning blend in a separate bowl, then toss with the steak cubes, being sure to coat all the pieces with the spices. Set aside.

In a small bowl, stir together the suya spice and neutral oil. Divide between 2 bowls. Arrange the red onions, bell peppers, and sirloin on skewers, alternating ingredients, about 3 pieces of sirloin per skewer. Brush half the suya-oil mixture over the kebabs, then cover and transfer to the refrigerator to marinate for at least 1 hour. When ready to cook, remove the kebabs from the refrigerator and allow to come to room temperature.

Meanwhile, preheat your barbecue grill to high, about 550°F (290°C). Place the kebabs on the heated grates and grill for 5–8 minutes, turning frequently using tongs or a grill glove, and basting with the remaining suya-oil mixture. The kebabs are ready when the vegetables and meat are slightly charred and the vegetables are tender. To serve, transfer the kebabs to a platter and sprinkle with additional suya spice and sea salt.

CHICKEN YASSA AND COUSCOUS

PREPARATION TIME: 20 MINUTES,
    PLUS UP TO 12 HOURS MARINATING
COOKING TIME: 1 HOUR
SERVES 4

FOR THE NOKOSS
7 oz (200 g) parsley
3 oz (100 g) green bell pepper
2 oz (60 g) each: leeks, shallots,
    scallions (spring onions), white
    onions, celery
¼ oz (10 g) fresh habanero chili
4 garlic cloves
2 teaspoons thyme leaves
2 teaspoons salt
2 teaspoons black peppercorns
4 fl oz (100 ml) olive oil

FOR THE CHICKEN
1 vegetable bouillon (stock) cube
    (I use Maggi)
2 lb (3 kg) bone-in, skin-on
    chicken thighs
¼ cup (2 fl oz/60 ml) corn oil

FOR THE COUSCOUS
2 cups (17 fl oz/500 ml) water
    or vegetable stock
2 teaspoons olive oil
2 tablespoons lemon juice
½ teaspoon (3 g) salt
1 cup (6 oz/180 g) couscous

FOR THE YASSA
2 lb 3 oz (1 kg) finely sliced
    white onions
9 oz (250 g) green bell pepper,
    finely sliced
1½ oz (40 g) ginger-garlic paste
1¾ oz (50 g) green onions, finely
    chopped
1 tablespoon white vinegar
1¾ oz (50 g) Dijon mustard
1¼ cups (10 fl oz/300 ml chicken or
    vegetable broth (stock), or water
¾ cup (100 g) pitted green olives
lemon juice
salt and pepper, to taste
1 lemon, cut into wedges, to serve

For special occasions like birthdays in Dakar, Senegal, my aunt would make chicken yassa and couscous. She taught me how to make this recipe when I was eight years old. It's always been my favorite dish because I couldn't get enough of the perfectly charred chicken. Though there are many ways of making it, my aunt's recipe is the one I love the most. Rather than the usual pairing of the chicken with rice, she pairs it with deliciously seasoned couscous, as here.

For the nokoss, chop the parsley, vegetables, chili, and garlic roughly, then add all the ingredients to a blender and blend together.

In a large bowl, toss together 7 oz (200 g) nokoss, bouillon (stock) cube, and the chicken thighs until well combined. Cover the bowl, then marinate in the refrigerator for at least 8 and up to 12 hours. Any leftover nokoss will keep in the refrigerator for up to 3 days, or freeze for up to 1 month.

Remove the chicken from the marinade, scraping off any excess. In a medium–large stock pot, heat the oil over medium–high heat. Add the chicken, skin-side down, and cook for about 5 minutes until browned, then turn and cook on the other side in the same way. Remove from the heat and set aside.

Lower the heat to medium, then add the white onions, bell peppers, and ginger-garlic paste to the pan and sauté, stirring frequently, for about 10 minutes, until softened and fragrant.

Add the green onions, vinegar, Dijon mustard, salt and pepper, and mix well. Cook for about 5 minutes.

Add the broth (stock), chicken, olives, and a little lemon juice into the pan, mix well, and continue to cook for 30–40 minutes, until the sauce is thickened and the chicken is cooked through. Season the chicken yassa with salt, if needed.

Meanwhile, for the couscous, put the water or stock, olive oil, lemon juice, and salt in a pan and bring to a boil. Stir in the couscous and return to a boil. Turn off the heat and cover, then let sit for 10 minutes.

Fluff the couscous gently and serve with the chicken and a few lemon wedges.

CHICKEN CASSAVA LEAF AND PEANUT BUTTER STEW

PIERRE THIAM

PREPARATION TIME: 20 MINUTES
COOKING TIME: 1 HOUR 10 MINUTES
SERVES 4

FOR THE NOKOSS
1 yellow onion, chopped
1 tablespoon dawadawa (fermented
  locust bean, optional)
1 clove garlic
1 teaspoon black peppercorns
½ teaspoon cayenne pepper (optional)

FOR THE CHICKEN
1 tablespoon sea salt, or more
  to taste
2 tablespoons fish sauce
4 boneless chicken thighs
½ cup (4 oz/115 g) smooth peanut
  butter
4 cups (12 oz/350 g) chopped cassava
  greens (leaves; okay if frozen)
4 tablespoons Nokoss (see above)
1 habanero pepper (optional)
1 cup (2½ oz/65 g) finely chopped
  okra (optional)
2 tablespoons red palm oil
cooked fonio or rice, to serve

This recipe is from Casamance, the southern region of Senegal where my family originates. It's usually prepared with cassava or sweet potato leaves. I particularly love this approach to cooking, which is one that upcycles the leaves of these root vegetables that are often wasted. The recipe is also very forgiving; if you don't have cassava or sweet potato leaves, any leafy vegetable will do. This recipe uses peanut butter as a substitute for the traditional peanut flour. In this recipe, I use chicken, but it can also be served with any meats or seafood, or even vegan style with firm tofu, potato, or cauliflower over fonio or rice.

Cassava leaves can be substituted with sweet potato leaves or collard greens (spring greens).

Place all the nokoss ingredients into a blender or a mortar. Blend or pound with the pestle until well combined and then put into a sterilized jar with a lid. Nokoss can be saved in a refrigerator for up to 1 week.

In a large pot, bring 8 cups (64 fl oz/1.9 liters) of water to a boil over high heat. Add the salt, fish sauce, and chicken thighs. Cook on medium heat for approximately 10–15 minutes until the chicken is cooked through. Remove the chicken, set aside to cool, then shred to bite-size pieces.

Add the peanut butter to the broth and return to a boil for 1 minute. Reduce the heat to medium–low and stir with a wooden spoon to dilute the peanut butter into the broth for approximately 2–3 minutes, until the peanut butter is completely dissolved. Add the chopped leaves and bring to a boil by turning the heat to high for approximately 1 minute. Reduce to low heat and simmer for 15–20 minutes until the leaves are soft.

Add the nokoss and a whole habanero pepper, if using. Stir the mixture with a wooden spoon and continue to simmer for another 10–15 minutes. Return the cooked and shredded chicken to the stew. Add the chopped okra, if using, and palm oil, and gently stir with a wooden spoon, being careful not to crush the whole haba-nero pepper into the stew (or else it may be too spicy). Simmer for another 10–15 minutes, stirring occasionally. Adjust the seasoning, remove the habanero pepper, and set aside. Serve over fonio or rice. The habanero pepper can be served on the side, if desired.

PLANTAIN FRITTATA

MATSE UWATSE

PREPARATION TIME: 30 MINUTES
COOKING TIME: 20 MINUTES
SERVES 4-8

vegetable oil, for deep-frying,
  cooking, and greasing pan
1 ripe plantain, cut into 1-inch
  (2.5-cm) circles
1 sausage, cut into small circles
  or thick strips
10 eggs
½ tablespoon garlic powder
¼ tablespoon dried Italian seasoning
¼ tablespoon ground black pepper
¼ tablespoon chili powder (optional)
¼ tablespoon paprika
salt
1 bouillon (stock) cube (optional)
½ green bell pepper, diced
½ red bell pepper, diced
½ yellow bell pepper, diced
½ red onion, diced

This plantain frittata was born out of fusing African and Italian cuisine, and I created this dish by using easily available ingredients in Nigeria. Upon sharing it online, it went viral in Nigeria, as people greatly embraced the dish. Locally, I call this recipe "dodo frittata," bringing two terms together as fried ripe plantains are called *dodo* in Nigeria, while *frittatas* are egg-based, quiche-like Italian dishes.

This recipe can be eaten for breakfast, served with hot beverages or cornmeal (maize meal) polenta, also known as *pap*, *sadza*, or *ugali*. It can also be served as lunch or dinner with salads, meats, and fish. It is a flavor-packed dish and very enjoyable to eat.

Preheat the oven to 350°F/180°C/Gas Mark 4.

To deep-fry the plantain, heat a pot of oil until 400°F/200°C. Carefully add the plantain and deep-fry for 5 minutes until golden brown, then drain on paper towels and set aside.

Heat 1 tablespoon of vegetable oil in a pan on medium heat. Add the sausage and fry for 1 minute, then drain and set aside.

Break the eggs into a medium-size bowl, then add all the spices (garlic powder, Italian seasoning, black pepper, chili powder, and paprika), a little salt, and bouillon (stock) cube, if using, and whisk thoroughly. Add most of the peppers, onion, and fried plantain to the egg mixture, leaving a little to garnish the top before baking.

With a food brush and vegetable oil, grease a small pie pan or ovenproof skillet. Pour the mix into the greased pan, and use the remaining fried plantain and vegetables to garnish the top. Bake in the oven for 10–15 minutes. Let rest for 2 minutes and serve hot.

OMO TUO ARANCINI WITH COCONUT PEANUT BUTTER SOUP

NANA ARABA WILMOT

PREPARATION TIME: 30 MINUTES,
 PLUS 2 HOURS FREEZING
COOKING TIME: 2 HOURS
SERVES 4

2 cups (14 oz/400 g) jasmine rice, washed until the water runs clear
5 chicken wings
1 tablespoon garlic powder
1 tablespoon onion powder
1 tablespoon adobo seasoning
½ celery stalk, cut into medium dice
3 carrots, cut into medium dice
2 bay leaves
1 large yellow onion, peeled and whole
1 scotch bonnet or habanero pepper
2 large tomatoes, left whole
1 cup (8 oz/225 g) smooth peanut butter
4 eggs
2 cups (10 oz/280 g) all-purpose (plain) flour
3 cups (7½ oz/210 g) bread crumbs
canola (rapeseed) or vegetable oil, for frying
2 × 14 oz (400 g) cans coconut milk
salt and pepper
herb salad, to serve

FOR THE CHIMICHURRI
1 bunch parsley, chopped
1 bunch cilantro (coriander), chopped
2 tablespoons chopped garlic
1 shallot, minced
1 lemon, halved
1 tablespoon salt
2 cups (16 fl oz/475 ml) extra virgin olive oil

This dish— *omo tuo ne nkatenkwan* in Ghana's Twi language—is a favorite in my house. My brother and I loved it when my mom and grandma made it. I can remember the smell filling the house and how we ran down the stairs when it was ready. This version is a fun take on the classic—I added coconut milk and chimichurri sauce (from across the ocean in Argentina), which brightens the flavors, while lemon and herbs further lighten a traditionally heavy meal.

Place the rice in a rice cooker with 4 cups (32 fl oz/950 ml) of water and cook according to instructions. Alternatively, cook the rice in a medium pan using the same ratio of water to rice. You want it to be very soft. Once cooked, use a wooden spoon to mash the rice against the side of the pot, creating a smooth consistency. Set aside.

Season the chicken wings with the garlic and onion powders and adobo seasoning. In a medium pot, sear the wings until golden on each side. Stir in the celery, carrots, and bay leaves and sweat for 2–3 minutes. Add 4¼ cups (34 fl oz/1 liter) of water, bring to a boil, then reduce the heat. Add the whole onion, scotch bonnet, and tomatoes and cook on low heat for 30–40 minutes. Once the tomato, onion, and pepper are tender, remove from the pot to a blender. Blend until smooth, then add the purée back into the stock for your soup base.

In a separate bowl combine the peanut butter with 3 cups (25 fl oz/750 ml) of hot water. Pour the peanut mixture into the soup base and, stirring frequently, allow to cook for 45 minutes. Remove and discard the chicken wings, and strain the soup into a pan. (Or shred the chicken and add to the soup, if desired.) Return the pan to the stove on low heat—the longer it simmers, the better! Transfer the soup to a freezer-safe container and freeze for at least 2 hours.

Prepare for the next stage by placing the whisked eggs, flour, bread crumbs, and rice in separate bowls. Have a baking sheet (tray) or plate ready for the prepped rice balls.

Once the soup has solidified, take 1 tablespoon of rice and flatten it in one hand. With the other hand, scoop a ½ teaspoon of soup and place it in the center of the flattened rice. Bring the edges together to form a ball. Repeat this step until all the rice is used. One by one, coat the rice balls in flour and shake off excess. Dip the rice balls into the egg wash and then into the bread crumbs. Repeat until finished.

Pour enough oil into a medium pan to cover the rice balls, then heat to 375°F/190°C. Gently add the rice balls in batches, taking care not to overcrowd the pan, and fry for 3–5 minutes until golden brown and crispy. Lightly salt them as they leave the oil, and set aside.

Place the remaining soup in a medium pot on a low heat, stirring constantly. Add the coconut milk to thin out the soup and heat through. Season to taste and set aside.

To make the chimichurri, in a bowl combine half the chopped herbs with the garlic, shallots, and the juice of half the lemon.

To serve, add the coconut peanut butter sauce to a plate. Place the rice balls on top and dress with chimichurri. Garnish with the remaining herbs and squeeze over the juice of the other lemon half.

SEARED CHILEAN SEA BASS WITH CELERY ROOT PURÉE AND GOLDEN MUSHROOMS

RÔZE TRAORE

PREPARATION TIME: 30 MINUTES
COOKING TIME: 50 MINUTES
SERVES 2

FOR THE PURÉE
canola (rapeseed) oil, for frying
1 white onion, julienned
¼ cup (2 fl oz/60 ml) white wine
1 Yukon Gold (or other baking)
  potato, peeled and cut into
  1-inch (2.5-cm) slices
1 celery root (celeriac), trimmed
  and cut into ½-inch (1-cm) slices
4 cups (32 fl oz/950 ml) whole
  (full-fat) milk
1 stalk lemongrass
1 bay leaf
2 sprigs thyme
1 tablespoon (½ oz/15 g) butter
salt, to taste

FOR THE MUSHROOMS
canola (rapeseed) oil, for frying
1 bunch of white beech mushrooms,
  split into individual pieces
1 lemon wedge
1 tablespoon finely sliced chives
1 tablespoon finely sliced parsley
salt and pepper, to taste
1 teaspoon grated horseradish,
  to garnish

FOR THE SEA BASS
6 oz (175 g) sea bass
salt, for coating
canola (rapeseed) oil, for frying
1 tablespoon (½ oz/15 g)
  salted butter
2 sprigs thyme
2 sprigs rosemary
1 clove garlic, crushed

I've always felt a strong connection to the ocean, perhaps because I have fond memories of spending time on the beach with my grandparents in Grand Bassam, Côte d'Ivoire. My father was an offshore fisherman who spent months at a time on boats and came home with stories still vivid in my mind. For these reasons, I am drawn to cooking seafood both genetically and nostalgically.

This seared Chilean sea bass dish is special to me because it's similar to the preparation my father enjoyed when he'd share his catch of the day. It's fresh, delicate, and sophisticated, but simple enough for an ordinary weeknight. I love finding ways to elevate dishes by incorporating different cultures and techniques into a dish. In this recipe, the flavors of Côte d'Ivoire shine alongside classic French techniques.

To start, place a medium pan on low–medium heat and drizzle enough canola (rapeseed) oil to coat the pan. Add the julienned onion, then season with a sprinkle of salt and let it sweat for about 3 minutes, but don't let it brown. Add the wine and let the alcohol cook out for 2 minutes. Proceed by adding the potato and celery root (celeriac) into the pot along with the milk. Season with salt, then add the lemongrass, bay leaf, and thyme sprigs. Let this cook on low–medium heat for 25–30 minutes until your ingredients are tender and translucent.

Spoon out the onion, celery root, and potatoes, and add to a blender. Pour about ¼ cup (2 fl oz/60 ml) of the cooking liquid into the blender (avoid the lemongrass and thyme) and turn it on high. While the blender is on, add the butter and blend until all your ingredients are incorporated and smooth. Season to taste. Place it on the side to keep warm.

Preheat a medium pan on medium heat. Drizzle enough oil to coat the bottom of the pan, then add the mushrooms and season with salt and cracked pepper. Cook for about 5 minutes or until golden brown. Turn off the heat, then zest and squeeze the lemon wedge into the pan, followed by the chives and parsley. Place to the side to keep warm.

Season the fish with salt on both sides. Heat a pan on low heat. Drizzle enough oil to coat the bottom of the pan. Place the fish in the pan, skin-side down. Let the fish cook for about 4–5 minutes or until the skin is golden. Once crispy, turn the fish flesh-side down, and add the butter, thyme, rosemary, and garlic. Once the butter has melted and become partially foamy, turn off the heat. Spoon the butter on top of the fish and let it rest for 2 minutes. Remove the fish from the pan and begin with plating.

Place the fish on the plate and pour the purée next to it, then add the mushrooms on top. Garnish the mushrooms with horseradish and serve warm.

SHRIMP STEW

PREPARATION TIME: 15 MINUTES
COOKING TIME: 1 HOUR
SERVES 4

12 tiger shrimp (prawns)
juice of 1 lime
4 garden eggs (African eggplants/
   aubergines), halved
2 corn cobs, each cut into 4 pieces
1 small cassava
1 tablespoon tomato paste (purée)
1 large white onion, roughly
   chopped
2 cloves garlic
1 green bell pepper, deseeded
   and chopped
1 bay leaf
1 teaspoon minced fresh ginger
1 teaspoon allspice
4 large tomatoes, chopped
1 fresh green chili or jalapeño
2 tablespoons palm oil
salt, to taste

The smell of this dish marked my childhood, its incredible flavors filling our house as it was being cooked. It brings back many fond memories, especially since it was a meal that was served for festive occasions. Even my parents have stories of eating the dish during the holiday season in Togo when they were growing up. Back then, the dish was vegetarian; now it is common to see this stew made with shrimp (prawns) or other fish and meat.

Prepare the shrimp (prawns) by removing and setting aside the heads and shells, then set the shrimp aside in the lime juice. Place the garden eggs (African eggplants/aubergines) and corn pieces in a bowl, cover with water and set aside. Peel the cassava, then cut it into thick slices and place in a bowl of cold water to prevent it from oxidizing.

Combine the tomato paste, onion, garlic, bell pepper, spices, and salt in a blender. Add the tomatoes and blend until they form a purée.

Heat a medium, stovetop-safe casserole (or Dutch oven), pour in the palm oil, then add the shrimp carcasses and heads. Stir and gently crush the carcasses and heads for 1–2 minutes, keeping them intact. Pour in 2 cups (16 fl oz/475 ml) of water and stir to loosen the bits at the bottom of the pan. Pour in the purée, bring to a boil, then reduce the heat, add the whole green chili, and simmer for 20 minutes.

Remove and discard the carcasses and heads, then add the cassava and corn and cook for 15 minutes on high heat. Add the eggplants and shrimp. Reduce the heat to the lowest setting. Add salt and simmer for 20 minutes while stirring occasionally, until the sauce has thickened and the vegetables and shrimp are well coated.

Serve on deep plates. First place the vegetables and cassava on the plate, then arrange 3 shrimp on top, and finish with the sauce.

SCALLOPS WITH HIBISCUS SAUCE

AGNESS COLLEY

PREPARATION TIME: 30 MINUTES
COOKING TIME: 15 MINUTES
SERVES 4

1 tablespoon dried hibiscus flowers
2 tablespoons canola oil
1 green plantain, peeled and thinly
  sliced lengthwise
2 teaspoons (¼ oz/10 g) butter
1 clove garlic, lightly crushed
  but whole
2 slices back bacon, cut into
  16 pieces about 1½ inches
  (4 cm) long
12 sea scallops
½ glass (4 fl oz/120 ml) wine
salt and pepper, to taste
3 branches microgreens, to garnish

My family is very fond of scallops. While they can be found in markets along ports in Togo or Senegal, they are not used widely in West African cuisine. I cooked scallops for the first time in 2017 and this recipe was born in 2018. The hibiscus, which is a familiar ingredient across West Africa, helps with the acidity of the wine. Bringing the hibiscus and wine together in this dish is perfect for the scallops.

Bring 2 cups (16 fl oz/475 ml) of water to a boil, then add the hibiscus flowers. Turn off the heat, then cover and let infuse for 15 minutes. Pass the infusion through a strainer and keep the juice.

Heat the oil in a small stock pot on medium heat to 340°F/170°C. Add the plantain slices and fry for 3–5 minutes until browned. Then remove the plantain with a slotted spoon, drain excess oil on paper towels, and season with salt.

In a medium pan on medium heat, add the butter, garlic, bacon, and the scallops. Sear the scallops for 2 minutes on each side, or until cooked through. Remove the bacon and scallops (but leave the garlic clove) and set aside to cool to room temperature. Pour the wine and hibiscus infusion into the pan to deglaze. Cook over medium heat for 5 minutes until reduced and thickened. Add salt and pepper to taste.

Pour the hibiscus reduction onto a plate. Then place the scallops and bacon on top. Roll up the plantain slices and place around the plate. Season with salt, garnish with a few microgreens, and serve.

COCOYAM POTTAGE

PREPARATION TIME: 20 MINUTES
COOKING TIME: 25 MINUTES
SERVES 4

1 lb 2 oz (500 g) cocoyam
2 tablespoons salt
4 plum tomatoes
1 large onion
1 small piece fresh root ginger
1 large red bell pepper, deseeded
2 cloves garlic
3 yellow scotch bonnet peppers, deseeded
2 sprigs basil
1 sprig rosemary
1 sprig thyme
½ cup (4 fl oz/120 ml) palm oil
¼ tablespoon ground calabash nutmeg
2 tablespoons shrimp or crayfish powder
14 oz (400 g) smoked mackerel, deboned and broken into pieces
chives, finely chopped, to garnish

As the last-born child in a Ghanaian household, I often assisted my mom in the kitchen. I was in the kitchen with her so much that I became an expert on her cooking techniques. I loved when she made cocoyam (also known as taro) pottage or *mpotompoto,* a flavorful and aromatic one-pot dish. She would cut and boil the cocoyam, along with the tomatoes, onions, and ginger, but then take out the tomato mixture to blend it separately. Finally, once the cocoyam was cooked, she would pour the tomato purée on top. As she cooked, I asked her why she used each ingredient. One morning, I insisted on cooking the dish myself so she could have a break. As I prepared the ingredients, I asked her questions at each step, especially about the quantities, since she always eyeballed the measurements. She stood next to me and instructed me on when to add ingredients, stir, and taste. Thanks to her directions, the dish was a success! I was thrilled to have the chance to serve my pottage to the whole family, and to see how everyone enjoyed it.

Peel the cocoyam, rinse, and place in a large pot, then add a pinch of the salt and about 2 cups (16 fl oz/475 ml) of water, and bring to a boil. Add the tomatoes, onion, ginger, bell pepper, garlic, and scotch bonnet peppers and cook for 10 minutes.

When the tomatoes have softened, take out the tomatoes, onion, ginger, garlic, and peppers. Put them all into a blender with 1 sprig of basil, the rosemary and thyme, and purée until smooth.

Check on the cocoyam. You will know it's cooked by pricking it with a fork to test if it's softened. Pour in the puréed mix and simmer for about 5 minutes. Pour in the palm oil, then add the calabash nutmeg, shrimp or crayfish powder, and smoked mackerel. Stir in and simmer for another 5 minutes. Add the remaining salt and basil. Simmer for 2 minutes, then take off the heat. Pour into individual soup bowls and garnish with some chopped chives just before serving.

BASIL CASHEW PESTO
WITH HIBISCUS PICKLED ONIONS
AND TWICE-FRIED PLANTAINS

IKENNA AKWUEBUE
BOBMANUEL

PREPARATION TIME: 30 MINUTES,
  PLUS 3 HOURS PICKLING
COOKING TIME: 15 MINUTES
SERVES 2

FOR THE BASIL CASHEW PESTO
2 cups (1½ oz/40 g) packed basil
  (ideally African)
⅓ cup (1½ oz/45 g) raw cashews
4 tablespoons lemon juice
6 cloves garlic
½ teaspoon kosher salt,
  or to taste
3 teaspoons ground fennel
honey, to taste
¼ cup (2 fl oz/60 ml) olive oil
black pepper, to taste

FOR THE HIBISCUS PICKLED ONIONS
1 large red onion, thinly sliced
¼ cup (2 fl oz/60 ml) apple cider
  vinegar
¼ cup (1¾ oz/50 g) granulated sugar
2 teaspoons salt
½ tablespoon cloves, toasted
¼ cup (¼ oz/10 g) dried hibiscus
  flowers

FOR THE PLANTAINS
1 green plantain (slightly ripe)
canola (rapeseed) or other oil of
  your choice, for deep-frying
salt, to taste

I like using local ingredients in my dishes, and this recipe is no exception. The idea for it came to me as I was making a staple Ghanaian dish called *kontomire abom*, which is made with cocoyam leaves. It was during the process of using the mortar and pestle to grind some of the ingredients that I considered creating a pesto with African basil, or *akokomesa* as we call it in Ghana. This wild basil has a lemony flavor and stands out in the pesto.

If you do not have African basil available, other types of basil will do. But, be assured, the African basil is worth finding for this dish.

For the basil cashew pesto, add the basil, cashews, lemon juice, garlic, salt, fennel, honey, and pepper to a food processor, and blend until a paste starts to form. Make sure there are still some bits of cashew chunks.

While the food processor is running, slowly drizzle in the olive oil until the ingredients are well combined. Scrape down the sides as you go, if necessary. Adjust seasoning and consistency, if desired. Store in a sealed container in the refrigerator and use within 1 week.

For the hibiscus pickled onions, put the thinly sliced onion in a large bowl and set aside. Put ¼ cup (2 fl oz/60 ml) of water with the vinegar, sugar, salt, cloves, and hibiscus flowers in a saucepan and bring to a boil. Remove from the heat, then carefully strain over the onions. Let steep and cool for 1 hour. Once cool, place in a sterilized jar, cover, and place in the refrigerator to chill for 2 hours. Store in the refrigerator for up to 2 weeks.

Cut the stems off the ends of the plantains and carefully slice down the skin. Using a spoon or your finger, peel the plantain from its skin and cut into 1-inch (2.5-cm) round slices.

Fill a cast-iron skillet, Dutch oven, or casserole, with frying oil about ½ inch (1 cm) deep. Heat the oil on medium-high until it is hot and shimmering, then place the plantain slices flat-side down and fry for 3–4 minutes until golden. Flip and repeat on the other side. Remove from the oil and reduce the heat to low.

Using a plate or another flat item wrapped with plastic wrap (cling film), carefully press the plantain slices until flattened. Once you have pressed all the plantains, bring the heat back up to medium–high. Add the pressed plantains back into the oil and cook for 1 minute on each side until crisp. Remove from the oil and place on a plate lined with paper towels to drain the excess. Sprinkle salt on top.

Serve the plantains with the pickled onions and basil pesto.

BUTTERED BAMBARA WITH VEGETABLES, RODO OIL, AND TOASTED EGUSI RELISH

IKENNA AKWUEBUE
BOBMANUEL

PREPARATION TIME: 30 MINUTES
COOKING TIME: 45 MINUTES
SERVES 2

FOR THE BUTTERED BAMBARA
4 tablespoons canola (rapeseed) oil
1½ red or white onions
1 sprig thyme
2 bay leaves
½ garlic bulb, peeled
2 teaspoons ground turmeric
1 teaspoon ground cumin
1½ cups dry white wine
½ cup (4 oz/115 g) bambara beans,
  cooked
1½ tablespoons lemon juice
½ bouillon (stock) cube (optional)
salt and pepper, to taste

FOR THE ROASTED VEGETABLES
2 small beets (beetroot), peeled
  and quartered
2 baby carrots, blanched and
  quartered
½ cup (2¾ oz/75 g) cauliflower
  florets
2 tablespoons melted ghee
1 sprig thyme

FOR THE TOASTED EGUSI RELISH
1 tablespoon canola (rapeseed) oil
4 cloves garlic, thinly sliced
¼ cup (1 oz/30 g) egusi seeds,
  toasted
handful cilantro (coriander),
  chopped
½ tablespoon shrimp powder
lemon zest, to taste, plus
  1 tablespoon lemon juice
3 teaspoons cayenne pepper

RODO OIL
2 star anise
1 teaspoon cloves
5 atarodo or scotch bonnet peppers
6 cloves garlic
½ cup (4 fl oz/120 ml) palm oil

My introduction to bambara beans took place at the bustling Nima market in Accra, Ghana, where a plethora of local ingredients dazzled my senses. Upon discovering their creamy texture, akin to chickpeas, I excitedly dubbed them "West African chickpeas," sparking my enduring fascination with incorporating bambara beans into my culinary creations. From crafting hummus to using them as a sauce thickener or in vegan patties, these versatile beans have become a staple in my kitchen.

In this recipe, I showcase the versatility of bambara beans by preparing buttered bambara with vegetables, a dish known as *ewa agonyi* in Yoruba culture and *gobe* among Ghanaians. The beans' creamy consistency, complemented by the vibrant hue and fragrance of turmeric, combined with the irresistible flavor of white wine, creates a delightful dish.

Cultivated in West Africa, bambara beans are small, hard, spherical seeds similar in size to chickpeas. Like peanuts, they mature underground, exhibiting a range of colors from black, dark brown, and red, to white and cream, or a blend of these hues. Their nutty, earthy flavor is a cross between chickpeas and pinto beans.

For the buttered bambara, heat the oil in a medium sauté pan on medium heat. Add the onions and sauté for 4 minutes until translucent. Add the fresh thyme, bay leaves, garlic, turmeric, and cumin. Sauté for another 3 minutes to activate their flavors. Add the white wine to deglaze and cook down for 3–5 minutes. Add the cooked bambara and some water, if needed, and simmer for 10–12 minutes. Season with salt and pepper (and a squeeze of lemon or the bouillon stock cube). Purée until smooth, then set aside.

Preheat the oven to 300°F/150°C/Gas Mark 2.

For the roasted vegetables, place the vegetables in a roasting pan, then drizzle the melted ghee on the vegetables, add the thyme, and season with salt and pepper, to taste. Roast in the oven for 8–10 minutes until slightly charred.

Meanwhile, for the toasted egusi relish, in a small sauté pan on medium–low heat, add the oil. Add the garlic and sauté for 3 minutes until aromatic. Add the toasted egusi seeds and cilantro (coriander), stir, and cook for about 2–3 minutes. Add the shrimp powder, lemon zest, lemon juice and salt and pepper to taste.

For the rodo oil, heat a pan on medium heat. Add the star anise and cloves and dry-toast for 4–5 minutes until fragrant. Slightly smash the peppers and garlic using the side of your knife with a gentle hit. Add all the ingredients to a small saucepan and cook on very low heat for 20–30 minutes to confit. Let cool, then store in a container.

To plate, place a circle of the bambara purée on the bottom with the vegetables stacked on top to create height. Add the egusi relish on top of the veggies and drizzle with the rodo oil (or drizzle the oil around the spherical base of bambara purée).

TOMATO STONE FRUIT SALAD WITH JOLLOF VINAIGRETTE

NANA ARABA WILMOT

PREPARATION TIME: 15 MINUTES
COOKING TIME: 5 MINUTES
SERVES 4-6

2 plum tomatoes
2-3 stone fruit (plums, mangoes, peaches, or nectarines)
2 tablespoons curry powder
1 shallot, thinly sliced into rings
1 tablespoon dried rosemary
1 teaspoon garlic (powder or grated fresh)
pinch of salt
2 cups (16 fl oz/475 ml) olive oil
1 bunch tarragon, leaves picked

FOR THE BLOODY MARY MIX
2 cups (16 fl oz/475 ml) tomato juice
½ cup horseradish
¼ oz (40 ml) lemon juice
2 teaspoons Worcestershire sauce
2 teaspoons Tabasco
1 teaspoon salt
1 teaspoon ground black pepper

When I was invited to create a menu for an Afro–Parisian brunch party, I sought to make something unique yet familiar. I wanted the essence of jollof rice, the famous West African tomato-based dish, without actually having it on the brunch menu. Drawing on this inspiration, I began to deconstruct the flavor profile of my jollof recipe—curry, tomato, and rosemary—to make the vinaigrette. Paired with the tomato stone fruit salad, this recipe was a hit at the party and will be unforgettable at yours.

Cut the tomatoes and the flesh of the stone fruits evenly into medium dice for maximum spoonful satisfaction, then place in a bowl. Set aside and refrigerate.

In a medium mixing bowl, combine the Bloody Mary ingredients.

In a small saucepan, dry-toast the curry powder on low–medium heat for about 2 minutes, stirring constantly: toasting will allow the curry powder flavor to open up and be fragrant so the spice can shine through this cold dish. Take off the heat and allow it to cool.

In a small mixing bowl, add the shallot, curry powder, rosemary, garlic, and salt. Slowly pour in the olive oil, incorporating with a whisk. Add the Bloody Mary mix. The vinaigrette should have a light curry tomato taste that won't overpower the fruits, but rather enhance it. Mix the vinaigrette with the cut fruits and serve in a big bowl. Garnish the salad with fresh tarragon and serve chilled.

GHANA SALAD

NANA ARABA WILMOT

PREPARATION TIME: 20 MINUTES
COOKING TIME: 5 MINUTES
SERVES 4-6

1 × 14¾-oz (418-g) can red salmon
½ red onion, thinly sliced
¼ cup (2 fl oz/60 ml) red wine
  vinegar
8 hard-boiled eggs
1½ cups (8 oz/225 g) frozen peas
  and carrots
5 cups (9 oz/250 g) spinach,
  roughly chopped
1 head Cos or romaine lettuce,
  roughly chopped
1 head iceberg lettuce, roughly
  chopped
2 plum tomatoes, thinly sliced,
  then each slice quartered

FOR THE DRESSING
1 cup (8 fl oz/240 ml) mayonnaise
½ × 12-oz (350-g) can evaporated
  milk
¼ cup (2 oz/60 ml) white vinegar
salt, to taste

My mother's Ghana salad was basically a celebrity in our community. It made a memorable appearance at every party. Friends of our family would ask my mom to make them special batches for their parties, and with the help of my grandmother, she would labor in the kitchen to make sure the salad was ready. My job was limited to watching them, and occasionally sneaking an egg out of the beautifully layered ingredients to secretly enjoy. Now, as I make it myself, the love and memories of that time guide my fingers as I meticulously layer each ingredient with pride.

This recipe will make you the Ghana salad queen of your community, just like my mom.

Drain the canned salmon and debone; the salmon should be mixed up, not mashed. Place the red onions in a bowl with the red wine vinegar to soak. Peel the hard-boiled eggs and slice them into rings. Set aside.

Bring a half-filled pan of water to a boil. Set a colander over the top, ensuring it doesn't touch the water. Add the frozen peas and carrots and steam for 2–3 minutes.

To make the dressing, place the mayonnaise in a bowl and slowly add the evaporated milk to thin it out. The consistency should be runny but still coat the back of the spoon. Add the white wine vinegar, a little at a time, and finish with salt to taste. Set aside.

In a large bowl, begin to layer each ingredient one at a time—starting with half the spinach, Cos, and iceberg. Add half the peas and carrots, followed by a layer of half the red onions and tomatoes. Top with half the salmon, eggs, and then the dressing. Repeat, so you can make 2 layers of each item. Take to the table so your guests can see the layers, and mix as you serve.

FONIO SALAD WITH PASSION FRUIT VINAIGRETTE

IKENNA AKWUEBUE
BOBMANUEL

PREPARATION TIME: 20 MINUTES
COOKING TIME: 30 MINUTES
SERVES 6

FOR THE PASSION FRUIT VINAIGRETTE
½ cup (4 oz/115 g) passion
   fruit pulp
1 tablespoon honey
½ cup (4 fl oz/120 ml) olive oil
zest of 1 lemon and juice of ¼
salt, to taste

FOR THE FONIO
pinch of salt
1 cup (6 oz/180 g) fonio grains
12 cherry tomatoes, halved
½ cup (2½ oz/70 g) cashew nuts,
   crushed
2 small radishes, sliced on
   a mandoline
scant 1 cup (1¾ oz/50 g)
   chopped mint
3½ oz (100 g) mixed greens
   (salad leaves)
¼ cup (1¼ oz/35 g) raisins or ¼ cup
   (¾ oz/20 g) chopped dates
pomegranate seeds, to garnish

Embark on a culinary journey with me as I recount my first encounter with fonio, a treasured grain native to the heartlands of West Africa. In northern Ghana, the resilient farmers of Chereponi toiled under the sun, nurturing the very essence of this nutritious gem. Their quest for recognition led them to the bustling streets of Accra, Ghana's vibrant capital, seeking a culinary maestro to weave fonio's magic into the fabric of urban cuisine. I was ready to embrace the challenge and elevate fonio from humble grain to culinary masterpiece, and together we embarked on a gastronomic adventure, experimenting with flavors and textures, from fluffy pancakes to comforting porridges and vibrant salads. Thus, the Chereponi fonio salad was born—a tribute to the farmers who bestowed upon us this gift of nature and the bond forged through our culinary exploration. Join me in celebrating the essence of fonio, honoring its origins, and savoring the harmony of flavors in every mouthful of this exquisite salad.

Combine all the vinaigrette ingredients except the lemon zest in a blender or food processor. Blend until smooth and emulsified. Taste for seasoning and add more salt and pepper if needed. Add the lemon zest. Use right away or refrigerate in a lidded glass jar.

Using a bao steamer lined with a straining cloth, bring 1½ cups (12 fl oz/350 ml) of water to a boil with the pinch of salt. Stir in the fonio, cover with the cloth and lid, and steam, stirring occasionally, until soft, about 25–30 minutes. Set aside to cool.

In a mixing bowl, combine the steamed fonio with the rest of the ingredients (tomatoes, cashew nuts, radish, mint, mixed salad greens/leaves, and raisins or dates). Garnish with the pomegranate and serve with the passion fruit dressing alongside.

BEAN FRITTERS

PREPARATION TIME: 20 MINUTES
COOKING TIME: 10 MINUTES
SERVES 8-10

1 cup (5¾ oz/165 g) dried black-
  eyed peas (beans), rinsed
3 habanero peppers
½ red onion, peeled
½ teaspoon salt, or to taste
1 bouillon (stock) cube (optional)
4¼ cups (34 fl oz/1 liter) vegetable
  oil, for deep-frying

Bean fritters are street food that I enjoyed as a child. They are usually sold in the mornings or evenings in Nigeria. While they are quick to make, we ordered them when my mom was too tired to cook the dish. Locally, the dish is called *akara* and commonly eaten for breakfast or as a snack. It is very popular and a part of most Nigerians' childhood. It can be eaten with cornmeal (maize meal) polenta (also known as *pap*, *sadza*, and *ugali*), bread, oats, or custard.

Put the black-eyed peas (beans) into a blender or food processor, adding enough water to cover the beans. Pulse for 3 seconds, taking breaks until the skin comes off the beans. Pour into a colander and separate the skin from the beans, then rinse with water until clean. Set aside.

Put the cleaned beans, peppers, and onion into the cleaned blender, then add ¾ cup (6 fl oz/175 ml) of water and blend until silky smooth. Add the salt and the bouillon (stock) cube, if using, and blend some more until it mixes in thoroughly.

Transfer the batter into a bowl and whisk with electric beaters, or use a stand mixer, until the batter doubles in size and looks like ice cream.

Heat the oil in a wok on medium heat until 400°F/200°C. Do not let the oil get too hot, as it can burn the bean fritters. Using an ice cream scoop, add dollops of the whisked batter into the oil, creating round balls of akara. Cook for 3–5 minutes on both sides until golden brown. You may need to do this in batches. Drain on paper towels in a colander. Serve hot.

FATAYA WITH
KANI SAUCE

PREPARATION TIME: 30 MINUTES,
  PLUS 2 HOURS RESTING
COOKING TIME: 35–40 MINUTES
MAKES 15–20

FOR THE PASTRY
3½ cups (1 lb 2 oz/500 g)
  all-purpose (plain) flour,
  plus extra for rolling
1 teaspoon kosher salt
½ cup (3¾ oz/110 g) unsalted
  butter, melted
⅓ cup (2¾ oz/80 g) egg yolks

FOR THE FILLING
½ cup (4 fl oz/125 ml) corn oil
4½ cups (1 lb 2 oz/500 g) ground
  (minced) beef
1 cup (7 oz/200 g) finely diced
  white onions
1 oz (30 g) finely chopped garlic
⅓ cup (2½ oz/70 g) tomato paste
  (purée)
2½ teaspoons white vinegar
2½ teaspoons liquid seasoning
  (I use Maggi)
½ teaspoon kosher salt
pepper

FOR THE KANI SAUCE
2 tablespoons corn oil
3 cups (1 lb 9 oz/700 g) finely
  diced white onions
¾ oz (20 g) finely chopped garlic
⅓ cup (1½ oz/40 g) tomato paste
  (purée)
2½ teaspoons white vinegar
4 teaspoons chili powder
½ tablespoon granulated sugar
1½ teaspoons kosher salt
1 teaspoon black pepper
2 teaspoons liquid seasoning
  (I use Maggi)
1 Scotch bonnet pepper, finely diced

Fataya, a deep-fried Senegalese pastry, is one of my favorites. Not only is it delicious, but it's always present at celebrations in Senegal, from weddings to baby naming ceremonies; it's a dish that loves a party. I love seeing it sold on street corners, where people stop by vendors to grab it as a snack. In restaurants, a *fataya* may show up as an appetizer.

Traditionally, *fataya* is made with tuna or sardines, which are available in Senegal's many markets. It can also be made with chicken or beef. It's often paired with kani sauce—a spicy chili sauce—which can be enjoyed by splitting open the *fataya* and spreading the sauce in the middle or simply drizzling it on top.

Combine all the pastry ingredients with 1 cup (8 fl oz/240 ml) of water in the bowl of a stand mixer fitted with a dough hook and mix until well combined. Cover with plastic wrap (cling film) and let the dough rest at room temperature for 1 hour until doubled in volume.

Roll out the dough on a floured surface to your desired thickness— for a chewier texture, roll it a little thicker; for a crispier texture, roll it thinner—then cut, using a large cookie cutter, into circles. Transfer the cut dough to a baking sheet and let rest in the refrigerator for at least 1 hour.

For the filling, heat the oil in a medium-size pot on medium heat. Add the ground (minced) beef, onions, and garlic, and cook for 10 minutes until fragrant and the beef is cooked. Stir in the tomato paste (purée), vinegar, and liquid seasoning and mix well. Simmer until the sauce is thick. Adjust taste with salt and pepper if needed. Let cool down completely before using.

For the kani sauce, gently heat the oil, then add the onions and garlic, and cook until fragrant. Add in the tomato paste, stir well, and cook for 10 minutes until caramelized. Add in the vinegar, chili powder, sugar, salt, black pepper, liquid seasoning, and scotch bonnet, and cook until reduced. Taste and adjust seasoning.

To assemble, place some beef filling in the middle of a fataya dough circle. Lightly brush with a little egg wash and seal the edges. They can now be frozen or fried right away.

To deep-fry, heat a pot of neutral oil to 350°F/180°C. Add the fataya and cook on each side until golden brown, about 5–6 minutes. Serve with the sauce alongside or on top.

FRIED YAM WITH
NIGERIAN TOMATO SAUCE

PREPARATION TIME: 20 MINUTES
COOKING TIME: 25 MINUTES
SERVES 2-4

1 tuber yam, or 4 smaller yams
½ teaspoon salt
oil, for deep-frying

FOR THE NIGERIAN TOMATO SAUCE
¼ cup (2 fl oz/60 ml) vegetable oil
4 tomatoes, diced
2 habanero peppers, minced
1 red onion, diced
½ teaspoon curry powder
¼ teaspoon dried thyme
1 bouillon (stock) cube (optional)
salt, to taste

Fried yam is a dish that I enjoyed so much when I was young that I could not even wait until my mom was done cooking to start indulging. Whenever my mom was cooking the dish, I would sneak into the kitchen and quietly take some without her noticing. Then, I would run into our shared children's bedroom, climb to the top of the bunk beds, and feast on the dish in absolute privacy, away from my siblings who had noses like hound dogs.

Locally called *dundun*, the dish gets its name from the Yoruba tribe of western Nigeria. It is made with the puna yam, a tuberous root vegetable. It is eaten for breakfast or dinner in most homes and commonly sold as street food. This recipe is a slightly tweaked version of the traditional recipe.

The tomato sauce is an age-old recipe engrained in Nigerian culture. It greeted me at birth and continues to be a part of my daily life. Most Nigerian families have different recipes for the dish. It can be made from smoothly ground tomato mixes, chopped tomatoes, or even squashed tomatoes. It is an accompaniment for rice, beans, bread, yam, potatoes, and plantain dishes, and can be enjoyed with my *dodo* frittata (Plantain Frittata, page 216) and here with fried yams.

Note that a ½ teaspoon of curry powder and ¼ teaspoon of dried thyme can be added when cooking the yam before frying, to change the taste profile. The flavor profile is spicy but not hot.

Cut the yams into 2-inch (5-cm) thick circles, approximately 4 pieces per yam. Peel off the skin. Rinse and place in a pot with enough water to cover them. Add the salt, bring to a boil, and cook for 15–20 minutes until a toothpick (or cocktail stick) passes through.

Meanwhile, for the tomato sauce, heat the oil in a medium-size pan. Add the tomatoes, habanero peppers, and onion, and cook on medium heat for 3–5 minutes. Add the curry powder, thyme, bouillon (stock) cube, and salt, to taste, and cook for 5 minutes, or more, if needed, until softened and wilted.

Fill a wok 3 inches (7.5 cm) deep with the oil and place on medium heat. Remove the yams from the water in the pot and let them drain. Then place them in the hot oil and fry for 3 minutes, turning on both sides. Drain in a paper towel-lined colander. Serve hot with the tomato sauce.

MILLET CRINKLE SCONES

JOSEPH ODOOM

PREPARATION TIME: 10 MINUTES
COOKING TIME: 20 MINUTES
SERVES 12

1½ cups (8 oz/225 g) millet flour
1½ cups (8 oz/225 g) cake flour,
  plus extra for dusting
5 teaspoons baking powder
1 teaspoon ground cinnamon
½ teaspoon cayenne pepper
1 teaspoon allspice
pinch of salt
generous 1 cup (3½ oz/100 g)
  shredded (desiccated) coconut
scant ½ cup (2¾ oz/80 g) superfine
  (caster) sugar
7 tablespoons (3½ oz/100 g)
  unsalted butter
2 eggs, whisked with ⅓ cup
  (2½ fl oz/80 ml) milk
confectioners' (icing) sugar,
  for dusting
berry compote, to serve

Scones are the first pastries I learned to make in the kitchen. Yet I came up with this recipe by happenstance, as I was in the process of making *hausa koko,* a West African millet-based breakfast porridge. Not wanting to waste the leftover chaff of millet strained to make the *hausa koko,* I thought I'd try making scones with it. Though my chef colleagues were skeptical about the idea, I didn't let that deter me. In fact, they were pleasantly surprised to see that it worked. Whenever I make and serve this dish, people are amazed that it is made with millet chaff and are always curious about the recipe.

Preheat the oven to 350°F/180°C/Gas Mark 4. Line a baking pan (tray) with parchment (baking) paper or grease the baking pan with nonstick spray.

Sift all the dry ingredients, except the coconut and sugar into a mixing bowl. Add the coconut and sugar and mix together. This can be done with your hands or with a stand mixer using the paddle attachment. If using your hands, rub the butter into the dry ingredients, making sure to use your fingertips to allow aeration. Rub until a sandy or crumbly texture is formed. If using a stand mixer, mix at slow speed until you reach the texture described.

Make a well in the center of the dry ingredients and add in the whisked eggs and milk. Gently mix until a nice, unified dough ball has formed.

On a floured surface, roll out the dough to a ¾-inch (2-cm) thickness. Using a round cutter dusted with flour, cut out the scones. Repeat until all the dough has been cut out.

Arrange on the baking pan and dust a generous amount of confectioners' (icing) sugar on each scone. Place in the oven and reduce the temperature to 325°F/160°C/Gas Mark 3. Bake for 20 minutes, or until a skewer comes out clean when inserted in the middle of the scones. Let cool and serve with a berry compote of your choice.

GHANAIAN DARK CHOCOLATE PUDDING

IKENNA AKWUEBUE
BOBMANUEL

PREPARATION TIME: 45 MINUTES,
  PLUS OVERNIGHT SOAKING AND
  CHILLING
COOKING TIME: 20-25 MINUTES
SERVES 4

FOR THE CHOCOLATE PUDDING
2 prekese (substitute with cardamom,
  if necessary)
1½ tablespoons cloves, toasted
2 cups (16 fl oz/475 ml) whole
  (full-fat) milk
½ cup (4 oz/115 g) honey
  (for more sweetness increase
  the measurement)
½ cup (2 oz/55 g) unsweetened
  cocoa powder
3 tablespoons cornstarch (cornflour)
¼ teaspoon salt
2 large egg yolks, beaten
1½ tablespoons (¾ oz/20 g) unsalted
  butter
¼ cup semisweet (dark) chocolate,
  melted
2 teaspoons vanilla extract

FOR THE BAOBAB CHANTILLY
1 cup (8 fl oz/250 ml) cold heavy
  (whipping) cream
½ tablespoon vanilla extract
2 tablespoons lemon juice
¼ cup baobab powder
4 tablespoons granulated sugar

FOR THE MAIZE CRUMBLE
½ cup (2 oz/55 g) fine cornmeal
  (maize meal), sieved
¼ cup (2 oz/55 g) granulated or
  brown sugar (I like to do half
  and half)
½ teaspoon ground cinnamon
  (optional)
4-6 tablespoons (2-3 oz/60-85 g)
  salted butter, melted
salt, to taste
cocoa nibs, finely crushed,
  to garnish

You can't live in Ghana without somehow engaging with chocolate. As one of the country's main resources, it's literally everywhere. When the opportunity came to visit a cocoa farm, I couldn't pass it up. Finally, I was going to see the soil that birthed the plant that gives us chocolate. At the farm, I saw the journey of the cocoa plant from seed to chocolate. I also saw innovative ways the plant could be used for products beyond food, sparking my imagination about food and sustainability. As you make this chocolate pudding, I hope you indulge delightfully and let it transport you to the soil it comes from.

This recipe includes *prekese*, a woody, angular pod plant native to Western and Central Africa that releases a sugary-sweet aroma and taste.

For the chocolate pudding, activate the prekese by scoring the soft edges and slightly charring for 5 minutes over the flame of a stove. Cut into respective halves (I call this method "prekesify").

In a bowl, combine the toasted cloves, charred prekese, and milk. Cover with plastic wrap (cling film) and refrigerate overnight to allow the spices to infuse the milk. Then strain and set aside.

In a medium saucepan, whisk together the honey, cocoa powder, cornstarch (cornflour), salt, and egg yolks until well blended. Whisk in the infused milk and place on medium heat, stirring often, for about 5–8 minutes. Once the mixture starts to bubble, turn the heat down to low and continue cooking, whisking often, for about 1–2 minutes until thickened.

Prepare a bowl of ice water. Remove the pan from the heat and immediately whisk in the butter, melted chocolate, and vanilla. Stir until smooth. Temper the chocolate pudding by placing it in an ice bath. Note that the pudding will be pourable, but it will continue to thicken as it cools.

For the baobab chantilly, pour the heavy (whipping) cream, vanilla, lemon juice, baobab powder, and sugar into a medium bowl. Using the whisk attachment of a stand mixer, whip the ingredients together on medium speed for 2–3 minutes until a soft peak forms. Cover with plastic wrap and refrigerate.

For the maize crumble, in a medium bowl, combine the sieved cornmeal (maize meal) and sugar. Add the cinnamon, if desired. Slowly drizzle the butter into the bowl while stirring the crumbs with a fork. I like to start with 3–4 tablespoons and add more as needed until the crumbs form. Season with salt to taste. Do not overmix (you do not want this to become like dough).

On medium heat, pan-bake the crumble using a nonstick pan for 5–10 minutes until nice and golden. Set aside to cool; it becomes crunchy when cool.

Pour the chocolate pudding into ramekins and allow to set in the refrigerator. Top with the maize crumble and a beautiful quenelle of baobab chantilly, then finish with some crushed cocoa nibs.

CONGO
BROWNIE

PREPARATION TIME: 20 MINUTES
COOKING TIME: 30-40 MINUTES
MAKES 8-10

2½ cups (1 lb 2 oz/520 g) butter,
   at room temperature
3 cups (1 lb 5 oz/600 g) granulated
   sugar
1 lb 2 oz (520 g) whole shelled
   eggs
1¼ cups (7 oz/200 g) all-purpose
   (plain) flour
2 teaspoons (¼ oz/10 g)
   baking powder
14 oz (400 g) semisweet (dark)
   chocolate, chopped
3½ cups (10½ oz/300 g) sweetened
   shredded (desiccated) coconut

This brownie is my ode to Africa. I created this recipe for the menu at Alkebulan, the African Dining Hall, for Dubai's 2020 World Expo. With ingredients directly sourced from Africa, including chocolate from the mountains of Ghana and coconut from Côte d'Ivoire, this dessert shines with rich flavors. I love making this dish as a gift to serve my friends and family.

Preheat the oven to 350°F/180°C/Gas Mark 4. Line an 8 × 8-inch (20 × 20-cm) baking pan with parchment (baking) paper.
   In a stand mixer fitted with the paddle attachment, cream together the butter and sugar until light and fluffy. Add the eggs, a quarter at a time, mixing until combined between each addition. Add in the dry ingredients (flour, baking powder, chocolate, and coconut) and mix just until combined.
   Place in the lined baking pan and bake in the oven for 30–40 minutes or until a toothpick (or cocktail stick) comes out clean.
   Let cool before cutting into squares.

BISSAP

PREPARATION TIME: 10 MINUTES
COOKING TIME: 35 MINUTES
SERVES: 10-12

2 cups (2¾ oz/80 g) dried
  hibiscus flowers
1½ tablespoons (¾ oz/20 g)
  chopped fresh root ginger
1¾ cups (14 oz/400 ml)
  pineapple juice
3 cups (1 lb 5 oz/600 g) granulated
  sugar
2 teaspoons rose water

There are a variety of ways to make bissap in Senegal. Everyone makes this hibiscus drink their own way. I wasn't a fan of it growing up, though my aunt would make it often. My mom would make it with rose water, while my aunt would add pineapple and ginger. This recipe combines both of their recipes. Today, I like it topped up with a little sparkling water.

In a large pot, add 5 cups (40 fl oz/1.2 liters) of water, the hibiscus, and the ginger. Bring to a boil, then reduce the heat, and let simmer for 20 minutes.

Add the pineapple juice and sugar and continue to cook until the sugar is completely dissolved, about 10 minutes. Remove from the heat and let cool slightly.

Prepare a bowl of iced water. Strain the liquid into a separate bowl and place the bowl in the ice bath to cool down completely. Once cool, add the rose water. Pour over ice and serve.

HIBISCUS DRINK

PREPARATION TIME: 15 MINUTES,
  PLUS 1 HOUR CHILLING
SERVES 4

2 limes
1 Gala apple
1¼ cups (1¾ oz/50 g) dried
  hibiscus flowers, rinsed
10 mint leaves
2 teaspoons ground cinnamon
1½ tablespoons (¾ oz/20 g) honey
1 mint sprig, to garnish
slices of apple or lime, to garnish
  (optional)

My father has diabetes, so adapting recipes to adhere to his diet is truly lifesaving. I remember that one summer, I decided to make him this hibiscus drink, from the hibiscus flower, which our family enjoyed when I was growing up. My mother would infuse hibiscus in various thirst-quenching juices. She would make the infusion with the skin of various fruits and hibiscus, then add a small amount of sweetener and serve it hot. Adjusting this recipe for my dad, I replaced the refined sugar with fruit and honey, and it is still truly delicious.

Peel the limes and section the flesh. Then peel, core, and cut the apple. Put all the ingredients into a blender with 2½ cups (20 fl oz/ 600 ml) of water and process until smooth.

Pass the mixture through a fine-meshed sieve to recover only the juice. Put the juice in the refrigerator to chill for 1 hour prior to serving. Garnish with a mint sprig, and slices of apple or lime, if desired.

TAMARIND AND COFFEE MOCKTAIL

JOSEPH ODOOM

PREPARATION TIME: 15 MINUTES
COOKING TIME: 25 MINUTES
SERVES 4-6

FOR THE TAMARIND COMPOTE
generous 2 cups (9 oz/250 g)
   tamarind pulp
½ cup (3½ oz/100 g) superfine
   (caster) sugar
scant ½ cup (3½ oz/100 g)
   brown sugar
2 grains of Selim
3 lemongrass stalks

FOR THE SIMPLE SYRUP
1 cup (7 oz/200 g) sugar

FOR THE COCKTAIL
½ cup (3½ fl oz/110 ml) Tamarind
   Compote (see above)
⅔ cup (5 fl oz/150 ml) espresso
   coffee
3½ tablespoons (2 fl oz/50 ml)
   simple syrup
lemon rind and 1 star anise,
   to garnish

My journey with coffee started in 2018 when I started baking desserts like chocolate cake and brownies in Accra. I always loved putting coffee into the mix, as it enhances the chocolate flavor, making it more pronounced. In search of the right coffee blend to use, I chanced upon a dark roasted coffee with origins in South Africa, and a roast intensity of 9. I loved how it smelled every time I used it in my cake batter, and how floral yet nutty it was. I later found myself brewing it for myself. Since then, I've been a coffee lover, having a cup in the morning to keep me alert during service.

While playing around with flavors, I chanced on tamarind and paired it with my coffee out of curiosity. This recipe was born and I haven't looked back since. The tamarind adds a tangy and earthy note to the floral caramel of the coffee. Feel free to adjust the sugar quantity depending on how tangy or sour you want the compote to be. Note that the compote thickens as it cools down; it should be almost the consistency of pancake syrup or honey. To test for the desired thickness, scoop a little with a spoon, let cool, then check the consistency; once you're happy you can remove it from the heat.

To make the compote, place the tamarind pulp in a medium-size pan. Add 1 cup (8 fl oz/250 ml) of water, both sugars, the grains of Selim, and 2 of the lemongrass stalks. Over medium heat, bring to a boil, then reduce the heat, and let simmer for 5 minutes.

Pass through a sieve if you prefer a finer texture, and return the liquid to the pan. Add the last lemongrass stalk and return to medium heat for about 6–8 minutes until reduced and a syrup consistency is achieved. If you prefer a more concentrated or thicker compote, let it simmer for a few minutes longer until your desired thickness is achieved.

To make the simple syrup, in a pan, combine the sugar with ½ cup (4 fl oz/125 ml) of water and bring to a gentle simmer for about 5–8 minutes until thickened. Let cool, and use as desired.

To make the cocktail, in a shaker, combine all the liquids, and 5 ice cubes, and shake until uniformly mixed. Put some ice in flute glasses and pour in the mocktail mix. Garnish the edge of the flutes with some lemon rind and star anise.

GIN 'N' GINGA

NANA ARABA WILMOT

PREPARATION TIME: 5 MINUTES
SERVES 1

4 tablespoons (2 fl oz/60 ml) gin
1 tablespoon (½ fl oz/15 ml)
  sweetened lime juice
½ cup (4 fl oz/120 ml) ginger beer
1 slice of lime, to garnish
rosemary, to garnish (optional)

When I was young, my parents frequently entertained at our house. My dad took pride in his stereo system, setting the vibes with his collection of all the best Ghanaian music like Highlife and Hiplife, while my mom, grandma, and aunties satisfied our taste buds with Ghanaian flavors. At these parties, alcohol was always in stock, especially gin. It was served traditionally at outdoor events (baby naming ceremonies), weddings, and funerals. As I got older, I was introduced to the local fermented gin, palm wine, or *akpeteshie*—which is higher in alcohol content, produced by distilling palm wine, and can be considered a Ghanaian moonshine. I call this Gin 'n' Ginga, an ode to *akpeteshie*.

Fill a glass with ice. Pour the gin and lime juice over the ice. Top up with ginger beer, then add the lime and rosemary garnish, if using, and serve.

When entertaining, this can be batched (gin and lime juice mix only) in a pitcher (jug) ahead of time. Top with ginger beer and garnish when ready to serve.

MICHAEL ADÉ
ELÉGBÈDÉ

I hope that my work in Nigeria and abroad brings a greater understanding of who we are as West Africans. I aim for people to better grasp the indigenous spices, flavors, and techniques that shape our cuisines, understand their cultural significance, and how they've influenced food cultures across the diaspora. Cuisines across West Africa, as a result of migration, either forced or otherwise, have played an immense role in the way people around the world celebrate food. I hope that visibility of the undeniable thread that links us brings a long-overdue acknowledgment and celebration of West African food traditions in global culinary narratives.

ABOUT
THE CHEFS

●

Zein Abdallah was born and raised in Uganda, where he embarked on a remarkable journey that has taken him to the pinnacle of the culinary world. With over a decade of experience in high-volume kitchen environments, he blends international and local cuisine with his diverse culinary expertise. At the heart of his journey lies a profound influence that shaped his passion for cooking: his mother's extraordinary skills. From a young age, he found himself captivated by the tantalizing aromas and flavors that emanated from his family's kitchen.

Zein's unwavering dedication, creativity, and commitment to excellence, as well as his experience in diverse gastronomical landscapes have enriched his repertoire and fueled his passion for creating unforgettable dining experiences. From the rich flavors of Uganda and Zanzibar to London's vibrant restaurant scene and the multicultural melting pot of Dubai, Chef Zein has honed his craft in a multitude of settings, including Twangale Park in Zambia. Each place has contributed to his culinary expertise, shaping him into the visionary chef he is today.

●

Agatha Achindu is the author of *Bountiful Cooking*; the founder of Yummy Spoonfuls, a line of fresh-frozen organic food for kids; and, since 2006, on an unrelenting mission to make families and communities healthier. A certified integrative nutrition health coach and yoga instructor, she extends her mission further as a respected voice and speaker, amplifying her message of whole living for modern times.

Agatha grew up on an organic farm in Cameroon, where eating fresh food from the earth was a right, not a privilege. This notion was the driving force behind how she fed her own family, as a married mother of three with a demanding career. Teaching other time-strapped mothers how to make nutritious meals from scratch became the foundation for the career she leads today as a food activist, advocate, and business-woman. A voice of authority and respected leader in her field, Agatha has appeared in notable media outlets such as NBC, CNN, CBS, *Today Show*, *Marie Claire*, *Forbes*, *Fortune*, and *People*, and her work has been published in *Parents* and *The Washington Post*.

●

Eric Adjepong is a first generation Ghanaian-American, passionate about introducing West African cuisine to the world, and is well known for infusing West African flavors into his dishes, taking inspiration from the meals he shared with his family.

After graduating with degrees in Culinary Arts and Nutrition from Johnson & Wales, Rhode Island, Eric went on to obtain his Master's in International Public Health & Nutrition from the University of Westminster in London. From there, he cooked in several Michelin-starred restaurants before taking his talents to TV's *Top Chef*. He was a finalist and fan favorite on season 16, and competed on *Top Chef All-Stars*. Eric is now a personal chef and nutrition professional, and continues to appear on TV food shows, and is the author of *Sankofa: A Culinary Story of Resilience and Belonging*, the story of a young boy's culinary journey 400 years into the past to reconnect with his African roots.

●

Selassie Atadika is chef and founder of Midunu, a lifestyle company celebrating Africa's cultural and culinary heritage, as well as a nomadic and private dining enterprise in Accra, Ghana, that embodies "New African Cuisine." She is also a founding member of Trio Toque, the first nomadic restaurant in Dakar, Senegal. After years of self-teaching in the culinary arts, Chef Atadika completed a course at The Culinary Institute of America (CIA) in New York. In 2017 she was honored as one of the

Global Top 50 Plant-Forward Chefs by the EAT Foundation and the CIA; in 2018 she served as a Stone Barns Center for Food and Agriculture Exchange Fellow; and in 2019 she was a finalist for the Basque Culinary World Prize.

She holds a Master's in International Affairs from Columbia University's School of International and Public Affairs, and a Bachelor's in Geography with Environmental Studies from Dartmouth College. She has been sought for her thought leadership by CNN's *African Voices*, *The Financial Times*, The Danish Broadcasting Corporation (DR), and OmVärlden, as well as featured in *Vogue*, *National Geographic*'s The Plate, *Entrepreneur*, and *Ebony*.

●

Ikenna Akwuebue BobManuel is a chef dedicated to creating memorable culinary experiences and contributing to the growth of African gastronomy, on a mission to promote the rich and diverse edible culture of West Africa. His perspective on food and culture is deeply influenced by his Nigerian heritage and extensive travels throughout the region. A graduate of the prestigious Red Dish Culinary School in Nigeria, he started his career as a young chef at HSE Gourmet, a restaurant owned by chef Nkesi Enyioha.

Chef Ikenna is currently based in Accra, Ghana, and can be found hosting popups and immersive dining experiences. He is an instructor at the School of Culinary Arts, and actively contributes to the Ghana Food Movement, a network that promotes sustainable food systems. He believes that food is a great connector and an opportunity to initiate conversations and find local solutions to local problems. He also masterminded the menu at Ghana's premiere eco-lodge "Meet Me There." Through his roles, he continues to inspire and educate others about West Africa's culinary treasures, fostering appreciation for the region's gastronomic heritage.

●

Clara Kapelembe Bwali, popularly known as "Black Garlic," is a food stylist, food photographer, and recipe author. She holds degrees in Computer and Information Sciences from Monash University in Melbourne, Australia. Her work has been featured internationally on many websites, including Black Foodie, Dine Diaspora, Food Blogger Pro, Food for Mzansi, Food24, My Cookery Zone, and My Burnt Orange.

Clara was recently featured on SABC's TV show *Afternoon Express*, representing Zambian cuisine during Africa Month, and the *Expresso Show*. She was selected as one of the African food influencers for the Every Plate Counts Challenge by the United Nations Environment Programme and Food and Agriculture Organization, the World Wildlife Fund, and the Future Food Institute. Locally, she has collaborated with a number of chefs, as well as Zambia's celebrated The Wood Kitchen, on several projects, including a five-part Zambian food video series and The Good Food Cooking Class.

●

Akram Cherif was born in Bizerta, north of Tunisia, where he studied hotel management in Hammamet, before graduating from the Institut Supérieur de la Gestion Hôtelière in Namur, Belgium. During his thirty-year career, he has worked his way up from acting manager in the Meridien Hotel chain to manager of several hotels in Tunisia and Marrakesh.

He has crossed the globe from Sri Lanka, India, and Vietnam to South Africa, Morocco, and Dubai; from Spain, France, and Italy, to Russia, Poland, and Hungary. His passion for cooking led him to become chef of the restaurant-lounge Le Quai Bizerta, where he combined seafood products and local dishes. He has worked as a consultant to restaurants and taught at the Vagatop Institute of Tourism in Bizerta. He has also been a guest chef at Alkebulan: The African Dining Hall in Dubai.

He is manager at the five-star Hotel Medina Solaria & Thalasso in Tunisia. He is also a member of the Tunisian delegation of the Académie Nationale de Cuisine in France, and of the Chefs' Manifesto organization.

●

Anto Cocagne was raised in Gabon, and she studied culinary arts at the Grégoire Ferrandi School of French Cuisine in Paris, followed by the Culinary Arts School in Rhode Island. She then moved to France, working with chefs such as Alain Hascoët and Éric Pras, before setting up a home cooking business, as well as consulting on African cuisine. She hosts a TV cooking show, *Rendez-vous with Chef Anto*; is co-author of *Saka Saka: Adventures in African Cooking, South of the Sahara*, and *Goûts d'Afrique*; and artistic director of *Afro Cooking* magazine.

In 2016 she received the prize for African Female Revelation of the Year at the Gala Africa COP22 in the gastronomy category. She was also a finalist of the La Cuillère d'Or competition in 2018 and winner of the Eugénie Brazier Prize, rewarding creativity. Founder of the We Eat Africa festival, which promotes African chefs and products, her aim is to make African cuisine more visible around the world.

●

Agness Colley—known as Aguyness—is a trained pastry chef and entrepreneur. In 2017 her passion pushed her to train in the culinary arts with Thierry Marx, and her time in the kitchen of La Régalade in Paris quickly reinforced this change of direction. Her cuisine is generous, authentic, delicate, comforting, and uninhibited, and she puts sharing, exchange, and authenticity at the center of her priorities. It is a cuisine of instinct, spirituality, and creativity—asserting her Africanness and telling the story of a life's journey, full of history and tradition.

She is keen to highlight the products of her Togo origins, as well as Black cuisines through creative and modern Afro-Caribbean dishes.

●

Michael Adé Elégbèdé was born and raised in Nigeria, and started cooking at a very young age. His mother and grandmother were both trained in the culinary arts, and they ran restaurants and cooking schools. He studied at the Culinary Institute of America Graystone, and worked at some of the top restaurants in the United States. He returned to Nigeria in 2016 to explore the diverse cultures and traditions that make up the cuisine, traveling to the more remote areas of the country to experience and learn about the unique nature of their cuisine and ingredients.

He set up the ÌTÀN Test Kitchen in Ikoyi, Lagos as a space in which he could utilize local ingredients and create fresh narratives and remarkable dining experiences around Nigerian cuisine. The space hosts curated dinners and aims to become a hub in which Nigerian and African chefs can experiment and grow. He is also a co-founder of Abòri, a local collective movement aiming to facilitate sustainable growth in Nigeria's food system. In 2022 he was named a La Liste Young Talent of the Year, and one of the World's 50 Best Next.

●

Moustafa Elrefaey is from Tanta, Egypt, and he studied culinary arts at Henry Ford College (HFC) in Michigan, where he developed his unique style. Moustafa traveled to all corners of Egypt to understand the different flavors, techniques, and hidden treasures of Egyptian culinary heritage, and to manifest those learnings in his work.

He is executive chef, cofounder, and partner of Zooba, an Egyptian restaurant with branches in Cairo, New York City, and Riyadh. In 2023, Zooba was ranked ninth in the prestigious Middle East & North Africa's 50 Best Restaurants awards. In addition, he is a board member and treasurer of the Egyptian Chefs Association; a certified executive chef of the American Culinary Federation; the Egyptian Ambassador at the World Chefs Without Borders; winner of Borough Market's Falafel

Festival 2016 competition in London; and winner of the Estrella Damm N.A. Chefs' Choice Award 2023.

It is his mission to empower people—he serves as a chef instructor at HFC, and provides coaching to a new generation of upcoming chefs.

●

Arnaud Gwaga is an entrepreneur who started cooking at his home in Burundi in 2020, and he developed a passion for hosting family and friends. Arnaud and his wife Ninette organized their first barbecue event—the Meat Gala—in Burundi with a small guest list of just fifty people. Other sold-out events were organized in Bujumbura, with 300 guests, and in 2023 they hosted their first event in neighboring Rwanda. They have now hosted eight Meat Galas in two countries, and interest in these gourmet events continues to grow, as they allow a real opportunity for participants to experience Burundi's rich culinary culture.

●

Mohamed Kamal is a passionate Nubian chef, researcher, and food developer with a burning desire to keep the culture and culinary traditions of his people alive. Hailing from Egypt, he has earned accolades and recognition for his culinary expertise and dedication to preserving the Nubian heritage through food.

His mission goes beyond simply cooking; it is about safeguarding and celebrating the identity and customs of his people. He is known for his innovative approach, pushing boundaries, while staying true to the roots and essence of the ancient traditions. Hibiscus, dates, and grains are among Mohamed's favorite ingredients, and he artfully weaves them into his dishes to showcase the essence of Nubian cuisine.

Having honed his skills over the years, he had the honor of being part of the Egypt national soccer team's culinary crew during the African Cup of Nations held in the UAE.

●

Kudakwashe Makoni, also known as "The Black Chef," is a culinary arts management graduate of New York's Culinary Institute of America, and he is passionate about the culinary arts and hospitality in general. He started out front of house—as a cashier, supervisor, assistant restaurant manager, and manager—and has gone on to run highly profitable kitchens in the United States, UAE, Bahrain, and Zimbabwe. He is a member of the Groupe Sebastien leadership, in which he serves as group executive chef based in Accra, Ghana, overseeing five culinary units. He has worked for leading organizations such as Radisson Blu, Shade, Starbucks, The Coffee Club, The Foundry, IHG Hotels & Resorts, Innscor Africa Limited, News Cafe, and Cafe Nush.

Kuda has an avid love for Pan African/Afro-fusion cuisine, especially merging the lesser known cuisines of Southern Africa with the more visible cuisines of Western, Northern, and Eastern Africa. He tells the stories of how ingredients across the African continent have distinct similarities and how they translate across people, culture, art, fashion, music, and history—expanding beyond the continent into the diaspora. He hopes and believes that Zimbabwean cuisine can share the stage alongside the more familiar cuisines of Africa.

●

Dieuveil Malonga is the owner of Meza Malonga, a culinary lab in Kigali, Rwanda. Born in Linzolo, near Brazzaville, Congo, Malonga was trained at Adolph–Kolping Schule in Münster, Germany. He honed his culinary skills at Michelin-starred restaurants Schote, La Vie, and Aqua. His work is guided by the spirit of Pan-Africanism, a celebration of unity of peoples of Africa. He develops his philosophy of Afrofusion as a subtle blend of tradition, innovation, and cultures; a bridge between African cuisines. Since its opening in 2020, Meza Malonga has already been acclaimed by Travel + Leisure and Food & Wine as one of the "world's best restaurants." He's also been recognized by The World's

50 Best Restaurants for his efforts: in 2021 he was listed among the organization's "50 Next" as an "Empowering Educator," and in 2022 was named its Champion of Change for his efforts in nurturing African culinary talent.

In 2016, he launched Chefs in Africa, a social enterprise committed to shedding light on Africa and diaspora gourmet rising stars. With 4,000 chefs, the enterprise has earned support from the World Tourism Organisation and UNESCO. He was a finalist of the Basque Culinary World Prize 2018, recognizing his community engagement to promote and transmit the culinary heritage of Africa through the valorization of its terroirs, its products, and its chefs. Malonga is also building a Culinary Innovation Village in Musanze, Rwanda—an integrated ecosystem with farm, culinary center, and restaurant for the transmission of African gastronomy based on local and sustainable products.

●

O'miel Moundounga is a Gabonese chef, who embodies the spirit of modern African cuisine, combining tradition and innovation with unwavering passion. Born in Libreville, Jr O'miel was introduced to the secrets of cooking by his paternal grandmother, leading him to discover the deep values of sharing and respect for products, valuable lessons that he applies to every dish he creates.

At age twenty, he walked through the doors of a professional kitchen for the first time, and he hasn't looked back since. His vision of cooking as an act of authentic and profound love has guided each of his steps. After seven years of perfecting his art, Jr O'miel felt the need to return to his roots and share the culinary wealth of his country with the world. His exceptional culinary skills were recognized when he won the prestigious Best Dish award at the Bocuse d'Or in 2018 in Marrakesh, Morocco. The following year, he opened the doors of his restaurant in Akanda, a true temple of Gabonese gastronomy where each dish is a work of art, a sensory experience where each bite transports you to the heart of Gabonese culture.

●

Mwaka Mwiimbu is a passionate Zambian home cook and TV chef. She has always had a passion for food, and she loves to work with ingredients indigenous to Africa and to put her own spin on recipes, while staying true to natural and traditional flavors. Her ultimate goal is to elevate African cuisine and showcase the rich diversity of flavors and ingredients the continent has to offer. As host of *My Zambian Plate*, a TV program dedicated to showcasing the beauty and versatility of Zambian food and ingredients, she has found a platform to advocate for her culinary beliefs.

She received a Bachelor of Social Sciences, majoring in History, Politics, and Governance, at the University of Cape Town, then continued her studies at the University of the Witwatersrand. Her passion for food and global issues led her to acquire a high-level certificate in Sustainable Global Food Systems from the University of Edinburgh. This blend of academic expertise in politics and food systems, as well as a passion for social change, has uniquely positioned her to tackle complex issues at the intersection of food security, international relations, and development.

●

Forster Oben Oru is from Cameroon, and for almost ten years gained experience working around Cameroon, Qatar, and Dubai, including the preparation of fine-dining cuisine at the Burj Al Arab in Dubai, and leading the chef team of Deseo Restaurant in Dubai. Forster has developed a reputation for his ability to combine a wide range of flavors to create novel culinary creations that enhance the experience of diners, and has an eye and talent for high-end presentation of dishes.

In 2022, he represented the UAE in the World Tapas Championships in Valladolid, Spain, and in 2023 he undertook a four-month internship programme in Cenador De Amós, a 3-Michelin starred restaurant in northern Spain. Currently, he runs supper clubs in Dubai, and undertakes private dining events.

●

Joseph Odoom is an Afro-fusion chef with influence from his Ghanaian roots. He is the head chef for Restaurant Momi in the Netherlands, a Ghanaian/West African fine-dining restaurant. He is said to be one of the top five chefs in Ghana, and one of Africa's rising culinary stars. In 2021, he won the first season of DSTV Honey's *House of Chefs*, and he was featured in *Ebony* magazine's "Dry January" edition 2023 and on the Cuisine Noir podcast. He has worked with top chefs including Siba Mtongana and Fatmata Binta.

Joseph combines his culinary training, experience, and contemporary approach with a blend of fine dining using indigenous African ingredients. He loves to bring to light the endless possibilities of these ingredients and share his knowledge, flavors, and culture.

●

Thabo Phake is a South African chef, who studied at the Johannesburg Culinary and Pastry School. He interned at The Cube Tasting Kitchen, a French gastronomic restaurant, and Urbanologi, one of the Top 10 bars in Africa. He then relocated to Abuja, Nigeria, where he worked in CF1 Cafe and La Taverba Abuja, and consulted for culinary establishments. In South Africa, he was head chef at Proud Mary in Johannesburg.

In 2021, he appeared on DSTV Honey's *House of Chefs*.

●

Coco Reinarhz is a Burundian chef at the forefront of modern African cuisine, reinventing traditional dishes through a contemporary lens. He learned his love of cooking from his mother, in her restaurant in Kinshasa, before training at Ecole Hotelière de la Province de Namur in Belgium.

He has worked in Belgium, Holland, Democratic Republic of Congo, Côte d'Ivoire, and South Africa, opened a dining outlet at the Kigali Arena in Central Africa, and was named among the 100 Most Influential Africans in 2022 by *New African Magazine*. He featured as a guest chef at the opening of Alkebulan: The African Dining Hall, and is now head chef at his own restaurant, Epicure, in Johannesburg.

He has also been a celebrity chef on *MasterChef South Africa* and an ambassador for TWISPER, the social travel app.

●

Mostafa Seif discovered his talent and passion for cooking in an army mess hall at the age of twenty, and his first culinary experience was working on a Kebda and Sogoa street food cart in Cairo. After graduating from the Culinary Arts Academy of Giza in 2013, he was one of the first to attempt to redefine and create the New Egyptian cuisine.

He is the 2018 winner of MBC's *Top Chef* Middle East and executive chef of Pier88 Group and Khufu's restaurant, a La Liste Hidden Gem Award winner in 2023.

●

Mogau Seshoene, also known as "The Lazy Makoti," is a trained chef and bestselling cookbook author. She left the corporate world in 2014 to pursue her love for food and preserving South African cuisine and heritage. What began as lessons for a friend—a bride-to-be who was afraid of being labeled "The Lazy Makoti" (the lazy daughter-in-law) because she couldn't cook—has evolved into a platform that offers cooking classes, food styling, and recipe development.

Mogau has since made the *Mail & Guardian* 200 Young South Africans list, and the *Forbes Africa* "30 under 30" list. She is a contributing food writer at Woolworths *Taste* magazine, and her debut cookbook, *The Lazy Makoti's Guide to the Kitchen,* was the bestselling cookbook of 2019–20 in South Africa. It also won a Gourmand World Cookbook Award. Her second cookbook, *Hosting with Lazy Makoti*, is also a bestseller and won the Luxe Award for Cookbook of the Year 2022.

●

Sinoyolo Sifo is a self-taught cook in South Africa with a passion for home cooking. He was raised in Eastern Cape in a small village called Kwanonkobe in Mthatha, and it was watching his mother cook that made him interested in learning how to cook. He also draws a lot of inspiration from his hardworking father. His aim is to break the stereotype that surrounds male figures in the home kitchen and encourage them to cook, while celebrating South African food culture.

A pharmacist by profession, Sinoyolo is creator of Sifo the Cooking Husband site on social media, where he shares simple and delicious meals.

Sinoyolo's cookbook, *Sifo The Cooking Husband*, is an invitation to readers to share in the joy of making memories through food. Inspired by the nostalgia of home and family, the book brings together simple and accessible recipes that are also wholesome and delicious; it won a Gourmand World Cookbook Award in the Family category in 2022.

●

Mame Sow draws her inspiration from seasonal and local ingredients, spices, colors, the juxtaposition of sweet and savory flavors, and her love of architecture. Born and raised in Dakar, Senegal, she moved to New York City in her teens. She is a graduate of Park West High School where she studied under C-CAP (Careers through Culinary Arts Program) and ultimately garnered a scholarship to the celebrated New York International Culinary Center.

Chef Mame's talents were cultivated under Marcus Samuelsson at Aquavit, Riingo, and Merkato 55. She also worked as a pastry chef at luxury hotels around the United States, such as Hotel on Rivington, Bardessano Hotel and Spa, and SLS Hotel South Beach's The Bazaar by Jose Andres. She was culinary director for Zaha Hadid's One Thousand Museum in Miami. She was also pastry chef at Spot Dessert bar in New York when it won Best Dessert Bar NYC 2010, and at The Cecil when it was named Best New Restaurant in America by *Esquire* magazine.

Chef Mame's favorite ingredient to work with is chocolate, and she aims to show the immense diversity of African flavors in her desserts. She is currently the executive chef of Alkebulan: The African Dining Hall in Dubai.

●

Sophia Teshome is the founder and executive chef of High Altitude Kitchen in Addis Ababa, Ethiopia, a contemporary restaurant, bar, and catering business that has crafted a uniquely Ethiopian-American soul food fusion menu in a vibrant yet relaxed atmosphere. It also gives a glimpse into the vast culinary landscape of Ethiopia through sharing innovative recipes, culinary experiences, inside tips, and the best places to eat and drink in Ethiopia. A self-taught cook, Sophia specializes in comfort food classics and a unique approach to Ethiopian-American fusion cuisine using fresh, organic, and locally sourced ingredients.

Sophia is also an experienced global health practitioner on the African continent, who dually works in real estate management and development, as she continues to explore her passion in culinary entrepreneurship.

●

Pierre Thiam is a celebrated chef, restaurateur, award-winning cookbook author, and entrepreneur. Born and raised in Senegal, he is known for his innovative cooking style, at once modern and eclectic, yet rooted in the rich culinary traditions of West Africa. He is the chef and owner of critically acclaimed New York-based restaurants Teranga, serving fast-casual West African fare, and the founder of Yolélé, a purpose-driven food business that makes African ingredients available to home cooks and restaurants, while connecting smallholder farms in West Africa with the global food economy. He is the author of four highly acclaimed cookbooks: *Yolele! Recipes From the Heart of Senegal*, *Senegal! Modern Recipes From the Source to the Bowl*, *The Fonio Cookbook*, and *Simply West African*.

●

Rōze Traore is a chef, media personality, and entrepreneur. He is the creator of unique dining experiences for clients and iconic brands such as *The New York Times*, Veuve Clicquot, American Express, and Louis Vuitton. He was also named one of *TIME* magazine's Next Generation Leaders. Born in Washington D.C., he was raised between Seattle and Côte d'Ivoire.

During his recovery from heart surgery as a child, he looked towards the kitchen as a place of healing, leading to his lifelong passion for the culinary arts. At age eighteen, he enrolled in Le Cordon Bleu, and from there, he worked in some of the most prestigious kitchens in the world, including Eleven Madison Park and The NoMad. Inspired by the different cultures and flavors experienced during his travels, Rōze has perfected a distinct ability to translate elements of elevated fine dining into approachable techniques for the enthusiastic home chef. Throughout his career, he has made it his mission to help those of every socio-economic background, to bring the pleasures of eating fresh, beautiful food to communities facing food insecurity. This mission is now front and center in his latest business venture, La Fourchette de Rōze, a boutique hotel in Grand Bassam, Côte d'Ivoire. He also founded an artist residency program, inviting selected artists from around the world to collaborate and create within the hotel's inspiring atmosphere.

●

Matse Uwatse is a multiple-award-winning radio personality and a leading Nigerian food blogger. Through her work at Wazobia FM in Lagos in 2007, she has won numerous awards, including an ELOY award, The Future Awards Africa, and an African Voices Award. In 2011, Matse joined Nigeria Info FM. Matse has appeared on *Chefrican* on EbonyLifeTV; as a Master Chef at the GTCO Food & Drink Festival in 2019; and as a celebrity chef in *Big Brother Naija: Pepper Dem*. She has also written for the culinary section of *Malimbe*, the in-flight magazine found on many Nigerian airlines.

Since 2013, she has focused solely on her food blog, Matse Cooks, to provide insightful information about food and drinks that are culturally significant to Africans. The positive reception led her to launch her own spice company, MatseCooks Seasonings. In 2016, she was listed as one of the 100 Most Inspiring Nigeria Women by YNaija, and in 2020 she was named one of the top 121 food bloggers in the world by Social Animal. She was honored as a "Creator" in the 2021 edition of the Dine Diaspora 31 Days of Black Women in Food initiative, which celebrates achievements and advancements of black women worldwide in the food and beverage industry.

●

Alfonso Videira is an Angolan-born Belgian. After working at several of Europe's renowned restaurants, including Château de la Chèvre d'or and Château de Berne in France, The Jane Antwerp and La Truffe Noire in Belgium, among others, he decided to move towards what is really close to his heart: promoting and introducing African culture to the whole world through revisiting traditional African dishes. Alfonso now travels around East Africa to train, share, and consult, to help the African hospitality sector and African youth to grow and improve their skills.

Nana Araba Wilmot is a chef and owner of Georgina's Private Chef and Catering Co. Nana started cooking at an early age with her grandmother, the source of her love of cooking for others. After graduating with two degrees in Culinary Arts and Culinary Management from The Art Institute of Philadelphia in 2013, Nana worked for Wolfgang Puck Catering and Jose Garces' restaurants. She also worked at Le Coucou, a Stephen Starr restaurant collaboration with Chef Daniel Rose in New York that garnered a James Beard Award for Best New Restaurant in 2017 and one Michelin star in 2018; then moved on to work with chef Marie Rose at La Mercerie.

Nana returned to Philadelphia in late 2020, where she started the Love That I Knead Supper Club, a West African focused dinner series that celebrates Black history and foodways across the diaspora. Reimagining that lens, Nana explores her identity on a plate while also helping others to "find their way back"—spanning different locations in Philadelphia, New York, and Accra, Ghana. Nana has had opportunities as chef in residence at the Philadelphia Museum of Art, a chef residency with Meet Resident in NYC, and a partnership with the AfroFuture (formerly Afrochella) music festival in 2022. She has been featured in a variety of media outlets including *Bon Appetit*, *The New York Times*, Radio Cherry Bombe, *Cherry Bombe* magazine, *Forbes*, and *Eater*.

Rubia Zablon is a Kenyan chef who has been fascinated by the art of cooking since a young age; he came to realize how powerful food is in its ability to bring people of all walks of life together. He attended culinary school at Utalii College in Kenya and has worked at a variety of five-star hotels in Kenya and abroad. He has traveled to various continents and worked with chefs throughout the world, learning and picking up ideas about different cuisines, including Chinese, Arabic, Thai, French, and Italian. Currently, he lives and works in between Gaborone, Botswana and Durban, South Africa.

Rubia's main objective as a chef is to provide modern gourmet dining experiences that will exceed people's expectations. His style of cooking is Afro-continental cuisine, as this allows room to infuse some of the local cuisines with different food cultures to create a new dining experience.

Farida Zamradje is originally from Marrakesh. After studying hotel management and gaining experience in her hometown, notably with the Barrière Group, she decided to celebrate her roots by joining Sahbi Sahbi ("sister souls") restaurant in Marrakesh, as a chef. It is an all-female-run restaurant offering a contemporary take on traditional Moroccan cuisine using local produce, while coordinating the talents of women from different regions of Morocco around a collective and immersive experience.

Her cuisine celebrates her gastronomic heritage, and represents a return to her roots and a desire to highlight traditional cuisine, handed down from generation to generation and exalting Moroccan cuisine and its conviviality.

ABOUT
THE AUTHORS

Alexander Smalls is a master of culinary curating and storytelling. His most recent undertaking has been the creation—the founding and orchestrating—of Alkebulan: the first modern contemporary African dining hall, which opened in October 2021 for Dubai Expo 2020.

Smalls has been featured on television on numerous occasions. He appeared twice on the CBS Saturday Morning show *The Dish*. He was also spotlighted, with Chef Kwame Onwuachi, on the CBS This Morning podcast *Trailblazers*, a series that features trailblazers, luminaries, and trendsetters who defied the odds and achieved extraordinary accomplishments. In 2021, he was on the national ABC special: *Juneteenth: A Celebration of Overcoming*, with Deborah Roberts, to celebrate the African-American holiday Juneteenth.

Additionally, Smalls has had a role on many food shows. He served three times as a celebrity chef judge on Bravo's *Top Chef*, appeared on ABC's *The Chew* with Carla Hall, Cooking Channel's *Extra Virgin* with Debi Mazar and Gabriele Corcos, and Hallmark Channel's *Meet The Peete's* with actress Holly Robinson Peete. He has been a four-time judge on Food Network's *Throwdown with Bobby Flay* and a judge on *Recipe for Success* about food entrepreneurs. In 2020, he was celebrated and featured in *Food & Wine* magazine's cover story.

Alexander Smalls' prolific path is marked by a plethora of copious achievements: he is a James Beard Award-winning chef, author, and raconteur. He was the visionary co-owner of renowned restaurants Minton's and The Cecil—New York City's first Afro-Asian American restaurant, which was named "Best New Restaurant in America" by *Esquire* in 2014. Over the past three decades, this South Carolina native has traveled the world, studying the cooking techniques and food-ways of the African diaspora.

Smalls has always brought elements of his birthplace into his menus. As the former chef-owner of celebrated restaurants, including Café Beulah, the first fine-dining African American restaurant in New York, Sweet Ophelia's in SoHo, and Shoebox Café at Grand Central Terminal, Smalls has received great acclaim in the restaurant scene. He cooked at the James Beard House, and he was named a *Zagat* "NYC Restaurant Power Players You Need to Know."

Smalls has had many awards bestowed upon him. He was honored with the 2014 Legacy Award from the *Amsterdam News*, one of the oldest African American newspapers in the country. He received a 2019 James Beard Award, with chef JJ Johnson and Veronica Chambers, for their cookbook *Between Harlem and Heaven*. In 2020, Smalls received the Creative Spirit Award from the Black Alumni of Pratt by his dear friend the inimitable Ms. Cicely Tyson. He also received recognition for his other written work, dating back to his first memoir and cookbook, *Grace the Table*, with a foreword by Wynton Marsalis, which features recipes from his upbringing that he calls Southern Revival cuisine. His most recent book, *Meals, Music & Muses: Recipes from My African American Kitchen*, has been acclaimed by *The New York Times* and the *Los Angeles Times*.

Smalls is also a world-renowned opera singer and the winner of both a Grammy Award and Tony Award for the cast recording of George Gershwin's *Porgy and Bess* with the Houston Grand Opera. He debuted his album *Let us Break Bread Together* in 2022.

Alexander Smalls sees his career in the world of hospitality as an activist and advocate for the foodways of the African diaspora. He is dedicated to elevating, educating, and expanding the narrative, visibility, and brilliance of African food in the world. When he's not traveling, Alexander Smalls resides in Harlem, New York City, where he is active in the community on nonprofit boards and with various initiatives.

ABOUT
THE AUTHORS

Nina Oduro is the Ghanaian-American CEO and co-founder of Dine Diaspora, a Black- and women-owned company based in Washington, D.C. that connects people and brands to African diaspora food culture. Nina leads strategy and creative direction, centering Black foodways through marketing initiatives for top global companies. She has worked with hundreds of food professionals and entrepreneurs, connecting them to opportunities and resources for their individual and collective growth of African diaspora contributions to food around the world.

Oduro co-founded Black Women in Food (BWIF) to address the gap in support and opportunities for Black women's advancement in the food and hospitality industry. Since its inception, BWIF has supported over 1,000 women across the food system around the world through funding, resources, networks, and recognition. Nina has also contributed to strengthening diversity, equity, and inclusion initiatives through training and advising for the James Beard Foundation.

As a champion for equity in the food and beverage industry, she has been featured as a Change-Maker in the D.C. Food System by *Washington City Paper*. Her work has been featured in publications such as *Food & Wine*, *Sweet July*, and *Washingtonian*. She has been recognized as a Top 30 Under 30 honoree by Future of Ghana and DAWNer of the Year by the Diaspora African Women's Network. Her writing has been featured in *Black Enterprise* magazine, *Cuisine Noir* magazine, and *The Africa Report*.

Nina received her Master's degree from Columbia University and a Bachelor's from University of Virginia. She also holds a certificate in Diversity, Equity, and Inclusion from eCornell.

DIRECTORY OF CHEF RECIPES

INDEX

WITH THANKS

First and foremost I want to acknowledge and give thanks and appreciation to the ancestral trust from which we come. Respect and recognition for the contributions of our forefathers and mothers who have inspired and empowered all of us to hold near their legacy and teachings. Our story is their story. Our lives are a continuation of theirs. As long as we breathe life, their customs, culture, and rituals live through us. I am grateful and appreciative of their wisdom and grace.

This book has been a labor of love, a family reunion, and a celebration of fellow creatives, chefs, cooks, and culinary practitioners across Africa. I want to humbly thank the tribe of contributors who touched this manuscript, with wisdom, creativity, and kind hands. Who showed up on these pages to present their culinary offerings and share their unique stories—chefs and food writers reinterpreting traditional heirloom recipes with a modern, contemporary feel for today's palate. These are change-makers who put their heart on a plate.

I want to thank Phaidon Press for joining me on this very special exploration. Their guidance and expertise were pivotal to this journey. To Emily Takoudes, my editor, who embraced my need to tell this story and was all in from its inception. She brought all of her resources and experience to bear, including her secret weapon, Rachel Malig. Never wavering, they were steady and sure-footed as we traversed the terrain. To, Gabrielle Guy—thank you for bringing the book to life through your wonderful design. And thank you to Beatriz da Costa and Cyd Raftus McDowell for the incredible photography throughout.

To my dear friend Nina Oduro, project manager, partner in crime, nurse, therapist, recipe chaser, editor, babysitter, all-out warrior, and organizer—you are a lifesaver and fixer. I can't thank you enough for your care, kindness, hard work, and no-nonsense approach to getting the job done. Truly my ride or die, and the constant heartbeat through these pages.

And to all of you who happened upon this wonderful book, led by your curiosity and love of Africa on a plate. I thank you for gracing the table with us. Blessings.

I want to thank my fellow chefs who generously contributed their voices. I greatly appreciate that your thoughts live within the pages of this work.

Selassie Atadika
Anto Cocagne
Michael Adé Elégbèdé
Coco Reinarhz
Pierre Thiam

To my participating tribe. My chefs and culinarians on the frontline, who have taken on the task of creating the everyday culinary expressions in their cities and countries on the continent. They are the fabric of our culinary trust. Our gathered harvest.

Zein Abdallah
Agatha Achindu
Eric Adjepong
Ikenna Akwuebue BobManuel
Clara Kapelembe Bwali
Akram Cherif
Agness Colley
Moustafa Elrefaey
Arnaud Gwaga
Mohamed Kamal
Kudakwashe Makoni
Dieuveil Malonga
O'miel Moundounga
Mwaka Mwiimbu
Forster Oben Oru
Joseph Odoom
Thabo Phake
Mostafa Seif
Mogau Seshoene
Sinoyolo Sifo
Mame Sow
Sophia Teshome
Pierre Thiam
Rōze Traore
Matse Uwatse
Alfonso Videira
Nana Araba Wilmot
Rubia Zablon
Farida Zamradje

Alexander Smalls

RECIPE NOTES

●

Butter should always be unsalted, unless otherwise specified.

●

All herbs are fresh, unless otherwise specified.

●

Eggs are medium (US large) unless otherwise specified.

●

Individual vegetables and fruits, such as onions and apples, are assumed to be medium, unless otherwise specified.

●

All milk is whole (3% fat), homogenized, and lightly pasteurized, unless otherwise specified.

●

All salt is fine sea salt, unless otherwise specified.

●

Exercise a high level of caution when following recipes involving any potentially hazardous activity, including the use of high temperatures, open flames and when deep-frying. In particular, when deep-frying add food carefully to avoid splashing, wear long sleeves and never leave the pan unattended.

●

Cooking times are for guidance only. If using a fan (convection) oven, follow the manufacturer's instructions concerning the oven temperatures.

●

All herbs, shoots, flowers and leaves should be picked fresh from a clean source. Do exercise caution when foraging for ingredients, which should only be eaten if an expert has deemed them safe to eat. In particular, do not gather wild mushrooms yourself before seeking the advice of an expert who has confirmed their suitability for human consumption. As some species of mushrooms have been known to cause allergic reaction and illness, do take extra care when cooking and eating mushrooms and do seek immediate medical help if you experience a reaction after preparing or eating them.

●

Exercise caution when making fermented products, ensuring all equipment is spotlessly clean, and seek expert advice if in any doubt.

●

When no quantity is specified, for example of oils, salts and herbs used for finishing dishes, quantities are discretionary and flexible.

●

All spoon and cup measurements are level, unless otherwise stated. 1 teaspoon = 5 ml; 1 tablespoon = 15 ml. Australian standard tablespoons are 20 ml, so Australian readers are advised to use 3 teaspoons in place of 1 tablespoon when measuring small quantities.

●

Cup, metric, and imperial measurements are used in this book. Follow one set of measurements throughout, not a mixture, as they are not interchangeable.

Phaidon Press Limited
2 Cooperage Yard
London E15 2QR

Phaidon Press Inc.
111 Broadway
New York, NY 10006

phaidon.com

First published 2024
©2024 Phaidon Press Limited

ISBN 978 1 83866 845 7

A CIP catalogue record for this book
is available from the British Library
and the Library of Congress.

The countries listed on page 7 are as
designated by the African Union.

Commissioning Editor: Emily Takoudes
Project Editor: Rachel Malig
Designer: Gabrielle Guy
Production Controller: Lily Rodgers
Photography: Beatriz da Costa
Food Stylist: Cyd Raftus McDowell

Printed in China

The publisher would like to thank
Vanessa Bird, João Mota, Claire Rogers,
Ellie Smith, Tracey Smith, and
Kathy Steer.